Interpersonality in Legal Genres

Linguistic Insights

Studies in Language and Communication

Edited by Maurizio Gotti,
University of Bergamo

Volume 191

PETER LANG
Bern · Berlin · Bruxelles · Frankfurt am Main · New York · Oxford · Wien

Ruth Breeze, Maurizio Gotti & Carmen Sancho Guinda (eds)

Interpersonality in Legal Genres

PETER LANG
Bern · Berlin · Bruxelles · Frankfurt am Main · New York · Oxford · Wien

Bibliographic information published by die Deutsche Nationalbibliothek
Die Deutsche Nationalbibliothek lists this publication in the Deutsche Nationalbibliografie; detailed bibliographic data is available on the Internet at ‹http://dnb.d-nb.de›.

British Library Cataloguing-in-Publication Data: A catalogue record for this book is available from The British Library, Great Britain

Library of Congress Cataloging-in-Publication Data

Interpersonality in legal genres / Ruth Breeze, Maurizio Gotti & Carmen Sancho Guinda (eds).
p. cm. – (Linguistic insights, studies in language and communication ; 191)
Includes bibliographical references and index.
ISBN 978-3-0343-1524-1
1. Law–Language. 2. Sublanguage. 3. Interpersonal relations. 4. Psycholinguistics. 5. Rhetoric. I. Breeze, Ruth, author editor of compilation. II. Gotti, Maurizio, author editor of compilation. III. Guinda, Carmen Sancho, author editor of compilation.
K213.I588 2014
340'.14–dc23

2014013766

Published with the support of Dipartimento di Lingue, Letterature Straniere e Comunicazione, Università di Bergamo, Italy.

ISSN 1424-8689 pb.
ISBN 978-3-0343-1524-1 pb.

ISSN 2235-6371 eBook
ISBN 978-3-0351-0725-8 eBook

Contents

Interactions between legal experts and mixed audiences

Interactions between legal experts and lay people

CARMEN SANCHO GUINDA / MAURIZIO GOTTI / RUTH BREEZE

Framing Interpersonality in Law Contexts

1. Interpersonality as a fuzzy paradox

Few concepts in Discourse Studies are so versatile and intricate and have been so frequently contested as *interpersonality*. This construct not only offers diverse perspectives and research topics depending on the linguistic schools and theoretical frameworks it is viewed from, or the instrumental tools employed in its analysis, but also across successive social spheres. It is moulded by national cultures, registers, disciplines, genres, and private intentions, as well as by the media and the communicative situation – the nature and size of audiences, for example – through which all of them are transmitted. Clearly, the notion is versatile due to the dynamism inherent in every social group, and particularly within specialized communities, where established conventions may change and new genres emerge and make use of the latest technologies to produce and disseminate knowledge. What is not so evident, however, is the boundary between the two basic elements assumed to integrate the interpersonality construct: *stance* and *engagement* (Hyland 2005). They hold a circular relationship (Sancho Guinda/Hyland 2012), fuzzy and full of overlaps, since engaging with interlocutors (or opting for not doing so) inevitably entails adopting a stance on them, and taking and disclosing such posture intentionally is per se an act of engagement.

In this sense, general scholarly labels such as *evaluation* (Hunston/Thompson 2000), *stance* as a conjunction of ideational, interpersonal, and stylistic stands (Biber/Finegan 1989, Biber 2006, Jaffe 2009, Gray/Biber 2012), *positioning* (Harré/van Langenhove 1999), *point of view* (Simpson 1993), *footing* (Goffman 1981) and *appraisal* (Martin 2000, Martin/White 2005) aptly reflect this circularity. The fuzziness intrinsic to interpersonality becomes even more patent when another superordinate term, *voice,* is invoked, often as a synonym. Do they in actual fact refer to the same phenomenon? The answer is yes and no. Both subsume stance and engagement (that is, the different kinds of stance), are qualified as dialogic, and imply a certain degree of subjectivity, but voice seems to incorporate an expressionist nuance of stylistic distinctiveness, of 'authorial imprint', either individual or collective – if there is really such a dichotomy, as Prior (2001) doubts, because society always mediates individual choices. Voice and interpersonality are *subjective* because they depend on the addressee's impression (Tardy 2012) to be identified, and may be metaphorically or literally *dialogic.* Recent investigations (e.g. Gil Salom/Soler Monreal 2014) have drawn on this aspect, which some might take as tautological given that dialogism (Bakhtin 1981) is connatural to language in interaction. In light of all this, interpersonality should be certainly understood as *fuzzy,* but also as *paradoxical* and *gradable:* it embraces two categories (i.e. stance and engagement) that in reality fuse in one (stance/evaluation/positioning or any other of the aforementioned 'general labels') and evolves along a multiple continuum of uniqueness (determined by a relative stability of its features within communities, despite its permanent dynamism), explicit dialogism, and subjectivity. Therefore, some texts are more interactive – more 'dialogic'– and easily recognizable, in stylistic terms, than others.

To complicate matters further, this interpersonal fuzziness may arise from several sources: the *openness* of the construct, its *motivation,* its *multifunctionality,* and its *multidimensionality.* The inventory of interpersonal devices is by no means closed, and researchers speak of 'potential features' (e.g. Hiltunen 2010, in relation to 'existential *there*' as readability resource and stage labeller in academic research articles). Among them, discourse areas such as rhetorical manipulation, interdiscursivity conceived as shared knowledge, the selection, prominence and ordering of contents, punctuation and layout/format, rhythm in speech and written prose (set by syntax, cadence, euphony and prosody and impinging on memorability), shifts in attribution, genre bending and manipulation for communal purposes, or choices regarding the medium and channel of dissemination, still constitute untapped sites of study for the applied linguist interested in pinning down the idea of interpersonality and refining its taxonomies.

Interpersonality may show accidentally, as a 'give-off' (Goffman 1959) betraying the speaker or the writer, but may also be intentional and seek alignment with the community of practice by complying with its conventions, or show deference towards its outsiders. These actions are not mutually exclusive and form the conceptual tandem *proximity/ positioning* (Hyland 2010), which turns interpersonality into a 'two-way street'. A case in point is the use of multifunctional metadiscourse in specialised texts: items such as evidentials (e.g. citations) simultaneously provide background information for those who need it, telling them where to obtain it, disclaim the knowledge being transmitted in accordance with the honesty and modesty code of academia or the profession, and show competence (i.e. scholarly authority), which creates a gap between the expert sender and his/her lay addressees.

Similarly, attitudinal boosters of the type *clearly*, *obviously*, *certainly*, *truly*, etc., draw a line between the knowledgeable insider and the uninformed listener/reader, yet signposting what is taken for granted among experts within their community – shared notions, perceptions and deductions considered elementary and that gauge the knowledge of non-members and cue them about the expertise they should acquire to join in. More vehement interactional items of this type, such as *needless to say* or *it goes without saying* embody this category of (superfluous?) tacitness-breakers that inform readers of the interlocutors' perceived relationship from either side. Of course, the interpersonal relationship or tenor between participants is partly shaped by the writer/speaker-reader/listener role, which includes the degree of interlocutor-considerateness (i.e. more or less reader/listener-responsibility, pointed to by Purves 1988 or Hyland 2004) and the higher and lower foregrounding/ backgrounding of the content or the person behind it in the national and disciplinary cultures. Another central issue is what 'community membership' actually means, because inside the specialist group coexist multiple communicative purposes and there are asymmetrical power relationships as well, and not everyone may wish to become an insider or think it is beneficial.

When communicative multifunctionality transcends sentence-level and affects the social repercussion of the whole text, we may be witnessing ‘genre manipulation’ (Hyland 2004) or ‘discursive appropriation’ (Bhatia 2004). Genres fulfil broad and narrow purposes and implement them through interpersonal devices, which span a cline whose poles are the informational and persuasive goals. The promotional component, every day more pervasive, is ‘colonizing’ (Bhatia 2004) texts that were strictly informational in the past. For example, at the time Vázquez and Giner (2009) held that judgments were seldom promotional, the U.S. National Transportation Safety Board was just beginning to divulge online its highly reader-oriented case appeal decisions (see Sancho Guinda, this volume), which in addition brand the institution as transparent and democratic, following the Freedom of Information Act’s guidelines, so representative of the all-American spirit. This promotional matter may go unnoticed to genre users, as not all instances of social purposes are expressed overtly and prototypically, resembling one another and making up genre families and colonies (Bhatia 2004). Its detection depends instead on the user’s ability to read between the lines.

Interpersonality is not determined by the social purpose of the genre, but the two interact (again fuzzily and circularly) on several planes: topical, rhetorical, sentential, phrasal, lexical, phonological, phonetic, proxemic, and kinesic within the text (Bhatia’s 2012 ‘text-internal factors’), which generate – and are in turn generated by – communal expectations concerning aims, audiences and situational contexts, assumptions of shared knowledge, the strategic management of gatekeeping, and intertextuality (‘text-external factors’, Bhatia 2012). *Internal* and *external factors* thus enmesh multidimensionally and bidirectionally (from the individual to society and vice versa) to convey different sorts of meaning. On the one hand, there is ideational opinion or stance, aimed to inform but in legal settings also normally expressed to persuade or influence. On the other, we must consider solidarity with the interlocutor in the form of deference/engagement, aimed to facilitate comprehension by making the text intelligible to outsiders. Between both, as an intersection, there are attitudinal meanings that may fluctuate from adherence and empathy to dissent, opposition, or rejection (e.g. 'affect', 'judgment' and 'appreciation', evaluating emotions, ethics and aesthetics according to systemic-functional classifications, Martin 2000). As Hafner and Mazzi remind us in their respective chapters (this volume), no text is ever completely impersonal, and in view of all the textual and contextual variables at play, accomplishing the claim made by Candlin, Bhatia and Jensen (2002) – to teach interpersonality explicitly across legal genres – becomes no easy task.

2. Interpersonality in legal discourse

It is commonly said that legal discourse is characterised by a highly impersonal style, and that features of interpersonality are scarcely present in it (Bhatia 1982, Hiltunen 1990, Tiersma 1999). The avoidance of the use of these features is not at all arbitrary, but derives from the main pragmatic principles specific to the legal field and the high degree of conservatism typical of the law. Although there are movements in many countries advocating use of more ordinary language, most legal specialists continue to follow the practices codified by centuries of use. An example of the avoidance of interpersonality is seen in the non-use of adjectival/pronominal anaphoric reference in legal texts. This kind of reference is familiar in common language but far less so in legal writing, where it is normally avoided in favour of lexical repetition. This preference stems from the need for maximum clarity and avoidance of ambiguity, a typical trait of legal discourse.

Important elements of a particular legal system are its drafting tradition and stylistic conventions. These may differ in civil law and common law texts: the former are mainly characterised by generality, while the latter prefer particularity. Indeed, it is commonly asserted that civil law statutes are written in terms of principle, whereas common law regulations are written in detail as "the civil code draftsman is eager to be widely understood by the ordinary readership, whereas the common law draftsman seems to be more worried about not being misunderstood by the specialist community" (Bhatia 1993: 137). This difference may be observed also in contracts: the common law rules typically give great authority to the wording of the document, while the civil law systems put more emphasis on the actual intent of the parties at the time when the agreement was entered into. This conceptual differentiation is reflected in the drafters' stylistic choices: in common law legislation sentences are very long, consisting of three or more main clauses, each modified by many subordinate clauses; this remarkable sentence length is required by the great number of details to be inserted and the need that specifications should be precise and clear. Civil law sentences are shorter, with a less strict use of paragraphing; this makes the understanding of the sentences easier, but renders the reconstruction of the relationship between the various sentences more complex. To limit the interpretative difficulties of statutes and contracts, in the last few years legal drafters have adopted a more interpersonal approach, with particular emphasis on explicit textual schematisation (Driedger 1982) dividing the text into ordered sections and subsections. By arranging content schematically, drafters can thus construct less cognitively-demanding texts.

One of the phenomena that most distinguishes legal discourse is compliance with the norms governing the construction of its different text genres. There is usually a close link between the type of legal text and its structure, which in turn implies a number of correlations between the conceptual, rhetorical and linguistic features that characterise the text itself. Genre not only provides a conventional framework but also affects all other textual features and constrains their conceptual and rhetorical development. With time, several text types have arisen – some derived from genres common in general language, others crafted specifically to meet the needs of specialists. Through training and professional engagement, specialists learn to follow given norms and patterns in each type of text. The conventional use of genres also produces certain expectations among readers, and whenever the rules are broken, a text may be misunderstood or rejected. Textual standardisation occurs in all disciplinary fields but it is stronger in legal genres.

Discourse analysts have discovered the importance of the genre concept for the interpretation of discourse, to get a better understanding not only of the linguistic characteristics of texts, but also of the macrostructure of these texts, which appears to be organised according to genre expectations and conventions rooted in the socio-cultural context. For this reason, in recent years genre theory has looked more broadly at context, paying particular attention to a more comprehensive understanding of text/context interactions and focusing not simply on the form and content of genres, but more importantly on how genres are constructed, interpreted, used and exploited in the achievement of specific goals in highly specialised contexts. Indeed, any communicative situation combines several contextual factors, making it difficult to attribute a given linguistic peculiarity to a single originating factor. This awareness has led scholars to group together the contextual factors capable of identifying the parameters which distinguish different genres within a specialised language.

According to this perspective, also the analysis of interpersonal features has acquired greater importance. Thus, for legal language, Danet (1980) adapted Joos' (1961) stylistic categories for degree of formality to the different modes of text production (distinguishing between WRITTEN and ORAL, with the former subdivided into COMPOSED and SPONTANEOUS). By this route she developed a sociolinguistic scheme for the genres of legal language, which characterises each legal genre in terms of its style (frozen, formal, consultative, or casual). There are genres – e.g. wills, contracts and insurance policies – which combine highly formal traits with features typical of the written mode. Others, although written and formal (e.g. statutes, briefs, appellate opinions) exhibit a less frequent use of standard and repetitive clauses, on a par with that of witness examinations and motions, which belong to the oral mode. Even oral texts, however, may contain highly formal traits, as observed for example in verdicts, wedding vows and oaths. These genres are highly codified and typically exhibit standardised, easily predictable sentences, often amounting to formulaic expressions. There are also less predictable genres, however, which allow for a greater degree of spontaneity and variation, both in content and expressiveness. They are usually oral and take on different levels of formality: higher in witness examinations or expert statements, lower in non-expert statements and client-lawyer conversation, right down to the informality of private conversation between lawyers.

The analysis of legal genres has also shown the use of specific discursive conventions based on the exploitation of specific interpersonal features. For example, analyses of courtroom interactions during legal proceedings (Gibbons 2003, Anesa 2012) have shed light on the considerable divergences between the standard norms of verbal interaction and legal norms, especially in the case of cross-examination of suspects and witnesses, which may be crucial to the outcome of the trial. The examining lawyer exploits all his linguistic skills to obtain admissions, substantiation, contradictions and other evidence to prove his version of the facts.

As regards recent studies on interpersonality in legal genres, while there is a vast body of literature on the construction of interpersonality in academic, scientific, and technical genres, this topic remains under-researched in legal contexts. Some of the interpersonal aspects that have been investigated in recent studies on legal discourse are the communicative impact of modality and performativity (Garzone 2001, Charnock 2009, Takahashi 2009, Williams 2009), metadiscourse and other types of deference towards the audience (Buscetti 2006; Pascual 2006; Breeze 2011), the use of vagueness (Endicott 2000; Bhatia *et al.* 2005, Arinas Pellón 2012), the observance of the Cooperative Principle (Frade 2002; Pavličková 2010), argumentation and the interpersonal dimension of judgments (Bowles 2002; Mazzi 2007), strategies of textual simplification and easification (Bhatia 1993, 2010), as well as investigations in the fields of identity (Sala 2010, Gotti 2011a), power relationships and appeals to authority (Gotti 2011b, Hafner 2013).

As has been seen in this brief overview, studies on the relationship between writer/reader and speaker/audience in the legal field have been, although very valuable, still scarce, dispersed, and limited to a narrow range of genres and a restricted notion of interpersonality, most often confined to modality and the Gricean cooperative principles. This is the main reason that prompted us to co-edit this volume, by means of which we intend to help bridge this gap. We have thus invited the submission of current research-based chapters written by specialists adopting a genre approach and doing a systematic analysis of language to show the realisation and distribution of interpersonal features in specific legal genres. The aim was to achieve an expansion of the concept of 'interpersonality', which besides modality, Grice's maxims and other traditionally interpersonal features (such as metadiscursive guidance, pragmatic presuppositions and implicatures, politeness devices, style, voice, tone, pronominal use, etc.), might comprise or relate to ideational and textual issues like narrative disclosure, typography, rhetorical variation, or Plain English, among others. As will be seen in the presentation of the volume below and in the chapters themselves, the contributors have succeeded in offering their interpretative views by means of a wide range of theoretical frameworks and combined approaches, such as Genre Theory, (Critical) Discourse Analysis, Systemic Functional Linguistics, Corpus Linguistics, Stylistics, and Pragmatics.

3. Contents of the volume

3.1. Interactions among legal experts

The first five chapters in this book examine the interpersonal features of interactions between legal experts, with a scope that encompasses legislative practices, judgments and complaints, shipping contracts, and academic law research. In all of these areas, skilled members of the discourse communities of law can be seen to operate effectively within the interpersonal frameworks of specific genres that have evolved to fulfil concrete communicative purposes. In some cases, such as the 'charter party' used in shipping, the interaction may seem highly formalised, if not rigidly formulaic. In others, such as judicial or academic writing, experts muster a wide range of stance and engagement resources with a view to persuading their audience to accept their arguments. It is interesting to note that in certain cases, such as that of EU directives, legal writers take greater trouble to present their arguments more convincingly than might be expected given their authoritative role, presumably in order to preempt opposition of a political nature.

The discourse of judges has long been a key focus of interest for linguists interested in the interactions between language and the law. In the first chapter, Davide Mazzi uses the tools of corpus linguistics to explore interpersonality in judicial language at crucial moments in the decision-making process in common law and non-common law contexts, namely at the Supreme Court of Ireland (SCI), and at the European Court of Justice (ECJ). He found that the assertive tone adopted by SCI judges when proposing interpretations of key terms contrasted with a somewhat milder mode of expression used for identifying reliable sources. These judges also tended to adopt a pragma-dialectic mode of argumentation, based on the need to resolve perceived differences of opinion effectively and reasonably. On the other hand, ECJ judges appeared to be less likely to modulate their discourse or argue pragmatically: instead, their discourse suggested that they tended to speak in the name of the court, projecting their role as that of proceeding impersonally towards legal truth on the basis of accepted interpretations of their sources and the principles that inform them. The ECJ judges appeared to open up a smaller discursive space, and to devote less attention to the possible ambiguity of key terms, in a style that Mazzi characterises as 'less tolerant towards judicial dissent' than that of the Irish judges. Mazzi concludes that judges make use of different interpersonal strategies to construct their role as adjudicators at the highest courts of appeal in these two different settings. Irish judges show a propensity to negotiate their standpoint with the expert readership within their own tradition, while ECJ judges adopt an impersonal style, speaking in the name of 'the court', and avoiding reference to ambiguity or personal decision-making.

In chapter two, Tarja Salmi-Tolonen analyses an EU directive to investigate the interpersonal discursive means used by the EU to communicate with its member states. EU directives are prescriptive documents belonging within the category of legislation, which are used to direct the legislators of the member states to take measures that will implement their purpose. Their discourse is thus informative and directive, in accordance with the addressees' expectations. Since the primary addressees are the law-makers and law-providers in member states, who share the same professional language as the drafters of the directive, there is less attempt to adapt to the general public than there might be, say, in the case of national legislation. Notably, however, the drafters of the directives also appear to perceive a need to persuade stakeholders in member states to subscribe to the values and principles that shape the directive, and their framing includes explanations of the motives and background that underlie it. Salmi-Tolonen's analysis reveals a range of stance and engagement features that are used to negotiate interpersonal relations with addressees. Noteworthy among these are the interactional resources used to convince the law-takers of the law-makers' good intentions, with a heavy emphasis on 'individual rights' and 'respecting rights', which offsets competing discourses of 'harmonisation' within the EU. She also points out how directives make use of the vague phraseology that has been found to be typical in legislative texts. Importantly, the vocabulary of the directives includes many positive, inclusive terms which may be intended to exert a persuasive function on the recipients, in order to draw them into 'furthering the cause' sponsored by the directive itself. She also includes an analysis of *shall*, *should* and *may* in this context, exploring the way in which EU directives tend to use *shall* for mandatory duties and norms, *should* for correct procedures, and *may* for conferring discretionary powers. Her chapter thus offers interesting material for comparison with analyses of other legislative genres.

In the next chapter, María de los Ángeles Orts investigates the interpersonal structure of 'charter parties', that is, the contracts made out between ship owners and the persons who charter a vessel, usually in order to transport freight. Charter parties generally consist of a set of complex clauses drafted in classically archaic legal English and specialised maritime terminology. Orts analyses the charter parties issued by the Baltic and International Maritime Council (BIMCO) in terms of their lexical and syntactic features, as well as their pragma-linguistic structure. She contends that in pragmatic terms, unlike many types of contract, the charter party is less an exchange of symmetrical promises than an asymmetrical set of directives issued for the benefit of the ship owner. The distribution of rights and obligations is thus patently uneven, and there is a striking absence of commissives that would bind the owners. Orts's analysis sheds light on the sophisticated use of interpersonality (including impersonality) in steering the discourse of the document to protect the shipowners' interests while protecting the face of both parties. She concludes that the success of these contracts in achieving the desired transactional outcome means that their use is actually increasing in the international shipping community. This is an instance in which a well-organized professional group has successfully managed to develop and administer a genre that structures reality to further its own ends.

Next, Michele Sala's chapter explores interpersonality in a very different legal setting, namely that of academic research. He focuses on interrogatives, which are particularly prominent in legal academic work, perhaps under the cross-influence of other discipline-related discursive practices such as are found in courtroom language. The model he uses to investigate these interrogative resources is designed around a complex framework which accommodates the pragmatic, textual and morpho-syntactic levels of analysis. Sala examines various types of interrogative, including leading questions (or 'conducive' questions), which have an evaluative function, real questions (or 'non-conducive' questions), which are instrumental in introducing meanings, and 'mention' questions, which aid the cognitive processing of information. He also devotes particular attention to pseudo-dialogical question-answer pairs, which serve strategically to close down certain areas of discussion and focus the reader's attention on the writer's argument. Sala contends that the informative and persuasive character of research papers in law (compared, say, with research articles in empirical disciplines) means that the writer has to bring to bear a wide range of interpersonal resources, in order to convince his/her audience. The writer thus compensates for what may be missing, questionable or problematic at the ideational level by constructing claims which are acceptable not because their content is incontrovertible, but because of the convincing way they are phrased. The specific role played by interrogative forms, especially the more *evaluative* formulations, in this dialogic process goes a long way towards explaining their high frequency in legal academic texts.

Finally, Christoph Hafner's chapter addresses the issue of interpersonal resources in the barrister's opinion, a document intended to provide a balanced legal view on a particular case for the solicitor representing the client involved. Such opinions have a twofold purpose: to provide an objective assessment of the lay client's legal position, and to give subjectively-oriented advice on how to proceed in tactical terms. This means opinions are also subject to a certain tension between the need to present a clear opinion, and the duty to indicate to the reader where uncertainty may lie. Hafner contrasts opinions written by practising barristers and those composed by postgraduate law students in order to shed light on areas of difficulty in the acquisition of an appropriate professional voice. One particular area of interest that emerges concerns the handling of uncertainty. Experienced barristers show a variety of ways of dealing with the need to indicate areas that are not clear without sacrificing the confident, authoritative tone of their opinions. Uncertainty concerning facts tends to be signalled through negative constructions, which serve to limit the scope of what is stated to situations in which the positive information holds. Uncertainty about the adversary's position is expressed through a range of classic epistemic stance devices. Uncertainty about a legal argument, on the other hand, is often indicated through the use of conditional sentences. Thus, experienced legal opinion writers succeed in indicating areas of uncertainty without undermining their own authoritative presentation of the case. In writing by novice lawyers, however, the management of uncertainty causes some difficulty: the excessive use of inappropriate epistemic devices tends to undermine the writer's argument and make the opinion appear hesitant and unprofessional. Hafner also points to other features that reinforce the writer's authoritative voice, such as the striking use of the first person singular: the solicitor who receives the barrister's opinion has requested a confident analysis from a professional with considerable expertise, and the frequent use of *I* enables the barrister to invoke the personal authority that is expected in this situation. He concludes that novice writers must align themselves with the values and discourses that prevail in their profession in order to attain full membership of the disciplinary community.

3.2. Interactions between legal experts and mixed audiences

The second section of this book explores the discursive interaction between lawyers, on the one hand, and heterogeneous audiences, on the other. Such situations arguably present a particular challenge to legal experts, because they have to engage with audiences whose expectations and knowledge may vary widely, as may their command of the language and terminology of the law. Although maximum clarity and transparency might seem to be the most obvious solution to the problem of communicating with laypeople, the type of discourse generated may not satisfy the more exacting requirements of the specialist community. The chapters in this section offer analyses of various approaches to resolving this conundrum.

In his chapter on interpersonality in statutory writing, Vijay Bhatia addresses some of the crucial issues inherent in the contextual configuration of legislative writing, relevant to the so-called depersonalisation of statutory writing, and clarifies some of the interpersonal constraints and tensions in modern-day statutory drafting practices. He revisits the process by which statutes are drafted, which is shaped by two key institutional players, namely the legislature, which has the political power to present bills and pass laws, and the governmental executive bodies which give expression to legislative intention and work with parliamentary draftsmen to bring the legislative text into being. The complexity of their task is compounded by the other side of the coin, which is the relationship these bodies have with potential readers of the text, who include legal professionals of many kinds, politicians, and also the ordinary citizens of the country, who could arguably be regarded as the main addressees of such texts. Since legislative texts have at least two clearly demarcated audiences who do not share the same legal background, Bhatia makes a case for producing two different versions of the text: a simplified version designed for the general public, and an easified version for specialist audiences meant to meet the genuine professional needs that arise, which would be clear, precise, unambiguous and all-inclusive in its phrasing. He also proposes a number of different rhetorical strategies that might prove useful for drafting legislative provisions in a principled way.

After this, Carmen Sancho's chapter explores the interpersonal features of legal decisions on aviation accidents and incidents issued by the National Transportation Safety Board of the USA (NTSB), which functions as a court of appeal in this context. Focusing on a corpus of such decisions, she applies an extended framework of engagement, understood broadly to mean 'commitment', which includes the level of disclosure, interactivity with the audience, and aspects of reader-friendliness. She finds that these decisions have a mixed nature, since they address a broad and heterogeneous readership including many ordinary citizens. The nature of the addressees, together with current moves in the US legal world towards institutional transparency, means that the documents can be seen to be deeply engaged with non-expert readers, including the general public. However, this engagement does not diminish the discursive bonds with the expert communities of practice (aeronautical and legal) that are involved in generating the texts. The writers manage to reconcile *accessibility* and *informativeness* through a series of choices that can be interpreted in interpersonal terms. In particular, the decisions are written to be at once explicit and memorable, two properties which are achieved through use of a stable organisational format and the intercalation of narratives (both within the body of the text and as notes or addenda) which raise the level of disclosure and give expression to multiple voices. Far from being impersonal and uncommitted, these decisions reveal a major concern with addressing real audiences of both an expert and a non-expert nature.

Moving to a completely different area of the law, Christopher Williams centres his attention on the interpersonal aspects of guides intended for people involved in drafting legislation. Unlike drafting manuals, which are usually specific to one jurisdiction, are principally written for fellow drafters, and are of little interest to non-experts, guides may be written not only for fellow drafters but also for readers who may have little knowledge of the workings of the law. After he has reviewed the tendencies in drafting manuals and guides elsewhere, the main part of his chapter examines the Scottish government publication *Plain Language and Legislation*, published online in 2006, which addresses fellow drafters but also speaks to a wider readership of interested laypersons. In view of the nature of the subject matter and the diverse target readership, it is interesting to note that this booklet operates within a restricted range of interpersonal discourse. Writer invisibility is maintained, and there are few engagement markers in the text. Readers also have a low profile in this text, never being addressed as *you* or *the reader*, and only once being presented with a direct question. None the less, the widespread use of imperatives might be understood as creating the effect of involving the reader directly. At the same time, attitude markers, boosters and hedges abound: these are used strategically to persuade readers of the usefulness of plain language, while indicating an awareness of the controversies surrounding this issue in the legal world. Williams concludes that the writers of such guides are heavily concerned with persuading their readers as to their own competence as authorities on the subject, and the rightness of their position on the polemical issue of plain language. On the other hand, unlike, say, many academic writers, the producers of this guide avoid explicit writer presence in the text, possibly in order to heighten the sense of objectivity, and reader presence is limited to the use of imperatives. In the context of guidelines concerning the use of plain language, the low writer presence and directive tone of this text could be thought to be particularly striking.

In chapter nine, Ignacio Vázquez takes on the challenging area of arbitration discourse, centring on the interpersonal dimension of World Intellectual Property Organisation (WIPO) domain name arbitration awards. His analysis focuses specifically on three aspects: authoritativeness, interpersonal reasoning, and legalese. Domain disputes of this kind concern Internet addresses registered by companies to be used as business identifiers, and generally arise when similar names have been registered by other companies, or a name containing the company's trademark has been registered by a third party for an unspecified reason. Misuse of brands and trademarks in this way is thought to result in considerable losses for the company involved. The WIPO arbitration process is designed to enable companies to resolve such disputes without the added complications and expense of a court case. However, although such arbitration is theoretically conducted along different lines from standard litigation, there is considerable discursive and terminological overlap with other areas of legal practice. The awards which communicate the panel's decision begin by being highly dialogic in nature, containing many examples of dialogic expansion in which they acknowledge the parties' differing points of view, thus meeting the expectations of their mixed audience (particularly the companies themselves and their chosen arbitrators). However, towards the end of the award, in the mandatory 'Discussion' and 'Findings' sections, the tendency is towards dialogic contraction. The arbitration rules set clear limits to what can be said in these sections, which results in a turn towards increasingly bureaucratic discourse. Moreover, since the purpose of the award is to make a clear decision, when different views have been entertained in the foregoing sections it is necessary to show which should prevail. The final part of the award, which encapsulates the operative decision, is entirely authoritative in nature. In terms of interpersonality these texts can thus be seen to be the product of the interplay of different kinds of interpersonal move, including the assertion of different panelists' voices, the alignment with bureaucratic discourses, and the culmination in an authoritative decision that puts an end to the dispute.

Moving to another area of intellectual property, Ismael Arinas's chapter tackles the issue of interpersonality in patents. To understand the interpersonal dimension of patents, it is necessary first to understand that lawyers consider that patents are drafted for two broad adversarial audiences: those concerned with *validity* and those worried about *infringement*. The former have to be persuaded that each patent application is useful, new, and non-obvious or, in other words, valid intellectual property. The latter have to be dissuaded from trespassing on some exclusive area of such property. In a study covering a large corpus of US patents, Arinas is able to show how the interpersonal metafunction is employed to overcome the objections of both these interest groups. The identification of an unsolved problem provides a basis for staking the claim of novelty, while stance markers are used to assert the deficiencies of prior inventions. Other strategies also play a role, so that use of vague language, particularly adjectives with the suffix *-able*, for example, can be seen to be crucial in encompassing the potential advantages and functions of the invention, while also protecting the company or inventor in cases of error. Through a combination of discursive and interpersonal features, patents thus persuade the gatekeepers (patent examiners or judges) of their novelty and non-obviousness while claiming as wide a right to intellectual property as possible.

3.3. Interactions between legal experts and lay people

The interaction between lawyers and lay people has long been regarded as one of the most fascinating areas of legal discourse. On the one hand, the lawyer has to meet the challenge of obtaining and providing the necessary information, ensuring the cooperation of lay people, and interpreting their contributions in the light of legal theory. On the other, he or she must ultimately inscribe the realities of the events and situations involving the lay participants into the discourses and cognitive frameworks of the law. In the four chapters which make up this section, we will see how in areas as diverse as letters to clients, mediation, jury instruction and public relations, professionals approach these same problems in different ways.

Letters of advice or opinion are essential in the legal world. In Ruth Breeze's chapter, she shows how the lawyer uses relational features to project an appropriate authoritative yet judicious professional identity, provide expert knowledge and construct a consensual understanding of the facts and issues. He or she extends a role to the client in which the particular situation he/she has lived through is reformulated in terms of legal roles and relationships. The lawyer also establishes a professional tone through specific lexical choices, and safeguards his/her professional reputation by demarcating the fields of certainty and contingency. Throughout such letters, the lawyer steers both participants and events towards what is legally feasible and/or expedient, through a process of discursive alignment.

Mediation, which forms the subject of Maurizio Gotti's chapter, is a form of alternative dispute resolution which has become widespread in many parts of the world. One of the principal attractions of mediation is that agreement is reached by the parties through the work of a neutral party, the mediator, who helps them analyse the various interests involved in the dispute. This person also identifies the differences implied in the parties' respective positions, leading them towards a resolution of the dispute without imposing any decision. Gotti analyses oral transcripts from mediation cases in order to investigate the main interpersonal strategies adopted in mediation discourse as it is shaped by its community of practice. He identifies the negotiation strategies commonly adopted by mediators to help parties to listen to and understand each other's concerns, empathize with each other, express feelings and confront emotions. To be effective, mediators must acknowledge participants' needs in terms of face as well as expectations, and adapt their discursive strategies to the particular requirements of the situation. By reformulating summaries and reports of the parties' positions with a different stance or shift of footing, mediators can clarify arguments and redirect the discussion, and also put forward arguments without assuming the responsibility for decision-making, which is always ultimately left to the parties themselves. The mediator's command of interpersonal discursive resources is thus vital to the outcome of this form of dispute resolution.

Patrizia Anesa tackles the issue of communication in situations of knowledge asymmetry in the case of instructions to jurors in US courts, where the language used bears witness to the tensions that arise between the legal requirement for technical precision and the practical need to communicate with lay jurors. She sets out to understand the way experts and laypeople interact in the jury instruction phase of trials, by reviewing the generic 'pattern' jury instructions widely used in US courtrooms and then analysing the transcription of a trial by jury to explore how such instructions are adapted to a real situation. Instructions of this kind are characterised as hybrids in a number of senses: though written, they are presented in oral mode and the text is often integrated with comments made by the judge; they are originally formal and impersonal, yet they may be interspersed with informal, personal language added by judges; their target is ostensibly the jurors, but judges in appellate courts may also be addressed, and so they are written in a blend of plain English and technical language which reflects the different possible addressees; they are general enough to fit a broad range of cases, but also have to be adapted to offer specific guidance for the case at hand. In her case study, Anesa illustrates how the judge explains the instructions to achieve maximum clarity. This includes strategic use of second person pronouns to address the jury, the use of the parties' names rather than abstract roles such as *plaintiff* and *defendant*, simple explanations with examples to achieve maximum clarity about specific key concepts (such as *what is evidence?*) and use of definitions, paraphrases and code glosses to present legal issues such as the burden of proof to the jurors. The predominant use of active forms is also interpreted as a concession to the jurors' status as non-specialists. However, at certain points, Anesa notes that the use of technicisms is inevitable, since major differences hinge on the definitions of specific actions before the law. Moreover, although the relationship established with the jury is partially mediated directly through use of second person pronouns, it is also partly framed through a more traditional third person narrative which assigns those present a role as 'the jurors'. This could be explained as an alternation between the judge's own reformulation and the text of the pattern instructions that he is using. This chapter sheds important light on the way in which generic texts such as pattern instructions are adapted to the interpersonal requirements of real situations, and points to some of the constraints which restrict the scope for simplification and non-technical language in such contexts.

Finally, Isabel Corona's chapter centres on press releases in international arbitration cases, showing how the interpersonal dimension of this public relations genre is adapted to deal with situations very different from the general advertising function with which we have come to associate it. The disputes that go to commercial arbitration generally place the corporations involved in a situation of considerably vulnerability, since their reputation and their investors' confidence may be at stake. Press releases published in such circumstances are conditioned by the rhetorical need to defend and justify the company's actions. Various dialogistic resources are used to argue for the legitimacy of the company's actions and reactions against the other party's (re)actions. The arguments to justify and legitimise the company's actions shape a specific text type with a pragma-dialectical argumentative structure reminiscent of that found in legal texts. On the basis of an appraisal analysis of press releases issued during the arbitration between Kraft and Starbucks, Corona examines how dialogic expansion resources are used to open up a space for negotiation at specific points during the ongoing process, but dialogic contraction similar to that found in legal argumentation is often employed to adjust expectations and narrow down the field of possible solutions. Corona argues that the genre of the press release is flexible enough to adapt to this new interpersonal function without modifying its basic underlying framework.

4. Closing remarks

This book has analysed the subject of interpersonality from a range of innovative perspectives, covering a broad spectrum of genres that are significant in the legal world. In doing so it has defined a *continuum* that runs from undialogized or slightly dialogized monogloss to heterogloss dialogicality and traverses every type of interaction: among experts, between experts and mixed audiences, and between experts and lay people. In expert circles, for example, at one extreme of this cline we find genres such as very specific contracts (charter parties) and judicial interpretations, which are fundamentally assertive and authoritative, whereas at the other extreme academic research displays a wider repertoire of interactional devices (e.g. different sorts of interrogatives) aimed at the negotiation of meanings and the recognition of other presences and voices. In between these two poles there is an intermediate zone of fluctuating interpersonality, occupied by international directives and barristers' opinions, whose degree of dialogicality varies, respectively, in function of the nature of the norm (obligation, recommendation, discretionary power) and the experience and status of the writer, which affect authorial visibility and the mitigation of uncertainty. In the communication between experts and mixed audiences, by contrast, the pole of restricted interpersonality agglutinates genres of little accessibility to non-experts and with low authorial visibility and few engagement markers, as is the case of statutes and legal drafting guides, while at the highly interpersonal end stand the decisions on aviation case appeals divulged online by the U.S. National Transportation Safety Board, strongly oriented to the general public due to their reader-considerateness and didacticism. Within the middle territory spanning those two poles, the subtle interpersonal devices of patents (e.g. mainly vagueness, marked rhetorical organisation and adjectival suffixes), which help addressees build expectations and decode technical meanings, give way to the increased but oscillating interpersonality – depending on the process stage – of arbitrations concerning intellectual property. To conclude, the asymmetrical interaction between experts and lay people shortens the distance between poles and blurs zone and discursive boundaries, with genres simultaneously one-sided and interlocutor-minded, such as the letter of advice and the arbitrations press release, and others overtly plural, deferential and conciliatory, such as jury instructions and mediations.

All in all, interpersonality is a key component in legal interactions which is not only audience-bound but may also vary with genres, genre stages, media, linguistic code, and the sender's circumstances. Among these factors, it is perhaps mixed audiences that most clearly uncover the tension between proximity and positioning – that is, in our context of study, between adhesion to an expert community of practice, by expressing authority through single ideational stances and little glossing of specialised concepts, or a position close to non-expert interlocutors, acknowledging alternative viewpoints and bridging to less-informed backgrounds. Obviously, we do not claim to be comprehensive and fill every slot in the dialogicality continuum, or to offer a complete, definitive account of interpersonality in the legal domain. Rather, we hope that the chapters in this volume will open up new perspectives, provide subjects for fresh discussion, and stimulate debate among all those scholars and practitioners interested in the interface between language and the law.

References

Anesa, Patrizia 2012. *Jury Trials and the Popularization of Legal Language: A Discourse Analytical Approach*. Bern: Peter Lang.

Arinas Pellón, Ismael 2012. How Vague can your Patent Be? Vagueness Strategies in U.S. Patents. *Hermes – Journal of Language and Communication in Business* 48, 55-74.

Bakhtin, Mikhail M. 1981. *The Dialogic Imagination: Four Essays by M.M. Bakhtin*. Ed. by Holquist, Michael (Emerson, Caryl / Holquist, Michael, trans.). Austin: University of Texas Press.

Bhatia, Vijay K. 1982. *An Investigation into Formal and Functional Characteristics of Qualifications in Legislative Writing and its Application to English for Academic Legal Purposes*, Ph.D. thesis. The University of Aston in Birmingham, UK.

Bhatia, Vijay K. 1993. *Analysing Genre: Language Use in Professional Settings*. London: Longman.

Bhatia, Vijay K. 2004. *Worlds of Written Discourse. A Genre-based View*. London: Continuum.

Bhatia, Vijay K. 2010. Drafting Legislative Provisions: Challenges and Opportunities. *The Loophole – Journal of the Commonwealth Association of Legislative Counsel* December issue, 5-15.

Bhatia, Vijay K. 2012. Interdiscursivity in Academic Genres. In Berkenkotter, Carol / Bhatia, Vijay K. / Gotti, Maurizio (eds) *Insights into Academic Genres*. Bern: Peter Lang, 47-65.

Bhatia, Vijay K. / Engberg, Jan / Gotti, Maurizio / Heller, Dorothee (eds) 2005. *Vagueness in Normative Texts*. Bern: Peter Lang.

Biber, Douglas 2006. Stance in Spoken and Written University Registers. *Journal of English for Academic Purposes* 5/2, 97-116.

Biber, Douglas / Finegan, Edward 1989. Styles of Stance in English: Lexical and Grammatical Marking of Evidentiality and Affect. *Text* 9/1, 93-124.

Bowles, Hugo 2002. How Judges Agree to Disagree: Social and Linguistic Patterns of Dissent in the English Legal Process. In Gotti, Maurizio / Heller, Dorothee / Dossena, Marina (eds) *Conflict and Negotiation in Specialized Texts*. Bern: Peter Lang, 143-164.

Breeze, Ruth 2011. Disciplinary Values in Legal Discourse: A Corpus Study. *Ibérica* 21, 93-115.

Buscetti, Stefania 2006. Tag Questions in Courtroom Discourse. In Flowerdew, John / Gotti, Maurizio (eds) *Studies in Specialized Discourse*. Bern: Peter Lang, 209-238.

Candlin, Christopher N. / Bhatia, Vijay K. / Jensen, Christian H. 2002. Developing Legal Writing Materials for English Second Language Learners: Problems and Perspectives. *English for Specific Purposes* 21, 299-320.

Charnock, Ross 2009. When *May* Means *Must:* Deontic Modality in English Statute Construction. In Salkie/Busuttil/van der Auwora (eds), 177-198.

Danet, Brenda 1980. Language in the Legal Process. *Law and Society Review* 14/3, 445-564.

Driedger Elmer A. 1982. Legislative Drafting Style: Civil Law versus Common Law. In Gémar, Jean-Claude (éd.) *Langage du droit et traduction / The Language of the Law and Translation*. Montreal: Linguatech / Conseil de la Langue Française, 63-81.

Endicott, Timothy 2000. *Vagueness in Law*. Oxford: Oxford University Press.

Frade, Celina 2002. The Legal Cooperative Principle: An Essay on the Cooperative Nature of Contractual Transactions. *International Journal for the Semiotics of Law* 15/4, 337-343.

Garzone, Giuliana 2001. Deontic Modality and Performativity in English Legal Texts. In Gotti, Maurizio / Dossena, Marina (eds) *Modality in Specialized Texts*. Bern: Peter Lang, 153-174.

Gibbons, John 2003.*Forensic Linguistics*. Oxford: Blackwell.

Gil Salom, Luz / Soler Monreal, Carmen (eds) 2014. *Dialogicity in Written Specialised Genres*. Amsterdam: John Benjamins.

Goffman, Erving 1959. *The Presentation of Self in Everyday Life*. New York: Doubleday Anchor.

Goffman, Erving 1981. *Forms of Talk.* Oxford: Oxford University Press.

Gotti, Maurizio 2011a. Identity Traits in Legal Texts. In Baccolini, Raffaella / Chiaro, Delia / Rundle, Christopher / Whitsitt, Sam (eds) *Minding the Gap. Studies in Linguistic and Cultural Exchange for Rosa Maria Bollettieri Bosinelli.* Bologna: Bononia University Press, 287-298.

Gotti, Maurizio 2011b. Exercising Power and Control in Arbitration Proceedings. *International Journal for the Semiotics of Law* 24, 179-193.

Gray, Bethany / Biber, Douglas 2012. Current Conceptions of Stance. In Hyland, Ken / Sancho Guinda, Carmen (eds) *Stance and Voice in Written Academic Genres.* Houndmills, Basingstoke, Hampshire (UK): Palgrave Macmillan, 15-33.

Grice, Paul 1975. Logic and Conversation. In Cole, P. / Morgan, J.L. (eds) *Syntax and Semantics 3. Speech Acts*. New York: Ablex. 41-58.

Hafner, Christoph A. 2013. The Discursive Construction of Professional Expertise: Appeals to Authority in Barrister's Opinions. *English for Specific Purposes* 32/3, 131-143.

Harré, Rom / van Langenhove, Luk / (eds) 1999. *Positioning Theory. Moral Contexts of International Action.* Oxford: Blackwell.

Hiltunen, Risto 1990. *Chapters on Legal English. Aspects Past and Present of the Language of the Law.* Helsinki: Suomalainen Tiedeakatemia.

Hiltunen, Turo 2010. 'There Are Good Reasons for This': Disciplinary Variation in the Use of Existential *There* Constructions in Academic Research Articles. In Lorés-Sanz, Rosa / Mur-Dueñas, Pilar / Lafuente-Millán, Enrique (eds) *Constructing Interpersonality. Multiple Perspectives on Written Academic Genres.* Newcastle upon Tyne: Cambridge Scholars Publishing, 181-204.

Hunston, Susan / Thompson, Geoff (eds) 2000. *Evaluation in Text: Authorial Stance and the Construction of Discourse*. Oxford: Oxford University Press.

Hyland, Ken 2004. *Genre and Second Language Writing.* Ann Arbor: The University of Michigan Press.

Hyland, Ken 2005. Stance and Engagement: A Model of Interaction in Academic Discourse. *Discourse Studies* 7/2, 173-192.

Hyland, Ken 2010. Constructing Proximity: Relating to Readers in Popular and Professional Science. *Journal of English for Academic Purposes* 9/2, 116-127.

Jaffe, Alexandra (ed) 2009. *Stance: Sociolinguistic Perspectives*. Oxford: Oxford University Press.

Joos, Martin 1961. *The Five Clocks*. New York: Harcourt, Brace and World.

Martin, James R. 2000. Beyond Exchange: Appraisal Systems in English. In Hunston/Thompson, 142-175.

Martin, James R. / White, Peter R.R. 2005. *The Language of Evaluation. Appraisal in English.* Basingstoke: Palgrave Macmillan.

Mazzi, Davide 2007. *The Linguistic Study of Judicial Argumentation. Theoretical Perspectives, Analytical Insights.* Modena: Il Fiorino.

Pascual, Esther 2006. Questions in Legal Monologues: Fictive Interaction as Argumentative Strategy in a Murder Trial. *Text & Talk* 26/3, 383-402.

Pavličková, Eva 2010. Legal Writing in Light of Grice's Cooperative Principle. In Kačmárová, Alena (ed.) *English Matters II: A Collection of Papers by the Department of English Language and Literature*. Prešov: Faculty of Humanities and Natural Sciences. <http://www.pulib.sk/elpub2/FF/Kacmarova2/pdf_doc/pavlickova.pdf>.

Prior, Paul A. 2001. Voices in Text, Mind and Society: Sociohistoric Accounts of Discourse Acquisition and Use. *Journal of Second Language Writing* 1-2, 55-81.

Purves, Alan C. (ed) 1988. *Writing across Languages and Cultures: Issues in Contrastive Rhetoric.* London: Sage.

Sala, Michele 2010. Interrogative Forms as Professional Identity Markers in Legal Research Articles. In Garzone, Giuliana / Archibald, James (eds) *Discourse, Identities and Roles in Specialized Communication*. Bern: Peter Lang, 301-320.

Salkie, Raphael / Busuttil, Pierre / van der Auwora, Johan (eds) 2009. *Modality in English. Theory and Description.* Berlin: Mouton de Gruyter.

Sancho Guinda, Carmen / Hyland, Ken 2012. Introduction: A Context-Sensitive Approach to Stance and Voice. In Hyland, Ken / Sancho Guinda, Carmen (eds) *Stance and Voice in Written Academic Genres.* Basingstoke: Palgrave Macmillan, 1-11.

Simpson, Paul 1993. *Language, Ideology and Point of View.* London: Routledge.

Takahashi, Hiroshi 2009. Modality in L2 Legal Writing: A Functional Analysis. *Language Research Bulletin* 24. < http://web.icu.ac.jp/ lrb/volume-24.html>.

Tardy, Christine M. 2012. Current Conceptions of Voice. In Hyland, Ken / Sancho Guinda, Carmen (eds) *Stance and Voice in Written Academic Genres.* Houndmills, Basingstoke, Hampshire (UK): Palgrave Macmillan, 34-48.

Tiersma, Peter M. 1999. *Legal Language*. Chicago: The University of Chicago Press.

Vázquez, Ignacio / Giner, Diana 2009. Authoritative Intervention and (In)directness in Legal Discourse. A Genre-Based Study of Judgments and Arbitration Awards. *XXVII AESLA International Conference.* Universidad de Castilla-La Mancha, 26-28 March.

Williams, Christopher 2009. Legal English and the 'Modal Revolution'. In Salkie/Busuttil/van der Auwera (eds), 199-210.

Interactions among Legal Experts

DAVIDE MAZZI

"The words are plain and clear…": On Interpersonal Positioning in the Discourse of Judicial Interpretation

1. Introduction

Over the last twenty years, interpersonality as a way to construct writer/reader or speaker/audience relationships at a variety of levels, has been profitably investigated in such areas as academic and scientific genres. With a view to academic essay writing, for instance, Barton (1995) highlights that connectives often occur in a two-part structure (e.g. *of course...but*), where the prominence of a non-contrastive connective invariably followed by a contrastive one can be seen as a face-saving move enabling the writer to maintain the degree of solidarity so highly valued between members of a shared academic community. At the same time, the frequency of contrastive claims is described by Barton (1995: 234) as an interpersonal metadiscourse marker of "shared emphasis between readers and writers in an academic discourse community that values contrast as a basis for creating knowledge via argumentation". More recently, Hirvela/ Belcher (2001) deal with problematic interpersonal aspects related to L2 writing skills. In this context, they discuss textual strategies of 'voice' as the process of establishing authorial presence or identity in expert writing. Furthermore, they call for the construction of an architecture of voice enabling students to acquire disciplinary competence "to locate the person behind the written words" (Hirvela/ Belcher 2001: 85, but cf. also Bowden 1999).

Despite the insights offered by these studies, the full potential of the study of interpersonality in legal and/or judicial settings remains to be fully explored. On the one hand, a number of studies have explored the interpersonal dimension of judgments associated with the expression of judicial dissent, thus focusing on the strategies to emphasize or downplay disagreement between peers or judges from different degrees of the jurisdiction, along with the related discourse tools (Bowles 2002; Mazzi 2006). On the other hand, available research still leaves much space to the quest for answers to such research questions as how judges construct their voice and professional identity as experts in a community of practice, how they legitimize their standpoints and eventual decisions, subjected as they are to strict public scrutiny on the part of their peers within and (often) beyond national borders, as well as the media and the general public in highly controversial cases.

In an attempt to contribute to filling this gap, this chapter focuses on the issue of interpersonal positioning (Ivanič/Camps 2001) in a key-genre of legal discourse, i.e. judgments. Based on the assumption that no writing is ever completely impersonal, Ivanič/Camps point out that writers make use of a variety of resources to convey messages about themselves. As they do so, they position themselves "in terms of their relative authoritativeness or tentativeness and in terms of [their] relationship with their readers" (Ivanič/Camps 2001: 4). This research draws on this conceptualisation in order to comparatively investigate issues of interpersonal positioning in judgments across two concurring and at times definitely overlapping legal systems, the Republic of Ireland and the European Union.

The relevance of interpersonality in judicial settings should come as no surprise. Indeed, it appears rather interesting to analyse the discourse of last-resort judges as they construct their profile as reliable adjudicating professionals. This can be properly appreciated if we think that judges have to fulfil tasks of both an integrative and a creative nature (Dworkin 1986): accordingly, if certainty of meaning must be the paramount aim of legal norms (Gowers 1962), the fact nonetheless remains that their meaning can sometimes be as slippery as not to be easily captured as a natural object (Hart 1961; Zirk-Sadowski 2012).

For this reason, the aim of the chapter is to examine the discourse strategies and the language tools through which judges position themselves interpersonally in cases where the controversy centres on the disputed interpretation of a term, phrase or passage of relevant legislation. This is a crucial moment of judicial decision-making, especially when the issues at stake are of paramount importance from a broader political or economic point of view: in the EU context, that seems to be the case of agriculture, a highly controversial subject-matter in which European institutions and Member States have been confronting each other for a few decades now.

How do judges resolve differences of opinion between parties that argue for different interpretations of the law? What interpretive and argumentative tools do they develop in order to establish their own credentials in arguing the case and pronouncing how the law is ultimately to be read? And how is their discourse shaped accordingly? These are the main research questions tackled in the study. In Section 2, the materials on which the research is based are discussed and analytical criteria are clarified, whereas Section 3 is dedicated to a presentation of findings to be discussed in Section 4.

2. Materials and methods

The study is based on two synchronic comparable corpora: the first one, the so-called ECJ corpus, includes the English version of 50 judgments issued by the Court of Justice of the European Union (279,604 words altogether); the second corpus, the SCI corpus, features 46 judgments delivered by the Supreme Court of Ireland (352,753 words). The choice of these two sources seemed good for two reasons. First of all, it reflects the use of English across native and non-native contexts; secondly, it is indicative of the fact that the creation of such supra-national bodies as the European Union has brought not only speakers but also different and at times heterogeneous legal systems closer together (Maley 1994; Barceló 1997). EU Membership has had a strong impact on common-law countries like the United Kingdom and the Republic of Ireland: from a legal point of view, these have yielded to Community law, i.e. a legal system largely influenced by the civil-law tradition, and they have had to create a new legal infrastructure to accommodate the influx of vast amounts of EC legislation in economic and social matters (Byrne/ McCutcheon 1996; Dimitrakopoulos 2001; Tomkin 2004). From a more inherently linguistic perspective, these English-native countries have had to come to terms with a distinct legal and judicial system, in which the use of English might not necessarily overlap with the standards and conventions they have traditionally been adopting in domestic legislation.

The criteria of corpus design were essentially fourfold. First of all, the homogeneity of the judicial subject-matter covered by the judgments was a key-parameter: for both corpora, only judgments concerning agriculture were selected.[1] Secondly, the homogeneity of the sources was secured, because the judgments were issued by two courts of last resort in the respective jurisdictions, i.e. EC law and the legal system of the Republic of Ireland. Thirdly, the two sources were chosen with a view to their capability of representing English in use in both an English-native national context – i.e. Ireland – and a supra-

1 ECJ judgments were downloaded from the official website of the Court of Justice of the European Union, i.e. <http://curia.europa.eu/juris/recherche.jsf?language=en&jur=C&td=ALL>. The URL directs users to a very detailed webpage, where one can set a wide range of search parameters – e.g. Period or Date, Authentic language, Subject-matter and Case status: in our case, *last 5 years* was set as Period or Date, *English* under Authentic language and *Cases closed* under Case status, whereas not only *Agriculture* but also other related terms suggested by the webpage itself were inserted as Subject-matter, e.g. *Agricultural structures*, *Animal feedingstuff*, *Beef and veal*, *Cereals*, *Coffee*, *Eggs and poultrymeat* etc. As regards SCI judgments, they were also downloaded from the Court's official website, namely <http://www.supremecourt.ie/Judgments.nsf/SCSearch?OpenForm&l=en>: the advanced search function allows one to insert any string in the quest for judgments, in addition to any judge's name one or more cases may be retrieved with. For the purpose of this study, the item *Agriculture* was used as the only search term in that it enabled us to come up with almost as many judgments as those already inserted in the ECJ corpus.

national context such as the EU, where English is not necessarily the language of the parties involved.[2]

Finally, we made sure that the two corpora were also quantitatively comparable: for the ECJ corpus, the carefully constructed search engine of the Court's website was used to retrieve the last 50 judgments delivered by the ECJ on agriculture and its related areas; in the case of the SCI, an equivalent advanced search based on the term *agriculture* was launched, with the effect of retrieving a total of 46 judgments. In an attempt to guarantee that the corpora reflect a comparable time span, the websites of the two courts were both accessed for the purpose of corpus design at the end of May 2012. In the context of EC law, however, where agriculture tends to be a hot and at times deeply controversial issue, the time span ultimately covered by the corpus turned out to be more restricted (22 December 2010 – 24 May 2012), because a large number of judgments is pronounced by the court on that topic; by contrast, since agriculture is less often an area on which the Supreme Court of Ireland is called upon to rule, the time span was predictably larger (23 February 2001 – 21 July 2011) for the SCI corpus.

2 Although this chapter is not intended to deal with language policy, the fact remains that language is indeed a major issue insofar as the two corpora are concerned. At an EC level, the language of proceedings is by rule the one used in the application, whereas judges conventionally deliberate in French as a common language (cf. Berteloot 1999 and <http://curia.europa.eu/jcms/jcms/Jo2_7024/>). This implies that in most cases, the English version of judgments is actually a translation from another language: this increases the interest in a variety of English, as it were, employed in a supra-national context across different legal systems, while it does not prejudice the reliability of the study in that it was shown elsewhere that neither the surface of text nor the generic structure of judgments are affected by potentially differing source-languages from which the English version was derived (Mazzi 2007). As for the Republic of Ireland, it seems equally interesting to note that Article 8 of the Irish Constitution defines Irish as 'the first official language of the country'. However, the Court's judgments are most often delivered in English, even though the SCI corpus also includes one judgment (*Ó Murchú v. An Taoiseach & chuid eile*) delivered in Irish and only subsequently translated into English (cf. Article 8.3 of the Constitution).

From a methodological point of view, this study combines the tools of corpus (Schulze/Römer 2008; Gabrielatos et al. 2012) and discourse (Ädel/Reppen 2008; Swales 2009) analysis for the purpose of a qualitative and quantitative analysis of the discourse tools and strategies associated with the courts' interpersonal positioning across ECJ and SCI corpus.

To begin with, a random sample of ten judgments was selected for each corpus.[3] These judgments were subjected to manual reading with a twofold aim: first of all, a rough estimate of the incidence of cases revolving around terminological disputes; secondly, a preliminary overview of any salient language feature correlated with the court's argumentation in clearing up doubts about controversial terms, phrases or passages of relevant legislation. This opening stage led to realize that in SCI cases, there is a steady relationship between the court's resolution of the cases in question and the occurrence of the reflexive terms *word*, *phrase*, *sentence*, *reading*, *meaning* and *interpretation*. On the other hand, since the ECJ appeared prone to resolve legal ambiguity by referring to whole chunks of relevant legal documents, its argumentation was largely tied to the occurrence of the metadiscursive terms *preamble*, *paragraph*, *subparagraph* and *meaning*.

This finding prompted the second stage of the analysis, where the above terms were lemmatized and subjected to a computer-assisted concordance-based analysis (Sinclair 2003) by means of the

3 The SCI sample included the following judgments: The Minister for Agriculture v. Albatros Feeds Ltd.; Rooney v. The Minister for Agriculture et al.; Ó Murchú v. The Taoiseach; Fuller et al. v. The Minister for Agriculture; Quinn v. Ireland, the Attorney general et al.; HMIL Ltd. v. The Minister for Agriculture; Kildare Meats v. The Minister for Agriculture; Philip et al. v. The Minister for Agriculture; Sparrow v. The Minister for Agriculture et al.; McDonnell v. Brady et al. In addition, the ECJ judgments included in the related sample were as follows: Hehenberger v, Republik Österreich; Bureau d'Intervention v. Beneo-Orafti; Groupe Limagrain v. Etablissement national des produits de l'agriculture; Danske Svineproducenter v. Justitsministeriet; Corman v. Bureau d'Intervention; Vlaamse Dienerartsenvereinigung et al. v. Belgium; Vlamex v. Hauptzollamt Hamburg; Republic of Poland v. European Commission; Hauptzollamt Koblenz v. Etling et al.; Camar v. Presidenza del Consiglio dei Ministri.

linguistic software package *WordSmith Tools 5.0* (Scott 2008). By looking at the terms in context, two major operations were performed in parallel: firstly, the regular collocational patterns of the concordanced terms were identified; secondly, the Court's argumentation was examined, with reference to both the legal tools employed by the two courts to clear legal ambiguities, and any widespread argument form (Van Eemeren et al. 1996; Van Eemeren 2001) detected around the occurrences.

3. Results

The aim of this section is to identify the main patterns in the data. For this purpose and for the sake of clarity, the findings about the Supreme Court of Ireland are dealt with first (3.1), to be followed by a review of the results from the ECJ corpus right next (3.2).

3.1. Interpersonal positioning in SCI judgments

A careful scrutiny of the ten random texts extracted from the SCI corpus provides solid evidence in two main respects. First of all, a significant number of cases appears to revolve around the interpretation of controversial language: this is not only true for cases where the Court is most obviously requested to rule with regard to the compatibility between domestic statutory law and the Irish Constitution, but also when it is to assess the conformity of domestic legislation with the regulatory framework of EU Law. Secondly, it may not be surprising that when relevant language is the core element of the dispute, the Court almost invariably uses such reflexive words as *word*, *phrase*, *meaning* and *reading* to reflect and comment upon the interpretive process.

An illustrative example is provided by Case No. 2005/63JR (*The Minister for Agriculture and Food and the Attorney General v.*

Albatros Feeds Ltd.). The judgment, delivered by Mr Justice Fennelly in 2006, concerned the import and distribution of animal feedstuffs by Albatros, the appellant. On the grounds that a portion of Albatros's cargo in County Cork allegedly contained bone spicules forbidden by EU Agricultural regulations, the Minister had issued notices bearing the heading 'Seizure and Detention Notice' to impound the cargo. Albatros lodged an appeal to the Supreme Court as it claimed to have suffered substantial losses as a result of the issuing of such instructions about a product liable to rapid deterioration. Interestingly, the Court's judgment eventually rested in working out the proper meaning of two lexical items of the utmost importance: these were *processed animal protein* and *so far as possible*.

The first was a key phrase because it was predictably necessary to determine whether bone spicules qualified as *processed animal protein*, this being the primary target of relevant EU regulations. Moreover, the adverbial phrase *so far as possible* turned out to be crucial, insofar as the Court was required to establish whether the Minister had a right to issue the contested instructions: in alleging that she had legitimately done so, the Minister relied on a passage of EU case law whereby the national court is declared to be bound to "interpret national law, so far as possible, in the light of the wording and purpose of the directive concerned" (*Pfeiffer and others v. Deutsches Rotes Kreuz*). In other words, the Minister argued, the end of the instructions, notably prohibiting the entry and marketing of illegal products within Member States, was what justified the means used to attain it, i.e. the 'Seizure and Detention Notice' itself.

The centrality of controversy on the disputed interpretation of a term, phrase or passage in legislation warranted the investigation of how Irish judges discursively construct their profile as trustworthy adjudicating professionals in such circumstances, at a wider corpus level. The concordance and context-based analysis of the key lemmas *word*, *phrase*, *sentence*, *meaning*, *interpretation* and *reading* showed that judges tend to construct their credibility in their expert readers' eyes by carefully combining a quintessentially assertive tone with a more tentative positioning.

To begin with, SCI judges tend to opt for a strong, assertive tone in two main contexts. In the first one, they stress that the natural meaning of words should be preferred in case of potential ambiguity. This means that either words are to be interpreted by referring to their plain meaning (cf. (1) below), or they ought to be understood in the light of the surrounding provisions of the same item of legislation (2).[4] At a discourse level, this discernible trend is indicated by the colligation between *word* and epistemic markers like *ought to*, *should*, *must* and *be the duty*, which concerns 8.4% of the 131 occurrences of the lemma:

(1) It is the duty of the court to construe section 16 in the light of the plain meaning of the *words* used and also in the contextual light of the surrounding provisions of the statute. Taking this approach my view is that 'absence from duty' bears the literal meaning, as held by the learned trial judge, of physical absence from the place of work. (Fuller et al. v. The Minister for Agriculture and Food et al.)

(2) The meaning which *words* ought to be understood to bear is not to be ascertained by any process akin to speculation: the primary duty of a court of law is to find the natural meaning of the words used in the context in which they occur, that context including any other phrases in the Act which may throw light on the sense in which the makers of the Act used the words in dispute. (Fuller et al. v. The Minister for Agriculture and Food et al.)

The second context where the SCI judge's authority is more straightforwardly perceived is instantiated by those passages where the Court firmly anchors the proposed interpretation of a controversial term or passage to its well established case law or, albeit less frequently, to teleological aspects of legislation and/or the EU legal framework the SCI finds itself to operate within. Emphasis on settled case law becomes clear in 21.5% of the 28 occurrences of *phrase* (see 3 below), whereas firm stance is taken towards issues of (mainly EU) legislation in 24% of the entries of *sentence* (4). In both cases, *phrase* and *sentence* are often observed to collocate with such boosters as *clearly* and *resolve any possible doubt*. Furthermore, SCI judges look naturally keen to assess the teleology, i.e. the overriding aim with which

---

4 In all numbered examples, the lexical item under investigation is in italics, whereas any salient collocate is underlined. Furthermore, the case the examples are taken from is indicated in brackets at the end of each example.

legislation was conceived, in 21.1% of the 19 occurrences of *reading*. As they do so, Irish judges find it useful to redefine the intended goal of a norm for chiefly refutative purposes, notably in the attempt to express their opposition to any competing interpretation they see as manipulating the only sensitive reading (5):

(3) The court then went on to consider the question as to whether what they described again as 'this power of adjudication' can be considered to be one normally and necessarily exercised by a legislature in a democratic state. The use of the latter *phrase* is clearly a reference to its use in the judgment of this court in Haughey v. Moriarty, where the court said: [...]. (Ardagh et al. v. Maguire et al.)

(4) "[...] the direct applicability of the measure empowering the Member State to take the national measures in question will mean that the national courts may ascertain whether such national measures are in accordance with the content of the Community regulation." Clearly, the last *sentence* refers to the right of the courts of the Member States to refer questions of interpretation to the Court of Justice pursuant to Article 234EC (then Article 177 of the Treaty). (Philip et al. v. The Minister for Agriculture, Food and Rural Development in Ireland et al.)

(5) The early part of this passage might be read as implying that, in some circumstances, the implementation of Community law is necessarily, by reasons of the demands of Community law itself, carried out by regulation. It is clear, however, from the second quoted paragraph that this *reading* is not what was intended; in any event, as shown above, Community law makes no such demands. (Philip et al. v. The Minister for Agriculture, Food and Rural Development in Ireland et al.)

The judges' voice sounds less commanding when they look for alternative sources to offer their interpretation of the key issue of the dispute. Judges thus seek to cite reliable sources to retain their credibility, although this frequently implies they adopt a somewhat milder tone which does not ward off counterclaims as peremptorily as in the extracts reported above. This aspect was remarkable in 2.3% of the occurrences of *word* instantiated in (6) and (7) below, where the Court respectively quoted a dictionary – an otherwise unqualified source to identify the appropriate (or possibly expedient) meaning of 'inherent'

– and a putatively plausible explanation provided by Lord Shaw decades before for 'intention'.

In (6), the judge does little more than merely specify that the entry of the *New Shorter Oxford English Dictionary* is the one he finds most convincing: there are no boosters in the passage, and the use of the first person in the following sentence appears to post-modify the choice by reappraising it as a rather subjective one. Notwithstanding Lord Shaw's authoritative voice in (7), the judge's choice of his view to disambiguate 'intention' is pre-modified by the hedge *perhaps*, which makes the argument sound less cogent and altogether more tentative:[5]

(6) The kernel of this case is whether members of the Dáil and/or Seanad in committee have inherent power to conduct an inquiry of the type in issue. The *word* 'inherent' is defined in the New Shorter Oxford English Dictionary as: [...] I adopt this definition. The question then is whether the power to conduct a public inquiry such as is in issue in this case is fixed, situated or contained in, or is existing in, members of the Houses as an essential or permanent characteristic, attribute or quality, or as a right, power or function under the Constitution of Ireland, 1937. (Maguire et al. v. Ardagh et al.)

(7) What 'intention' in that context means and how it is ascertained has been the subject matter of much judicial authority in respect of which no real controversy arises in the present case. Perhaps a convenient explanation of the *word* 'intention' in this context was provided by Lord Shaw in [...], when he said: [...]. (Igote Ltd. v. Badsey Ltd.)

---

5 Because Lord Shaw's opinion dates back to 1918, e.g. four years ahead of the birth of the Irish Free State, (7) raises the interesting issue of the value of English case law in Ireland. There seems to have been no judicial unanimity as to whether decisions of the House of Lords 1800-1922 are binding on the Republic's courts or merely have persuasive authority (cf. Henchy 1962; Byrne/McCutcheon 1996). Still, it should be noted that Article 50 of the Irish Constitution establishes that English laws no longer have force insofar as they are not consistent with the Constitution itself, and to the extent to which they may have been repealed or amended by the *Oireachtas*. This aspect was strongly emphasized by Supreme Court Judge Niall McCarthy ("In no sense are our courts a continuation of or successors to the British courts", *Irish Shell Ltd v. Elm Motors Ltd* [1984]).

One final remark on the discourse of SCI judges concerns the deployment of a widespread argument form the Court may formulate in cases where the interpretation of a contested term, phrase or paragraph proves particularly problematic. This is pragmatic argumentation (Bustamante 2013; Carbonell 2013), which has been a favourite subject of investigation in argumentation studies, where a range of different variants of it have been pointed out (Van Poppel 2012). In judicial settings, pragmatic argumentation has been defined as a consequentialist argument, whereby "judges often defend a decision by referring to the consequences of application of a particular legal rule in the concrete case" (Feteris 2002: 349).

In the SCI corpus considered here, pragmatic argumentation equally applies to the assertive and the more cautious attitude associated with the Court's discourse so far. In the former context, the Court's use of pragmatic argumentation is typically correlated with the term *meaning* co-occurring with statements that suggest the adverse effects of a decision other than that upheld by SCI judges:

(8) In his submissions on this point the appellant was not objecting to the fact that two distinct bodies are involved in the process but the Directive did not permit the absence of a single integrated assessment by one body. It seems to me that it would be absurd to interpret the Directive so as to suggest that in permitting two or more competent bodies to carry out an EIA of the factors referred to in Article 3, including the interaction between them, by each body at the relevant stage of the process with which it was concerned, that nonetheless it was intended that there must be one body only that carries out an assessment of all the factors as if there was only one stage in the process and it was the only body making the assessment. <u>This would run contrary to</u> the plain *meaning* of the provisions and scheme of the Directive. (Martin v. An Bord Pleanála et al.)

More specifically, the co-occurrence pattern between *meaning* and conditional/consequentialist statements applies to 3.2% of the 127 tokens of the noun in the corpus, where the undesirable effects brought about by competing decisions are framed within Van Poppel's (2012: 99-100) 'variant II' of pragmatic argumentation in the following terms:

Variant II	SCI text
1. Action X should not be performed	1. Action X (i.e. ruling that "there must be one body only that carries out an assessment of all the factors") should not be performed.
1.1a Action X leads to Y	
1.1b. Y is undesirable	1.1b. Y is undesirable ("it would run contrary to the plain meaning of the provisions and scheme of the Directive")
1.1a-1.1b' (If action X leads to Y and Y undesirable, then action X should not be performed)	1.1a-1.1b' (If action X leads to Y and Y undesirable ["absurd"], then action X should not be performed)

Table 1. Van Poppel's variant II of pragmatic argumentation in *Martin v. An Bord Pleanála et al.*

As can be seen from both the running text in (8) and the schematization in Table 1, the Court forcefully argues that the correct interpretation of the legislation involved cannot possibly be the one suggested by the appellant. In fact, should the appellant's view be embraced by the Court, this would have the undesirable effect of contradicting the plain meaning of the provisions, as well as the overall scheme of the Directive. Accordingly, the Court makes use of a consequentialist statement (*would run contrary to*) to show the grim scenario that would arise from the acceptance of the appellant's submissions.

Variant II also characterizes pragmatic argumentation advanced by the SCI within more tentative passages of judgments, as in 10.5% of the 114 corpus entries of *interpretation* where the noun collocates with hedges like *it seems*, *I would* and *appears to*:

(9) No finding, however, is made in either judgment of an obligation to provide a version of an Act simultaneously or at the same time. If it were the intention to do so, I consider it likely this would have been expressly stated. If, on the other hand, having regard to any ambiguity flowing from use of the words when/*nuair* in the relief sought and granted in the O'Beolain case, it could be understood that this was intended to reflect such a simultaneous obligation, I would disagree with such an *interpretation*, which does not flow from the plain language of Article 25, nor from the judgments. [...] This provision appears to me to follow closely upon the finding of Hardiman J. in O'Beolain v. Fahy, *supra.*, that the translations must be made available as soon as

> practicable. It also <u>seems</u> to me to be sufficient and appropriate compliance with the obligation of translation found in Article 25.4.4., of the Constitution. (Ó Murchú v. An Taoiseach)

Excerpt (9) is taken from a judgment dealing with a terminological issue typical of the Irish legal system, where English and Irish co-exist as the official languages of the country. The Court's opinion is at once discursively mitigated (*I consider it likely*; *I would disagree*; *seems to me*; *appears to me*) and argumentatively consolidated by recourse to pragmatic argumentation. In brief, the line of argument opposed to the Court's own – notably that it is mandatory to provide a version of an Act of the *Oireachtas* (Parliament) in English and Irish simultaneously – is refuted on the grounds that it would flagrantly violate the spirit of the relevant legislation, embodied as it is by Article 25 of the Constitution, and of the case law.

In other words, the Court's argument runs, the fact that both the *Oireachtas* and Irish jurisprudence have remained silent on the issue proves that there was no intention to have the law interpreted as one of the parties suggested. As far as (9) above is concerned, variant II of pragmatic argumentation applies as illustrated in Table 2:

Variant II	SCI text
1. Action X should not be performed	1. Action X (i.e. ruling that there is "an obligation to provide a version of an Act simultaneously or at the same time") should not be performed.
1.1a Action X leads to Y	
1.1b. Y is undesirable	1.1b. Y is undesirable (it "does not flow from the plain language of Article 25, nor from the judgments")
1.1a-1.1b' (If action X leads to Y and Y undesirable, then action X should not be performed)	1.1a-1.1b' (If action X leads to Y and Y undesirable ["if it were the intention to do so, I consider it likely this would have been expressly stated"], then action X should not be performed)

Table 2. Van Poppel's variant II of pragmatic argumentation in *Ó Múrchú v. An Taoiseach*.

3.2. Interpersonal positioning in ECJ judgments

A visible presence of cases where the wording of legal texts is controversial was also suggested by the ECJ texts. Among those included in the sample collected for the preliminary data survey (cf. Section 2), C-102/09 (*Camar Srl v. Presidenza del Consiglio dei Ministri*) shows some of the interpretive mechanisms later investigated at a broader corpus level. The judgment was delivered in 2010 and contributed to inscribing the final word in the ongoing national dispute between Camar, an Italian importer of tropical fruit, and the Italian Government. In particular, the Florence Tribunal had stayed the main proceedings to request the ECJ for a preliminary ruling under Article 234 of the EC Treaty, for the purpose of determining the veracity of Camar's allegations, based on Article 14 of the First Yaoundé Convention ("each Contracting Party shall refrain from any internal fiscal measure or practice that directly or indirectly leads to discrimination between its own products and like products originating in the territory of the other Contracting Parties"). Camar contended that the domestic tax introduced in 1964 by the Italian Government on the consumption of fresh bananas, which had increased over the years, was to be interpreted as discriminatory taxation in this regard. The Court eventually ruled that Article 14 of the Convention did not preclude a tax on bananas originating in Somalia such as that introduced in 1964, and it justified its decision by means of a restrictive reading of the Article, and most notably of the narrow legal scope defined by the phrase *like products*. In turn, this reading of the wording of the article was reinforced through a reference to a few selected paragraphs of settled case law, e.g. *Commission v. Italy* (C-184/85).

Camar v. Presidenza del Consiglio dei Ministri is indicative of a trend to be detected elsewhere in the corpus, too. More generally, in moving from SCI to ECJ judgments, one is led to appreciate a markedly different type of interpersonal positioning on the Court's part. In an EU judicial setting, the Court seems altogether less keen on negotiating its adjudicating role with its intended readership in terms of a cline between assertive and cautious approaches to the interpretation of controversial legislation. This means, first of all, that the Court rather impersonally proceeds to the quest for legal truth, as it were, by laying strong, unmediated emphasis on a preferred interpretation arising from a set of influential sources including (but not limited to) the Advocate General's opinions, the Court's settled case law, and fundamental principles such as equal treatment or proportionality. In argumentative terms, secondly, the Court tends to avoid expatiating on the issues at stake in the main proceedings. Rather, much can be observed to depend on the literal interpretation of selected sources, possibly read in conjunction with the wide discretionary scope of the mentioned principles.

One consequence of this systematic examination of legal sources is that the ECJ less often engages in the interpretation of single terms or uses lemmas like *word*, *phrase* or *sentence* so common in Irish texts, than it interprets disputed passages of legislation by way of brief, judiciously selected references to key parts – e.g. paragraphs or sub-paragraphs – of relevant legislation. The only exception to this trend is possibly *meaning*: this noun is attested as many as 337 times in the corpus and was therefore analyzed along with *paragraph*, *sub-paragraph* and *preamble* underlying the cross-textual references mentioned earlier on.

The lemma *meaning*, when relevant to the Court's argument, is embedded in contexts where the interpretation of any controversial passage sounds fairly straightforward. Accordingly, in 30.5% of its ECJ occurrences, *meaning* collocates with strong epistemic markers like *must* or *should*, and/or with such boosters as *is apparent from* and *is clear from*. In these entries, the Court is either satisfied with the plain meaning of a disputed term (cf. (10) below), or (and more frequently) it links up the putative clarity of its interpretation to the Advocate General's documents (11) and its own case law (12):

(10) It should be pointed out that that structure of subheading 0207 14 conforms to the normal *meaning* of the word 'offal', designating the edible parts other than the meat of animals for human consumption. It is therefore necessary to examine whether products such as those concerned in the main proceedings fall, as RLK claims, under the categories of offal other than livers, covered by subheading 0207 14 99. (Rakvere v. Põllumajandusministeerium)

(11) In that regard, as the Advocate General pointed out in point 47 of his Opinion, the fact that the fourth recital in the preamble to Regulation No 1626/94 states

that part of the coastal zone should be reserved for the most selective gear used by small-scale fishermen does not preclude the prohibition, in accordance with that recital, of fishing gear the use of which contributes excessively to the degradation of the marine environment. […] It follows from all those considerations that the answer to the questions referred is that Article 1(2) and Article 1(3) of Regulation No 1626/94 must be interpreted as *meaning*, first, that the entry into force of that regulation does not affect the validity of a supplementary national measure, a prohibition, which was adopted before that entry into force and, secondly, that those provisions do not preclude such a measure […]. (Panagiotis v. Ipourgos)

(12) […] it does not appear that a measure to recover restructuring aid [..] constitutes a measure that is manifestly disproportionate, within the meaning of the case-law cited at paragraph 77 above, in terms of the objective which the legislature of the European Union sought to pursue by introducing that aid, recalled at paragraph 45 above. The answer to the second part of the fourth question is, therefore, that Article 26(1) of Regulation No 968/2006 *must be interpreted* as *meaning* that, in circumstances such as those at issue in the main proceedings, if an undertaking has complied with its commitment partially to dismantle the production facilities of the factories concerned but not its commitment to renounce the quota, the amount of the aid to be recovered is equal to the part of the aid corresponding to the commitment that has not been complied with. (Bureau d'intervention v. Beneo-Orafti)

Regardless of the legal source cited by the Court in its support, whether a point of the Advocate's Opinion or a paragraph from a judgment close to the current case, the formulaic nature of the imperative phraseology *must be interpreted as meaning* is indeed noteworthy. It occurs as many as 92 times across ECJ corpus texts, where it serves as a preferred tool for the Court to close the debate about the correct interpretation of disputed law in rather peremptory terms.

The style of the Court's argumentation emerging from passages such as these appears less tolerant towards judicial dissent than in Irish judgments, where judges may also contemplate pronouncing verdicts under occasionally less stringent and more tentative, if acceptable and effective, argumentative guidelines. This widespread impresssion is strengthened by evidence on the use of *sub-paragraph* and *paragraph*. In 3.8% of the tokens of the former and in 25% of those of *paragraph* the Court is no more restrained in strengthening claims and expressing commitment to its authoritative interpretation of the law. With *paragraph*, in particular, the ECJ often reconciles its reading of key points of the legal norms involved with the cardinal principles of EU law, e.g. proportionality or equal treatment as in (13):

(13) Like the farmers who have applied for livestock aid, farmers who have applied for aid under Article 22 of Regulation No 1257/1999, [...], run the risk of the same legal consequences since, as is apparent from *paragraph* 43 above, the national authorities may [...]. In those circumstances, it would be inconsistent with the principle of equal treatment if the situation of farmers who applied for aid under Article 22 of Regulation No 1257/1999, which is subject to a condition relating to density of livestock, were treated differently from the situation of farmers who applied for livestock aid [...]. (Nagy v. Mezgazdasági)

In order to establish whether farmers applying for livestock aid and those applying for aid under Regulation No 1275/1999 are to be treated differently for any reason, the Court offers an insightful reading based both on what it explained earlier in the judgment and, more than anything, on the cogent nature of the principle of equal treatment. And this underlies yet another instance of variant II of pragmatic argumentation attributed to the Supreme Court of Ireland in 3.1, as can be seen in Table 3 below:

Variant II	ECJ text
1. Action X should not be performed	1. Action X (i.e. ruling that "farmers who have applied for livestock aid and farmers who have applied for aid under Article 22 of Regulation No 1257/1999" should be treated differently) should not be performed.
1.1a Action X leads to Y	
1.1b. Y is undesirable	1.1b. Y is undesirable ("it would be inconsistent with the principle of equal treatment")
1.1a-1.1b' (If action X leads to Y and Y undesirable, then action X should not be performed)	

Table 3. Van Poppel's variant II of pragmatic argumentation in *Nagy v. Mezgazdasági*

4. Conclusion

The aim of this chapter has been to combine the methodological tenets of corpus and discourse in order to observe how two courts of last resort position themselves interpersonally in the event of disputes concerning controversial terms or passages of relevant legislation. In spite of the frequency of such cases across the SCI and ECJ corpora chosen for the study, evidence suggests that judges make use of different strategies to construct their profile as trustworthy adjudicators in hard cases pertaining to agriculture, a most sensitive matter in the relationship between the European Union and its Member States. Recourse to these strategies does not merely shed light on heterogeneous discourse tools, but also on a number of argumentative devices whose application seems uneven across EU and Irish texts.

On the one hand, Irish judges seem to handle the problematic cases under investigation here in a way that shows a certain propensity to negotiate their standpoint with the expert readership most likely to approach their written opinions. As a result, the assertive tone embedding authoritative interpretations based on the Court's own case law, EU legislation or a decoding of the goals pursued by legislators, is counterbalanced by a more cautious attitude accompanying standpoints resting on other sources (e.g. legal opinions from various authors). From a discursive point of view, accordingly, the use of boosters alongside the key terms *words*, *phrase*, *sentence* and *reading*, underlying a sense of strong authorial commitment to the truth value of the Court's position, is well interspersed with the recurrence of hedges. These elements appear to qualify the Court's reliance on alternative sources in more tentative terms, possibly allowing judges to anticipate potential objections to claims by expressing statements with caution and deference to the views of colleagues (Hyland 1996).

On the other hand, the ECJ's impersonal style, whereby no individual judge is mentioned and verdicts are to be traced back to a kind of superordinate and collective entity ('the Court'), underlies the typically brisk, matter-of-fact and clipped tones in which the Court's interpretation arises as if necessarily following from paragraphs of case law or the Advocate General's words, to name but a few sources. It would indeed be of great interest to ascertain whether the kind of imperative style disclosed by the Court's discourse may be indicative of a judicial role that differentiates it from national courts such as the Irish one, with the former in a position of higher authority in stating what the law is and a spectrum of intended readers as wide as the whole of the EU Member State authorities.

On an argumentative note, an interesting tension is revealed by data that characterize both courts, albeit to varying extents. On the one hand, the tendency to mediate disputes of a mainly terminological nature by referring to the plain, natural meaning of disputed words might be interpreted as a welcome development in judicial language. This trait, to be readily identified in SCI texts, admittedly comes under the influence of the pressure exerted on public officials "to resolve to make your meaning plain to your reader even at the cost of some trouble to yourself" (Gowers 1962: 136).

On the other hand, the use of pragmatic argumentation – and mainly of Variant II thereof – testifies to the presence of a substantial degree of strategic maneuvering in judicial rhetoric, again with a slight predominance in Irish judgments. The notion of strategic maneuvering is a well-established acquisition of the so-called pragma-dialectic theory of argumentation. Within this framework, people are observed to be involved in argumentation in the attempt to resolve differences of opinion both reasonably and effectively, namely in agreement with the standpoint they have adopted or elected to represent. The simultaneous pursuit of the inter-related aims of reasonableness and effectiveness is a distinctive trait of argumentative discourse, and as such it underlies the notion of 'strategic maneuvering' referring to "the continual efforts made in all moves that are carried out in argumentative discourse to keep the balance between reasonableness and effectiveness" (Van Eemeren 2010: 40).

The deployment of pragmatic argumentation successfully fulfils this twofold function: on the one hand, the choice of the plain meanings of words, alongside the citation of such influential (let alone binding) sources as the Court's case law and the goals pursued by legislation or general principles, is perfectly reasonable. In fact, no one would dispute the lawful authority of the learned references invoked by courts in their support nor the commonsensical choice of the straightforward meaning of words as being of extreme clarity and honesty to even the lay reader. On the other hand, however, the role of pragmatic argumentation to warn against the side effects of a potential decision is of conclusive persuasive effectiveness. Indeed, depicting concurring decisions opposed by the court as absurd, not flowing from the wording of the law or the intended regulatory scheme of valid legislation (cf. Section 3), is an ingenious device in the judges' hands to conveniently legitimize their own view of disputed legislation.

It would be of genuine interest to expand the available corpus to further investigate to what extent the balance between reasonable legal tools employed in adjudication is combined with the pursuit of rhetorical effectiveness possibly guiding the preference for one interpretive tool (say, case law) over another (the meaning of a word or phrase as attested in a dictionary) in clearing doubts about the appropriate reading of controversial legal passages.

References

Ädel, Annelie / Reppen, Randi 2008. The Challenges of Different Settings: An Overview. In Ädel, Annelie / Reppen, Randi (eds) *Corpora and Discourse*: *The Challenges of Different Settings*. Amsterdam: Benjamins, 1-6.

Barceló, John J. 1997. Precedent in European Community Law. In MacCormick, Neil / Summers, Robert (eds) *Interpreting Precedents. A Comparative Study*. Aldershot: Dartmouth, 407-436.

Barton, Ellen L. 1995. Contrastive and Non-Contrastive Connectives. Metadiscourse Functions in Argumentation. *Written Communication* 12/2, 219-239.

Berteloot, Pascale 1999. Le droit à la langue de l'Union Européenne. In Jayme, Erik (ed) *Langue et Droit*. Bruxelles: Bruylant, 345-362.

Bowden, Darsie 1999. *The Mythology of Voice*. Portsmouth: Boyton/ Cook Heinemann.

Bowles, Hugo 2002. How Judges Agree to Disagree: Social and Linguistic Patterns of Dissent in the English Legal Process. In Gotti, Maurizio / Heller, Dorothee / Dossena, Marina (eds) *Conflict and Negotiation in Specialized Texts*. Bern: Peter Lang, 143-164.

Bustamante, Thomas 2013. On the *Argumentum ad Absurdum* in Statutory Interpretation: Its Uses and Normative Significance. In Dalman, Christian / Feteris, Eveline T. (eds) *Legal Argumentation Theory: Cross-disciplinary Perspectives*. Dordrecht: Springer, 21-44.

Byrne, Raymond / McCutcheon, Paul 1996. *The Irish Legal System*. London: Butterworths.

Carbonell, Flavia 2013. Reasoning by Consequences: Applying Different Argumentation Structures to the Analysis of Consequentialist Reasoning in Judicial Decisions. In Dalman, Christian / Feteris, Eveline T. (eds) *Legal Argumentation Theory: Cross-disciplinary Perspectives*. Dordrecht: Springer, 1-20.

Dimitrakopoulos, Dyonissis G. 2001. The Transposition of EU Law: 'Post-Decisional' Politics and Institutional Autonomy. *European Law Journal* 7/4, 442-458.

Dworkin, Ronald 1986. *Law's Empire*. London: Fontana Press.

Feteris, Eveline T. 2002. A Pragma-Dialectical Approach of the Analysis and Evaluation of Pragmatic Argumentation in a Legal Context. *Argumentation* 16, 349-367.

Hart, Herbert L. A. 1961. *The Concept of Law*. Oxford: Oxford University Press.

Gabrielatos, Costas / McEnery, Tony / Diggle, Peter J. / Baker, Paul 2012. The Peaks and Troughs of Corpus-Based Contextual Analysis. *International Journal of Corpus Linguistics* 37/2, 151-175.

Gowers, Ernest 1962. *The Complete Plain Words*. Harmondsworth: Penguin.

Henchy, Seamus 1962. Precedent in the Irish Supreme Court. *The Modern Law Review* 25, 544-558.

Hirvela, Alan / Belcher, Diane 2001. Coming Back to Voice. The Multiple Identities of Mature Multilingual Writers. *Journal of Second Language Writing* 10, 83-106.

Hyland, Ken 1996. Writing without Conviction? Hedging in Scientific Research Articles. *Applied Linguistics* 17/4, 433-454.

Ivanič, Roz / Camps, David 2001. I am how I sound. Voice as Self-Representation in L2 Writing. *Journal of Second Language Writing* 10, 3-33.

Maley, Yon 1994. The Language of the Law. In Gibbons, John (ed.) *Language and the Law*. London: Longman, 11-50.

Mazzi, Davide 2006. 'This is an attractive argument, but...': Argumentative Conflicts as an Interpretive Key to the Discourse of Judges. In Bhatia, Vijay K. / Gotti, Maurizio (eds) *Explorations in Specialized Genres*. Bern: Peter Lang, 271-290.

Mazzi, Davide 2007. The Construction of Argumentation in Judicial Texts: Combining a Genre and a Corpus Perspective. *Argumentation* 14, 21-38.

Schulze, Rainer / Römer, Ute 2008. Patterns, Meaningful Units and Specialized Discourses. *International Journal of Corpus Linguistics* 13/3, 265-270.

Scott, Mike 2008. *WordSmith Tools 5.0*. Liverpool: Lexical Analysis Software.

Sinclair, John 2003. *Reading Concordances. An Introduction*. London: Longman.

Swales, John 2009. Afterword. In Charles, Maggie / Pecorari, Diane / Hunston, Susan (eds) *Academic Writing. At the Interface of Corpus and Discourse*. London: Continuum, 291-294.

Tomkin, Jonathan 2004. Implementing Community Legislation into National Law: the Demands of a New Legal Order. *Judicial Studies Institute Journal* 4/2, 130-153.

Van Eemeren, Frans H. 2010. *Strategic Maneuvering in Argumentative Discourse*. Amsterdam: Benjamins.

Van Eemeren, Frans H. / Grootendorst, Rob / Snoeck Henkemans, Franciska 1996. *Fundamentals of Argumentation Theory*. Mahwah: Lawrence Erlbaum Associates.

Van Eemeren, Frans H. (ed.) 2001. *Crucial Concepts in Argumentation Theory*. Amsterdam: Amsterdam University Press.

Van Poppel, Lotte 2012. The Strategic Function of Variants of Pragmatic Argumentation in Health Brochures. *Journal of Argumentation in Context* 1, 97-112.

Zirk-Sadowski, Marek 2012. Interpretation of Law and Judges Communities. *International Journal for the Semiotics of Law* 25, 473-487.

TARJA SALMI-TOLONEN

Interpersonality and Fundamental Rights

The principles of fair trial cannot be met if defendants do not understand the language of the courts where their cases are tried. This should be obvious to everyone. The new European Directive on the Rights to Interpretation and Translation in Criminal Proceedings (2010/64/EU)[1] aims at strengthening and implementing the basic rights set out in the European Convention on Human Rights (hereinafter ECHR). This chapter explores the interpersonal and interdiscursive strategies used to communicate the legislative, executive and judicial functions of the Directive to the Member States, their legislators and judiciaries and to communicate how essential language rights are in view of the principle of fair trial.

Since this Directive is the first legislative instrument in the field of criminal law to be adopted under the Lisbon Treaty, the interdiscursive elements between those documents as well as the Charter of Fundamental Rights on the European Union (hereinafter the Charter) and ECHR will also be commented on here. Some concepts that appear in the Directive, such as *mutual recognition*, are borrowed from Europe's internal market, which seems to refer to further intertextual ties and properties. The aim of this chapter is therefore to analyse both the explicit and implicit features of communicating basic rights in European legislation.

1 <http://eur-lex.europa.eu/LexUriServ/LexUriServ.do?uri=OJ:L:2010:280:0001: 0007:en:PDF>. (Accessed on January 16, 2014)

1. Introduction

"[T]he law itself has no mind. Those who make the laws may certainly have purposes which they wish the law to achieve [...]" (Atiyah 1983: 72). This statement by Atiyah, a well-known legal theorist, reminds us of one characteristic that language and law have in common: namely that they themselves have no purpose or power but they become purposeful and powerful in the hands of those who possess institutional power (cf. Salmi-Tolonen 2008). The law-makers have a purpose, and in order to achieve that purpose they must persuade the law-takers to act – or abstain from acting – in a desired manner.

Law is generally seen as decontextualized and impersonal. However, law and language are intertwined, and as language philosophers Austin (1962), Searle (1969) and Grice (1975) most compellingly put it, language is social action. In real life, any representation of purposeful information in order to persuade people to act in a certain way requires language. Searle (1995) stresses that systems which are inherently social must be communicative. Since law is a consequence of continued human cooperation and interaction, law must be a communicative system. The rules of law not only regulate but also create possibilities for certain activities (Searle 1995).

Furthermore, legal language can be seen as possessing certain characteristics that are peculiar to it:

> (a) Legal language is always *normative*. It does not describe but obliges or gives instructions and confers competences.
> (b) Legal language is always *functional* (*e.g.*, cautioning) and it is always connected with some part of the legal system (*e.g.*, giving a ruling/ adjudication).
> (c) Legal language is *institutional*, *i.e.*, formally authorised, language of the art. It is both professional and institutional. The language of the legislature is specialised and regulated by the official system. (Salmi-Tolonen 2008: 46)

How these characteristics manifest themselves in the context of the European conception of basic rights is the main concern of this chapter. An EU Directive (2010/64/EU) will be analysed in order to see what kind of linguistic means the EU as a supranational organisation uses to accomplish the interpersonal functions of communication in relation to the Member States, and how the principle of fair trial is expressed. Figure 1 illustrates the relationship between the supranational and national laws when their end purpose is the same: to guarantee fair trials and the fulfilment of fundamental rights.

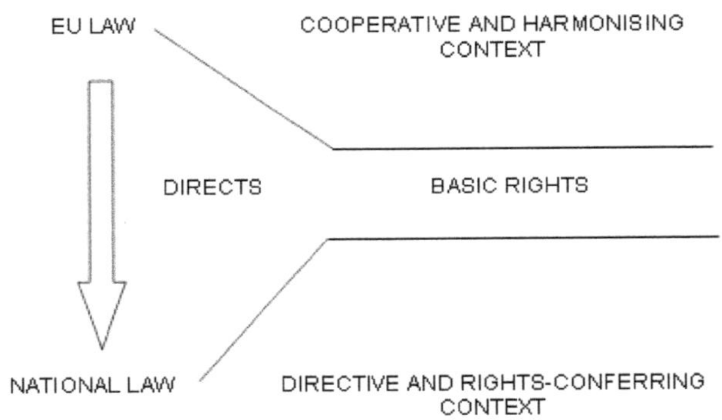

Figure 1. The two contexts of law (adapted from Salmi-Tolonen 2008: 42).

The legal context can be understood broadly as comprising both the legislative and interpretative or applicative contexts. Where there is a conflict of norms, EU law takes precedence and thus directs national law. They both have the same objective to ensure: in the case of the directive analysed here, the basic right of the suspects or defendants in public courts.

In analysing the grounds of the European Court's decisions on interpretation (the law-applying context), the principles of the Court can be divided into *semiotic criteria* based on the linguistic features of the language used in legal norms, *contextual criteria,* which place the emphasis on the static perspective, and *systemic criteria* which are used to draw inferences from different interrelated norms (Bengoetxea 1993). The dynamic criteria of interpretation can be further divided into three types of argument – functional, teleological and consequential – which are related to the dynamic context in which the norms operate. Bengoetxea (1993) draws his arguments from the conception that norms are to be interpreted in such a way that they function effectively, or from the objectives they are pursuing either explicitly or implicitly and from the consequences to which the interpretation of the norms leads. MacCormick and Weinberger (1986: 17) point out that a legal system is a thought-object or a conceptual construct:

> Such a representation of legal orders and legal processes presupposes that the logically formalised picture of legal phenomena is to be understood as a rational reconstruction which states the substantive meaning of the law as this results from interpretation of raw legal texts. It is not a matter of simply reducing to schematic order the exact utterances in the national language which constitute the texts of statutes, decisions etc.[2]

In this light, the language event – the regulative text chosen for analysis here – constitutes only part, but a very important part, of this complex construction. However, studies of the texts which are constructed in the process and which further constitute law and its application and interpretation will contribute to our understanding of the overall construct and context.[3]

2. Right to language and linguistic rights

A person's own language embraces one's experiences, thinking and creativity, in fact, one's view of the world and identity; it is something fundamental, inseparable and inalienable. It is an essential element for performing cognitive operations and for a person's mental well-being. Throughout history, the authorities have always known this, as allowing or denying people the use of their own language has been used as a powerful tool of control. Jean Jacques Rousseau once said that

---

2 See also Tuori (1998: 282).

3 See also the discussion in Salmi-Tolonen (2008: 103-105).

"the antithesis of the freedom of speech is not censorship but excommunication" (cited in Harris 1990: 157). In any modern democracy and constitutional state, language rights are essential in ensuring that a number of legal principles are fulfilled in a justice system, including the right to a fair trial. Therefore, the right to language and linguistic rights are among the basic rights of any human being, although these rights as such have not been included in legally binding instruments. A Finnish emeritus professor of constitutional law has collected and categorised them on the basis of constitutions and international instruments in the following way:

- Freedom to use one's own language in a civil society,
- Freedom from discrimination exercised on the basis of language,
- Right to linguistically equal treatment before the authorities,
- Right to one's linguistic identity,
- Right to education and acquiring information in one's own language,
- Right to political and social participation using one's own language.

(Jyränki 1999: 92, my translation)

In Finland, the present author's home country, the transposition of the Directive requires amending at least twelve Acts. I am citing them to illustrate how onerous the task can be simply from a technical perspective, let alone taking other contingencies into consideration. The fundamental rights addressed by the Directive are fragmented and distributed in a number of different instruments in the Statute Book of Finland. The Constitution of Finland provides for these fundamental rights, but to give an example of the other relevant legislative instruments, I list below the various instruments containing provisions concerning translation and interpretation in Finland:

- Administrative Judicial Procedure Act 434/2003, 26 §
- Administrative Procedure Act 586/1996, 77 §, amendments 435/2003
- Criminal Investigations Act 449/1987, 37 §
- Act on the Status and Rights of Patients 785/1992, 3 §, 5 §
- Health Care Act 1326/2010, 6 §
- Act on the Status and Rights of the Clients of Social Services 812/2000, 5 §
- Act on the Integration of Immigrants and Reception of Asylum Seekers 493/1999
- Act on Furthering the Integration of Immigrants 30.12.2010/1386, 5 §

- Aliens Act 301/2004, 10 §, 203 §
- Language Act 423/2003, 18 §
- Sami Language Act 1086/2003[4]

In addition to domestic regulation, the following international conventions constitute part of the people's basic rights.

- European Convention on Human Rights (ECHR), Article 6 (e): [Everyone has the right] to have the free assistance of an interpreter if he cannot understand or speak the language used in court.
- UN Covenants of Human Rights
- Decree on the Assertion of the International Covenant on Civil and Political Rights (ICCPR) and its Supplementary Protocol, Article 14 (f): [Everyone has the right] to have the free assistance of an interpreter if he cannot understand or speak the language used in court in civil and criminal proceedings.

Finland is a bilingual country, so our Statute Book provides for the linguistic rights and the right to translation and interpretation of speakers of the national languages (Finnish and Swedish) in the Language Act; the rights of speakers of Sami are contained in the Sami Language Act. The regulative context is therefore rather complex and scattered across various instruments.

3. Material and Methods

The text analysed in this chapter is the English text of Directive 2010/64/EU of the European Parliament and the Council of October 2010. It illustrates what kind of strategies a supranational, multilingual legislator chooses to communicate with its members and citizens in order to advance the principles of fair trial. The date on which the Directive was to be transposed was October 27, 2013. Given the complex network of regulative instruments, it is too soon to tell how

4 See government proposal HE 63/2013 at <http://www.finlex.fi/fi/esitykset/he/2013/20130063> (Accessed on January 16, 2014)

well the Member States have complied or will comply with the Directive. Implementation of directives has been one of the problems in the Member States since Directives require amendments to national legislation: the deletion of provisions which are not in accordance with new directives, the addition of new provisions or even the enactment of new laws in cases where the national legislation lacks the required norms, and in some cases the updating of standards. As can be deduced from the Finnish example above, the task of the national legislator can be quite extensive.

It is clear that before the drafting of the Directive there was a problem with the varying standards of legal interpreting and translation available in criminal proceedings throughout the EU. All Member States are signatories to the ECHR, which is a requirement for joining the EU, and the ECHR provides that anyone facing a criminal charge has the right to be provided with the services of an interpreter free of charge if he or she does not understand the language of the proceedings. This requirement was obviously not complied with in a satisfactory way in all EU Member States.

The analysis of one directive cannot render statistically significant results, but it is possible to compare the results with those from earlier studies (Salmi-Tolonen 2008) and studies on other genres such as academic dissertations (Hyland 2005). The size of the sample directive is 8 pages, 4,299 words, 22,533 characters, 708 types, with a type token ratio of 16.47 (WordSmith Tools 6, Scott 1999).

3.1. Metadiscourse

The concept of metadiscourse offers a framework for understanding communication as social engagement (Hyland 2005: 4). In this chapter, the framework is used to discover how the EU negotiates the principles of fair trial and how the interpersonal meaning is manifested. Although the Member States have previously signed the ECHR, major defects were found. One of the issues that unfortunately must be considered every time, even when it is a question of fundamental rights, is how these measures are to be financed. In the case of providing translation and interpretation to suspects and defendants, the

Member States bear the costs. Therefore, the Council of Ministers have to take particular care in pursuing their cause.

3.2. Interpersonal metafunction

Interpersonality, by definition, refers to the ways in which the writers project themselves and their audience in the discourse: in other words, it plays a role in setting up and maintaining social relations, and indicates the roles of the participants in communication (Halliday 2004/1994). Language is always used for some specific purpose: to influence the recipients' attitudes and behaviour, to provide information in order to persuade them to take some action or abstain from other actions. Consequently, how language is used is also a factor determining the success of communication between the law-makers and the law-takers. What are the linguistic means to accomplish this? Halliday (2004/1994) points out that interpersonal meaning can be expressed by mood, modality and key. Later he specifies the pronoun system, attitudinal modifiers and rhythmic features of words. It is apparent that different genres use a different selection of these means. The following analysis is an attempt to clarify which ones are used in the regulative genre.

Metadiscourse is "the means by which propositional content is made coherent, intelligible and persuasive" (Hyland 2005: 39). The interpersonal use of conjunctions is perhaps most apparent in the use of concessive forms as these both mark what the writer anticipates will be unexpected and monitor the reader's response to the discourse. Tracking the reader's expectations is a vital interpersonal strategy since interpersonal meaning orients to non-linguistic phenomena (Hyland 2005).

4. Analysis of interpersonal markers

According to Hyland (2005) the two types of metadiscourse – interactive and interactional – have two main purposes: the first organises the information in a way that the audience is likely to find coherent and convincing, and the second acknowledges the need to adequately meet readers' expectations of inclusion and solidarity. Interactive resources are used to organise propositional information in a way that the intended audience, the law-takers, will find coherent and convincing. Interactional resources refer to features which involve readers and invite them to contribute to the discourse by making them aware of the writer's attitudes towards the propositional content and towards the readers themselves (Hyland 2005).

Article 1 of the Directive is an example of a text that expresses the attitudes of the writers and invites the readers to contribute. The beginning of the Article evokes the objectives of the Union: "The Union has set itself the objective of maintaining and developing an area of freedom, security and justice". The sentence refers to authorities: in other words, the drafters of the EU Charter. *Freedom*, *security* and *justice* are concepts no one would like to deny or be excluded from furthering. Thus, this is an appeal to the readers' solidarity, making them participants in the communicative situation. In this way the second purpose mentioned by Hyland (2005: 54) is also fulfilled: "rhetorically positioning the audience, pulling readers into the discourse". This extract also contains a *frame marker* used to sequence the text, in Hyland's terms (2005: 51), announcing a discourse goal and providing framing information about the discourse elements that follow. Article 1 of the Directive then goes on to establish its present purpose:

(1) […] the *principle of mutual recognition* of judgments and other decisions of judicial authorities should become the *cornerstone of judicial cooperation* in civil and criminal matters within the Union because enhanced *mutual recognition* and the necessary approximation of legislation would facilitate coopera-

> tion between competent authorities and the judicial protection of individual rights. (Article 1, 2010/64/EU) [5]

This long sentence introduces one of the key concepts – *mutual recognition* – borrowed from internal market texts, where it is an economic concept (if an item is suitable for sale in one Member State, then all Member States should accept it for sale without further question) (see Morgan 2011/2012). The use of this concept connects the event to *internal* communication and positions the readers in the EU context. Furthermore, the Directive does not give a definition of *criminal proceedings*: this legal concept must be interpreted in the light of the case law of the ECHR with respect to the field of application of Article 6 of the ECHR. Thus there is also an intertextual link to both the ECHR and case law.

This directive is the first step in a programme designed to increase mutual trust between Member States in relation to their criminal justice systems. The purpose is to protect fundamental rights in the EU and to facilitate the operation of mutual recognition between judicial authorities in the EU. The Directive expresses this explicitly:

> (2) Although the Member States are party to the ECHR, experience has shown that that alone does not always provide a sufficient degree of trust in the criminal justice systems of other Member States. (Preamble: 6, 2010/64/EU)

Implicitly the Directive also communicates the notion that previously there were various standards and the level of trust was not sufficient, and that without the present Directive not all Member States would respect the basic rights of the defence. According to Caroline Morgan of the European Commission and the surveys done while the Directive was being prepared, translators and interpreters work in very poor conditions and sometimes a cellmate is used as an interpreter (Morgan 2011/2012: 7). The lack of competent interpreting may amount to denial of a fair trial.

Article 8 contains an important non-regression clause: "Nothing in this directive shall be construed as limiting or derogating from any

---

5 All italics in this and the following quotations from the Directive are mine.

of the rights and procedural safeguards that are ensured under the ECHR, the Charter, other relevant provisions of international law, or the law of any Member State that provides a higher level of protection." In other words, the Directive ensures only minimum standards. Table 1 gives examples of the interactive properties in the Directive. The categorisation and definitions are Hyland's and are borrowed from his interpersonal model of metadiscourse.

Category	*Function*	*Resources*	*f*
Transition markers • addition • comparison • consequence	express relations between main clauses	but, and	3
Frame markers	refer to discourse acts	for the purpose(s)	5
Endophoric markers	refer to information in other parts of the text	without prejudice, acting in accordance	4
Evidentials	refer to information from other texts	ECHR, the Charter, Article 47, Article 82(2), the Roadmap	7; 7; 1; 1
Code glosses	elaborate propositional meanings	such as, namely, *inter alia*	3; 1

Table 1. Interactive resources (modified from Hyland 2005: 49).

Of the transitional markers *but* is used three times in the Directive. The first occurrence (3) indicates an additional aim of the programme adopted by the Council in accordance with the Tampere Conclusions:

(3) The introduction to the programme states that mutual recognition is 'designed to strengthen cooperation between Member States *but also to enhance* the protection of individual rights'. (Preamble: 2, 2010/64/EU)

The other two occurrences of *but* are found in (4). They also serve not only the purpose of connecting the clauses but also function as an emphasis evoking the purpose and extent of the Directive in the readers' or law-takers' minds:

(4) Mutual recognition of decisions in criminal matters can operate effectively only in a spirit of trust in which *not only judicial authorities but all actors* in

> the criminal process consider decisions of the judicial authorities of other Member States as equivalent to their own, implying not only trust in the adequacy of other Member States' rules, *but also trust that those rules are correctly applied.* (Preamble: 4, 2010/64/EU)

The references to other parts of the text or other legislative texts are commonly done through phrases that are typical of legislative texts, such as *for the purposes of* or *without prejudice to*. In this respect the Directive and legislative texts in general deviate from other types of texts and can be considered to contain genre-specific markers. Although expressions like the ones above are formal, they also meet the readers' expectations of a legislative text:

(5) *For the purposes of the preparation of the defence*, communication between suspected or accused persons and their legal counsel in direct connection with any questioning or hearing during the proceedings, or with the lodging of an appeal or other procedural applications, *such as an application for bail*, should be interpreted where necessary in order to safeguard the fairness of the proceedings. (Preamble: 20, 2010/64/EU)

Example 5 also contains a *code gloss*, the purpose of which is to elaborate the propositional meaning. *Such as* is an expression which can cause misunderstandings because punctuation or the lack of punctuation before it renders different meanings, namely whether *such as* is followed by an example or whether the provision or prescription concerns that explicit item. *Namely* is another *code gloss* used in this Directive. It reminds the readers of the objective expressed earlier in the text:

(6) Since the objective of this Directive, *namely establishing common minimum rules*, cannot be sufficiently achieved by the Member States and can therefore, by reason of its scale and effects, be better achieved at Union level, the Union may adopt measures in accordance with the principle of subsidiarity as set out in Article 5 of the Treaty on European Union. (Preamble: 34, 2010/64/EU)

The occurrences of interactive markers are not statistically significant but sometimes even low occurrences are meaningful and worth noting from a genre-specific point of view. In this case what is noteworthy is that in all the categories used in this legislative text we find markers which are typical of any text. The difference is that only a limited selection is used and in some cases they are markers which are entirely genre-specific. Table 2 displays the interactional devices used by the law-maker. Again the framework is borrowed from Hyland's (2005) interpersonal model of metadiscourse, although *writer* and *reader* are replaced by *law-maker(s)* and *law-taker(s)*. These expressions have been used throughout this chapter because the writer and reader or recipient can better be defined by those terms.

Category	*Function*	*Noun*	*Verbs*	*Adverbs/ adjectives*
Hedges	law-maker's comment	without delay	might be	free; adequate
Boosters	emphasize the objective	cornerstone; fairness; right	safeguard; ensure; enhance	necessary; essential; individual
Attitude markers	law-maker's attitude	in a spirit of trust; approximation	facilitate; compromise	efficient; effectively; effective; more consistent; potentially weak
References to self	explicit reference to the law-maker	the Union; the Council		
Engagement markers	explicitly build relationship with the law-taker	protection; fair trial	welcome	mutual; individual rights

Table 2. Interactional resources (modified from Hyland 2005: 49).

The categories suggested by Hyland (2005) are those that in some studies – for instance, Salmi-Tolonen (1993) – have been referred to as 'markers of epistemic modality', the purpose of which is to modify the writer's attitude to the propositional content. Such expressions and utterances are commonly used in academic writing. The writers try to establish a position among the academic community and wish to appear humble, protect themselves and/or convince the readers of the correctness of their findings depending on whether they are aspiring researchers or already established ones. In the text of the Directive these expressions and utterances are used to convince the law-takers of the law-maker's good intentions and the good cause and draw them into the discourse and make them participants in furthering this cause.

At the outset, one cannot help noticing the very positive rhetoric the law-maker has opted for in all categories. Although the basic purpose of the Directive is *approximation of legislation*, *facilitating cooperation* and *mutual recognition* – in other words, *harmonisation*, an objective at the Member State level – much attention is paid to *individual rights*, guaranteeing the *right of defence* and *respecting those rights*. Thus the rhetoric used in the Directive clearly addresses individuals as well as public bodies. The Directive is the first EU instrument within the domain of criminal law and the first step in the Roadmap for strengthening the procedural rights adopted by the Council in 2009. One cannot help but notice a certain strategy and a tool intended for use in domestic politics, bearing in mind that the implementation of the Directive will mean an increase in the budgets of the judiciaries of the Member States, which, in many cases, are already suffering from severe cuts. Example 7 contains the expression *without delay,* which is placed in the category of hedges. It is one of the vague expressions often found in legislative texts. An exact time-line would cause further problems (see generally Endicott 2000). The interpretation of *delay* will be defined by judicial practice and is thus left to the courts of the Member States to decide:

(7) Interpretation for the benefit of the suspected or accused persons should be provided *without delay*. However, where a certain period of time elapses before interpretation is provided, that should not constitute an infringement of the requirement that interpretation be *provided without delay*, as long as that period of time is reasonable in the circumstances. (Preamble: 18, 2010/64/EU)

In (8) the Council expresses the fact that there are varying practices among the Member States in certain legal areas. The use of the modals *may/might* expresses the Council's willingness to allow the States a certain amount of 'wiggle room' as far as how to apply the Directive:

(8) In some Member States an authority other than a court having jurisdiction in criminal matters has competence for imposing sanctions in relation to relatively minor offences. That *may be the case*, for example, in relation to traffic offences which are committed on a large

> scale and *which might be established* following a traffic control. In such situations, it would be unreasonable to require that the competent authority ensure all the rights under this Directive. (Preamble: 16, 2010/64/EU)

Free and adequate is an expression which conveys the law-makers' attitude and are supposed to ensure a minimum standard. Again, the final definition will depend on future case law, and the text of the Directive gives the Member States discretionary powers, thus making them party to the success of the law-makers' intentions:

(9) This Directive should ensure that there is *free and adequate* linguistic assistance, allowing suspected or accused persons who do not speak or understand the language of the criminal proceedings fully to exercise their right of defence and safeguarding the fairness of the proceedings. (Preamble: 17, 2010/64/EU)

Example 10 contains the purpose and background of the Directive and the Roadmap. *Mutual recognition* and *cornerstone* are powerful expressions in order to draw the law-takers into the discourse:

(10) [...] *the principle of mutual recognition of judgments and other decisions of judicial authorities should become the cornerstone of judicial cooperation* in civil and criminal matters within the Union because enhanced mutual recognition and the necessary approximation of legislation would facilitate cooperation between competent authorities and the judicial protection of individual rights. (Preamble: 1, 2010/64/EU)

Example 11 is the non-regression clause mentioned above. It assures Member States that they have the right to provide better services to suspects or accused persons. Thus it explicitly builds up the relationship between the law-maker and the law-taker:

(11) Nothing in this Directive shall be construed as limiting or derogating from any of *the rights and procedural safeguards* that are ensured under the European Convention for the Protection of Human Rights and Fundamental Freedoms, the Charter of Fundamental Rights of the European Union, other relevant provisions of international law or the law of any Member State which provides a higher level of protection. (Article 8, 2010/64/EU)

Example 12 expresses the Council's attitude and care for persons who may be even more disadvantaged:

(12) The duty of care towards suspected or accused persons who are in a *potentially weak* position, in particular because of any physical impairments which affect their ability to communicate effectively, underpins a fair administration of justice. (Preamble: 27, 2010/64/EU)

In sum, the law-makers of this Directive have used a number of interpersonal means to communicate their good purpose to the law-takers and secure the law-takers' cooperation in furthering the cause at both the individual and public levels.

4.1. Analysis of the words of authority as markers of interpersonality

In Halliday's (2004/1994) thinking, most of the fundamental purposes in any exchange involve giving, taking or demanding a commodity of some kind. He further suggests that these commodities be termed *information* and *goods-service*. Table 3 presents the basic speech roles according to Halliday.

role / commodity	goods-service	information
giving	offer	statement
demanding	command	question

Table 3. Basic speech roles according to Halliday (1994).

A regulative text both gives and demands. It gives information and demands goods-service by commanding or directing. In other words, it is both descriptive and prescriptive and also falls into the categories given above: normative, functional, and institutional. In other genres, commanding or directing is most commonly done using the imperative mood; however, as is well known, regulative texts written in English use the modals *shall, should* and *may* to represent the imperative and are words of authority. *Shall* expresses a mandatory rule, imposing a duty to do something, and *may* is used to confer discretionary powers. Table 4 shows the frequency with which various modal verbs occur in the Directive.

Modal auxiliaries	*f*
SHALL	30
SHOULD	35
MAY	8
MIGHT	1
CAN	3
WOULD	2
WILL	1

Table 4. The occurrence of modal auxiliaries in the Directive.

4.1.1. Mandatory shall

Mandatory *shall* first occurs in *Article 1* – Subject matter and scope:

(13) The right referred to in paragraph 1 *shall apply to persons from the time that they are made aware by the competent authorities of a Member State*, by official notification or otherwise, that they are suspected or accused of having committed a criminal offence until the conclusion of the proceedings, which is understood to mean the final determination of the question whether they have committed the offence, including, where applicable, sentencing and the resolution of any appeal. (Article 1: 2, 2010/64/EU)

The use of *shall* is often criticised by reformers of legal language because, in their view, proper drafting uses both the indicative mood and the imperative mood. A bill-drafting guide (<http://www.le.wa.gov/Legislature/_template>) explains that the proper role of the imperative mood is to create a legal duty or to prescribe a rule of conduct, as in the example above, whereas the imperative mood should not be used merely to state a legal result. Therefore, its use, as in (14), is a false imperative because the purpose of the provision is achieved by declaring the very act of the legal result (Salmi-Tolonen 2008):

(14) *There shall be no requirement* to translate passages of essential documents which are not relevant for the purposes of enabling suspected or accused persons to have knowledge of the case against them. (Article 3: 4, 2010/64/EU)

In this Directive *shall* occurs most often in the company of *ensure*:

(15) *Member States shall ensure* that suspected or accused persons who do not speak or understand the language of the criminal proceedings concerned are provided, without delay, with interpretation during criminal proceedings before investigative and judicial authorities, including during police questioning, all court hearings and any necessary interim hearings. (Article 2: 1, 2010/64/EU)

(16) *Member States shall ensure* that, where necessary for the purpose of safeguarding the fairness of the proceedings, interpretation is available for communication between suspected or accused persons and their legal counsel in direct connection with any questioning or hearing during the proceedings or with the lodging of an appeal or other procedural applications. (Article 2: 2, 2010/64/EU)

(17) In proceedings for the execution of a European arrest warrant, the executing *Member State shall ensure that its competent authorities provide* persons subject to such proceedings who do not speak or understand the language of the proceedings with interpretation in accordance with this Article. (Article 2: 7, 2010/64/EU)

Out of the 30 instances of *shall*, ten occur in the company of *ensure* in clauses that impose duties on the Member States, as demonstrated in the examples above. This, of course, is to be expected, as the Directive is primarily addressed to the Member States. Other main verbs imposing duties on the Member States in this text are: *apply, include, decide, request, meet (the costs)*, and *take (measures)*. An earlier study (Salmi-Tolonen 2008) on a larger EU sample – 110,603 words – found 102 occurrences of *shall*, and the highest frequency (34 cases) occurred with *take measures,* which, again, was to be expected. The fact that in the text at hand *shall ensure* is the most frequently used example of *shall* can be associated with an interpersonal feature: namely taking into consideration that, as noted above, some Member States have already taken the measures in question before signing the ECHR, and the Council takes this into consideration and simply wants those Member States to check that the measures have, in fact, been taken. This use of *shall* can, therefore, be assigned to both interpersonality and interdiscursivity.

4.1.2. May *conferring discretionary powers*

Another genre-specific auxiliary in regulative English is the auxiliary verb *may*. It is used to confer discretionary powers: a right, privilege or power. In the current text it occurs eight times, showing that discretionary powers are more often conferred on other subjects than the Member States or their official bodies, such as the Union in (18):

(18) Since the objective of this Directive, namely establishing common minimum rules, cannot be sufficiently achieved by the Member States and can therefore, by reason of its scale and effects, be better achieved at Union level, *the Union may adopt measures* in accordance with the principle of subsidiarity as set out in Article 5 of the Treaty on European Union. In accordance with the principle of proportionality, as set out in that Article, this Directive does not go beyond what is necessary in order to achieve that objective. (Preamble: 34, 2010/64/EU)

Discretionary powers may also be conferred on the defendant, on suspected or accused persons or their legal counsel:

(19) The competent authorities shall, in any given case, decide whether any other document is essential. *Suspected or accused persons or their legal counsel may submit a reasoned request to that effect.* (Article 3: 3, 2010/64/EU)

(20) The suspected or accused persons or the persons subject to proceedings for the execution of a European arrest warrant should have the right to challenge the finding that there is no need for interpretation, in accordance with procedures in national law. That right does not entail the obligation for Member States to provide for a separate mechanism or complaint procedure in which such *finding may be challenged* and should not prejudice the time limits applicable to the execution of a European arrest warrant. (Preamble: 25, 2010/64/EU)

In the instances where *may* confers discretionary powers on the Member States, it usually allows them exceptions to the rules, as in (21):

(21) As an exception to the general rules established in paragraphs 1, 2, 3 and 6, an oral translation or oral summary of essential documents *may be provided* instead of a written translation on condition that such oral translation or oral summary does not prejudice the fairness of the proceedings. (Article 3: 7, 2010/64/EU)

The use of *may* also allows the competent authorities to use other forms than the traditional face-to-face methods, as in (22):

(22) Where appropriate, communication technology such as *videoconferencing, telephone or the Internet may be used*, unless the physical presence of the interpreter is required in order to safeguard the fairness of the proceedings. (Article 2: 6, 2010/64/EU)

Thus *may* serves as the expression of a right to deviate from the norms which are the main purpose of the Directive.

4.1.3. Should *communicating the correct procedure*

The auxiliary verb *should* communicates the correct procedure. Whereas *shall* in English regulative texts denotes a mandatory rule, *should* is also used as a directive verb, as Garner (1995) points out. As can be seen in the examples above, this is also the case in the Directive, where *should*, the softer word, should be used. In legislative texts *should* is often used in post-qualifying subordinate clauses, as shown by the following example taken from the United Kingdom's Sex Discrimination Act of 1975:

(23) In applying subsection (3) account *shall* be taken of –
(a) whether and how far it is reasonable to expect that the accommodation *should* be altered or extended, or that the further alternative accommodation *should* be provided [.] (Salmi-Tolonen 2008: 163)

In Directive 2010/64/EU *should* is used differently. It occurs the most frequently – 35 times – of all the words of authority. As the examples below show, *should* is used to describe the desired procedure and outcome of the Directive:

(24) the principle of mutual recognition of judgments and other decisions of judicial authorities *should* become the cornerstone of judicial cooperation. (Preamble: 2, 2010/64/EU)

This Directive respects the linguistic rights of the accused and should be implemented accordingly:

(25) Common minimum rules *should* lead to increased confidence in the criminal justice systems of all Member States, which, in turn, *should* lead to more efficient judicial cooperation in a climate of mutual trust. Such common minimum rules *should* be established in the fields of interpretation and translation in criminal proceedings. (Preamble: 9, 2010/64/EU)

The correct procedure is often related to a particular outcome, as the example above shows. Thus *should* is also used to impose a duty on inanimate subjects in a way to which Garner (1995) and the advocates of plain language strongly object.

4.2. Discussion of the words of authority

The findings of the analysis of the three main words of authority (*shall*, *should*, and *may*) are well in accordance with the purpose of the Directive. *Shall* imposes mandatory duties and norms on the Member States; *should* communicates the correct procedures for applicants. The examples of the expressions where *should* is used involve a principle rather than a rule. *May*, again, confers discretionary powers: in other words, rights and competences. It also gives permission or allows possibilities, but that function is secondary in terms of illocutionary force, as is the case in general language. This auxiliary verb deserves more attention in a pedagogical setting because giving permission or allowing a choice is often wrongly understood to be its only function in legislative texts. Generally speaking, this auxiliary deserves a much closer analysis in legislative texts than it has received so far.

5. Conclusions

The primary function of a European Union directive is prescriptive – imposing duties and conferring rights – and it can be assigned to the legislative genre. It directs the legislators of the Member States to take measures that will implement the purpose of the directive and the values and principles of its background. Generally speaking, one might think that the textual function would be informative and directive. However, the analysis above shows that the communicative function is also expository. In order to achieve the desired end, it is necessary to explain the motives and background of the directive to the relevant bodies in the Member States. There is no doubt that it is crucial for the recipients, the legislative bodies, to get the information that the Council wants to convey. If we pursued only this informational approach, we would ignore the participants in the discourse and their background understandings and expectations. These interpersonal dimensions influence how the recipients interpret and respond to the message and act upon it. Not everything that occurs in directive and informational genres works only to convey norms. The law-makers want to ensure that the information concerning the norms is understood and accepted and consequently acted upon. The recipients, be they legislative bodies of the Member States or individuals, are drawn in, engaged and motivated to follow along and participate.

The directive genre is tied to conventions and context perhaps more than any other genre; therefore, the text of a directive is shaped by its drafters according to the expectations and requirements of the receivers – the law-takers. EU directives are basically designed with the legislators of the Member States in mind, who can be considered to have developed a shared language, and only secondly thinking of the citizens of the EU. Therefore, the diversity among the audience is perhaps not considered to be as great as it would be in the case of statutes, which directly address the citizens and are designed to be used in different ways. Unexpectedly, the analysis presented above reveals quite an extensive use of interpersonal and interactive metadiscursive devices. An earlier study of an international model law (the UNCITRAL Model Law) revealed that the primary function of the model law was expository rather than directive, as would be the case with national laws (Salmi-Tolonen 2003). It seems that, similarly, the drafters of supranational legislative texts need to help their audience by offering explanations and background and using persuasive devices so that the audience can more easily interpret and identify with the values represented in the directive.

References

Atiyah, Patrick S. 1983. *Law and Modern Society*. Oxford: Oxford University Press.

Austin, John L. 1962. *How to Do Things with Words*. Oxford: Oxford University Press.

Bengoetxea, Joxerramon 1993. *The Legal Reasoning of the European Court of Justice. Towards a European Jurisprudence.* Oxford: Clarendon Press.

Braun, Sabine / Taylor, Judith L. 2011/2012. *Videoconference and Remote Interpreting in Criminal Proceedings*. Oxford: Intersententia. Online book <http://www.videoconference-interpreting.net/BraunTaylor2011.html> (Accessed on January 16, 2014).

Endicott, Timothy 2000. *Vagueness in Law*. Oxford: Oxford University Press.

Garner, Bryan A. 1995. *A Dictionary of Modern Legal Usage*. Oxford: Oxford University Press.

Grice, H. Paul 1975. Logic and Conversation. In Cole, P. / Morgan, J.L. (eds) *Syntax and Semantics 3. Speech Acts*. New York: Ablex. 41-58.

Halliday, Michael A.K. 2004/1994 *An Introduction to Functional Grammar*. London: Edward Arnold.

Harris, Roy 1990. On Freedom of Speech. In Joseph, J. / Taylor, T. (eds) *Ideologies of Language*. London: Routledge. 153-161.

Hyland, Ken 2005. *Metadiscourse*. London: Continuum.

Jyränki, Antero 1999 (ed.) *Oikeuden kielet. Oikeus ja oikeudellinen ajattelu monikielisessä maailmassa.* [The Languages of Law. Law and Legal Thinking in the Multilingual World.] Turku: Turun Yliopisto.

MacCormick, D. Neil / Weinberger, Ota 1986. *An Institutional Theory of Law: New Approaches to Legal Positivism.* Dordrecht: Reidel.

Morgan, Caroline 2011/2012 The New European Directive on the Rights to Interpretation and Translation in Criminal Proceedings. In Braun/Taylor (eds), 5-10.

Salmi-Tolonen, Tarja 1993. Epistemic Modality or the Author's Comment in Academic Writing. In Suojanen, Matti K. / Kulkki-Nieminen, A. (eds) *Folia Fennistica & Linguistica,* Publications of the Department of Finnish and General Linguistics No. 16, Tampere: University of Tampere. 263-282.

Salmi-Tolonen, Tarja 2003. Arbitration Law as Action: An Analysis of the Finnish Arbitration Act. In Bhatia, Vijay K. / Candlin, Christopher N. / Gotti, Maurizio 2003. *Legal Discourse in Multilingual and Multicultural Contexts. Arbitration Texts in Europe*. Bern: Peter Lang. 313-336.

Salmi-Tolonen, Tarja 2005. Persuasion in Judicial Argumentation. The Opinions of the Advocates General at the European Court of Justice. In Halmari, H. / Virtanen, T. (eds.) *Persuasion across Genres.* Amsterdam: John Benjamins.

Salmi-Tolonen, Tarja 2008. *Language and the Functions of Law: A Legal Linguistic Study*. Turku: Painosalama.

Scott, Michael 1999. *WordSmith Tools, Version 6.* Oxford: Oxford University Press.

Searle, John 1969. *Speech Acts: An Essay in the Philosophy of Language*. Cambridge: Cambridge University Press.

Searle, John 1975. Indirect Speech Acts. In Cole, P. / Morgan, J. (eds) *Syntax and Semantics 3: Speech Acts*. New York:Academic Press.

Searle, John 1995. *The Construction of Social Reality*. New York: The Free Press.

Tuori, Kaarlo 1998. Lainsäädäntö politiikan ja oikeuden välissä. [Legislation between politics and justice] *Oikeus*. 1998:3, 251-259.

MARÍA ÁNGELES ORTS LLOPIS

Contractual Commitment or Obligation? The Linguistic Interactions in Charter Parties

In the words of the International Maritime Organization (IMO), the history of the world is one of "conquest, trade and exploration by sea".[1] Nevertheless, and despite the importance of shipping trade in the present-day globalized world – it is calculated that 90% of global trade is carried out by sea, and this volume is on the increase −, few studies have been carried out on the linguistic meaning and the wording of the documents which regulate such trade and its control, such as bills of lading, insurance policies and charter parties (Orts 2006: 170). Specifically the latter, which constitute the focus of this chapter, have also attracted little critical analysis, with some exceptions (Van Hooydonk 2003; Bhatia 2010). These studies have been carried out from the point of view of legal interpretation and understanding, and not from any linguistic perspective. With the present analysis of the genre constituted by charter parties, I intend to shed some light on the mechanics that articulate this particular form of contract as a genre and on the interactions that take place between the *dramatis personae* involved in them.

1 International Maritime Organization: International Shipping Facts and Figures <http://www.imo.org/KnowledgeCentre/ShipsAndShippingFactsAndFigures/TheRoleandImportanceofInternationalShipping/Documents/International%20Shipping%20-%20Facts%20and%20Figures.pdf>.

1. Charter parties in context

Chartering, and particularly voyage chartering, is the oldest way of exploitation of commercial ships. Indeed, maritime law – a normative body which consists of rules and regulations related to the shipping industry – has its roots in ancient times, when trade and commerce through sea routes became a flourishing business. Within maritime law, contracts of affreightment for cargo ships are embodied in a singular instrument, the so-called 'charter party' (from the Latin *charta partita*, a divided legal paper), which is made out after a verbal agreement (a 'fixture') between vessel owners and charterers (i.e., the people who wish to hire a vessel). Such agreement is usually arrived at through a broker. The name comes from the fact that the document is written in duplicate, with one half retained by each party, meaning that both sides are aware of the rights given to them under law by the agreement. By virtue of this contract between the ship-owner and the charterer, vessels are rented out for a period of time or a specific journey, to be used for freight transport.

There are two main differing kinds of charter: a 'time charter' which allows the hiring of a vessel for a specific period of time, covering any number of journeys made within that time, and a 'voyage charter' – according to Carr (2005: 164), the most commonly used type of charter, and the one which will constitute the object of our study – which covers one specific journey from a point of departure to one of arrival. Among time charters there is also a subset named a 'demise' or 'bareboat charter', in which the charterer takes full legal responsibilities over the vessel and all crewing and maintenance matters, becoming the *de facto* owner of the boat for the duration of the charter. While contractual conditions may vary widely among charters, it will be seen below that standard language is currently used to describe the basic undertakings of the parties.

The law governing charter parties is a difficult issue to clarify. In principle, unlike bills of lading, charter parties are not subject to mandatory applications of The Hague and The Hague-Visby Rules or to statutory obligations. Ostensibly, a charter party is a contract negotiated in a free market where the trading power of the parties is highly dependent on the factor of supply and demand. Accordingly, charters are governed by the ordinary law of contracts either in the domestic or the international legal scenario, depending on the context of the deal. However, Maniruzzaman (2006: 658) points out that:

> Neither municipal law nor international law is appropriate or suitable for dealing with international commercial disputes when parties from different countries are involved. In their view, a national legal system may not be sensitive to the expectations of a disputing party from a different national legal background, and international law proper may not be adequate to deal with cross-border commercial transactions. Thus, a third legal order, popularly known as the *lex mercatoria*, which is neither national nor international law but a mixture with the characteristics of both, is an attractive option. The so-called third legal system has been described in the literature by various names, such as 'transnational law', 'transnational commercial law', and 'the *lex mercatoria*', and 'international law of contracts'.

This *lex mercatoria*, or 'Law Merchant', as it has usually been called in England, was the general law (*ius commune*) applicable in all countries of Western Europe until the fifteenth century (Tetley 1999: 36). Today, the law is a system of norms which has as its main purpose self-regulation within a defined category of trade (De Ly 1992: 208). In the maritime shipping industry, such self-regulation includes the standard forms of charter parties and bills of lading, as well as the York/Antwerp Rules and the Uniform Customs and Practice for Documentary Credits, among others (Montori Díez 2009: 65). Consequently, as was pointed out above, charter parties are, indeed, contracts, and thus liable to be interpreted in the light of the basic principles of contract law. Nonetheless, when used transnationally, they become a body of self-regulating norms with their own interpretational regime, in tune with the background of custom and commercial usage of the shipping industry.

In law there is no requirement that charter parties should be in writing, but these contracts have been, in general, standardized in English due to the international character of the industry. Only in 1995 did the IMO designate English as the official language for mariners, but this language has been the working communication tool in the specific area of merchant marine transportations for a long while (Ziarati *et al.* 2009: 2), probably due to the central role of the Common Law in the marine world since the expansion of the country's maritime trade in the 18th century (Tetley 1999: 10). It is undeniable that the shipping community is an international one and, following the general spirit of standardization of the IMO, a range of universal forms for charters has been available in the market for a while, some for use with all cargoes and some with special cargoes, for different types of vessel, different types of trade, and different forms of chartering. The process of standardization has been carried out mainly by organizations such as the Chamber of Shipping and, mainly and more importantly, by the Baltic and International Maritime Council (BIMCO). BIMCO is an independent organization that aims at protecting the interests of the international shipping industry by providing and applying global regulatory instruments. BIMCO is the largest of the international shipping associations, represents ship-owners, controls around 65 percent of the world's tonnage and has members in more than 120 countries, including managers, brokers and agents, as well as many other stakeholders with vested interests in the shipping industry. It is not strange, thus, that the standard forms for contracts coming from such a prominent institution should be leaders in the market.

As mentioned above, international and domestic law (with the exception of English Common Law, which inspires most of the marine documents and instruments in current use, The Hague-Visby rules among them) has a relative role in the matter of the international carriage of goods by sea (Maniruzzaman 2006: 658) and, therefore, the *lex mercatoria* of the trade is the law in charge of the regulatory activities of this industry. The central claim of our study is that to standardize the activities of the trade through their contracts of affreightment models, the powerful group of ship-owners represented by BIMCO invest themselves with the authority to control how transactions take place and how disagreements should be resolved, against the framework of their own interests and welfare.

2. Charter parties as a genre

Charter parties are made up of a set of complex – and quite hackneyed – clauses, drafted in the most orthodox style of Legal English as the *lingua franca* of maritime communication (Bocanegra 2013: 3570). The clauses, as I intend to demonstrate, are ostensibly difficult to understand by the lay reader, no matter how standardized and widely used they may be. Despite this fact, and that the use of private contracts in an international environment poses problems in terms of interpretation and applicable law, the truth is that the texts in hand – i.e., the different types of charter parties BIMCO offers for time, voyage and bareboat – have achieved international scope and influence in all countries, transcending the difficulties that those problems may pose, both of comprehension and/or application. This chapter aims to prove that the reason for that transcendence is, precisely, the power of the communicative community it emanates from.

Following the traditional definitions of the concept of specialised discourse community provided by Swales (1981, 1985, 1990) and Bhatia (1993, 2002), a genre may be defined as a very well-structured communicative event that is ultimately envisaged for a due community to legitimately attain its professional (and, sometimes, personal, according to Bhatia 2002: 7) purposes. Hence, getting to know how a specific kind of genre works amounts to acquiring familiarity with the communicative resources that the specialised community that issues the genres in question deploys to accomplish those legitimate goals. It follows that the more generic knowledge one may acquire of a profession, the more inside, privileged knowledge he/she will have about the mechanisms that articulate the communication within such a community. The text under study arises from the transfer of power to an elite of professionals – BIMCO in this case – who, in constituting a powerful group of vessel suppliers, have also established themselves as the providers of the norms. To what extent this elite, as the specialised community that emits these texts, is willing to give up the complexity of the language for the benefit of its users, the charterers, as they seem to suggest,[2] is something that remains to be seen.

Hence, the purpose of this chapter is to analyse charter party clauses in depth – and, more specifically, those of GENCON voyage charters –, both as an illustrative example of English legal discourse and as a genre in its own right, seeking to unravel the interactive entanglement between the participants (suppliers and customers, or, here, ship-owners and charterers) in the communication act that the contract constitutes. More concretely, the present study will focus on the linguistic, discursive and pragmatic peculiarities of the genre constituted by this modality of charter party. Indeed, our analytical approach contemplates genre at large as "a communicative vehicle for the achievement of goals" (Swales 1990: 46), and thus the generic analytical model proposed divides the research process into three different levels: the formal level (with lexical and syntactic sublevels), the discursive or textual level, and the pragmatic level, which has to do with the charter party as a communicative event in context. All in all, the research process has suggested the efficacy of the method as an analytical and enlightening tool.

2.1. The formal level

The formal level deals with the study of the surface elements (Crystal/Davy 1969: 201) – that is, with the substance or raw material of the text, as well as with the peculiar combinations of that substance –, which can develop into higher units. Taken in isolation, the presence or absence of certain formal traits is an unreliable indicator of analysis; together and in their context they can supply very useful information about their discursive/pragmatic function.

Our analysis has a lexical part in which those vocabulary choices which depend on the type of legal genre that charter parties

2 BIMCO pride themselves of endeavouring to attain "the harmonisation and standardisation of all shipping related activity" by promoting "fair business practices, free trade and open access to markets" (<https://www.bimco.org/en/About/About_BIMCO.aspx>).

constitute as instances of legal discourse will be considered, namely the use of archaisms, technical terms, and formal and ritual language.

The first step of our lexical analysis concerns the level of terminological precision. In this context, it is pertinent to study the very specialised words or *terms of art* of legal language (Mellinkoff 1963: 63) but not only, since the text also belongs to the area of marine activity, thus constituting "a unique language that only men and women of the sea will understand" (Pritchard 2002: 14).

Lexical rituality and formality go hand in hand with archaic forms in French, English and Latin, which, in turn, are remnants of the time when the English legal profession was trilingual. As Lakoff has pointed out (1990: 100), formality in the context of the courts serves to remind participants that this is an adversarial context. The rituals and formal parts of a legal document are marked by the presence of often polysyllabic words and archaic or unusual grammatical forms, normally of Latin origin, or infrequent prepositional combinations such as *hereby* or *theretofore*. The trace of these will be searched in our document as well.

In the area of syntax and discourse of legal English, complexity is also the rule. Sentences around a hundred words long or more are common, when the average norm is for lawyers to include 20-30 words per sentence at most. Syntax is made up of complex structures embedded into one another, in an attempt to capture every possibility of regulation, and conditionals with complex prepositional phrases are overused. Nominalizations and passive structures obscure the agent of the sentence and make the prose heavy and unclear. The discourse focuses on exceptions and negatives rather than on basic principles, placing what negates, limits, or constitutes an exception at the front of the sentence or paragraph, and relegating the main principle to the end of the line. Such a convoluted syntactical trend makes comprehension difficult and gives a negative, threatening connotation to legal texts.

2.2. The discursive level

Once the formal analysis is concluded, GENCON is to be analysed as an instance of text or written discourse from the basic rules of linguistic organisation that makes it work. The textual elements of professional language at large are visible in its supra-organisation or macrostructure, which is a very definite part within the text, and frames the textual segment, assisting the reader in its global comprehension. The macrostructure represents the dominion of the text in its functional level, revealing the way in which the elements of a textual typology operate. This textual structuring reflects the conventionalised social knowledge at the disposal of the discursive or professional community, BIMCO, besides the strategies or tactic choices used in general to render the discourse more effective for the communicative purpose of such a community.

2.3. The pragmatic level

Finally, genres are the stratified discourse of a very specific specialised community. This, broadly speaking, is shown both in their external and internal structure and in their communicative function and sociopragmatic conventions. Looking at language from its communicative perspective implies introducing a description of language in use, the specification of its pragmatic discursive meaning, combining the linguistic aspects of textual construction and interpretation, together with the sociocultural factors that integrate the text. At this pragmatic level, the charter party will be studied from the point of view of speech act theory: as a peculiar generic type of legal agreement in which commitment between the parties is not established in the form of a symmetrical relationship or commissive act, whereby both parties equally oblige themselves for the sake of a mutual benefit (Trosborg 1995: 33). Rather, charter parties are established as a directive, i.e. an obligation issued by a party – the powerful group of ship-owners as represented by BIMCO, the profferer of these policies, in their various forms – over the other, namely charterers, who in hiring the vessel for the transportation of cargo assume all sorts of risks and liabilities.

3. Genre in context: Analysis of GENCON

As has been advanced, charter parties are classified into three basic types: *voyage*, *time* and *demise* (or *bareboat*), according to the regime of charter they seek to cover. I have also mentioned that voyage charter parties are the commonest type of contract for the transportation of goods. By virtue of this particular contract of affreightment, the owner of the ship agrees to lease the cargo to the charterer for a particular voyage in exchange for freight payment, retaining control of the vessel and the crew (the charterer being responsible for the number and destination of voyages) and for the deployment of the ship itself. In addition to the express clauses agreed by the parties limiting mutual obligations and rights in the charter, there are also implied obligations and rights which are automatically incorporated into the contract in the absence of agreement to the contrary (Bhatia 2010: 115).

The voyage charter party – a voyage-bound trip charter with availability of crew – is one of the most famous charter parties, and GENCON is the standard form recommended by BIMCO for the transportation of general cargo. Since first being issued in 1922, the GENCON form has been revised in 1976 and 1994. As will be seen when the macrostructure of the text is discussed, the form contains two main parts: the first is made up of 26 sections (or boxes) for the owner and charterer to provide the specific details of the transaction in question, while the second contains 19 standard clauses which refer to the rules governing the charter party. Despite being one of BIMCO's most widely-used general-purpose voyage charter party forms, used for all kinds of trades and for various types of cargoes, and the one recommended by the UNCTAD Secretariat, the clauses in GENCON have given rise to much criticism for their obscurity and ambiguity, and their construction is the usual cause of litigation between the parties.[3]

3 See as examples Louis Dreyfus & Cie v Parnaso Cia Naviera SA (The Dominator) [1959] 1 QB 498, and Salamis Shipping (Panama) SA v Edm van Meerbeeck & Co SA, (The Onisilos) 2 QB 500.

3.1. Formal aspects of GENCON

3.1.1. The lexicon of GENCON

The lexicon of BIMCO's voyage charter party shares many of the terminological traits of legal discourse in general, and more specifically of the lingo that characterizes contracts in Common Law. Nevertheless, a thorough search of the document has revealed its rich linguistic idiosyncrasy. Discarding words of low information value such as ordinary prepositions and determiners (articles, demonstratives and the like), the lexical world of the text – which has almost 5,800 words in all – is reduced to a group of more or less definable categories, such as the *dramatis personae* in the contract (the Owner, the Charterer, the Vessel, the Charter Party, the Shippers, the Stevedores and the Agents), a sizable number of very specialised words referring to maritime transport and risks, and an interesting, more limited number of words pertaining to the legal lexicon. The tables below provide an illustration of the lexical study. Frequencies have been obtained with MonoConcPro and etymologies with *Merriam Webster Dictionary Online*. Also, marine terms were classified as such in the light of Tetley's *Glossary of Maritime Terms* and legal terms according to *Black's Law Dictionary*:

Term	*Occurrences*	*Origin*
owner	79	Middle English from Proto-Germanic
vessel	79	Old French
charterer	51	Old French from Latin
master	19	Old English from Latin
agent/s	10	Middle English from Latin
stevedores	8	Spanish
shippers	4	Middle English from Proto-Germanic
charter party	4	Old French from Latin

Table 1. The *dramatis personae* in GENCON.

Term	*Occurrences*	*Origin*
afloat	2	Old English
ashore	1	Old English
average	6	Middle French
berth	4	Middle English
bill of lading	3	Old English
cargo	71	Spanish
carriage	6	Anglo-French
carrier	1	Anglo-French
collision	3	Middle English from Latin
consignee	2	Middle French
crew	10	Middle French
deadfreight	1	Dutch
deadweight	1	Old English
discharge	26	Anglo French
dunnage	4	Proto-Germanic
freight	33	Dutch
gear	8	Old English
hold	2	Old English
lash	1	Middle French
laytime	15	Old English
layday	1	Old English
load, loading	61	Middle English
mariner	1	Anglo French
pilot	2	Middle French
piracy	1	Latin
port	70	Old French
readiness	6	Middle English
sail	4	Proto-Germanic
salvage	3	Old French
(un)seaworthiness	2	Old English
(summer) loadline	1	Middle English
stow, stowage	1	Old English
trim	1	Proto-Germanic
shipment	2	Middle English from Proto-Germanic
tally	1	Anglo-French
tow	1	Proto-Germanic
trim	1	Old English
voyage	11	Old French
winch	3	Old French

Table 2. Marine terminology in GENCON.

Term	*Occurrences*	*Origin*
broker, brokerage	4	Anglo French
cancel	13	Anglo French
claim	8	Old French
compliance	2	Old French
commencement	4	Old French
condition	5	Middle French
contract	11	Middle French
damage	14	Middle French
deem	8	Old English
default	4	Old French
delay	5	Old French
demurrage	14	Old French
disbursement	1	Old French
due	11	Old French
due diligence	2	Old French
expiration	2	Middle French
indemnify	2	Middle French
howsoever	3	Old English
liability	4	Old French
lien	3	Middle French
loss	8	Old English
negligence	3	Middle French
notice	14	Middle French
notwithstanding	1	Old English
null and void	3	Middle French
option	12	Old French
ownership	1	Old English
party	34	Old French
provision	9	Middle French
reasonable, reasonably	5	Middle French
shall	106	Old English
right	1	Old English
strike	9	Old French
terminate	2	Middle French
thereby	2	Old English
thereof	2	Old English
thereon	1	Old English
thereto	2	Old English
warrant	1	Middle French
wear and tear	1	Old English
will	4	Old English

Table 3. Legal Terminology in GENCON.

The lexical analysis carried out points to several textual features:

1. The *dramatis personae* taking part in the agreement are given clear prominence. Notably, 'the Vessel' acquires as much significance as the parties to the contracts themselves. The relevance of this factor will be discussed later on, when dealing with the aspects of GENCON as a discourse type.
2. Terminological precision is evident: marine vocabulary – both naming the main parties or elements in the contract and other terms describing the maritime activity – is also salient, most of the terms (such as *dunnage*, *laytime* or *stow*) being highly specialised. Nevertheless, the legal flavour of the corpus is patent: even if the number of words that have been classified as pertaining to the legal area is lower than that in the marine field, the most frequent word in the corpus overall is the verb *shall*, used in legal texts to convey a strong sense of obligation (Tiersma 1999: 139). There is also a sizable and representative group of terms indicating contractual obligations, options, and contingencies.
3. As the tables show, the language of the different specialised areas is very archaic in origin, with words from Anglo-French, but also from Proto-Germanic and from Old and Middle French and English, and occasionally from Spanish and Dutch, confirming what has been asserted before: that legal English used to be filled with legal expressions in French and that the marine activity harks back to the very beginning of commercial transactions. The vestiges of Dutch, English, French and Spanish exist in English because these were once great imperial powers and the only nations with full-fledged fleets (Garcia-Herrera *et al.* 2003: 6).
4. Formality and rituality, typical of contractual language, is manifest in occasional binomials (such as *null and void* or *wear and tear*), the use of polysyllabic words of Latin origin (*disbursement*, *indemnify*, *commencement* or *expiration*), in the uncommon combinations of *there+preposition*, typical of legal discourse – clear indicators, as will be seen, of anaphorical, cataphorical and exophorical reference –, in the above-men-

tioned use of *shall*, and in the deployment of long connectors such as *notwithstanding*, *howsoever* and *whatsoever*.

These lexical phenomena acquire their full meaning when contextualized in the subsequent levels of analysis, making GENCON a peculiar instance of legal discourse, a genre which responds to the communicative needs of the community that articulates the message, BIMCO, with a significant role in the complex and fascinating field of international marine normative.

3.1.2 .The syntax of GENCON

Sentence length is the distinctive seal of legal discourse, and this is not an exception in the present text. Indeed, the contract is made up of long and quite convoluted sentences, the average being 70 words in length, where the shortest is made up of 28 words and the longest reaches 209. Remarkably, the lengthiest syntactical constructions are to be found both in the clauses having to do with payment and compensation for damages (the 'Both to Blame Collision Clause' with 139 words and the 'General Average/New Jason Clause', with 197 words) and in the compensation for extraordinary risks (the 'Strikes', 'General Ice' and 'War' Clauses, with 139, 110 and 197 words per sentence, respectively). If the average length of legal sentences reaches 50 to 80 words per sentence (Gustaffson 1975; Hiltunen 1984), it is obvious that some of the most interpretation-sensitive clauses in the contract exceed this length by far. Complexity is also apparent in the preference of subordination to coordination and the frequent use of legal qualifications to introduce exceptions or inclusions in the sentences, and conditional sentences with *if*, *unless* or *provided that* abound.

Another consequential trait in the text is the common use of passive structures. The impersonality of legal texts as a symbol of the impartiality of the law and its institutional weight has been highlighted as one of the features that characterize legal discourse. The desire for impersonality is also present in our corpus through its passive constructions, which make the universality and impartiality of these texts visible. As a genre in its own right, GENCON also uses this resource to convey the authority-obedience relationships between the actors, as well as the expression of the ubiquitous nature of uncertainty that is especially present in the world of marine trade. All of this will be discussed in the subsequent levels of analysis.

3.2. Textual aspects of GENCON

The perception that texts are linguistically coherent segments reveals to us how our corpus works at a structural level. BIMCO's voyage charter party has been studied as a discourse instance, that is, from the basic linguistic rules of the text, analyzing the recurrent devices that provide its informational role. The textual elements of professional language are visible in the supra-organisation or macrostructure, which frames the textual segments, and assists the reader in his/her global comprehension. It also reflects the conventionalised social knowledge at the disposal of the discursive or professional community. The macrostructural rigidity of GENCON as a standard contractual form is unquestionable, with a peculiar and predetermined bipartite structure, already referred to, that has changed little over time.

1. Part I, containing, in boxes, all the details of the ship and the voyage, as follows:

Data	*Box*
the name and the address of the shipbroker	1
the date and the place where the charter party was concluded	2
the name and the address of the contracting parties	3/4
the name and a short description of the ship	6/7
the position of the ship	8
the date the ship is expected to load	9
the loading and charging ports or places	10/11
the cargo	12
the freight	13/14

Table 4. Part I, details.

2. Part II, the text part with the printed clauses, which contain the terms and conditions agreed between the parties.

Clause	*Name*
1	No specific name: Preamble
2	Owners' Responsibility
3	Deviation Clause
4	Payment of freight: Subclauses a) (unnamed) b) Prepaid c) On Delivery
5	Loading/Discharging Costs
6	Laytime: Subclauses a) Separate laytime for loading and discharging b) Total laytime for loading and discharging c) Commencement of laytime (loading and discharging)
7	Demurrage
8	Lien Clause
9	Cancelling Clause
10	Bills of Lading
11	Both-to-Blame Collision
12	General Average and New Jason
13	Taxes and Dues: Subclauses a) On Vessel b) On Cargo c) On Freight
14	Agency
15	Brokerage
16	General Strike
17	War Risks: 1 to 6 Subclauses
18	General Ice: Port of Loading a), b), c) subclauses / Port of Discharge a), b), c) subclauses
19	Law and Arbitration: a) b) c) subclauses for lieu of arbitration

Table 5. Part II, the clauses.

As it is structured, the text has a visible, coherent organization of its terms by categorizing those provisions topically, including explicit headings dealing with each topic and arranging the categories in a proper sequence. Theoretically, organizing the terms of an agreement in this way enables the parties to locate the provisions or details that they need in an easier way. Such a distribution obeys a pre-established organization with stereotyped formulae and conventional schemata which are usually present in general charter party contracts. That is the case of some standard clauses – also included in other contracts of affreightment and Bills of Lading –, like the Both to Blame Collision Clause or the New Jason Clause. Specifically, the former has a very confusing wording and sometimes is the cause of deceitful interpretations. Still, allegedly, it is normally introduced in charter parties and imposed by P&I Clubs[4] as a mandatory requirement to protect ship-owners' liability in case of collision (Barder/Fordam 2009: 18). This could be applicable to the rest of the text at large: the macro-structural clarity belies the fact that comprehension is generally thwarted by the long-windedness and complexity of the constructions and the peculiarity of the terminology overall.

As far as cohesion and textuality devices are concerned, the text is set to reflect the enforceable promises that are the expression of the parties' intent, fulfilling the goal of the text to create pacts between ship-owners and charterers. Nevertheless, expressions of prohibition and condition are often concealed into apparently impartial expressions, being substituted with nominalizations and passives, or obliterated by the 'fallacy of the Vessel', a concept that will be explained later on with regard to the peculiarities at generic level.

Finally, intertextuality shows the presence of other texts in the charter party, but not in the way that this usually takes place in legal agreements. Regular contracts reflect the legal constraints that limit the private scope of rights and duties of the parties by means of the citation of the relevant laws in force, having to do with a spirit of legal compliance. This also happens in GENCON, whose main references as to jurisdiction are to English or US law ('York-Antwerp Rules 1994') but with some peculiarities, since the main references are to other parts or the text (or *Boxes*) and to other documents generated by BIMCO itself. In a type of contract like this, for the international transport of cargo by sea, legal references are ambiguous, as has been explained above, because they are part of the *lex mercatoria*, which is transnational. The placing of the charter within the context of Anglo-Saxon law, and the continuous references to concepts generated by BIMCO itself, convey a sense of security which is, to my understanding, unreal, inasmuch as it refers to the world created by one of the parties, namely the ship-owners or their representatives.

---

4 Protection and Indemnity Associations, organizations providing cover for its members, typically ship-owners and ship operators.

3.3. The pragmalinguistics of GENCON

As Trosborg (1995) points out, contrary to legislation – where there exists an asymmetry between the legislative power and the citizens – in contracts, parties have a symmetrical relationship between them, based upon a common interest ('promise' and 'consideration'). Citing Searle's (1976) taxonomy, she states that regulative speech acts in contracts may have the illocutionary force of the law when an obligation is issued by one party over the other – thus constituting a 'directive' – or they may be 'commissive' acts, i.e. those which commit the participants in the interaction to do or refrain from doing something. Aiming at isolating the pragmalinguistic realization patterns of directives and commissives in contractual texts, Trosborg further develops a taxonomy of different categories in a scale that ranges between the direct directives of obligation and permission (with the subcategories 'assignment of rights' and 'limitation of liability' for the granting of benefits to the parties) to the unmarked character of constitutive rules (statements of legal effect with unidentifiable pragmatic realizations), to commissives, as set out in Table 6.

Category	*Meaning*	*Fulfilment*
Direct directives ⇩ Obligation	Illocutionary force of order	*Shall*+verb *Be*+to, *must, have to, obligate* *Shall* +passive (face redress)
Permission ⇩	Symmetrical relationship	*May* Lexical verbs (*grant, give, Allow*)
Assignment of rights/ limitation of liability	Rights/Exemptions for either party	*Shall*+right *Shall* +limitation of liability
Constitutive rules	Establishing the terms of the contract Spelling out conditions as to price or date	Lexical verbs (*mean, apply, include, exclude*) Constructions *be+responsible, be+deemed*
Commissives	The parties commit themselves before the law	Lexical verbs: *agree, undertake, warrant, accept, acknowledge*

Table 6. Trosborg's regulative speech acts in English contracts.

The hypothesis of the current study – which has been present throughout the rest of our scrutiny of BIMCO's charter party – is that this type of contract, due to its sociopragmatic peculiarities, is less an exchange of symmetrical promises that characterize commissive acts than a directive, an asymmetrical act issued for the benefit of the profferer, the Owner, and at the cost of the recipient, the Charterer. A faithful application of Trorsborg's taxonomy through a manual tagging of the different speech acts contained in the 19 Clauses of GENCON has, indeed, rendered the results below. For the purposes of our scrutiny, though, it is relevant to point out that, in order to increase illocutionary force, the act was solely attributed to the parties to the contract, namely 'the Owner' and 'the Charterers'. Sentences with *the Vessel*, *the Master* or *the operators* as subjects were attributed to the party ultimately in control of the speech act, ie, *the Owners*.

Clause	*Shipowner*	*Charterer*
1. Preamble (unnamed)	2 right (vessel) 1 commissive	1 obligation 1 commissive
2. Owners' responsibility	2 obligation (1 with redress) 1 limitation of liability	
3. Deviation clause	1 right (vessel)	
4. Payment of freight	1 obligation (1 with redress) 1 limitation of liability	3 obligation (1 with redress) 1 right
5. Loading, discharging	3 permission 1 right (master) 1 constitutive rule	9 obligation (1 with redress) 1 constitutive rule
6. Laytime	2 obligation with redress 1 right (vessel) 2 constitutive rule	3 obligation with redress 2 limitation of liability 1 constitutive rule
7. Demurrage	1 right 1 permission	2 obligation with redress
8. Lien clause	1 right	
9. Cancelling clause	1 obligation 2 constitutive rule, 1 with redress	1 obligation with redress 3 right 1 constitutive rule
10. Bills of lading	1 obligation (master)	1 obligation

11. Both to blame collision clause	1 right 1 constitutive rule (owners, operators)	1 obligation (owners of the cargo)
12. General average and new jason	1 right 1 limitation of liability 1 constitutive rule	3 obligation (owners of the cargo, consignees, shippers) 1 constitutive rule
13. Taxes and dues clause	1 obligation 1 right	2 obligation (1 with redress)
14. Agency	1 right	
15. Brokerage	1 constitutive rule	1 constitutive rule
16. General strike clause	1 obligation 5 right (master, owner,vessel) 1 limitation of liability	1 obligation with redress 1 right 1 limitation of liability
17. War risks	1 constitutive rule 8 right 6 limitation of liability	2 obligation 1 constitutive rule
18. General ice	6 right (vessel, one with redress) 1 constitutive rule	2 obligation with redress 1 commissive
19. Law and arbitration	1 obligation 10 constitutive rule	1 obligation 10 constitutive rule
Total	obligation 9 (4 with redress) permission 5 right 29 limitation of liability 10 constitutive rule 29 commissive 1	obligation 33 (10 with redress) permission 0 right 5 limitation of liability 3 constitutive rule 16 commissive 2

Table 7. Regulative speech acts in GENCON.

There are several phenomena worth pointing out in the Clauses, as follows:

- The text shows a case of clear asymmetry in mandatory character: regarding the obligations of the parties, it is patent that the structures of *shall+verb*, *be+to* and *must*, or those with *shall+passives* – when face redress is used as a mitigating device (Brown/Levinson 1987: 13) –, were much more abundant – 33 out of 42 – in the sentences where the Charterers were the subject. Contrarily, direct directives of obligation were scarce – 9 in all – in those cases where the Owner was, directly or indirectly, the subject of the duty. Power to grant permission is very irregular too, all the occurrences being assigned to Owners.

- There is also a patent unevenness in the granting of rights, with 29 occurrences for Owners and 5 for Charterers, as well as limitation of liability, with 10 cases for Owners and 3 for Charterers. An indication is to be given there though, because in the inordinate yielding of benefits for the Owners a phenomenon I have termed 'the fallacy of the Vessel' takes place: the ship, under the power and control of the Owners by virtue of this specific kind of charter, i.e., the voyage charter, acquires the stature of a *dramatis persona*, being given the animate qualities (as in the recurrent sentence "the Vessel has the liberty to"), and, in this case, rights, of a human being. Reification is not rare in legal instruments, but in this case the strategy of personification, of considering human something that is not, is a way to conceal the lack of balance of the document: the Owners are, indeed, in control, but the Vessel is the decoy used to pretend they are not so much so.
- Constitutive rules in the text take different shapes, and are almost always used to explain or define words in the charter (as in "for the purposes of this clause, the words … shall mean", in clause number 17, War) or to supply information concerning the application of the contract (as in "Time used before commencement of laytime shall count", in Laytime, Clause number 6). The situation in which they are placed indicates that norms are more explanatory for Owners in the charter, in 29 cases, than for Charterers, with 16 occurrences. This may be due to the fact that in the absence of express clauses the charter is to be explained implicitly. The text keeping silence in some indications for Charterers could mean yet another device to remit the clauses to the *stored knowledge patterns* (De Beaugrande/ Dressler 1980: 197) of the profession, the specialised community of ship-owners that is BIMCO.

- Finally, the absence of commissives is striking in a text that should be based upon the exchange of promises and which is, in fact, a compilation of indications to the client, the unknowing Charterer.

4. Concluding remarks

The voyage charter parties issued by BIMCO are set to be contracts, understood as the exchange of binding promises in the interest of the parties under the law. In fact, this chapter has endeavoured to prove that they are not. The power and authority of BIMCO as the profferer of these policies and its role as the world representative of one of the parties involved, the ship-owners, together with the ubiquity of its contracts of affreightment in the world of carriage of goods by sea, has turned what should be a 'convivial act' (Leech 1983: 104) of agreement for the benefit of both parties into a directive for the benefit of the speaker and at the cost of the recipient, the Charterer. Actually, they are unlike any other type of lease contract in two senses. First, because of the kind of asset which is leased: ships are a singular, extraordinarily valuable property, a huge investment to be protected by their owners with utmost care. Second, because of the community that issues them, and in this sense they are similar to other agreements such as the Institute Cargo Clauses, where the powerful communicative group issuing these marine insurance policies has become the sole authority in the field. In my generic analysis in its different levels I have tried to demonstrate this fact, in attempt to unveil the sophisticated way in which the group of ship-owners provide a text with a visible, coherent organization where stereotyped formulae and conventional schemata belie the complexity of its wording and the sensitiveness of interpretation of the mandatory requirements which the policy sets out. Such an imperative character is concealed in the face redress usage of passive constructions to issue orders to the recipient and in the constitution of the persona of the vessel, which is none other than the ship-owner.

Such a state of affairs, in sum, is not the result of a scheming conspiracy on the part of the professional community that issues the text of the charter party. On the contrary, the popularity and wide expansion of these peculiar contracts has to be regarded in the context of international transactions, where the rules of the game have to be negotiated between the parties and where BIMCO charter parties constitute one more instance of a well-organized communicative group successfully administering its genres to the community at large.

References

Barder, Ena / Fordam Stephen 2009. The Both to Blame Collision Clause. *Wikborg Rein's Shipping Offshore*. At <http://e-pages.dk /wikborgrein/3/18> Last retrieved 18th June 2013.

Beaugrande De, Robert / Alain Dressler, Wolfgang 1980. *Introduction to Text Linguistics*. London: Longman.

Bhatia, Kailash L. 2010. *Textbook on Legal Language and* Legal *Writing*. New Delhi: Universal Law Publishing.

Bhatia, Vijay K. 1993 *Analysing Genre: Language Use in Professional Settings.* London: Longman.

Bhatia, Vijay K. 2002. Applied Genre Analysis: A Multi-perspective Model. *Ibérica* 4, 3-19.

Bocanegra Valle, Ana 2013. Maritime English. In C.A, Chapelle (ed.) *The Encyclopedia of Applied Linguistics*. Oxford: Wiley-Blackwell, 3570-3583.

Brown, Penelope / Levinson, Stephen 1987. *Politeness. Some Universals in Language Usage*. Cambridge: Cambridge University Press.

Carr, Indira 2005. *International Trade Law*. London: Routledge.

Crystal, David / Davy, Derek 1969. *Investigating English Style*. London: Longman.

De Ly, Filip 1992. *International Business Law and Lex Mercatoria.* London: Emerald Group Publishing.

García-Herrera, Ricardo / Prieto, Luis / Gallego, David / Hernández, Emiliano / Gimeno, Luis / Können, Gunther P. / Koek, Fritz / Wheeler, Dennis / Wilkinson, Clive / Prieto, María R. / Báez, Carlos / Woodruff, Scott 2003. *CLIWOC Multilingual Meteorological Dictionary.* EU contract EVK2-CT-2000-00090. At <http://epic.awi.de/17064/1/Gar2003b.pdf>. Last retrieved 19th June 2013.

Gustafsson, Marita 1975. *Some Syntactic Properties* of *English Law Language*. Publication. No. 4. Turku, Finland: University of Turku, Department of English.

Hiltunen, Risto 1984. The Type and Structure of Clausal Embedding in Legal English. *Text* 4/1-3, 107-123.

Lakoff, Robin T. 1990. *Talking Power: The Politics of Language.* New York: Basic Books.

Leech, Geoffrey 1983. *Principles of Pragmatics*. London: Longman.

Maniruzzaman, Abdul F.M. 2006. The Lex Mercatoria and International Contracts: A Challenge for International Commercial Arbitration? *American University International Law Review* 14/3, 658-734.

Mellinkoff 1963. The Language of the Law. New York: Little Brown.

Merriam Webster Dictionary Online, at <http://www.merriam-webster.com/>.

Montori Díez, Agustín 2009. *Manual del Transporte Marítimo*. Barcelona: ATEIA-OLT.

Orts, María Ángeles. 2006. *Aproximación al discurso jurídico en inglés*. Madrid: Edisofer.

Pritchard, Boris 2002. On Some Issues in the Standardization of Maritime English – Pedagogical Implications. *Proceedings of the International Seminar on Maritime English, Istanbul Technical University*. Istanbul, 20-22 March.

Searle, John R. 1976. The Classification of Illocutionary Acts. *Language in Society* 5, 1-24.

Swales, John 1981. Definitions in Science and Law – Evidence for Subject-specific Course Component. *Fachsprache* 3/4 106-111.

Swales, John 1985. Citation Analysis and Discourse Analysis. *Applied Linguistics* 7/1 40-56.

Swales, John 1990. *Genre Analysis*. Cambridge: Cambridge University Press.

Tetley, William 1999. Maritime Law as a Mixed Legal System. In *Tulane Maritime Law Journal* 23, 317-350. At <http://www.mcgill.ca/maritimelaw/comparative/marlawmix/>. Last retrieved 17th June 2013.

Tetley, William ²2004. *Glossary of Maritime Law Terms*. At <http://www.mcgill.ca/maritimelaw/glossaries/maritime>. Last retrieved 18th June 2013.

Tiersma, Peter 1999. *Legal Language*. Chicago: University of Chicago Press.

Trosborg, Anna 1995. Statutes and Contracts: An Analysis of Legal Speech Acts in the English Language of the Law. *Journal of Pragmatics* 23, 31-53.

Van Hooydonk, Eric (ed.) 2003. *English and Continental Maritime Law: After 115 Years of Maritime Law Unification – A Search for Differences Between Common Law and Civil Law*. Antwerp Maritime Seminars. Antwerp: Maklu.

Ziarati Martin / Ziarati Reza/ Calbas, Bahar/ Moussley L. 2009. *Improving Safety at Sea by Developing Standards for Maritime English*. Helsinki, Finland: IMLA.

MICHELE SALA

Interpersonal and Interactional Markers in Legal Research Articles

1. Introduction

The present chapter investigates interpersonal resources in legal research articles (RAs) focusing specifically on interrogative formulations, that is, those strategies that more openly than others presuppose and reveal a recognizable dialogical framework between the writer and the readers by appealing to them and rhetorically expecting a response on their part. The role and the function of questions in legal RAs are highly strategic. As a matter of fact, legal research – being primarily devoted to the discussion of legal principles and their application (or applicability) to practical cases – is very much a discourse-based phenomenon rather than an evidence-based one, and argumentation needs to be compelling in order to compensate for the lack of undisputable, quantifiable, and objective data with which to persuade the reader. For this reason, scholarly discourse about legal matters has often been claimed to benefit considerably from a detached and depersonalized treatment of the content, so as to rhetorically minimize the role of the writer in presenting claims and downtone the risk of bias (hence the preference for impersonal or passive constructions, cf. Hiltunen 1990). However, many authors of such texts are also professionals of the Court and expert users of forensic discourse, which is eminently interactional in that it linguistically presupposes a responding (if silent) audience whose possible doubts and objections need to be anticipated and neutralized (Pascual 2002, 2006; Gibbons 2003; Anesa 2012). Interrogative formulations are very effective resources to achieve this purpose, thus making claims more easily acceptable and the argumentation compelling. Thus, the main assumption of this investigation is that legal research and its way of exploiting the language reflects both roles of the legal experts, i.e. the legislator and the defender, conflating the semantic precision of the statute and contract drafter with the pragmatic effectiveness of the experienced lawyer.

More specifically, legal RAs, not relying upon measurable evidence but rather on varyingly interpretable factors (actions or situations), cannot benefit from an orderly and "careful step-by-step description [and from] the kind of explicitness that we associate with standard academic description" (Swales 1990: 169). At the same time, very often legal RAs, when discussing human behaviours, resort to high-level claims, those which "are likely to be important but risky" (Swales 1990: 117) in that they include informatively significant statements questioning or challenging accepted and established views, thus contributing dramatically to the debate on a given topic. Given the face-threatening potential of this type of communication, in order to avoid aversive reactions on the part of the audience, mitigate assertion and compensate for the lack of self-explanatory evidence, writers need to make their argumentation more engaging at the interpersonal level, and "questions clearly facilitate this kind of engagement" (Hyland 2002: 538).

Despite their rhetorical potential and strategic function, interrogative forms in academic written texts tend to be generally contained (Hyland 2002). As a matter of fact, the use of such resources in a monologic genre like the RA is quite marked in that, not only do they imply the 'reader-in-the-text' (Thompson 2001), but they openly address the audience and invite them to find suitable responses to crucial points. By doing this, they both reveal the writer's stance, bias interpretation, and "have a direct appeal in bringing the second person into a kind of dialogue with the writer" (Webber 1994: 268). From a pragmatic and cognitive perspective, questions expressly presuppose an asymmetrical power and knowledge balance between writers and readers, those who 'know' and those who 'don't' (or 'are simply not aware of knowing', in the case of rhetorical questions). It is precisely owing to the face-threatening potential intrinsic in their directness and impact that interrogatives are usually very limited in scholarly written discourse, especially when addressing specialized audiences (rather than trainees), as is typically the case with RAs (Swales/Feak 1994; Chang/Swales 1999; Hyland 2002). These factors, together with the influence of discipline-related epistemological paradigms and the specificity of their discursive practices (i.e. courtroom monologues, cross-examination, etc. for legal experts, cf. Breeze 2009), may explain the level of variation that can be encountered in the use of questions when comparing RAs written in different domains, which is part of the present analysis.

This chapter examines interrogative collocations as argumentative devices exploited to introduce informative gaps which are eventually going to be filled in the ensuing text. In this case these resources acquire a marked metadiscursive function (Thompson 2001, Hyland 2002, 2005a) which affects the interpersonal tenor in the text without directly assessing the ideational and propositional meaning of the claim. In other words, interrogatives modify the degree of acceptability of the content both by codifying evaluative and affective meanings (Hyland 2005a, 2005b), by implying a certain level of engagement, solidarity and cooperation towards the reader, and, especially, by presupposing a comparable level of competence and commitment and a similar ideological positioning on the part of the recipient. More in detail, questions will be here investigated according to their pragmatic meaning (i.e. their being *conducive* vs. *non-conducive*), their textual function (i.e. *repository, evaluative* or *mention*), and their morpho-syntactic representation (i.e. *polar* vs. *open*) in a corpus of 80 legal RAs, and will at the same time assess the distinctive use of such resources in legal studies by comparing their occurrence with a reference corpus of 240 RAs in applied linguistics, economics and medicine.

2. Material and methodology

The corpus selected for the present analysis is taken from CADIS (Gotti 2006, 2012) and consists of 320 RAs published between the year 1990 and 2012 in four different disciplines, each of which is represented by 80 texts. The corpus totals about 2,574,000 running words thus distributed: over 905,000 words in legal RAs (LARAs), over 804,000 in applied linguistics (ALRAs), 624,000 in economics (ECRAs) and 380,000 in medicine (MERAs).

WordSmith Tool 5.0 (Scott 2007) and Adobe Acrobat (pdf program) search options were used for quantitative searches. The result yielded by such programs were then filtered through a stage of manual revision to filter out non-relevant instances (i.e. question marks found in web addresses, tables, quotations, references, etc.), classify spurious cases and clarify ambiguities. The qualitative analysis focuses on the interpersonal dimension of discourse as conceived in terms of the systemic functional approach (Halliday 1994; Halliday/Matthiessen 1999). According to these parameters, whereas the ideational function of language governs the propositional meaning – i.e. the representation of ideas and experiences – and the textual one accounts for its linguistic and rhetorical realization, the interpersonal function concerns the interplay between the participants in negotiating meaning and is manifested by those resources which, at various degrees of explicitness, codify interaction by presupposing pragmatic roles for the interactants and by expressing evaluation, engagement and group membership. In metadiscursive terms, such interactional resources function as engagement markers conflating several communicative purposes:

> [B]ringing the interlocutor into an arena where they can be led to the writer's viewpoint […] questions arouse interest and encourage the reader to explore an issue with the writer as an equal, sharing his or her curiosity and following where the argument leads. (Hyland 2005a: 153)

As a matter of fact, within the RA, an eminently monologic genre, interrogatives are not exploited for their primary function, i.e. to request information, but rather to anticipate informative gaps, elicit curiosity, strengthen coherence and connectedness between different text parts and, at the same time, by presupposing an active and participating role on the part of the audience, they reinforce the degree of solidarity and cooperation in the process of meaning negotiation between the participants (Webber 1994; Thompson 2001; Hyland 2002; Giannoni 2008).

The model adopted here to examine interrogative resources is a complex framework which accommodates three different levels of analysis, i.e. the pragmatic, the textual and the morpho-syntactic. The pragmatic investigation assesses questions in terms of their contextual purpose, effectiveness and impact, and, on this basis, interrogative formulations can be distinguished into *non-conducive* and *conducive* (Greenbaum/Quirk 1990), the former being meant to emphasize informative gaps, whereas the latter presuppose "a questioner's expectation of and preference for a given answer" (Piazza 2002: 510) in that they contain elements already pointing to a specific response. The second level of analysis will enquire the function of questions as text-organizing resources and coherence markers, either used to introduce new meanings (*research questions*), or as transition markers signalling the switch between different conceptual units (*question-answer pairs*), or, finally, designed to reproduce the recipient's voice (*clausal and word level questions*, cf. Pascual 2002, 2006). Eventually, from a morpho-syntactic viewpoint, interrogatives can be further distinguished into *polar* and *open* forms, respectively those offering an alternative between two possibilities (in terms of acceptance or rejection) and those needing a more complex and content-based response.

3. Results

3.1. The pragmatic level

Functional and semantic approaches to grammar distinguish interrogative clause types on the basis of their discourse function into two broad groups, namely *non-conducive* and *conducive questions*. *Non-conducive* interrogatives (or *non-assertive* and *real* questions, cf. Hudson 1975; Tench 1988; Downing/Locke 2006) are those formulations "to which the speaker does not think he or she already knows the answer, but thinks that the addressee does" (Thompson 1995: 239). If this function is obvious and implicit in oral contexts, where both interactants take turns in the communicative event, in written monologic genres questions lose this distinctive purpose. As a matter of fact, in RAs such strategies are not primarily meant for the reader to respond to, but rather aimed to highlight an information gap for it to be eventually filled, yet rhetorically maintaining their peculiar interactional and dialogic character, as can be seen in the following examples:

(1) How have Chinese intellectuals perceived and responded to the Bush Doctrine? Naturally, there are many divergent viewpoints, but the main perspective can be easily identified (LARA 42)

(2) What has prevented this cooperation from occurring? How can international law contribute to bringing it about? To answer these questions, it is necessary to examine conditions favoring cooperation without the threat of external enforcement. (LARA 22)

As is evident in the extracts above, in academic writing by using such structures:

> Proficient writers attempt to second-guess the kind of information that the reader might want or expect to find at each point of the unfolding text, and proceed by anticipating their questions about, or reactions to, what is written. The text is built as a series of writer responses to these anticipated reactions. (Thompson 2001: 58)

For these reasons, *non-conducive* formulations have both a marked text- and discourse-structuring role, in that they make explicit what is missing in the given information so as to justify the introduction of new meanings and to coherently organize them within the text (as will be discussed in depth in section 3.2).

Conducive interrogatives (or *leading, biased, checking, assertive, loaded* or *rhetorical*, cf. Hudson 1975; Thompson 1995) are those resources "that are biased according to the kind of answer the speaker expects, towards a neutral, positive or negative assumption" (Downing/Locke 2006: 201), thus being "interrogative in structure but [with] the force of a strong assertion" (Greenbaum/Quirk 1990: 240).

This presuppositional character and bias towards preferred answers stems directly from lexical and syntactical elements (Keenan/Hull 1973; Bublitz 1981; Piazza 2002) like strong markers of affirmation and negation, such as, respectively, *really, truly, indeed, after all,* etc. – presupposing a preferred negative answer – or *no, not, never, ever,* etc. – pointing to a positive answer – as well as markers of contrast and concession, or *if*-clauses wording out conditions which imply or point to the relevant response, as the texts below exemplify:

(3) *If* 'integration through law' had worked so well in Europe, why should *not* a similar mechanism succeed on a global level? (LARA 15, emphasis added)

(4) Coordination of research policies is legally and politically possible in spite of some difficulties; *but* is ERA an adequate means to implement it in any case? (LARA 12, emphasis added)

In all the cases above, the possible answer is obvious, in that it "seeks confirmation of what the speaker has explicitly assumed [...] to be agreed truth" (Greenbaum/Quirk 1990: 467).

The table below lists the distribution of *non-conducive* and *conducive* formulations in LARAs,[1] and, for the sake of comparison, also in RAs in other domains. For this purpose, frequencies are expressed in normalized terms.

	LA	AL	EC	ME
non-conducive	**4.26**	3.72	2.28	3.88
conducive	**1.19**	0.20	0.31	0.22
total	***5.45***	*3.92*	*2.59*	*4.10*

Table 1. Occurrence of *non-conducive* and *conducive* questions.

The most striking piece of evidence resulting from the comparison presented in the table above is the remarkably higher occurrence of interrogative forms in LARAs than in other disciplines, which evidences the openly interpersonal nature of legal academic language with

1 Table 1 does not count *mention questions* (see section 3.2) since, given their peculiar textual character, they can hardly be accounted for in terms of conduciveness.

respect to other scholarly discourses (Breeze 2009). More distinctively, we also notice a proportionally significant frequency of *conducive questions* (four to five times more used in LARAs than in other domains). This adds to the dialogic dimension (exemplified by the occurrence of *non-conducive* forms) an expert-to-expert character by implying shared knowledge and common grounds, thus exploiting the sense of community membership as a persuasive device to make claims readily acceptable.

3.2. The textual level

In relation to their pragmatic aspect, interrogative forms may acquire a specific structuring or interpretive function on the basis of which they can be distinguished into three broad categories (Webber 1994; Hyland 2002; Pascual 2006; Giannoni 2008; Sala 2010):

- *repository questions*, those *non-conducive* forms which are instrumental in introducing meanings by stressing semantic coherence and cohesively organizing the argumentation;
- *evaluative questions*, those *conducive* formulations emphasizing commitment to what is said, expressing affect and evaluation, and presupposing preferred answers (which are not necessarily lexicalized);
- *mention questions*, those direct questions which are meant to word out the gap-filling cognitive mechanisms required for the processing of information and the correct assimilation of a given meaning.

These three categories will be discussed in detail in the following subsections. According to the definition provided by Pascual (2006: 388), the category of *repository questions* includes those strategies used to organize an argument in courtroom monologues. In RAs they function as textual mapping devices in that they help structure the text "by pointing to information provided later on" (Giannoni 2008: 220). More specifically, such questions guide interpretation by highlighting both the overall cognitive outline of the text and the interconnectedness and interdependence of its various parts, thus controlling and facilitating 'the flow of information' (Hyland 2002: 541). As such, they "provide a framework for the discourse [...], arouse the reader's interest and create anticipation" (Webber 1994: 261-262). These resources can be further divided into two classes, namely, *research questions* and *question-answer pairs*, on the basis of their position within the text and the type of information they convey.

Research questions, very frequent in academic writing, are usually positioned in the opening parts of the RA or its various sections. They "provide an initial framework for the discourse" (Hyland 2002: 540-541) by establishing the niche of the research being carried out and making explicit the gaps in the existing literature (Swales 1990) which are then going to be dealt with in the ensuing text. Some examples can be found in the excerpts below.

(5) By doing so this paper deals with two questions which may be sorted to two different levels of constitutional thinking. The first question is: who is the legitimate body to decide on a constitutional design? The second question is: which constitutional design is the appropriate one that should be implemented by a jurisdiction of prudent inhabitants? (LARA 21)

(6) The central question that arises in relation to the topic of this paper is; how does the eastern enlargement differ from the previous enlargements; why does diversity matter so much? (LARA 11)

These formulations are not followed by a relevant answer, but by a dissipated one, distributed over the whole text of the RA and usually synthesized in the closing paragraphs. In some cases (proportionally very few) *research questions* may also be found in the concluding sentences of a section or of the whole RA. In the former case, they are meant to lexicalize problems arising from what has been discussed up to that point, and are instrumental in cognitively introducing (interrogatively rather than assertively) the content of the upcoming section and cohesively linking the various parts of the text. In the latter case, *research questions* closing a RA are exploited to point to problematic aspects possibly resulting from the current research which are left to be investigated and clarified by future studies (Webber 1994).

Question-answer pairs are those pseudo-dialogical clusters placed in non-initial position (typical for *research questions*) where the first part, the probing question, implies the possibility of multiple relevant answers (thus requiring the reader to imagine alternative scenarios which could fill an informative gap), and the second part, the answer sequence, poses one such possibility as the only relevant one, implicitly ruling out all the others. The response sequence may be either very brief and of a polar type (i.e. *yes/no* or equivalent forms), more articulated and gradually expressed in a declarative or narrative way "immediately after the question [...] or distributed over several sentences" (Giannoni 2008: 219, see 7), or inter-semiotic (see 8), that is to say, expressed through other semiotic codifications such as pictures, tables, graphs, mathematical formulae, etc. (this being very seldom the case found in LARAs but not infrequent in other domains). Examples of *question-answer pairs* can be observed in the examples below:

(7) How did the AG arrive at this revolutionary conclusion? Relying on Article 22 of the DSU, the AG adopted the position that WTO members have no legal choice but to comply with DSB rulings. (LARA 45)

(8) [W]hy should a green tax reform absolutely be based on the most complete and complex assessment? A classification as in Table 3 will always lead to intense discussions but every system can be improved and refined over time. (LARA 66)

These clusters have both a marked discourse-structuring function, in that they help synthesize given information and prepare the ground to cohesively introduce new informative elements, and an interactive one, facilitating comprehension and 'providing a focus' (Greenbaum/ Quirk 1990: 466) for an effective interpretation of the meaning, thus "helping [the writer] communicate her information and leading the audience to both interpret and structure it coherently" (Bowker 2006: 64).

Evaluative questions are represented by those *conducive* formulations where the answer is presupposed by the wording of the interrogative itself or is self-evident with respect to a given context. For this reason, whether it is provided or missing, the answer is alluded to as being obvious; therefore, even if present, its lexicalization is redundant. Such resources, although resembling fully fledged questions, have the pragmatic force of a declarative (Giannoni 2008), in that, not only are they not meant to be answered, but they have the function of guiding and controlling interpretation. In semantic terms, *evaluative questions* embody a counterclaim as to their own propositional content (i.e. positively marked questions point to a negative answer, and vice-versa, see section 3.1), and this can be achieved in either *neutral* or *confrontational* terms.

Neutral evaluative questions are those strategies which favour given meanings without critical undertones, simply "presenting an opinion as an interrogative so the reader appears to be the judge, but actually expecting no response" (Hyland 2005a: 153), as can be seen in the following examples:

(9) A safe solution would be to say that the European Principles only apply if both parties to the transaction are European community "citizens", and their contract must be performed in the European Union. Is not this too restrictive? (LARA 25)

(10) Are they [Interinstitutional Agreements] merely an instrument to smooth the functional interplay of the organs and therefore comparable to other formal or informal interrelations between political institutions? (LARA 13)

As we can see, these resources are used to implicitly negotiate the meaning with the reader by discarding given views without explicitly and polemically questioning or attacking them.

Confrontational evaluative questions are *conducive* forms meant to bias interpretation by being markedly critical, by inferring strong affective meanings, implying judgement, casting doubts as to the truthfulness of a preceding claim or pointing to paradoxes deriving from the comparison between two meanings. In most cases the confrontational aspect is not explicit in the sentence, but can be inferred from co-textual elements, as the extracts below indicate:

(11) Even if we assume that this would be the case – notwithstanding what has been noted above –, I am not sure that it would be a desirable goal to pursue. In other words: do we really want parties to engage in this costly convergence exercise? (LARA 53)

(12) Assuming that the regime of international human rights applies in such a situation, are there circumstances in which a targeted killing would *not* be regarded as a violation of the victim's right to life? (LARA 16, emphasis in the original text)

Strategies like the one above are exploited to refute and reject given viewpoints but are formulated in such a way as to make the reader participate in the negotiation of such a judgment, that is to say, so as to make the audience share rather than merely accept the writer's opinion.

Mention questions are represented by those formulations which are intended to quote or discursively exemplify the various phases of the cognitive process needed to fully comprehend a given meaning. They may be placed in brackets or be separated from the co-text (clausal level questions, see 13) or syntactically integrated in a sentence as phrasal elements (word level questions, see 14), as illustrated by the following examples:

(13) The age-old terminological confusion around *ius gentium* – universal private law or law of nations? – was instrumental to legitimate the use of Roman law and the *ius commune* to determine what the rules of natural law and the new *ius gentium* were. (LARA 61)

(14) Rather than asking 'are wee for or against using international law to protect women's right?' we might consider which rights of which women we want to protect, and in what ways international law should be interpreted to protect them. (LARA 40)

These formulations, despite their syntactic aspect, do not have the function of interrogative sentences since, in the case of clausal questions, they follow their relevant answer and simply illustrate the steps required to get to such an answer, whereas, in the case of word level collocations, they function as positive semantic units, positing meanings rather than questioning their propositional content. The table below shows the occurrences and distribution of questions with respect to their textual function.

	LA	AL	EC	ME
Repository questions				
Research questions	**1.94**	2.39	1.08	2.43
Question-answer pairs	**2.32**	1.33	1.20	1.45
Sub-total	***4.26***	*3.72*	*2.28*	*3.88*
Evaluative questions				
Neutral questions	**0.80**	0.20	0.29	0.22
Confrontational questions	**0.39**	-	0.02	-
Sub-total	***1.19***	*0.20*	*0.31*	*0.22*
Mention questions	**0.48**	0.27	0.17	0.31

Table 2. Occurrence of *repository, evaluative* and *mention* questions.

The data in the table indicate that, as far as *repository strategies* are concerned, unlike other domains, in LARAs *question-answer pairs* are more frequently used in structuring the argumentation than *research* resources. This is indicative of the fact that in legal academic discourse guiding readers through the various steps of the argument and helping them to coherently process new meanings with respect to given information or shared knowledge is considered to be more strategic than to simply provide the audience with the outline of and the reasons for the discussion (which is the distinctive purpose of *research questions*). Along the same lines the frequency of *evaluative* resources is to be interpreted, especially those with a *confrontational* value. On this basis it appears that LARA writers do not consider it dangerous to suggest not only what meanings should be preferred and what discarded, but also what value judgment should be attributed to them. Finally, the contained but noticeable occurrence of *mention* structures rhetorically corroborates reader inclusion and implies writer guidance, thus conferring reader-friendliness especially to the textualization of complex meanings.

3.3. Morpho-syntactic level

A further classification of interrogative forms is based on their morpho-syntactic structure, according to which it is possible to distinguish between *polar* and *open questions* (Greenbaum/Quirk 1990; Downing/

Locke 2006), on the basis of their pointing to either a circumscribed or extended range of responsive options.

Polar questions (or *yes/no* questions) are those formulations syntactically introduced by an inversion of the subject and the auxiliary operator, where only the polarity or truthfulness of the propositional content is questioned. Through such resources "the speaker asks for confirmation or denial of the clause content, to be expressed by yes or no" (Downing/Locke 2006: 183). Within this category it is possible to include also *alternative questions,* those collocations where two interrogatives are linked by a marker of alternative (*or, otherwise, on the other hand,* etc.), thus restricting the range of possible responses to two, only one of which is going to be relevant. Some examples of *polar* formulation can be observed in the following extracts:

(15) Can it be said that a convention dealing with the use of a substance or thing that is known to cause significant damage to human health does not deal with a health matter? […] Would a convention dealing with the legality of nuclear weapons really be a convention dealing with a health matter? (LARA 98) (LARA 78)

(16) Moreover, should court assess the overall efficiency of the standard document as a whole, or should they proceed on an issue by issue (i.e. clause by clause) basis? (LARA 52)

As is clear from the examples above, the interrogatives found there presuppose a limited negotiating role on the part of the reader, since the response can only be expressed in terms of affirmation or negation, or by accepting one option and implicitly discarding the alternative one, yet in both cases the alternatives are readily provided by the writer.

Open questions are interactional resources which "typically expect a reply from an open range of replies" (Greenbaum/Quirk 1990: 232), filling the slot introduced by interrogative items such as *who, what, where, which, why, when, how,* etc. More precisely, these formulations "contain an element of missing information which is embodied in the *wh*-word. What the speaker is seeking […] is the identity of that element" (Downing/Locke 2006: 185). For this reason these devices are also referred to as *content* or *information* questions (Payne 1997: 299). Some examples can be found in the following extracts:

(17) Who makes the rules, fills the gaps, and resolves the conflicts and ambiguities in this complex transnational regulatory arena? What is the role of corporate actors in this drama? (LARA 62)

(18) Why an environmental principle has been so much in the fore in the field of health protection? (LARA 20)

Open questions are more reader-responsible than *polar* forms in that the addressees are required to think of an elaborate and substantiative answer (Sadock/Zwicky 1985, Kellermann 2007), scanning their competence for the missing information. The presupposition on the part of the writer is that the addressee is not only an active but also a competent participant with adequate knowledge to participate in the negotiation of meaning (or, at least, he/she is rhetorically treated as such for inclusive purposes). The following table illustrates the occurrence of *polar* and *open questions* in our corpus.

	LA	AL	EC	ME
polar questions	**2.82**	1.65	1.27	1.80
open questions	**3.11**	2.64	1.49	2.61
total	***5.93***	*4.19*	*2.76*	*4.41*

Table 3. Occurrence of *polar* and *open questions*.

As we can see from the data above, in line with RAs in other disciplines, LARAs display a preference for *open* reader-responsible formulations. However, a closer look at the occurrences reveals that *polar* structures are proportionally more frequently found in legal academic writing than in other domains. This tendency is possibly related to the typically discursive and argumentative (rather than evidence- or corpus-based) nature of LARAs and is likely to be intended for inclusive as well as focalizing purposes. As a matter of fact, *polar* questions are meant to actively involve the addressee in the reasoning and, at the same time, limit and control interpretive alternatives in order to allow the reader only few and selected options. This makes the transfer of the meaning challenging and stimulating, the reasoning more cohesive, the argumentation compelling and, ultimately, the claim more convincing.

4. Discussion

The data collected in the previous sections, though partial like all those yielded by corpus-based analyses, are nonetheless representative and indicative of the way interpersonality is discursively constructed and organized in legal research. More specifically, they illustrate the ways questions are used to structure a cohesive argument, both in quantitative and qualitative terms, and provide solid grounds to evaluate the functions performed by such resources in scholarly discourse dealing with legal matters. The significant presence of interactional interrogative formulations in LARAs observed in the sections above may be explained on the basis of three different, yet interrelated, factors, namely, the epistemology of the discipline, the influence of discursive and persuasive practices typical of forensic language, and the alignment to Plain Language Movement (PLM) policies.

As to the epistemological factors it must be noted that, unlike other academic disciplines which deal with the observation of empirical phenomena (i.e. the broad category of natural sciences) or description of quantities, their measurements, and their significance with respect to specific parameters (i.e. corpus-based approaches like AL or case-based ones like ME), legal research focuses on human behaviour and, more specifically, on the principles that (should) govern social interaction, on the one hand (i.e. when discussing human right issues or national and international laws), and possible instances of deviation from conventionally accepted behaviours, on the other (i.e. when examining criminal cases), with the purpose of eventually offering an interpretation of practical (deviant) cases in the light of established and accepted criteria. Moreover, especially for those writers stemming from or discussing cases relevant to Common Law contexts – as is mostly the case of English native speakers (cf. Gibbons 2003) or experts operating in Anglophone countries (which is the case of 70% of the writers in our corpus) – the discussion of the content is more a matter of interpretation and argumentation (both discursive functions) than observation and description. This may be due to the lack of a stable reference point such as a civil code establishing norms meant to regulate, judge and proscribe social activities, but rather having to refer to 'precedents' and their arguable pertinence to the case at hand. Indeed, "for many social and historical issues there may be more than one convincing explanation and interpretation" (Freeden 2003: 17). On the basis of this, given the informative and persuasive character of RAs, the need to convince the audience has to confront the scarcity of self-evident elements, and writers have to compensate for what is missing, questionable or problematic at the ideational level by exploiting interpersonal resources, thus constructing claims which are acceptable not because their content is *per se* acceptable, but because of the convincing way it is worded out. This is the specific role played by interrogatives forms, especially by *question-answer pairs* and *evaluative* formulations. As a matter of fact, *question-answer* clusters, by presenting an information gap to be subsequently filled by the writer, guide interpretation of the content along specific lines, thus favouring (almost forcing) the access only to some meanings, and focusing the reader's attention on specific elements, as well as preventing interpretations which are contrary to or dangerous for the establishing of the writer's viewpoint. Similarly, *evaluative* formulations in LARAs (especially of the type *Are we really sure that... ? Is this truly the case?*) are very strategic in that they falsify or even negate the propositional content of a given claim. More specifically, writers, when confronted with problematic meanings, may decide to present them interrogatively and conducively, even in a confrontational way, thus rhetorically avoiding answering questions which might otherwise be perceived by the reader as totally legitimate and necessitating a more substantial reply.

The emphasis conferred to the interpersonal level of discourse may also be a trace of the type of language used in the Courtroom. By a cursory glance at the bibliographical footnotes which are usually linked to LARA authors' name it is possible to notice that most of them (with very few exceptions) are also practitioners of the Court or teachers in forensic disciplines, thus they are familiar with forensic rhetoric and its peculiarities, particularly its marked interactional character (Walter 1988; Cotterill 2003; Gibbons 2003; Anesa 2012). This is especially the case of Common Law Courtroom monologues (Pascual 2002, 2006) – both on the part of the prosecution and the defense – which are not aimed at evidencing the applicability of existing norms to specific actions, but are rather primarily "designed to convince the court" (Tiersma 1999: 141), that is, the judge and the jury. Given the adversarial nature of this procedure and the fact that lawyers will not be interrupted by observations or objections that the floor may have, in order to make their point more cohesive, clear and convincing, defense and prosecutors need to anticipate and respond to possible doubts. They often do so by framing such problematic aspects in the form of question (Breeze 2009) – thus suggesting their possible legitimacy – and subsequently discarding their validity and contextual relevance by providing answers which corroborate a given viewpoint. In this sense, monologues at trial can be said to be "used to win, not to help the courts to discover facts" (Jacquemet 1996: 9) within an activity which may defined "not so much as a search for the truth [but] as an institutionalized search for answers" (Pascual 2006: 399-400). Traces of these discourse practices can be found in the type of interrogatives used in LARAs. The questions used here, in fact, are not primarily meant to provide the argumentative design of the text and its goal orientation (i.e. *research questions*), but rather to actively involve readers in the process of meaning construction, through *question-answer* strategies designed to represent underspecified or unanswered elements in the given information so as to create a discursive space within which to introduce and justify new claims.

This tendency towards challenging the recipient into active reasoning is also reflected in the frequency of *conducive questions*, which, as seen above, are not intended to be answered but rather to rhetorically align readers towards given positions and consequently bias their interpretation. Another significant aspect in this respect is the high number of *polar questions* (which is not far below that of *open questions*). *Polar questions* are, in fact, particularly strategic in engaging the audience, in that, unlike *open* formulations, they do not offer a whole range of responsive alternatives, but only one possibility is lexicalized. Readers are expected to either confirm or reject it on the basis of their competence and of the fact that the preferred response needs to be coherent with and presupposed by the surrounding text. These strategies are less reader-responsible than *open questions* (or even more 'manipulative', in that limiting the interpretive options to only two, whereas multiple answers could be possible) and, at the same time, less intimidating as they allow the recipient little margin of choice but also for mistake.

Another possible explanation of the interpersonal character found in legal RAs may be related to the influence of PLM. Originating from the awareness that English in written legal texts had become increasingly convoluted, in some cases to the detriment of comprehensibility (Mellinkoff 1963), PLM is aimed at the simplification of legal language to make documents, statutes, norms, contracts, etc. understandable to the layperson. Beside suggesting measures like the limitation of archaic forms and redundant formulations, or the reduction of sentence length and nominalizations – PLM questions the necessity of the highly impersonal style often found in legal writing (Maley 1985, Tiersma 1999, Williams 2007). In fact, although considered "to reinforce the idea of impartiality and authoritativeness" (Williams 2004: 114), it is not *per se* a guarantee of truthfulness, relevance or clarity. When synthesizing the main requirements of PL, Adler (2012) invites writers to "adopt as informal a tone as is appropriate in the circumstance (which include the reader' and the writer's preference and the relationship between them)" (2012: 77). This inclusive and engaging language is also found in LARAs and is epitomized by interrogative structures, in that, much more than other personalizing resources (such as the use of the first and second person pronouns and directives), questions not only imply personalization, but presuppose cooperation and interaction between the participants. Most typically, in LARAs inclusion is reflected in the predominance of cognition-based (*question-answer pairs*) and *evaluative* questions, which are explicitly designed to rhetorically involve the reader, and by the distinctive presence of *mention* forms, meant to simplify complex concepts by representing them as the answer to (a series of) questions worded out as if through the reader's voice, as if quoting his/her mental processing, thus implicitly suggesting the cognitive steps to follow in order to fully comprehend given ideas.

5. Concluding remarks

Legal research, as a discipline pertaining to social sciences, is epistemologically based on discourse and interpretation and, as such, it combines a descriptive character with an intrinsically evaluative one, being aimed to describe actions, actors and situations, and judge them with respect to recognizable parameters. Within this type of text the writer's stance is usually quite foregrounded, if not explicit, and, having to deal with negotiable and debatable claims, which usually cannot be uncritically accepted, the primary need for writers is to align the audience to their point of view. As we have seen in the previous sections, this task may be effectively performed by strategically exploiting interpersonal resources such as interrogative forms, by which writers may achieve several purposes. On the one hand, by resorting to *non-conducive research questions* they provide the general framework of their discussion: this helps readers navigate the text and find their way through the articulations of meaning. On the other hand, with *question-answer pairs* writers manage to make their argumentation more cohesive by preparing the ground for the introduction of new claims and making the shift between meanings seem almost necessary. Moreover, *mention* and *conducive evaluative questions* indicate how certain meanings are to be processed and evaluated, thus rhetorically guiding the readers to understand and accept the writer's opinion.

References

Adler, Mark 2012. The Plain Language Movement. In Tiersma, Peter / Solan, Lawrence (eds) *The Oxford Handbook of Language and Law*. Oxford: Oxford University Press, 67-83.

Anesa, Patrizia 2012. *Jury Trials and the Popularization of Legal Language: A Discourse Analytical Approach*. Bern: Peter Lang.

Bowker, Janet 2006. Referential and Affective Force in Oral Business Presentations: The Role of Narration. In Bamford, Julia / Bondi, Marina (eds) *Managing Interaction in Professional Discourse: Intercultural and Interdiscoursal Perspectives*. Roma: Officina Edizioni, 58-71.

Breeze, Ruth 2009. Issues of Persuasion in Academic Law Abstracts. *Revista Alicantinade Estudios Ingleses* 22, 11-26.

Bublitz, Wolfram 1981. Conducive Yes-No Questions in English. *Linguistics* 19, 851-870.

Chang, Yu-Ying / Swales, John M. 1999. Informal Elements in English Academic Writing: Threats or Opportunities for Advanced Non-native Speakers? In Candlin, Christopher N. / Hyland, Ken (eds) *Writing: Texts, Processes and Practices*. London: Longman, 145-167.

Cotterill, Janet 2003. *Language and Power in Court: A Linguistic Analysis of the O.J. Simpson Trial.* Houndmills: Palgrave Macmillan.

Downing, Angela / Locke, Philip 2006. *English Grammar. A University Course*. London: Routledge.

Freeden, Michael 2003. *Ideology. A Very Short Introduction.* Oxford: Oxford University Press.

Giannoni, Davide S. 2008. Popularizing Features in English Journal Editorials. *English for Specific Purposes* 27, 212-232.

Gibbons, John 2003.*Forensic Linguistics.* Oxford: Blackwell.

Gotti, Maurizio 2006. Creating a Corpus for the Analysis of Identity Traits in English Specialised Discourse. *The European English Messenger* 15/2, 44-47.

Gotti, Maurizio (ed.) 2012. *Academic Identity Traits*. Bern: Peter Lang.

Greenbaum, Sidney / Quirk, Randolph 1990. *A Student's Grammar of the English Language*. London: Longman.

Halliday, Michael A. K. ^{2}1994. *An Introduction to Functional Grammar*. London: Edward Arnold.

Halliday Michael A. K. / Matthiessen, Christian 1999. *Construing Experience Through Meaning: A Language-Based Approach to Cognition*. London: Cassell.

Hiltunen, Risto 1990. *Chapters on Legal English. Aspects Past and Present of the Language of the Law*. Helsinki: Suomalainen Tiedeakatemia.

Hudson, Richard 1975. The Meaning of Questions. *Language* 51/1, 1-31.

Hyland, Ken 2002. What Do they Mean? Questions in Academic Writing. *Text* 22/4, 529–557.

Hyland, Ken 2005a. *Metadiscourse: Exploring Interaction in Writing.* London: Continuum.

Hyland, Ken 2005b. Stance and Engagement. A Model of interaction in Academic Discourse. *Discourse Studies* 7, 173-192.

Jacquemet, Marco 1996. *Credibility in Court: Communicative Practices in the Camorra Trials*. Cambridge: Cambridge University Press.

Keenan, Edward / Hull, Robert 1973. The Logical Presuppositions of Question and Answers' In Petöfi, János / Franck, Dorothea (eds) *Präsuppositionen in Philosophie und Linguistik.* Frankfurt: Athenäum, 441-466.

Kellermann, Kathy 2007. Persuasive Question-Asking: How Question Wording Influences Answers. Paper presented at the Annual Meeting of the State Bar Association of California, September 27, 2007, Anaheim, California.

Maley, Yon 1985. Judicial Discourse: The Case of the Legal Judgment. *Festschrift in Honor of Arthur Delbridge. Beitrage zur Phonetic und Linguistik* 48: 159-173.

Mellinkoff, David 1963. *The Language of the Law*. Boston: Little, Brown & Co.

Pascual, Esther 2002. *Imaginary Trialogues: Conceptual Blending and Fictive Interaction in Criminal Courts.* Utrecht: LOT Dissertation Series 68.

Pascual, Esther 2006. Questions in Legal Monologues: Fictive Interaction as Argumentative Strategy in a Murder Trial. *Text & Talk* 26/3, 383-402.

Payne, Thomas E. 1997. *Describing Morphosyntax: A Guide for Field Linguistics*. Cambridge: Cambridge University Press.

Piazza, Roberta 2002. The Pragmatics of Conducive Questions in Academic Discourse. *Journal of Pragmatics* 43/5, 509-527.

Sadock, Jerrold / Zwicky, Arnold 1985. Speech Act Distinctions in Syntax. In Shopen, Timothy (ed.) *Language Typology and Syntactic Description, Volume 1, Clause Structure.* Cambridge: Cambridge University Press, 155-196.

Sala, Michele 2010. Interrogative Forms as Professional Identity Markers in Legal Research Articles. In Garzone, Giuliana / Archibald, James (eds) *Discourse, Identities and Roles in Specialized Communication.* Bern: Peter Lang, 301-320.

Scott, Mike 2007. *WordSmith Tools Version 5.0.* Oxford: Oxford University Press.

Swales, John 1990. *Genre Analysis: English in Academic and Research Settings.* Cambridge: Cambridge University Press.

Swales, John / Feak, Christine A. 1994. *Academic Writing for Graduate Students: Essential Tasks and Skills.* Ann Arbor, MI: University of Michigan Press.

Tench, Paul 1988. *The Roles of Intonation in English Discourse.* Frankfurt: Peter Lang.

Thompson, Geoff 2001. Interaction in Academic Writing: Learning to Argue with the Reader. *Applied Linguistics* 22/1, 58-78.

Thompson, Susan 1995. Teaching Intonation on Questions. *ELT Journal* 49/3, 235-243.

Tiersma, Peter 1999. *Legal Language.* Chicago: University of Chicago Press.

Walter, Bettyruth 1988. *The Jury Summation as Speech Genre: An Ethnographic Study of What it Means to those Who Use It.* Amsterdam: John Benjamins.

Webber, Pauline 1994. The Function of Questions in Different Medical English Genres. *English for Specific Purposes* 13, 257-268.

Williams, Christopher 2004. Legal English and Plain Language: An Introduction. *ESP Across Cultures* 1, 111-124.

Williams, Christopher ²2007. *Tradition and Change in Legal English. Verbal Constructions in Prescriptive Texts*. Bern: Peter Lang.

CHRISTOPH A. HAFNER

Stance in a Professional Legal Genre: The Barrister's Opinion

> I think it's fair to say it's the area of my opinion where I am least certain... but I can't say to the solicitor, 'I'm not sure' because he's paying me to give a view, as long as I caution him about it I think that's fair enough. (B1, Interview)

In many common law contexts, a distinction is maintained between two kinds of lawyers: barristers, who specialize in courtroom advocacy and have expert understanding of relevant procedural rules and trial tactics; and solicitors, who are primarily engaged outside the courtroom, for example in the negotiation and formal documentation of agreements for their clients. In cases that seem likely to go to trial, a solicitor may request a written opinion from a barrister on the merits of the case of a particular 'lay client'. Such a barrister's opinion is centrally concerned with taking up a stance in order to provide a balanced legal view on the case in question. The purpose of the genre is two-fold: to provide both an objective assessment of the lay client's legal position and subjectively-oriented advice on how to proceed from a legal tactical perspective (Hafner 2008, 2010).

However, as the quote above shows, there is an inherent tension in this genre. The barrister is required to provide a definite opinion about something that is fundamentally uncertain, that is, the legal outcome of a trial. In order to manage this tension the barrister must be able to clearly communicate their professional opinion, while at the same time evaluating that opinion and 'cautioning' readers if there is any uncertainty. Thus, conveying an appropriately nuanced stance to readers is crucial for this genre. This is especially true given the stakes involved: the barrister's opinion is meant to be relied upon by readers as a basis for real-world action that could have far-reaching consequences for the individuals concerned. This chapter explores the range of interpersonal linguistic resources that writers of the barrister's opinion draw on in order to resolve the tensions involved in adopting an appropriate stance and engaging with a diverse audience. It will be argued that the linguistic and discursive features described index cultural values common to the legal community.

1. Stance and evaluation

Following Halliday (1994), any clause simultaneously realizes three main kinds of meaning: ideational, interpersonal and textual. There has recently been considerable scholarly interest in aspects of interpersonal meaning, which is now seen to play an important role in genres, like the scientific research article, traditionally considered impersonal and objective in nature. One important element of interpersonal meaning is stance, which can be broadly defined as the position adopted by the writer vis-à-vis the text created (Jaffe 2009). This category is referred to in the literature in a range of ways: in addition to *stance* (Biber 2006), major treatments refer to the concept in terms of *appraisal* (Martin/ White 2005), *evaluation* (Hunston/Thompson 2000), and *metadiscourse* (Hyland 2005a). With these competing theoretical orientations, a commonly agreed definition of stance has been elusive.

Jaffe points to the importance of stance in discourse, saying: "Although some forms of speech and writing are more stance saturated than others, there is no such thing as a completely neutral position vis-à-vis one's linguistic productions, because neutrality is itself a stance" (Jaffe 2009: 1). Similarly, according to Thompson and Hunston, stance (or *evaluation*, in their terms) is an important object of inquiry for linguists because it functions: "1) to express the speaker's or writer's opinion, and in doing so to reflect the value system of that person and their community; 2) to construct and maintain relations between the speaker or writer and hearer or reader; 3) to organize the discourse" (Thompson/Hunston 2000: 6). As Jaffe

(2009: 2) points out, the existing literature treats stance as essentially concerned with the adoption by the speaker/writer of a position: this can be a position towards what is said, a position towards the audience or a position towards some larger context, within which the discourse is situated. This implies that stance is a discursive and intertextual phenomenon (see also Martin/White 2005: 10): stance is developed across the boundaries of clause, sentence and text as speakers/writers implicitly or explicitly refer to and evaluate their own text and related prior texts.

Consider first of all, how speakers/writers adopt a position towards their own text. In this sense, stance can be divided into *affective stance* and *epistemic stance* (Biber 2006; Jaffe 2009). Affective stance refers to the attitudinal position that the author adopts towards the text, i.e. it is a judgment in terms of value. Epistemic stance refers to the position adopted towards the text in terms of truth and knowledge, i.e. it is a judgment of the strength/weakness of the claims presented. Epistemic stance can be expressed through epistemic modality, including modal verbs (e.g. *may, must*), adverbs (e.g. *possibly, definitely*), adjectives (e.g. *possible, certain*) and other pragmatic devices described in the literature on hedging and boosting (Hyland 1998, 2005a). Epistemic stance can also be expressed through the use of evidential markers (e.g. *according to*), which signal the source that forms the basis for claims made. Such evidentials and the intertextual referencing that accompanies them are particularly important in the legal context, because, in order to succeed, legal arguments must be supported by appropriate appeals to authority (Hafner 2013).

Secondly, stance can refer to the way that speakers/writers adopt a position towards their audience, creating and maintaining a social relationship. Clear examples of this are linguistic devices that explicitly involve the audience in the discourse (this can of course also be done implicitly). Hyland (2005b: 177) refers to this kind of stance as *engagement*, "an alignment dimension where writers acknowledge and connect to others, recognizing the presence of their readers, pulling them along with their argument, focusing their attention, acknowledging their uncertainties, including them as discourse participants, and guiding them to interpretations." As Hyland notes, this kind of stance can be constructed through the use of reader pronouns (e.g. *you*, *the reader*), directives (e.g. *consider*), questions, appeals to shared knowledge, personal asides and any discursive strategies that rhetorically position the audience or are designed to meet audience expectations. Indeed, some of these strategies not only involve the speaker/writer in positioning themselves towards their audience, but also in positioning themselves towards the wider context (e.g. appeals to shared knowledge). This final element of stance involves alignment (or, perhaps, a refusal to align) with shared cultural values and can be enacted by the observation of tacitly agreed conventions in speech/writing production.

In the applied linguistic domain, much of the work on stance in writing has focused on the academic context, exploring how academic writers draw on linguistic resources in order to convey an appropriate stance and balance their claims. The findings have tended to show disciplinary variation, with different disciplinary writers drawing on the available resources in ways that are subtly different and can be seen to index community values. However, less attention has been paid to the realization of stance in professional legal writing of the kind under consideration here (see, however, Tessuto 2006). Even less work has sought to identify the kinds of difficulties that novice professional legal writers encounter in adopting an appropriate stance. This chapter attempts to fill some of these gaps, by providing an analysis of stance in barrister's opinion texts written by both novice and expert legal professionals.

2. Stance in the barrister's opinion

Two main genre analytic studies have considered the barrister's opinion and both provide some insight into the construction of stance in this genre (Hafner 2010; Tessuto 2006). Hafner (2010) provides a detailed analysis of the communicative context, move structure and lexico-grammatical realization of the genre. The study emphasizes the intertextual nature of the barrister's opinion, with the barrister responding to written 'instructions to Counsel' drafted by a solicitor. These instructtions summarize the facts relevant to the lay client's case and request advice. The resulting opinion follows a 6-move structure: 1. Heading; 2. Opening; 3. Discussion; 4. Conclusion/Opinion; 5. Giving advice; 6. Closing. Move 2, the Opening, contains sub-moves (2a. Identifying key issues; 2b. Identifying material facts; 2c. Limiting the scope), as does move 3, the Discussion (3a. Raising an issue; 3b. Stating the law; 3c. Providing authority; 3d. Applying the law to the facts; 3e. Providing a conclusion/opinion). In this analysis, the generic structure of the Discussion can be seen to follow a common pattern of legal reasoning: identifying and resolving issues, often through the deductive application of law to facts. In addition, it is clear that some moves, especially those that call for the provision of legal conclusions and opinions, are more stance-laden than others.

As was noted earlier, stance-taking is crucial to the genre and Tessuto's (2006) study describes this aspect in some detail. First, he notes the conventional use of self-mention by barristers, who typically adopt the first person pronoun *I*, occasionally alternating with *we* or *one*. In addition, the analysis shows that barristers combine epistemic modality with other, pragmatic hedging strategies in order to qualify the barrister's commitment to the truth value of propositional content expressed. In support of his analysis, Tessuto draws upon Hyland's (1998) study of hedging in scientific research articles, in which hedging is characterized as a mix of epistemic devices and pragmatic strategies. According to Hyland, scientists strategically hedge knowledge claims in their writing by referring to limitations in the state of available knowledge. In Tessuto's study, the barrister's opinion genre similarly involves pragmatic hedging strategies, which signal what he characterizes as a 'lack of information' or 'deficiency in advice model' (2006: 300). It is the aim of the present chapter to build on these insights and develop a more complete model of factors that affect stance, especially the strategic management of uncertainty, in the barrister's opinion genre.

3. The study

The data for this study draws on a comparative genre analysis of the barrister's opinion, which is based on writing samples from five expert barristers and 19 novice lawyers completing the vocational stage of legal education at a university in Hong Kong. In Hong Kong, this vocational stage of legal education is known as the Postgraduate Certificate of Laws, or PCLL for short, and it is analogous to professionally-oriented legal practice courses in other jurisdictions which are attempted after completion of an academic legal qualification (e.g. LLB) and are designed to prepare novice lawyers for the world of legal practice. All of the novice lawyers who took part in this study were taking a course in Conveyancing and Probate as part of their PCLL studies, on which they were assigned to complete a barrister's opinion based on a simulated fact situation. The fact situation, referred to as 'Hibiscus Court', involved a dispute about a potential breach of contract in the sale and purchase of residential property. The five expert barristers were also provided with simulated instructions on two other fact situations, also in the general area of land law: 'Villa Rouge', a dispute about what items could be included in a sale and purchase of residential property, and 'Hair Flair', a dispute about whether a commercial lease had been created and could be enforced. Two of the experts wrote on the 'Villa Rouge' topic and the other three on the 'Hair Flair' topic.

The expert barristers who took part in this study included three women and two men. Two of the women were of Hong Kong Chinese ethnicity while the other barristers were of Caucasian extraction. Between them, the experts had an average of eight years' experience as barristers in Hong Kong. The least experienced barrister had been practising for less than a year, but had six years' prior experience as a solicitor, while the most experienced barrister had been practising for 22 years at the time of the study. As for the 19 novice writers, nine were men and ten were women, with ages ranging from the low twenties to over 40 years. They were generally highly educated: most had another university degree in addition to their LLB and about a quarter of the novices had master's degrees of some kind. The majority of them reported completing some stage of their education overseas, for example in the U.K., with only five completing their entire education in Hong Kong. In addition, all of the novices had some kind of prior work experience, either full-time work or law-related temporary/part-time work (e.g. a summer internship in a law firm). Of the 19 novices, 16 considered Cantonese to be their first language, with the other three indicating English. All had passed the IELTS test to get into the PCLL, with scores ranging from seven to nine and an average score of 7.8.

A qualitative, multi-perspective genre analysis (Bhatia 2004) was performed. This approach holds that, in order to reach a satisfactory understanding of the genre, it is necessary to go beyond a simple analysis of text to include other sources of data. Thus, in this study, data sources include relevant community texts and legal writing guides on the barrister's opinion genre, focus group interviews with the 19 participating novice writers, individual interviews with the five experts and the results of a questionnaire designed to elicit background information about the writers. The primary data analyzed consist of the barrister's opinions themselves: five expert texts (8,476 words; 1,695 words on average) and 19 novice texts (46,588 words; 2,452 words on average). With respect to the novice texts, which were graded, it was also possible to obtain (with the consent of participants) the scores awarded. These range from 19 to 37 (out of 40), which indicates that a range of abilities are represented. The text analysis proceeded as follows. An initial genre analysis was performed on the five expert texts, identifying moves and sub-moves. This analysis was checked with experts at an individual interview and necessary modifications were made. A similar analysis was then carried out on the novice text, identifying genre moves. The examples of stance in the barrister's opinion genre which are described below emerged as a result of this genre analysis.

In the following section, the primary source of data relied on is the expert writing, demonstrating the expert discursive management of stance. In addition, in order to illustrate potential pitfalls in stance-taking, a qualitative analysis contrasting one expert and novice text is provided. This qualitative approach aims to illuminate the way that the linguistic features of stance are strategically combined to greater or lesser effect across stretches of discourse.

4. Stance towards audience

As noted above, the barrister's opinion is highly intertextual in nature and is specifically written in response to solicitor's instructions. The immediate audience is rather narrow and includes the instructing solicitor and the lay client, whose case the solicitor is handling. Thus, the barrister's opinion is a hybrid genre, which mixes generic elements of business correspondence (in Opening and Closing moves) with other elements more typical of a legal judgment (in Discussion and Opinion/ Conclusion moves). In the Opening and Closing moves, the barrister explicitly involves other participants, using linguistic resources to establish a particular kind of relationship with them. Consider the following examples from the Opening, written by experts (salient features are highlighted in italics throughout the analysis):

(1) *I am instructed* to advise on the enforceability of a tenancy agreement between *lay client, Hair Flair Limited* ('Hair Flair') and New Wave Limited ('New Wave'). (B3, Opinion)

(2) *Instructing solicitors* act for *Hair Flair Limited ('Hair Flair')* who were in negotiations with New Wave Limited ('New Wave') for the lease of premises in the basement of New Wave World, Nathan Road, Hong Kong, ('the Premises'). (B5, Opinion)

Significantly, there is no use of the pronoun *you* to refer to the readers. Instead, the barrister refers to institutional roles: 'instructing solicitors', 'lay client' or, in the case of the client, by name. This choice serves to keep the reader at a respectful distance: the reader is involved only in terms of formal role. This strategy extends to the formulation of requests:

(3) I would be grateful if *those instructing me* would confirm, that the silk panels can therefore be removed from the wooden panels. (B2, Opinion)

Very occasionally (four times in the expert corpus) the inclusive pronouns, *we* or *our*, are used by barristers, as below:

(4) Although *our case* is less strong, I believe that there is a reasonable chance [...]. (B3, Opinion)

(5) [...] in the case of the silk panels *we must consider* the method and extent to which the silks have been attached to the walls of the house [...]. (B2, Opinion)

In example (4) the use of *our* has the effect of aligning the barrister with both the instructing solicitor and the lay client. It involves the readers by acknowledging their role as active participants, at the same time expressing professional solidarity. Similarly, the usage in example (5) also has the effect of involving the reader, when compared to alternatives like 'one must consider' or 'it is necessary to consider'. In addition, the choice of the first person has the effect of aligning writer and reader to a wider community. Here, *we* appears to mean 'we, as members of the legal community'.

Frequently, the texts end with a Closing move that appeals to the solicitor audience.

(6) I trust this advice *is helpful* and would be pleased to advise further *if so instructed.* (B4, Opinion)

(7) Should *instructing solicitors* have any questions arising from the above, I would be pleased to deal with these by telephone or e-mail. (B1, Opinion)

In example (6) the presence of the solicitor is implicit. To make it explicit would require the addition of 'solicitors' after 'helpful' ('helpful to solicitors') and 'instructed' ('instructed by solicitors'). Example (7) refers to the audience explicitly, but again in a form that avoids the second person pronoun, *you*, and thereby maintains a certain professional distance. In summary, then, in this genre the audience is involved in the writing, but the institutional language used (e.g.

'instructing solicitors', 'lay client') generally serves to keep the audience at a respectful distance.

5. Stance towards claims

As mentioned earlier, taking a stance towards claims is of central importance to the barrister's opinion genre. The genre requires barristers to develop an opinion on the legal outcome of the case. However, this can pose a challenge, as acknowledged in the following writing manual:

> It is very rare that you will be able to say yes or no, win or lose. But what the practitioner cannot do is say, 'I can give no answer'. There may be no *definite* answer, but there *must* always be *an* answer. (Inns of Court School of Law 2007: 27: emphasis in original)

It is difficult for barristers to commit to a legal outcome with certainty because ultimate authority lies not with the barrister, but with the court, and many factors can affect judicial decision-making. Thus, the opinion that the barrister gives is subject to a range of uncertainties. The pragmatic challenge that such underlying uncertainty poses in terms of writing is how to provide an opinion which accurately reflects the risks as the barrister perceives them. In this section, three main kinds of uncertainty are identified and elaborated:

1. Uncertainty about facts;
2. Uncertainty about adversary's position;
3. Uncertainty about the legal argument.

5.1. Uncertainty about facts

In order to ascertain the facts of a given case, the barrister must rely on the account provided by the instructing solicitor and lay client, as well as relevant documentation (letters, agreements and so on).

Unfortunately, this account could be both biased and incomplete. As a result, barristers must carefully analyze the facts, a process that may be time-consuming and difficult. As noted by one expert, the process can be even more challenging than the legal analysis proper: "It's analyzing the facts which causes most of the problem" (B3, Interview). As a result, one pragmatic strategy that expert writers employ regularly, is to draw attention to uncertainty about the facts, limitations in evidence/ knowledge about what actually happened. An example of this is provided below:

(8) The facts and correspondence are summarised in my instructions. *I have not seen any draft witness statement* from Mr Thomas Tung, the director of Hair Flair who conducted the negotiations for the lease. *I assume that no material matter*, such as contents of conversations and oral negotiations, *has been omitted from my instructions*. (B1, Opinion)

In example (8), the barrister both acknowledges and resolves uncertainty about the facts. First, uncertainty is acknowledged by highlighting a potential gap in the documentation ('I have not seen [...]'). Such a gap could refer to an entire document, as above, or just part of a document, as in this example: 'The relevant clause [...] does not provide that alterations can be made' (B5, Opinion). It could also refer to a gap in the solicitors' instructions: 'I am not informed of any issue of the respective directors' capacity [...]' (B3, Opinion). As these examples suggest, uncertainty about facts is often signalled by the use of the negative. In example (8), this uncertainty is subsequently resolved, through the explicit statement of an assumption ('that no material matter [...] has been omitted'). This strategy, also observed in other expert writing, serves to limit the scope of the opinion to those situations where the assumption holds.

5.2. Uncertainty about adversary's position

A second source of uncertainty is the position that the other party to the dispute will take, in terms of its analysis of the legal and factual situation. Barristers occasionally acknowledge this source of uncertainty by an explicit reference. In the expert writing, such uncertainty is normally both raised and resolved, as in the following examples:

(9) *New Wave Ltd does not give reasons* for its contention that the agreement is not binding. *We may speculate* that its stance will be that the negotiations and correspondence were all, in effect, 'Subject to Contract' [...]. (B1, Opinion)

(10) *Unless the other side raises this issue* in due course, *I believe it would be safe to assume* that this is the case. (B3, Opinion)

In example (9), the barrister explicitly refers to a lack of knowledge about the adversary's position ('does not give reasons'). This uncertainty is tentatively resolved through the use of the epistemic verb *speculate*, which is employed to suggest a possible position. In example (10) the barrister makes their assumption contingent on the position of the 'other side'. Again, uncertainty introduced is tentatively resolved through a range of epistemic devices ('believe', 'safe to assume').

5.3. Uncertainty about the legal argument

Another potential source of uncertainty is the legal argument itself, including interpretation of the law and its legal effect for the parties, considering the facts of the case. In appellate judgments, this is the most actively contested element, with parties arguing for an interpretation of the law that favours their interests. In contrast, in the barrister's opinions analyzed here, this source of uncertainty is only occasionally acknowledged, perhaps because the case files used involved relatively 'easy' cases that drew on well-settled law. Example (11) shows how one barrister acknowledged potential uncertainty about legal effect in order to introduce an alternative argument.

(11) *Even if I am wrong regarding the effect* of the correspondence, section 3(2) of the Conveyancing and Property Ordinance provides that an action may still be

> brought on the oral agreement if there has been an act of part performance by Hair Flair. (B3, Opinion)

The *if*-clause here acknowledges a possible limitation in the barrister's argument, which is resolved in the subsequent text. A more extensive example from the expert corpus can be seen in the comparative analysis below.

5.4. Resolution of uncertainty in expert and novice texts

The analysis so far describes how sources of uncertainty are typically *acknowledged* and *resolved* by expert writers. In this section, an expert text is compared to a novice text in order to illustrate potential challenges in stance-taking for novice writers. The expert text is written by the most experienced of the barristers (B1), while the novice text was identified as problematic by law school graders, being awarded the lowest mark out of all the novice texts (S14). As such, the comparison is instructive though not necessarily representative. It identifies potential challenges, which novice writers can and do encounter, when they are managing uncertainties in the barrister's opinion in order to take a stance towards their claims. The texts are reproduced in Appendices 1 and 2.

In Text A, paragraph 13, the barrister considers the issue 'is the memorandum a binding agreement for a lease?' This is followed by two alternative possible interpretations of the law as applied to the facts of the situation. Here the barrister hedges the propositional content of the text by using the epistemic modal verb *may* (line 3, line 7), clearly indicating both possibilities are uncertain and contingent. It is interesting to note the use of the appeal to authority (line 12) which supports both of the interpretations offered, and leads into the following issue: 'which of these interpretations is correct?' Taken as a whole, this paragraph serves to acknowledge uncertainty in the legal argument, with the barrister raising two possible alternative constructions of the law.

Paragraph 14 resolves this uncertainty. It begins with a clearly worded opinion, 'it seems to me that the memorandum provides for all the terms of the lease' (lines 16-17). The effect of the initial epistemic device, 'it seems to me', is to reduce the writer's commitment to the following proposition. At the same time, it also serves to clearly attribute the opinion to the writer, presenting the claim as individually held and contingent. This is an interpersonal strategy that involves the reader, by acknowledging that the reader may or may not reach the same conclusions, i.e. the validity of the claim is presented as dependent on the reader. In spite of this evaluation, which places limitations on the claim, the effect of the paragraph as a whole is to present a confident judgment.

This confidence is achieved by a general avoidance of epistemic devices after 'it seems to me'. First, the propositional content of the opinion (lines 16-17) is not itself hedged, with 'the memorandum *provides* for all the terms of the lease'. Next, the opinion is supported by a series of factual statements, all expressed in indicative mood ('the main terms are', 'the rest of the terms are to be', etc.). The argument concludes with a principle of law, which doubles as a reinforcement of the barrister's position: 'In the absence of any words of contingency or condition, *the bargain is immediately binding*' (lines 23-24). The manner in which law and opinion are combined in this one sentence makes it rhetorically forceful, as the opinion is both indistinguishable from legal principle, and supported by legal precedent (lines 25-26). Furthermore, in discursive terms, the opinion has evolved from a hedged opinion at the beginning of the paragraph to an unhedged statement near the end. Thus, while this expert writer clearly signals a degree of uncertainty, this uncertainty is skilfully resolved, in such a way that the barrister's opinion appears not only clear but well argued. This is possible because of the skilful use of discursive resources, including generic structure, stance and appeals to authority.

Let us now refer to the novice text, Text B, in Appendix 2. Text B considers the issue of whether a vendor has misled a purchaser about the existence of an illegal structure on a property, which is the subject of an agreement for sale and purchase. The state of knowledge of the vendor plays a role in the legal analysis, and this introduces an interesting element of uncertainty, as it is difficult to know, as a matter of fact, whether the vendor was aware that the illegal structure (a balcony) had been built in contravention of the Buildings Ordinance.

The novice writer here begins with a clear statement of opinion that the vendor in this situation has not disclosed information to the purchaser (lines 1-3). Subsequently Text B, like Text A, recognizes an uncertainty in the facts of the situation ('I do not have evidence' in line 8). This uncertainty is portrayed as problematic: 'the absence of such evidence makes it difficult to establish the Vendor was innocent' (lines 11-12). Thus the perceived uncertainty raises the question 'can the vendor be established as innocent?' This issue must be resolved in the following paragraph, and in order to do so, the novice must draw on effective discursive resources.

Paragraph 13 fails to resolve the issue raised in paragraph 12 largely because of the inappropriate use of stance throughout. The paragraph is punctuated by a large amount of hedging (contrast this with paragraph 14 in Text A which is characterized by its one single interpersonal hedge). What is particularly striking here is the writer's frequent use of epistemic devices, continuing to acknowledge (rather than resolve) the factual uncertainty and limitations on the writer's knowledge. In addition, the amount of hedging applied to a single proposition is in some cases extreme, with the writer weakening the following proposition three times:

(12) The Vendor has been occupying the Property since 1998 *suggests* that the period of the Vendor's occupation was long enough for him to have been *aware of the possibility* that the Balcony *could be* illegal.

For the most part, the facts are treated as merely suggestive. It is not until lines 21-25 that the writer begins to use less tentative language ('this clearly indicates the Vendor would have been aware', lines 23-24). However, the final statement of opinion is circuitous at best, beginning with a rebuttal of the vendor's assumed stance ('I do not support the argument that the Vendor was innocent', lines 25-26), before a hedged conclusion ('the circumstantial evidence suggests to me', lines 27-28).

The novice writer apparently lacks the discursive resources to effectively manage the uncertainty inherent in the barrister's opinion genre. In paragraph 13 in particular, the writer fails to *resolve* the uncertainties introduced. The opinion put forward is tentative throughout (with the exception of lines 21-25), with heavy use of epistemic devices. Furthermore, in the conclusion the writer fails to assert *his/her own view*, instead arguing *against the view* of the Vendor. The overall effect of this writing is to leave the reader in doubt about the writer's position/stance. This contrasts markedly with the expert writing in Text A, where discursive resources are effectively deployed to present a clear and confident view.

5.5. Self-mention and boosting

As the examples above illustrate, the barrister's opinion genre is characterized by the use of self-mention by the author, with first person pronouns (*I/me/my*) employed throughout. This observation accords with Tessuto's findings, mentioned earlier. In move 4, the final Conclusion/Opinion, this usage appears to be obligatory. In this move, all of the expert barristers drew on the strategy of self-mention, always through the use of some form of first person pronoun, e.g. 'my views are', 'I consider', 'I believe'. In addition, the strategy was frequently seen when providing conclusions as part of move 3, the Discussion (sub-move 3e). In this sub-move, three of the experts exclusively used first person, coupled with epistemic lexis, e.g. 'it seems to me', 'in my opinion'. The other two experts mixed personal and impersonal forms, also introducing forms like 'it is clear that', 'it seems unlikely'. Thus, there appears to be a very strong preference in this genre for use of the first person as a means of intruding into the text at those points where a conclusion or opinion is called for.

This strategy has the effect of attributing reasoning and conclusions directly to the barrister concerned as the arguments of a single, expert professional. As noted, the use of the first person is frequently associated with epistemic lexis, which serves to weaken speaker commitment and makes the opinion contingent on acceptance by the reader. An interesting compensatory strategy, a form of pragmatic boosting, can be seen in the Conclusion/Opinion move of some of the expert opinions:

(13) I have taken into account all the circumstances and I am of the view that […]. (B4, Opinion)

(14) Having taken all the circumstances into account, and having regard to the authorities which I have referred to above, I consider that […]. (B2, Opinion)

(15) Having perused the correspondence between the parties, I believe that […]. (B3, Opinion)

In these examples, barristers refer to their own research process, emphasizing its completeness and thoroughness. Thus, the final opinion, while an individual view, is nevertheless presented as an expert view that has been reached only after careful consideration of all relevant matters. Apart from this pragmatic strategy, the use of boosters (e.g. *certainly*) to indicate confidence is rare. However, some individual variation was observed, with one expert barrister indicating in interviews a preference for strong opinions. This barrister used boosters in conclusions, as in the example below:

(16) The two documents can *definitely* be read together under the joinder of documents rule. (B5, Opinion)

6. Discussion and conclusions

This chapter reports an exploratory study that is based on a limited set of data, and findings should be interpreted with this limitation in mind. The analysis shows how, in this professional genre, features of stance play an important role, as barristers take up positions towards their audience and towards their own claims. Such positions appear to overlap, with one clause capable of expressing a stance towards both audience and claims. With respect to stance towards claims, this study builds on existing work to show how the expression of stance is achieved not only through the use of linguistic devices but also through discursive resources. The pragmatic model described shows that, in order to hedge claims, barristers strategically refer to a lack of knowledge in three key areas: 1) uncertainty about facts; 2) uncertainty about adversary's position; 3) uncertainty about legal position. This use of pragmatic hedging is similar to that identified in academic research articles, where writers reference limited knowledge, limitations in model theory or method, limitations in experimental design (Hyland 1998). However, the sources of uncertainty identified are specific to the genre. In delineating these sources of uncertainty, this study sheds light on important aspects of writing considerations for the barrister's opinion. Barristers must find a way to clearly establish, for themselves and for their readers, an accurate representation of the facts of the matter, relevant legal arguments and the likely stance of their professional opponents.

The analysis has also consistently shown how, in their writing, expert barristers not only *acknowledge* these sources of uncertainty, they also carefully *resolve* them. This resolution appears particularly important to meet the requirements of the genre, namely, to provide a 'clear opinion'. Resolution of uncertainty is achieved through: the explicit statement of assumptions; the appropriate use of epistemic devices coupled with a preference for conventional use of language to introduce conclusions: e.g., 'it seems to me', 'I believe'. As the comparison with novice writing demonstrates, for barristers to succeed in resolving the various sources of uncertainty raised, the use of epistemic devices must be appropriately limited. Excessive use of such expressions can prevent the writer from taking up a position effectively. Nonetheless, resolution of uncertainty does not necessarily amount to a complete removal of all doubt from the opinion. Instead, by stating assumptions, speculating about a rival position, arriving at a hedged conclusion supported by analysis of facts and law, the expert barrister advances the argument, developing, step-by-step, plausible questions and plausible answers. As we have seen, the final opinion is always presented as a contingent one, the writer's individual view dependent on final acceptance by the reader.

An explicit stance towards audience is taken up in the texts analyzed, most visible in Opening and Closing moves, but not limited to them. Reference to the reader(s) is to be expected, as the genre is, in effect, a form of specialized business correspondence that both responds to and draws upon accounts provided by the lay client and the instructing solicitor. The formal, institutional tenor that is adopted establishes and maintains a respectful, professional distance to readers, referred to as 'instructing solicitors', 'lay client' but not by use of the personal pronoun, *you*. At the same time, barristers sometimes align with their readers, either as members of the same legal team, as shown in example (4) which refers to 'our case', or as members of a common disciplinary culture, as shown in example (5) with its use of the inclusive 'we must consider' to describe a legal test.

It is interesting to note that, while barristers avoid directly engaging their readers through the use of the second person pronoun, *you*, they nevertheless routinely involve themselves in the discourse through the use of the first person pronoun, *I*. This usage is perhaps at odds with the more distanced reader/writer relationship otherwise cultivated. Be that as it may, the use of self-mention here allows the barrister to clearly attribute arguments and conclusions to themselves, as individually held 'beliefs' and 'opinions'. This allows the barrister to present the arguments as contingent, dependent on the acceptance of the reader. In this way the barrister defers to the judgment of fellow professional readers, taking up the position that 'this is just my opinion, you are free to agree or disagree as you see fit'. Adopting such an individual stance is also consistent with, and serves to align the writer with, cultural values and beliefs of the legal community. In particular, these include the notion that legal problems are seldom susceptible to a single, 'correct' answer, instead being open to multiple, competing, individual interpretations.

This routine use of self-mention through use of the first person contrasts with that observed in academic genres. In the barrister's opinion, there is a strong preference for the use of the first person singular pronoun to express conclusions and opinions, with little variation. In contrast, a wider range of options appears to be available to writers of academic research articles. Previous research has shown that, in research articles in the hard disciplines, the first person singular pronoun is avoided completely, with a general preference for the use of *we*, even in single-authored articles (Kuo 1999). The first person singular is sometimes seen in research articles in the soft disciplines, for example in Philosophy, but is more likely to be a strategic choice, rather than the preferred option (Hyland 2001). In addition, it is quite common to avoid personal involvement altogether, through impersonal expressions, the use of the passive and so on. In contrast, personal involvement of the writer is expected in the barrister's opinion and appears to be an obligatory element of the genre.

This difference in emphasis between the professional genre of the barrister's opinion and the academic genre of the research article has to do with the communicative context of each. In particular, barristers, who have been invited to provide their opinion on a particular case, enjoy a higher status and greater power vis-à-vis their audience than do academic writers, who usually offer their writing to journal editors and reviewers and depend on these readers in order to get published. In the case of the barrister's opinion, the solicitor reader acknowledges the specialized, practical expertise of the barrister writer by drafting instructions that request advice from the individual barrister addressed. It is therefore not surprising that the use of personal warrants in support of the final opinion reached has become conventionalized in the genre. The use of *I* allows the barrister to invoke a personal authority, based on expertise recognized by the solicitor when the instructions were drafted and sent.

The overall picture of stance that emerges from this study, then, is one of a complex set of interacting discursive resources that can be explained with reference to features of context. The qualitative methodology that was adopted has shown how a range of different factors interact in the construction of stance: use of modality, epistemic devices, pragmatic hedging, appeals to authority and even the innovative use of generic structure all contribute to a careful management of sources of uncertainty in order to adopt an appropriate stance. As was noted at the outset, adopting a stance in this way is crucial to the successful composition of a barrister's opinion. This study further suggests that this is an area in which novice legal writers need support. In providing such support, existing research into stance-taking, based on written academic genres, serves as a useful starting point for practitioners of Languages for Specific Purposes. However, practitioners should also be aware of the unique features of stance in this professional legal setting. Stance in this professional genre indexes the particular cultural values with which novice writers must align if they are to progress towards full membership of the disciplinary community.

References

Bhatia, Vijay K. 2004. *Worlds of Written Discourse: A Genre-based View*. London: Continuum.

Biber, Douglas 2006. Stance in Spoken and Written University Registers. *Journal of English for Academic Purposes* 5/2, 97-116.

Hafner, Christoph A. 2008. *Designing, Implementing and Evaluating an Online Resource for Professional Legal Communication Skills* (Unpublished doctoral thesis). Macquarie University, Sydney.

Hafner, Christoph A. 2010. A Multi-perspective Genre Analysis of the Barrister's Opinion: Writing Context, Generic Structure, and Textualization. *Written Communication* 27/4, 410-441.

Hafner, Christoph A. 2013. The Discursive Construction of Professional Expertise: Appeals to Authority in Barrister's Opinions. *English for Specific Purposes* 32/3, 131-143.

Halliday, Michael A. K. [2]1994. *An Introduction to Functional Grammar*. London: Edward Arnold.

Hunston, Susan / Thompson, Geoff (eds) 2000. *Evaluation in Text: Authorial Stance and the Construction of Discourse*. Oxford: Oxford University Press.

Hyland, Ken 1998. *Hedging in Scientific Research Articles*. Amsterdam: John Benjamins.

Hyland, Ken 2001. Humble Servants of the Discipline? Self-mention in Research Articles. *English for Specific Purposes* 20/3, 207-226.

Hyland, Ken 2005a. *Metadiscourse: Exploring Interaction in Writing.* London: Continuum.

Hyland, Ken 2005b. Stance and Engagement: A Model of Interaction in Academic Discourse. *Discourse Studies* 7/2, 173-192.

Inns of Court School of Law 2007. *Opinion Writing.* Oxford: Oxford University Press.

Jaffe, Alexandra 2009. Introduction: The Sociolinguistics of Stance. In Jaffe, Alexandra (ed.) *Stance: Sociolinguistic Perspectives.* Oxford: Oxford University Press, 1-28.

Kuo, Chih-Hua 1999. The Use of Personal Pronouns: Role Relationships in Scientific Journal Articles. *English for Specific Purposes* 18/2, 121-138.

Martin, James R. / White, Peter R. R. 2005. *The Language of Evaluation: Appraisal in English.* Basingstoke: Palgrave Macmillan.

Tessuto, Girolamo 2006. Opinions of Counsel: An Exploratory Survey of Generic Features. In Bhatia, Vijay / Gotti, Maurizio (eds) *Explorations in Specialized Genres.* Bern: Peter Lang, 291-308.

Thompson, Geoff / Hunston, Susan 2000. Evaluation: An Introduction. In Hunston/Thompson (eds), 1-27.

Appendices

Appendix 1: Text A, Expert text (B1)

13. The memorandum *certainly* contemplated the drawing-up of a	1	Issue
formal lease but that alone *is not sufficient* to prevent the	2	
memorandum from being a binding agreement for a lease. *It may*	3	
be that all the terms had been settled and what was contemplated	4	App.
was merely their reduction into a more formal shape, *in which case*	5	
there was already a contract and the agreement was in no way	6	

conditional upon that reduction being carried out. *Or it may be* that	
what had been settled were only the main terms, or heads of	
agreement, and that what was to be executed was to embody further	
terms, *in which case* there was to be no contract until that had been	
done. *These alternative constructions are postulated by Sargant LJ*	
of the English Court of Appeal in *Chillingworth v Esche* [1924] 1	Au.
Ch 97 at 113. *Which of these is correct is a matter of interpretation*	Issue
of the agreement, which in this instance is contained in the letters	
and the memorandum.	
14. *It seems to me* that the memorandum *provides* for all the terms	Opn.
of the lease. The main terms *are* spelt out in the memorandum. The	App.
rest of the terms *are to be* those contained in the usual form of lease	
used by the landlord in respect of the development. Accordingly	
there was nothing left to be settled or negotiated: any further terms	
not stipulated in the memorandum *could be found* in the standard	
terms of the landlord. The memorandum *sets out* the terms of a	
concluded bargain between the parties. In the absence of any words	Law
of contingency or condition, the bargain *is* immediately binding.	
See the decision and approach of the Privy Council in *Elias v*	Au.
George Sahely Ltd [1982] 3 All ER 801.	

Note: the generic structure is recorded on the right: sub-moves listed are part of move 3, Discussion and are abbreviated to Issue, Law, Authority (Au.), Application (App.), Opinion (Opn.).

Appendix 2: Text B, Novice text (S14)

12. Applying to the present case, *it is clear to me* that *the*	Opn.
Vendor did not disclose to the Purchaser in the conversation or	
in the Agreement about the illegal nature of the Balcony. In	
Jumbo King, it was suggested that the limiting clause could	Law+Au.
have allowed innocent non-disclosure by the vendor. In the	
present case, it is a known fact that the Balcony existed when	App.
the Vendor bought the Property. But apart from this known	
fact, *I do not have evidence* regarding when the Balcony was	
erected, who erected the Balcony, and whether the persons	
who erected the Balcony obtained approval from the Building	
Authority for the erection. *The absence of such evidence*	Issue
makes it *difficult to establish* the Vendor was innocent about	
the illegal nature of the Balcony.	
13. In light of the above, I must therefore take into account the	App.

circumstantial evidence for which the Vendor disclosed the information. The Vendor has been occupying the Property since 1998 *suggests* that the period of the Vendor's occupation was long enough for him to have been *aware of the possibility* that the Balcony *could be* illegal. The Vendor knew a similar balcony was removed *suggests* that this incident *would have at least put him on inquiry* on the illegality of the Balcony. When the Vendor told the Purchaser that he did not notice any enforcement action against the Balcony, this *clearly indicates* the Vendor *would have been aware* the illegality of the Balcony. Putting all the *circumstantial evidence* in context, *I do not support the argument* that the Vendor was innocent about the illegal nature of the Balcony because *the circumstantial evidence suggests to me* that the Vendor ought to have known the Balcony was illegal as he has means to such knowledge.	Opn.

Note: the generic structure is recorded on the right: sub-moves listed are part of move 3, Discussion and are abbreviated to Issue, Law, Authority (Au.), Application (App.), Opinion (Opn.).

Interactions between legal experts and mixed audiences

VIJAY K. BHATIA

Interpersonal Constraints in Statutory Writing*

1. Background

Statutory writing at surface level is often characterized as one of the most impersonal and decontextualized forms of professional communication in the sense that its illocutionary force holds independently of whoever is the 'originator' or the 'reader' of the document (Bhatia 1993). However, when one considers the context in which it is designed and created, and ultimately used and interpreted, there seems to be an intricate web of interpersonal forces and tensions that tend to give it a highly complex interpersonality rarely seen in any other professional genre.

The complexity of statutory writing is not simply a function of its contextual constraints, but also a function of the communicative purpose it is meant to serve. It has always been intended to be clear, precise, unambiguous, on the one hand, and all-inclusive, with as detailed specification of legal scope as possible, on the other (Bhatia 1982). This may appear to be contradictory in nature, and may often make it inaccessible to its audiences, both specialists as well as ordinary citizens, thus often attracting negative publicity for being 'verbose', 'long-winded' and having 'tortuous and convoluted syntax'; however, the drafting community has always claimed that in the drafting exercise their first priority is to be faithful to the intentions of the Parliament or legislative institution, rather than to ordinary readers. This is one major interpersonal constraint that is responsible for the complexity of the drafting process.

* Some of the material and examples in this chapter draw on Bhatia (2010).

Drawing on the analysis of statutory writing from a number of different contexts, I would like to identify some of the crucial issues inherent in the contextual configuration, relevant to the so-called depersonalisation of statutory writing, and clarify the role of interpersonal constraints and tensions in modern-day statutory drafting practices, thereby illustrating some of the socio-pragmatic consequences of the use of what I have elsewhere referred to as 'simplification' and 'easification' strategies (Bhatia 1982, 1993, 2010) used in statutory drafting. Let me first elaborate on what I mean by contextual configuration.

2. Contextual configuration of statutory drafting

Statutory writing in all jurisdictions, and particularly in the common law tradition, has been considered problematic when it comes to its construction, interpretation, its use and exploitation of linguistic resources. It is generally believed that statutory writing is impersonal as it is independent of any writer or reader, in the sense that it is meant to apply to anyone who contravenes any of the provisions of the statute book. In my early study of legislative discourse, I pointed out that

> Legislative writing is highly impersonal and de-contextualized, in the sense that illocutionary force holds independently of whoever is the 'speaker' (originator) or the 'hearer' (reader) of the document. (Bhatia 1993: 102)

So in this conventional sense, statutory writing is meant to be least interpersonal, and therefore many of the commonly used interpersonal and interactive linguistic resources in other discourses, such as politeness devices, style, voice, tone, pronominal use, etc. are rarely found in statutory provisions. However, like many other professional discourses, statutes are also shaped and interpreted by diverse communities of practice, and as such, some of the linguistic considerations, like modality and even Gricean maxims, continue to play an important role in their construction and interpretation; the only difference is that these aspects of statutory construction are quite complex and have discipline-specific uses and interpretations.

Before we discuss contextual configuration of statutory writing in general, let me point out that the main function of statutory provisions is to impose obligations and to confer rights. As legal draftsmen are well aware of the age-old human capacity to minimize obligations and to maximize rights, in order to guard against such eventualities, they take special care to express obligations and rights, permissions and prohibitions as precisely, clearly and unambiguously, on the one hand, and all-inclusive, on the other, which tends to make statutory provisions unique. However, what makes the task of drafting incredibly complex is the nature and function of participant management that constrain legal actions associated with statutory provisions.

In order to identify and discuss a framework for the analysis of participant involvement and management in the context of statutory drafting and interpretation, I would like to draw on Goffman's (1981) notion of participation framework taking into account the nature and function of statutory provisions and their organization, identifying the role of participating institutions rather than individuals, which seem to influence and constrain the construction, accessibility, and interpretation of relevant and appropriate legal action in a given context. Referring to spoken interaction, Goffman (1981) suggests an insightfully powerful model of speaker-hearer participation, which can be decomposed into a range of different categories. Talking about the speaker, he suggests four different kinds of role. The *Animator* is the one who actually produces the talk, whereas the *Author* is the one who is responsible for putting speech acts into words and sentences. Similarly, the *Principal* is the party who is socially responsible for what is said, and the *Figure* is a character depicted in the Animator's talk. On the other side of the interaction, he classifies the *Hearer* in various categories, deconstructing it into different kinds of participants, who include bystanders, eavesdroppers, addressed and unaddressed hearers, and so on. He also points out that the talk can be embedded not simply in any speech event, but in action that the speech or talk is trying to achieve, and therefore he argues for the use of primary context for making sense of what the speaker is trying to do.

When we look at the contextual configuration of statutory construction and interpretation, we find a dynamic complexity of participation structure, which is rarely seen in any other form of professional writing. In Goffman's terms, the parliamentary draftsman is the *Author*, and the legislative institution (whether a Legislative Assembly, Parliament or any other statutory body) is the *Principal*; however, the factor that really complicates the construction process is the role of the governmental institution in the form of the Executive, which often has some role to play, not only in the construction but more importantly in the interpretation and execution of statutory provisions. So from the point of view of the construction of statutory actions, we find two major participating institutions (not necessarily individuals as is often the case in a number of other professional contexts), namely, the *legislature,* with the political power to negotiate legislative intentions, and the *government executive* bodies, in particular the legal affairs division, having the executive privilege to give expression to legislative intentions, which is then passed on to the parliamentary draftsmen to give it appropriate and valid form in language that is acceptable to the legislature. Unfortunately the draftsman, who has the main responsibility of giving expression to the will of the *Parliament,* is never present when the intentions are being discussed, which makes his task even more difficult.

This represents only one side of the coin, as it were. What adds additional complexity to his task is the other side, which concerns the nature of the recipient structure, the complicated relationship they seem to have with different recipients, and the nature of loyalty they are required to display in their drafting practice. On the one hand, their ratified readers are the members of the judiciary, legal community, including judges associated with the system of courts; on the other hand, they have the ordinary people with no legal background at all, who are often referred to as their 'unratified recipients', although it is possible to claim that they are also the real audience, who are governed by the statutory provisions they draft. So who is the legislative counsel or parliamentary draftsman supposed to be loyal to: the judiciary, who has the primary duty to interpret what they write, or the ordinary people ultimately governed by these provisions, or the legislature or Parliament referred to as the *Principal*? It is impossible to satisfy all these requirements at the same time because the three sets of audiences have very little shared background knowledge, although believers in plain language law claim that it is possible to write in language equally accessible to all of them, including ordinary people as well as the judiciary. The truth, however, lies somewhere in between. I shall come back to this issue a little later, but first I would like to make the recipient structure a bit more complex by adding one more participant to it, that is, the Executive with the privilege to interpret legislative intentions to suit socio-political decisions of the government, as far as possible. The complexity of participant structure can be visually represented as in the following diagram:

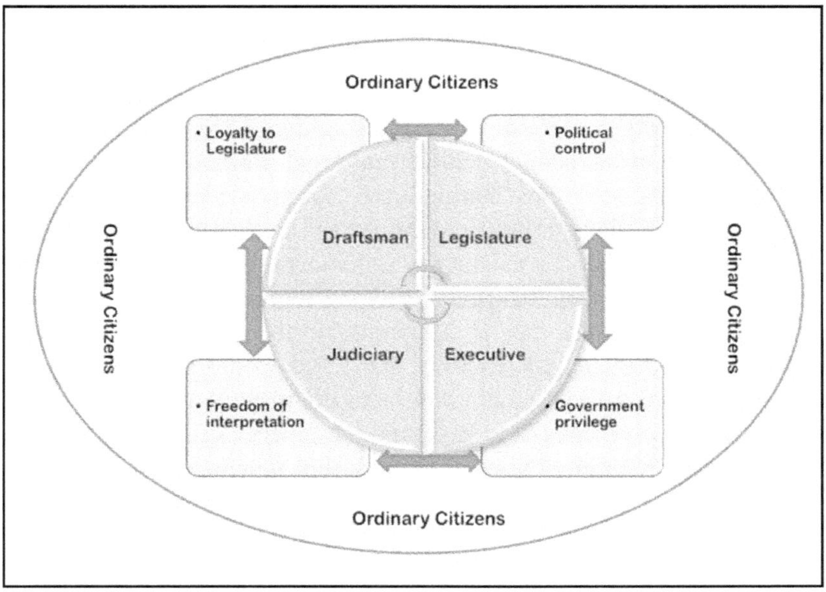

The participation framework briefly discussed here offers an interesting tool, not simply for the analysis of statutory drafting contextual constraints and tensions, but also for the discussion of a set of three other important related legal concepts, that of *Transparency*,

Power, and *Control.* Power and Control are seen as the function of the relationship between some of the main participants involved, directly or indirectly, not only in the drafting process, but also in the interpretation and use of legislative provisions. Different parties have some degree of power and hence control over, certainly some interest in, the construction and interpretation of legislative processes, though the amount is limited by their role, as well as their access to discursive resources. The real challenge in the construction of legislative discourse is the nature and extent of under- and over-specification of legal scope in the expression of legislative intentions. This also raises the issues of accessibility (comprehensibility and interpretability), transparency, power, and control in specific socio-political and legal systems. The issue of specification, or rather the lack of it, has been summed up in Bhatia (1982) when I have pointed out that legislative expressions are required to be clear, precise and unambiguous on the one hand, and all-inclusive, on the other. This may appear to be a contradiction, but a close analysis reveals that a clever balance between the two is the essence of the craftsmanship of legislative intentions. As an outsider, I believe that legal draftsmen have always been conscious of the institutional conflicts involved in the specification of legislative intentions as well as the legislative authority, especially in parliamentary democracies, where legislative authority is invested in the legislature as it represents the people who elect them. As a result, they (Parliament and the drafting community) zealously guard this right (Renton 1975) and would not like to hand over this role either to the judiciary or to the executive, which creates the possibility of a three-way institutional conflict. Edward Caldwell, a senior parliamentary counsel, frames this tension quite nicely as follows:

> There's always the problem that at the end of the day there's a system of courts and judges who interpret what the legislative counsel has done. It is very difficult to box the judge firmly into a corner from which he cannot escape [...]. (Quoted in Bhatia 1982: 25)

Another factor that complicates their task is that they also need to construct their statutory provisions in such a way as to avoid any potential conflict with any preceded or preceding legislation. Caldwell (quoted in Bhatia 1982), once again, points out that 'a new legislative provision is part of a jigsaw puzzle' and the legal draftsman often goes to great lengths to ensure that any statutory provision must express exactly what the legislative institution intends to say, that is precise or vague as necessary, on the one hand, and all-inclusive, on the other (see Bhatia 2005 for details). On the other side, to make matters even more difficult, draftsmen are almost universally criticised for making their provisions inaccessible to ordinary citizens, often questioning their loyalty to them.

3. Participation management in statutory drafting

In the context of what we have been discussing, I think there are two ways of looking at lack of 'comprehensibility' in legislative discourse, one resulting from syntactic complexity and all-inclusiveness leading to over-specification of legal scope as in common law drafting practice, and the other resulting from syntactic simplicity and under-specification of legal scope, as in civil law drafting tradition. The first one is likely to be more comprehensive and transparent, but may be relatively harder to comprehend, especially for the non-specialist ordinary readers. The second one is likely to be more accessible to lay persons, but can be contentious when it comes to interpretation in real life contexts, as in a court of law, giving the Judiciary and/or the Executive extensive discretionary powers to interpret the legislative intention (for more elaborate evidence of this issue, see Bhatia 2005). In the context of legislative drafting in the common law tradition, I would now like to propose two ways of handling legislative provisions for ease of accessibility and interpretation.

Considering the complexity of participant structure in statutory drafting, it is possible to analyse interpersonality in statutory drafting and interpretation in three rather different kinds of tensions:

- Firstly, there is always the tension between the legislative machinery and the judiciary, where the draftsmen are directed to write statutes in a way to 'box the judge in a corner' (Caldwell 1982) as much as the linguistic resources permit.

- Secondly, there is always a tension between the legislative institutions, such as the parliament or any other legislative council and the ordinary citizens. As mentioned earlier, the legislative draftsman, as the Author, has the first loyalty to the Principal who would like him to 'box the judge into a corner' so that he can interpret the statutory provision unambiguously. This tension between the interests of the legislative institution and the judiciary or the system of courts is the primary concern for the drafting community.
- Finally, there is the tension between the judiciary and the executive or the government, who is responsible for the execution of legal obligations. The judiciary has the privilege of interpretation and the executive has the duty to implement what the judiciary decides. So the executive has a two-way responsibility, one towards the legislature to make sure that their intentions are executed and the other towards legislature to ensure that there is no tension between the legislature and the judiciary.

Most of these tensions arise from the concerns that these different institutions seem to have and are the functions of three key issues: the accessibility of statutes to ordinary citizens; the transparency and all-inclusiveness of statutory provisions; and who gets the ultimate power and control in the interpretation and application of statutory provisions. In order to resolve some of these tensions, I would like to propose three different versions of statutes to serve somewhat different and often contested communicative purposes.

1. Original versions of statutes as drafted in conventional sense, clear, precise, unambiguous and as all-inclusive as linguistic resources permit.
2. 'Easified' versions of the original, which are also as clear, precise, unambiguous, and as all-inclusive as linguistic and other semiotic resources permit, without compromising the scope of legal effect in any way, yet making them more

accessible to specialists, i.e., ratified as well as nonratified recipients.

3. Plain language versions of statutes, which are clear, precise, and accessible to non-specialist bystanders or ordinary citizens, but not entirely unambiguous with limited specification of legal scope.

In the rest of the chapter, I would like give more substance to the argument I have suggested here, illustrating the three different versions I have referred to above, and the interpersonality associated with each of these versions, which include the 'conventional original version', the 'easified version', and the 'plain language version'.

As in most technical discourses, especially those that have public implications, we need at least two versions: one for specialists, and the other for ordinary citizens. This is a common practice in sciences, where we have the original research reports of various kinds, including journal articles, and also a popular version for uninitiated readers. Similarly, in statutory contexts we can have a conventionally written original version meant for specialists and a plain language version meant for ordinary non-specialist citizens. The two versions would serve two very different communicative purposes: one legislative, and the other informative. Both will need to have their own respective mechanisms, depth of specificity and levels of reader accessibility. However, it has been common knowledge that the conventionally written original version can be largely inaccessible even to specialists, especially to executives in the government and also to many other administrators in private corporations. In order to make the specialist versions easier for processing and interpretation, I have suggested 'easification' of legislative provisions, keeping them clear, precise, unambiguous, and all-inclusive, but at the same time, much more transparent and accessible than its conventional form. Thus it can still be relatively more accessible to its intended readership, specialists as well as non-specialists. The provision will still be equally authoritative, detailed, and adequately specified, serving the same legislative function in the court of law.

On the other hand, plain language versions for non-specialists are like popular or simple accounts of authoritative versions to inform the citizens about some of the main legislative intentions and their implications for their personal and public affairs. This plain language version may not necessarily be all-inclusive, and hence not authoritative, authentic, or complete in all respects, but is certainly informative and easily accessible to larger non-specialist readers. Such simplified versions should be meant for public awareness, which may even include legal intentions, explanations, and typical examples. A reasonable degree of awareness can also be achieved by involving ordinary people in the public consultation exercises, which are being increasingly used in many of the democracies almost everywhere. Let me now suggest and illustrate some of the common easification devices for making legislative provisions more accessible. My first example comes from a typical agreement between the author and the publisher, which though different from statutory writing in a conventional sense, is as legally binding as any statutory provision (adapted from Bhatia 2010).

> AGREEMENT BETWEEN PUBLISHER AND AUTHOR
>
> The author hereby warrants to the Publishers that the author has the right and power to make this Agreement and that the Work is the Author's own original work, except for material in the public domain and such excerpts from other works as may be included with the written permission of the copyright owners, and will in no way whatever give rise to a violation of any existing Copyright, or a breach of any existing agreement, and that the Work contains nothing defamatory or libellous and that all statements contained therein purporting to be facts are true and that nothing in the Work is liable to give rise to a criminal prosecution or to a civil action for damages or any other remedy and the author will indemnify the Publishers against any loss, injury or expense arising out of any breach or alleged breach of this warranty. The Publishers reserve the right to alter or to insist the Author alter the text of the Work in such a way as may appear to them appropriate for the purpose of removing or amending any passage which on the advice of the Publishers' legal advisers may be considered objectionable or likely to be actionable at law without affecting the Author's liability under this Clause in respect of any passage not so removed or amended. The foregoing warranties and indemnities shall survive the termination of this agreement.

The same provision can be rewritten to make cognitive structures somewhat more accessible and easier to process, as in the following version:

(1) The author hereby warrants to the Publishers that:
(a) the author has the right and power to make this Agreement, and
(b) the Work is the Author's own original work,
(except for material in the public domain and such excerpts from other works as may be included with the written permission of the copyright owners, and will in no way whatever give rise to a violation of any existing Copyright, or a breach of any existing agreement,) and
(c) the Work contains nothing defamatory or libellous, and
(d) all statements contained therein purporting to be facts are true and,
(e) nothing in the Work is liable to give rise to a criminal prosecution or to a civil action for damages or any other remedy, and
(f) the author will indemnify the Publishers against any loss, injury or expense arising out of any breach or alleged breach of this warranty.
(2) The Publishers reserve the right to alter or to insist the Author alter the text of the Work in such a way as may appear to them appropriate
(for the purpose of removing or amending any passage which on the advice of the Publishers' legal advisers may be considered objectionable or likely to be actionable at law without affecting the Author's liability under this Clause in respect of any passage not so removed or amended.)
(3) The foregoing warranties and indemnities shall survive the termination of this agreement.

Both these versions are authentic but the first one is the original version whereas the second one has been rhetorically revised using some of the 'easification strategies', to clarify cognitive structuring to map textual and rhetorical resources for easier processing. Let me now offer a simplified plain language version, which is very easy to process and interpret. It is a popular version, which is meant more for information to ordinary readers rather than the one with adequate details about specification of legal scope. It can be something like the following:

> The Author warrants (guarantees) that he has the right to enter into the Agreement, and that his work is original and contains nothing defamatory and is not liable to give rise to any criminal prosecution or to a civil action.
> If any loss arises as a breach of this warranty, the author will be responsible for it.
> The Author also agrees that the Publisher has the right to change the text of his work, if necessary.

Let me now take Chapter 148, Amendment to Gambling Ordinance 1977 (Hong Kong).

> *Section16. Cheating at gambling*
> Any person who, by any fraud, misleading device or false practice, before or after or in the course of or in connection with gambling or a lottery, wins from another person, for himself or for any other person ascertained or unascertained, any money or other property; or fraudulently or by any deception whatsoever by words or conduct, including a deception relating to the past, the present or the future and a deception as to the intentions or opinions of any person, directly or indirectly persuades, incites or induces another person to take part in gambling or a lottery, commits an offence and is liable on conviction on indictment to a fine of $1,000.000 and to imprisonment for 10 years.

This lengthy provision, once again can be rewritten as follows:

> (1) Any person who –
> (a) by any fraud, misleading device or false practice, before or after or in the course of or in connection with gambling or a lottery, wins from another person, for himself or for any other person ascertained or unascertained, any money or other property; or
> (b) fraudulently or by any deception whatsoever by words or conduct, including a deception relating to the past, the present or the future and a deception as to the intentions or opinions of any person, directly or indirectly persuades, incites or induces another person to take part in gambling or a lottery,
> commits an offence and is liable on conviction on indictment to a fine of $1,000.000 and to imprisonment for 10 years.

Here is the plain language version of the 'Cheating at gambling' section.

> Any person who wins from another person any money or property by fraud or fraudulently persuades another person to take part in gambling or lottery commits an offence and can be punished by imprisonment for 10 years and a fine of One million dollars.

My third example comes from a corporate investment brochure:

> The Bonds bear interest from 5th January, 1994 at the rate of 5.25 per cent per annum payable in arrears on 5th of January, 1995; 5.5 per cent. per annum

payable in arrears on 5th January 1996; and 5.75 per cent. payable in arrears on 5th January 1997 and each 5th of January thereafter (each such date being referred to an 'Interest Payment Date'), provided that, notwithstanding the foregoing, interest on the Bonds will be payable at 5.75 per cent. per annum from, and including, the IPO Listing Date. The Bonds will cease to bear interest (i) on the Interest Payment Date last preceding the Conversion Date (as defined below) subject to conversion of the relevant Bond in accordance with the provisions of Condition 7 (c) and subject to the provisions of Condition 7 (c) or (ii) from the due date for redemption thereof unless, upon surrender in accordance with Condition 10, payment of full amount due is improperly withheld or refused or unless default is otherwise made in respect of any such payment. In such event referred to in (ii) above, such Bonds shall continue to bear interest at the rate most lately applicable (both before and after the judgment) until one of the following dates, whichever is earlier of (a) the day on which all sums due in respect of such Bonds up to that day are received by or on behalf of the relevant holder and (b) the day seven days after the Trustees or the Principal Paying Agents has notified Bondholders of receipts of all sums due in respect of all the Bonds up to that seventh day (except to the extent that there is failure in the subsequent payment to the relevant holders under these conditions). If interest is required to be calculated for a period of less than one year, it will be calculated on the basis of a 360-day year consisting of 12 months of 30 days each and, in the case of an incomplete month, the number of days elapsed.

The easified version could be something like the following:

5.1. The Bonds bear interest from 5th January 1994 per annum payable in arrears at the rate of
(a) 5.25 per cent. on 5th of January, 1995;
(b) 5.5 per cent. on 5th January 1996;
(c) 5.75 per cent. on 5th January 1997 and on each 5th of January thereafter,
(*each such date being referred to an "Interest Payment Date"*).

5.2. Notwithstanding the provisions of section 5.1 above,
(a) *in the case of IPO listing*, interests on the Bonds will be payable at 5.75 per cent. per annum from and including the IPO Listing Date,
(b) *in the case of conversion under the provisions of Condition 7c*, the Bonds will cease to bear interest on the Interest Payment Date last preceding the Conversion Date, and
(c) *in the case of redemption*, the Bonds will cease to bear interest from the date Bonds become due for redemption.

5.3. *Where, upon surrender in accordance with Condition 10, payment of the full amount is improperly withheld, refused or otherwise defaulted,*

> Bonds shall continue to bear interest at the rate most lately applicable (both before and after the judgement) until one of the following dates, whichever is earlier.
> Either
> (i) the day on which all sums due in respect of such Bonds up to that day are received by or on behalf of the relevant holder,
> or
> (ii) the day seven days after the Trustees or the Principal Paying Agents has notified Bondholders of receipts of all sums due in respect of all the Bonds up to that seventh day
> (*except to the extent that there is failure in the subsequent payment to the relevant holders under these conditions*).
>
> 5.4. *If interest is required to be calculated for a period of less than one year*, it will be calculated on the basis of a 360-day year consisting of 12 months of 30 days each and, in the case of an incomplete month, the number of days elapsed.

My final example comes from Securities (Insider Dealing) Ordinance 1990, Government of Hong Kong SAR, which in my view has been drafted using the rhetorical and textual-mapping I was referring to earlier as part of easification procedures. In its original authentic form, it demonstrates the use of easification strategies.

> (1) If it appears to the Financial Secretary, whether following representations by the Commissions or otherwise, that insider dealing in relation to the listed securities of a corporation has taken place or may have taken place, he may in accordance with this section require the Tribunal to inquire into the matter.
> (2) An inquiry shall be instituted by the Financial Secretary by notice in writing to the Chairman of the Tribunal containing such particulars as are sufficient to define the terms of reference of the inquiry.
> (3) The object of an inquiry shall be to determine, within the terms of reference of the inquiry as defined under subsection (2):
> a. whether insider dealing in relation to the listed securities of a corporation has taken place;
> b. the identity of every insider dealer; and
> c. the amount of any profit gained or loss avoided as a result of the insider dealing.
> (4) Where the Tribunal identifies a corporation as an insider dealer under sub-section (3)(b) the Tribunal may also identify any officer of that corporation to whose breach of the duty imposed on him by section 13 the insider dealing in question is directly or indirectly attributable.

> (5) The Tribunal shall not identify any person as an insider dealer or as a person to whose breach of the duty imposed on him by section 13 the insider dealing by a corporation may be directly or indirectly attributable without first giving such person an opportunity of being heard.
> (6) Where the Tribunal identifies a corporation as an insider dealer under sub-section (3)(b), if the insider dealing took place with the knowledge, consent or connivance of any officer of the corporation then such officer as well as the corporation shall be regarded as having been so identified.
> (Securities (Insider Dealing) Ordinance 1990, Government of Hong Kong)

It is quite a complex and detailed statutory provision, which is not simply clear, precise and all-inclusive, but also rhetorically more accessible to specialist readership. However, for non-specialists, it is still beyond their processing reach as some of the details incorporated in this version make it inaccessible; so I suggest the following plain English version for informative purposes.

> The Financial Secretary may institute an inquiry by the Tribunal to determine whether insider dealing in the listed securities of a corporation has taken place in order to identity the insider dealer and the amount of any profit gained.
> As a result of the inquiry, if the Tribunal identifies a corporation as an insider dealer, it may then also identify if such dealing is attributable to any breach of duty on the part of any officer of the corporation.
> (Securities (Insider Dealing) Ordinance 1990, Government of Hong Kong)

What I have demonstrated here is that different stakeholders in the drafting and interpretation process have somewhat different back-grounds and interests, and in order to meet these separate demands and concerns it is possible to have three different ways of designing statutory information. What I have indicated is a sample of what I call 'easification and simplification devices', which are both rhetorical as well as syntactic. In addition, there could be a number of other semiotic strategies that can be used to make legislative provisions somewhat more accessible, and yet equally effective in terms of adequate specification of legal scope, with the expression of the required number of qualifications and contingencies.

4. Concluding remarks

In this chapter I have made an attempt to indicate the enormous complexity of the legislative drafting process, identifying a number of contextual factors that contribute to the intricacy of the entire process and have interpersonal repercussions. I have also tried to highlight some of the main challenges facing the drafting community. In doing so, I have also suggested ways of meeting some of them, which are unlikely to solve all the problems but certainly open a window of opportunity to understand and handle some of these difficulties in an informed and principled manner. Since the legislative provisions are addressed to very different audiences, who do not share the same level of legal background, I argued for two different versions of the provisions, a simplified version for informative communicative purposes, and an easified version for specialist audiences meant to serve the authentic legislative communicative purposes. I also suggested a number of different rhetorical strategies useful for drafting legislative provisions in a principled manner. Although it is not possible to illustrate all the rhetorical strategies in a paper of this kind, I have illustrated one of them taking examples from available legislative and other relevant contexts. I am also aware of the fact that there is greater awareness of these issues now than it was some time ago; however, I still feel that there is a need to pay more attention to some of these rhetorical and syntactic resources on a regular basis, rather than using them occasionally.

References

Bhatia, Vijay K. 1982. *An Investigation into Formal and Functional Characteristics of Qualifications in Legislative Writing and its Application to English for Academic Legal Purposes*, Ph.D. thesis. The University of Aston in Birmingham, UK.

Bhatia, Vijay K. 1987. Textual-Mapping in British Legislative Writing. *World Englishes* 6/1, 1-10.

Bhatia, Vijay K. 1993. *Analysing Genre: Language Use in Professional Settings.* London: Longman.

Bhatia, Vijay K. 2005. Specificity and Generality in Legislative Expression: Two Sides of the Coin. In Bhatia, Vijay K. / Engberg, Jan / Gotti, Maurizio / Heller, Dorothee (eds) *Vagueness in Normative Texts.* Bern: Peter Lang, 337-356.

Bhatia, Vijay K. 2010. Drafting Legislative Provisions: Challenges and Opportunities. *The Loophole – Journal of the Commonwealth Association of Legislative Counsel* December issue, 5-15.

Caldwell, Edward 1982. *Specialist Informant Interviews*, reported in Bhatia (1982).

Goffman, Erving 1981. Footing. In Goffman, Erving *Forms of Talk.* Philadelphia: University of Pennsylvania Press, 124-159.

CARMEN SANCHO GUINDA

Engagement in NTSB Decisions on Aviation Case Appeals

This chapter explores the singular interpersonal features of the legal decisions on aviation accidents and incidents issued by the *National Transportation Safety Board* of the United States of America (NTSB for short). Such distinctiveness instantiates the stylistic versatility of judgments noted by previous authors (see Mazzi, this volume) and is caused by two major factors that affect the status of the document and the degree and quality of the engagement between writer and reader, especially reader-considerateness: the *function of the agency* itself and the *legal framework* in which it operates.

1. Contextualizing the genre

1.1. Pedagogical and scholarly contexts

Since Candlin, Bhatia and Jensen (2002) made the case for the explicit teaching of the management of interpersonal stance in legal settings, very few didactic materials with a genre orientation (either language or content-based, printed or online, and for native or non-native speakers of English) have tackled the issue. Among those that do, some prefer not to offer a systematic theoretical input but to raise awareness through strategic questions aimed at self-discovery (e.g. Riley (1991), today a classic) and inform implicitly by means of several exemplars. Tone, attitude and figurative language may be touched upon, but tangentially and often in a dispersed manner, as in Volokh's (2007) writing manual for law review articles and seminar papers. On the whole, judgments, also known as decisions, judicial opinions or cases,[1] form an essential part of the genre repertoires included in ESP legal textbooks, monographs in the L1, and online resources for law students of any provenance, but the focus is invariably set on register (lexico-grammatical features) and the number and delimitation of moves to ensure reading comprehension. In addition, when the targeted readership is non-native, the main concerns are genre taxonomies and translation repercussions – along these lines are titles such as Alcaraz (1994), or the descriptions of legal genres and language by Russell and Locke (1992), Borja Albí (2007) and Campos Pardillos (2007). Likewise, much-visited websites familiarising law apprentices with judgments, like those of Clinton (1992), Kerr (2005), and the University of British Columbia (2008), also prioritise macrostructures and phraseologies. In this sense, the panorama depicted by Candlin, Bhatia and Jensen in the early 2000s has changed little, as the insights provided by the pedagogical literature remain at too general a level whatever their channel.

Contributions in Applied Linguistics research, however, may change the course of this trend. As Bhatia (this volume) underlines with regard to the drafting process of legal provisions, nowadays awareness of the need for accessible legal documents is greater. This has made scholars turn their gaze to the communicative impact of modality and performativity (Charnock 2008; Takahashi 2009; López Samaniego/Tarandilla 2012), metadiscourse and other types of deference towards the audience (Vass 2004; Buscetti 2006; Pascual 2006; Wagner/Cacciaguidi-Fahy 2008; Breeze 2011; Tessuto 2012), the observance of the Cooperative Principle (Frade 2002; Pavličková 2010), argumentation (Mazzi 2007a, 2007b, 2008), and even foray into the topics of identity (Sala 2010, Gotti 2011a), power relationships (Gotti 2011b), genre hybridation (Gotti 2011c) and cross-cultural variation (Bhatia/Candlin/Gotti 2003; Gotti 2007; Bhatia/Candlin/Engberg 2008; Gotti/Williams 2010). Corpus-based investigations of this kind

1 Technically speaking, a judgment is a particular kind of decision – the final one made by a court in a case, be it a lawsuit, a criminal prosecution or an appeal (*West's Encyclopedia of American Law,*[2] 2008 in *The Free Dictionary-Legal Dictionary* online). Sometimes the word 'decree' is used as synonymous with 'judgment'.

into legal interactions diagnose communicative gaps and may eventually close the circle by permeating through the didactic literature, helping to improve actual documents and speech. Nonetheless, while the genre and culture gaps are rapidly being plugged, concrete legal scenarios (e.g. maritime, corporate, family or religious law, etc.) have received far less attention. This chapter integrates some of the aforementioned research strands to study judgments in one of those scenarios – the aviation sector – in the Anglo-American culture.

1.2. Professional context

Although Aviation Law relates to other legal realms – administrative, civil, commercial, criminal, fiscal, customs, labour, etc. – governed by the internal orders of each state, some specialists (Díaz Rafael 2008, among others) hold that it should be considered autonomous. The reason is its international and dynamic character, which stems in turn from its numerous and complex normative provisions and regulations, public or private, to control flight, air travel, and associated legal and business matters at a national and international level. Internationally, general aviation rules are provided by the ICAO (International Civil Aviation Organization), a specialised agency of the United Nations. Nationally, virtually every country has its own domestic agencies for monitoring and regulating aviation safety.

There are two such federal agencies in the USA: the Federal Aviation Administration (FAA) and the NTSB. The FAA, working under the Department of Transportation and authorised by the Congress, is in charge of applied aspects of flight, whereas the NTSB is responsible for the independent investigation of any civil[2] aviation accident or incident within the USA,[3] for developing factual records, is-

2 When requested though – that is, when commissioned by the Congress – the NTSB may assist the military and foreign governments with accident investigation.

3 It may nevertheless investigate mishaps occurring outside the United States under certain circumstances. These may include accidents or incidents involving American-registered or American-owned civil aircraft or aircraft with U.S. manufactured components in foreign airspace. In case of resource limitations

suing safety recommendations aimed at prevention, and occasionally for advising other transportation investigative boards in countries that do not have the equipment or specialized technicians available to undertake all aspects of a complex investigation. It must be noted that only the FAA has enforcement authority: it can create regulations and invoke administrative law to punish those who violate them. The NTSB, by contrast, does not have legal authority to implement or impose the recommendations it issues (that duty falls on regulators at federal or state level or on individual transportation companies), but it performs an important role serving as 'court of appeals' for any airman/woman or mechanic whenever certificate action is taken by the FAA. This means that the Board issues orders that may affirm, modify, or reverse the judges' decisions, or remand cases to the judges for further proceedings.

The sequence of appeal steps (Figure 1) goes as follows: in the course of the *first appeal (to the judge),* a petition is filed with the NTSB's office of Administrative Law Judges, assigned a docket number, and acknowledged by the office's Case Manager. The FAA files a copy of the order of revocation, suspension or assessment of civil penalty issued to the respondent or certificate holder, together with a letter that designates the order as the FAA's complaint. The respondent must then file an answer admitting or denying each of the factual allegations stated in the complaint. The judge sets a hearing assigned to the case at an appropriate place and in it he/she makes an *initial decision* affirming, reversing, or modifying the FAA's action. In all cases, both the FAA and the respondent may file requests for discovery of information.

---

the NTSB may request the FAA's collaboration, for example, by collecting factual information at the scene of the accident.

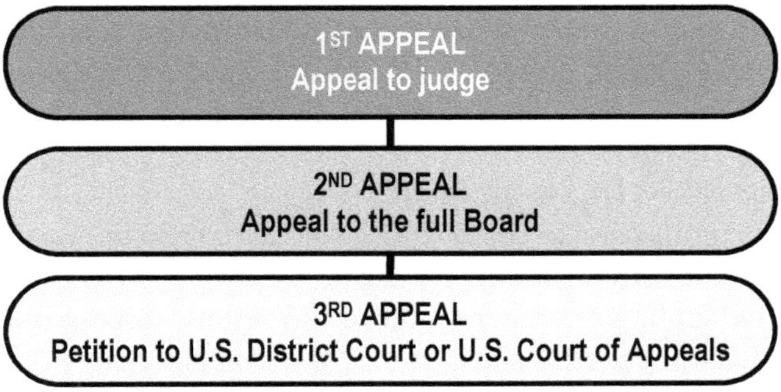

Figure 1. Sequence of steps in the appeal procedure.

In the *second appeal (to the NTSB),* the Office of Administrative Law Judges sends the appeal from the judge's decision it has filed to the Board's office of General Counsel, together with the case record or docket. This done, an appeal brief[4] and a reply brief are filed by the appealing and opposing parties, respectively. Next, the Board issues its affirming, modifying, reversing, or remanding order. A stay[5] of the Board's order may be requested if it ratifies the FAA's revocation, suspension, or civil penalty assessment and the certificate holder intends to appeal to the U.S. District Court or the U.S. Court of Appeals.

In the *third and last appeal (to the U.S. District Court or the U.S. Court of Appeals),* the appealing party files a petition in either of them. If in the District Court, it must be in the district where the party resides or where the action in question occurred. If the choice is the U.S. Court of Appeals, it must be in the D.C. Circuit (i.e. District of Columbia Circuit) or in the circuit[6] where the appellant resides. Finally, the Board prepares a Certificate of Record to be filed with the Court. According to the website of U.S. Courts, the court must affirm the NSTB's decisions unless: 1) the order is arbitrary, capricious, an

4 A *brief* is a document containing all the facts and points of law pertinent to a specific case, filed by an attorney before arguing it in court.

5 A *stay* is a suspension or postponement of a legal action or an execution.

6 A *circuit* is the judicial territory over which a court has the jurisdiction to hear cases.

abuse of discretion, or otherwise not in accordance with the law; 2) the order is not based on relevant factors or constitutes a clear error of judgment; and 3) the Board's factual findings are not supported by substantial evidence and therefore not conclusive. Consequently, the NTSB's decisions tend to prevail.[7]

This professional framing of NTSB judgments would be incomplete without referring to the *Freedom of Information Act* (FOIA),[8] whereby citizens are granted the right to access information from the federal government. The FOIA warrants a policy of transparency in every administrative account and is a pillar of American democracy. It has influenced the NTSB's option, since 2009, for proactively disseminating its decisions online instead of merely declassifying them. In other words, thanks to the FOIA the NTSB *makes its documents public* and does *not simply release* them. The benefit of public online dissemination is double: for one thing, it spares the consultation of documents *in situ* (at the NTSB's archives). For another, it enables readers, by clicking some buttons through the Agency's website, to delve into the nuances and details of the case by accessing legislation, descriptions of NTSB procedures, analogous cases, and even full reports of the accident or incident surrounding the appeal. None of these possibilities can be afforded by declassification or release.

7 In my corpus of 34 NTSB judgments from 2012, 17 cases were dismissed, 11 denied and only 6 granted or remanded.

8 It was enacted in 1966 and took effect on July 5, 1967, when the NTSB began its activity as an independent agency within the Department of Transportation (in 1974 the Congress conferred it the status of a complete separate entity). The Department of Justice's Office of Information Policy oversees the compliance of the FOIA by all agencies. Following the spirit of the FOIA, in 2009 the NTSB decided to publish directly online rather than on paper (it posts an average of 130 dockets each month) and conducts Board meetings and hearings in the direct view of the public.

2. Methodology

With an eclectic framework combining Corpus Linguistics, Discourse Analysis and Genre Theory, the decisions made by the NTSB along 2012 (an online corpus of 34 files from the NTSB's website, stripped of their attached case narratives from previous proceedings and totalling 46,970 tokens[9]) were examined both manually and electronically to study *engagement* (in this chapter not confined to dialogicality as in Hyland (2005b) but taken more broadly to mean 'commitment' and include the level of disclosure, the interactivity with the audience, and reader-friendliness) in format, rhetoric and language. The main focus was put on the genre layout and moves and on metadiscursive signposts of subjectivity (attitudinals), inference (transition markers), and various sorts of guidance (sequencers, stage-labellers, topic shifters, code glosses and endophorics), as well as on engagement markers 'proper' (questions, asides, shared knowledge items, directives and reader pronouns). All these metadiscoursal items were drawn from Hyland's (2005a, 2005b) notions and taxonomies.

Thus, engagement was divided into three categories: *organisational* (comprising genre moves and text sections), *metadiscursive,* and *embedded* (i.e. explanations and polyphonic narrative insertions with their specific types of reporting). Electronic analysis was accomplished with the aid of the concordance program *AntConc 3.2.1w* (Anthony 2007), and to determine the impact of the FOIA on the NTSB texts, findings were contrasted with the interpersonal traits of a multinational online corpus of 34 judgments (206,891 tokens) on aviation matters by other English-speaking courts: from Australia (South Wales), Canada (Alberta and British Columbia), Hong Kong, Ireland, New Zealand, Singapore, South Africa, The Isle of Man, and The United Kingdom.

9 The original corpus, of 107,298 tokens, contained initial decisions by the judges from previous proceedings attached to some of the NTSB decisions.

3. Findings: Engagement features

The three categories of engagement delimited here are closely interrelated, as metadiscourse and narrative and explanatory insertions shape the organisation of the text. Some headings and visual resources dividing it, for instance, may transcend their organisational role and also function as metadiscursive items of relevance and narrative epitomes, as happens with the ever-present NTSB caption reflecting the title and date of the case, the names of the parties in dispute, and of those involved. Explanations, on the other hand, are always narrative to a certain extent, because in the legal context they point back to established sources (legal literature and previous similar cases) through some kind or reporting or another. Logically, by calling our third interpersonal category 'narrative embeddings' we would have been implying that the judgment/decision, the matrix-text where they are inserted and which is narrative per se, could be of a different nature. Hence the simplified label 'embedded engagement'.

3.1. Organisational engagement

Compared with the macrostructures of the multinational corpus, the rhetorical organisation of the NTSB samples appears as more *stable,* more *detailed,* more *emphatic,* more *compact,* and more *complete.* In effect, the NTSB decisions' headings display less variation, contain more subdivisions and visual (typographic) highlights marking the hierarchy of ideas, and all throughout the contents develop in a more storytelling-like layout that allows for a fluid reading and bestows on the case more narrative compactness than a mere succession of numbered paragraphs. Furthermore, the account of the facts presented is fuller thanks to the attachment of transcripts of previous hearings. Table 1 provides an overview of the chief organisational features across the two corpora.

Judgment	*Attached proceedings*	*Numbered paragraphs*	*Foot-notes*	*Anticipated verdict*	*Fixed headings*
NTSB	yes	no	yes	No, but implicit in titles of grants and dismissals	yes
Alberta	no	yes	1 sample	no	no
Australia	no	yes	no	yes	no
British Columbia	no	yes	no	no	?
Hong Kong	no	yes	no	no	no
Ireland	no	yes	no	no	no
Isle of Man	no	yes	no	no	? (table format)
New Zealand	no	yes	1 sample	yes	no
Singapore	no	yes	no	no	no
South Africa	no	2 samples and rest indented	no	1 sample	no
UK	no	1 sample and rest indented	no	no	no

Table 1. Organisational engagement in the NTSB and the multinational corpora (the question mark indicates uncertainty caused by the insufficient number of samples).

Unlike other aviation judgments, NTSB decisions organise their text by means of a quasi-steady list of headings. This systematic division of the contents facilitates reading by creating expectations within a regular structure. First of all, the case citation and filing data (that is, the date and place of the decision, the court deciding the case – the NTSB acting as such – and the docket number) precede the body of the opinion, whose authorship (and this is another characteristic of the NTSB) is mentioned at the very end of the document and not at the beginning, among or after the citation data. This practice contrasts with the initial mention of the judge(s) by all multinational samples, seven of which (one from the United Kingdom and the rest from the

Alberta Court in Canada) credit authorship also at the closure. With its final mention of the Chairman, Vice Chairman and members of the Board responsible for the verdict, the NTSB might be directing our attention towards the orderly and transparent steps of the procedure, apparently agentless and encapsulated in the headings and subheadings, to enhance collegial (not individual) authority and embody the democratic principles of the FOIA. Judgments are, no doubt, 'stories of authority' (Johnstone 1987) that serve as argument to expose expert opinion (Gewirtz 1996), but their conflict is narrated polyphonically with a series of competing and embedding accounts and references, with 'controlled intertextuality' (Breeze 2013).

The NTSB underscores that polyphony/intertextuality and dilutes narrative control by inserting many of those accounts in the linear argument and in the paratext, glossing or expanding knowledge in footnotes and appending extra narratives of previous hearings to sustain the decision. The stamp of authority is postponed to the last heading 'ACCORDINGLY, IT IS ORDERED THAT', which is a public declaration that agglutinates the multiplicity of fragmented narratives, determines 'winners and losers' (Vázquez/Giner 2009), and links the past and the future interpreting facts and performatively setting a binding reference. Authoritativeness is reinforced by typography (the heading is presented in bold capitals) to signal its social importance, but at the same time writer and reader assume a sort of tacit contract, an understanding that the delayed placement of this heading in the text means that the authority of credibility is not a given (Brooks 1996). It must be earned by reading through the lines of reasoning deployed, so for the NTSB *ethos* (the status of the writer) depends almost entirely on *logos* (on the consistency of the argument) rather than on a persona prior to the argument, announced as part of the citation data and inducing to believe in the decision beforehand due to its expertise and prestige. The NTSB just presents the case, as if reminding us that judgments may be revised, refused, and re-made. What the performative phrase 'it is ordered that' does not leave clear is its antecedent. Hollander (1996) wonders whether it really applies to the whole of the opinion or to a specific section or statement.

We could regard the first and last NTSB headings – the case data and the performative verdict phrase – as a split 'coda' (a key element in the Labovian narrative scheme (Labov/Waletzky 1967)) evaluating the import of the document. In between them unfolds the core narrative: the *facts of the case* (the events that happened before it was filed), its *procedural history* (what happened after it was filed in court) and the *legal principles* that will be used to decide and reach an outcome. The sources of these principles may be the Constitution, statutes and regulations, and common law (i.e. former case decisions). Next comes the *disposition* (*sanction* in the NTSB samples), which informs of the action to be taken by the court with the case: affirm, reverse, vacate, dismiss, or remand it. After the verdict, the NTSB unfailingly includes the sentence reproduced in Example (1), as a closing and untitled section of *concurrences and dissents* with the judges' views of the case. In other judgments it is titled and incorporated only occasionally:

(1) [...], Chairman, [...], Vice-chairman, and [...], [...] and [...], Members of the Board, concurred in the above opinion and order.

This formulaic closure stresses the unanimous agreement among Board members and the collegiality mentioned earlier, which brand the NTSB as a solid professional institution without fissures. The prototypical structure of NTSB decisions, in sum, is fixed enough to be recognised by genre users but simultaneously flexible enough to admit sections specifying particularities of the case in question:

1. Background
a. Facts
b. Procedural Background / Evidence Presented at Hearing
c. Law Judge's Oral Initial Decision
d. Law Judge's Written Initial Decision (optional)
e. Issues on Appeal

2. Decision
a. Free specific headline (e.g. Comparison of this case to *X versus Y*)
b. Free specific headline (e.g. Credibility Findings, Reasonable Reliance, Incorrect Standard of Law, Scope of the Board's Review on Appeal, Substantial Justification, Prejudicial Errors, etc.)
c. Due Process Violation
d. Sanction

> ACCORDINGLY, IT IS ORDERED THAT: [...]
> Authors concurred in opinion and order

In the majority of multinational judgments, the content (at times excessively specific) and typography of (sub)headings fluctuate too much so as to pattern a progression recognizable by novice genre users. For example, headings may even consist of long direct questions (2) on case details that, in spite of their engaging purpose, interrupt the narrative flow, blur the sequence *facts of the case* → *law of the case* → *analysis,* and demand a more meticulous reading. In the next subsection I will be turning to metadiscursive engagement more fully.

(2) Does the use of undefined acronyms on the face of the waybill create a vague or ambiguous agreement?' *[Provincial Court of Alberta, Edmonton. Citation: Durunna v. Air Canada, 2013 ABPC 31]*

3.2. Metadiscursive engagement

Contrary to what might be expected, NTSB decisions comply with the accessibility code of the FOIA without relying so much on metadiscourse. Their repertoire of metadiscursive items is scarce and limited, and their higher use of certain categories in comparison with the multinational corpus (namely of inferential transition markers, sequencers, stage labellers, endophorics, and additive and chronological connectives) is not significant.

As can be seen in Table 2, the tendencies for some items are very similar in both corpora – sometimes identical (e.g. for topic shifters). Clearly, NTSB decisions guide readers more throughout the argumentation by signposting logical deduction, direct them more to other parts of the text to aid their comprehension of the content and remind them of relevant points, anticipate more the information to come and also recapitulate more, but they resort slightly less to glosses. That is to say, they do not explain, define or clarify contents as much as the samples of the multinational corpus. Latin jargon terms such as *per curiam, subjudice, pro se, de novo, affidavit, prima facie, sua sponte* or *res judicata* remain unglossed in both corpora, with a couple of exceptions from the NTSB in parenthetical form and within footnotes. Curiously, bracketed glosses as asides are more abundant in the NTSB judgments, especially to define the numerous acronyms they employ and to expand information (i.e. define, explain or add details) and not so much to cite other cases and legal literature, indicate the origin of typographic emphases or the omission of information, or formulate directives telling the reader where to go in the text or how to interpret it. NTSB decisions also outnumber multinational judgments in additive and chronological connectives, which may be a consequence of the story-like layout chosen by the Agency to disseminate its judgments: as there are no numbered paragraphs, internal cohesion (i.e. the story timeline intertwining case facts and procedural history in the past with the Board's analysis of the appeal in the present, the summation of arguments and their comparison) must be secured with metadiscourse.

Metadiscursive item	*NTSB*	*Multinational corpus*
Inferentials	6.9	4.4
Chronological markers	2.2	0.5
Sequencers	1.5	1.4
Contrast markers	1.4	1.7
Endophorics	1.1	0.9
Glosses	1.1	2.3
Additives	0.9	0.6
Stage labellers	0.4	0.2
Topic shifters	0.2	0.2

Table 2. Relative frequencies of metadiscursive items (per 1,000 tokens).

If metadiscursive guidance seems exiguous in the NTSB opinions, it is more so in those decisions granting and dismissing appeals, whose syntax is extremely simple. Grants and dismissals are brief texts where syntactic subordination is rare: sentences are short and follow each other after full stops, producing what could be described as a 'choppy style' (3). There are very few linking words, *however* being practically the only one to be found (and very seldom *because* and *furthermore*), always in formulaic expressions referred to the appellant's failure to meet established deadlines (4, emphasis mine). All in all, inter-sentence relationships reduce to coordination and apposition, and substitutional items are conspicuously absent, which implies the repetition of noun phrases. Although this repetition contributes to the stylistic choppiness mentioned above, it may also function as a textual beacon – to facilitate the spotting of actors – with disambiguating and guiding effects (5, emphases mine).[10]

(3) On November 30, 2012, the Administrator filed a motion to withdraw his complaint. Respondent subsequently filed a motion requesting the case be dismissed with prejudice. The Administrator does not oppose that request. *[NTSB Order No. EA-5643]*

(4) Respondent's brief was due on December 7, 2011, *however*, no brief has been filed. *[NSTB Order No. EA-5612]*

(5) Furthermore, the record from the hearing shows *the law judge* thoroughly briefed *respondent* on the importance of complying with the Board's filing deadlines. At the end of the hearing, *the law judge* clearly informed *respondent* of the requirement to file his brief within 50 days of *the law judge*'s oral decision. Initial Decision at 459. Because *respondent* was pro se. *[NTSB Order No. EA-5630]*

The traditional engagement devices (*shared knowledge, directives, asides, questions,* and *reader pronouns* in Hyland's (2005a, 2005b) model) have a low impact as well, but the incidence of NTSB asides[11] is almost four times as much as in the multinational corpus and the frequency of NTSB directives doubles that of the multinational samples (see Table 3). NTSB asides by means of appositive relative claus-

10 In addition to the lack of personal pronouns to substitute actors, the absence of definite articles before the appellant or anybody from his/her party is another idiosyncratic feature of the discourse of NSTB decisions. We may find *respondent* and *Counsel for respondent* but judges and members of the NTSB are always clearly delimited (e.g. *the law judge*, *the Administrator*). This intentional deictic absence does not occur in the multinational corpus.

11 In my count of asides I have discarded parenthetical ones containing years or numbers of sections and paragraphs (with or without pagination) for citation purposes, as the interpersonality they convey is very little. Analogously, I have not considered questions from the transcripts of previous hearings, since they are not posed by the writer/Board members in charge of the decision.

es are less frequent but nonetheless well over those of the multinational judgments.

Engagement marker	*NTSB*		*Multinational corpus*	
Asides	Parenthetical	Appositive relative	Parenthetical	Appositive relative
	3.8	0.4	0.4	0.06
Directives	2.0		0.4	
Questions	0.04		0.5	
Shared knowledge	0.7		1.3	
Reader pronouns	0.0		0.0	

Table 3. Relative frequencies of engagement markers (per 1,000 tokens).

Whereas appositive asides unmistakably convey a gloss, an opinion, a comment or an informative expansion (i.e. definitions, explanations and details), glosses and expansions conflate in the NTSB corpus whenever the meaning of an acronym is spelt out. Unconventionally, the aside brackets do not contain the gloss but the acronym, which is deferred and preceded by its unabbreviated form (6). In this manner, the aside indirectly helps to decode the acronym and ensures its future recurrent use for the sake of linguistic economy (its two ultimate goals), but also introduces it as additional information with a peripheral comment status.

(6) Respondent contacted an airmen medical examiner (AME) in Delaware, Ohio. *[NTSB Order No. EA-5611]*

As for directives, the predominant item is *see*, which urges readers to consult legislation and jurisprudence. It tends to go after commas or full stops in the body of text or in the footnotes, and is infrequently found between brackets. Questions, interestingly, are nearly non-existent in NTSB decisions. The two instances detected within the body of opinion (of two different samples) reproduce the original interrogatives in two formal documents: aviation regulations and an official medical certificate application. This dearth contrasts starkly with the ample use of rhetorical questions by some courts of the multinational corpus (Alberta, Australia, Ireland, New Zealand, Singapore and United Kingdom), either as headings, or within a section entitled 'Issues', 'The questions for the Tribunal', or 'The questions referred' (the last two in United Kingdom judgments), whose objective is to structure the argumentative discourse and isolate contradictions and unclear points. Perhaps questions of this type become superfluous in the NTSB texts because their elaborate organisational structure suffices to bridge the asymmetrical gap between experts and lay readers.

By the same token, shared legal knowledge is hardly marked by the NTSB, presumably because it seeks a balanced alignment with both its broad lay audience and the expert community of practice (i.e. aviation staff and law professionals). This desire to be acknowledged a member of the specialist circle – to achieve *proximity* (Hyland 2010), but also to attend to non-expert readers – might account for the tension between the little glossing of legal Latinisms and the minimal use of adverbs and adjectives such as *clearly*, *obviously* and *clear* through the argumentation (with a frequency of 0.6 per 1,000 tokens). Lastly, legal documents are formal written interactions that do not address a particular readership, and in consequence cannot include second-person pronouns or appellatives. This public dimension explains why they are disregarded as engagement strategy in all judgments.

Stance has been often separated from engagement, yet the divide is questionable: the choice between disclosing or silencing information, and mostly one's own positioning, is an act of engagement with the interlocutor. Authorial visibility, to start with, does reveal much about the communicative context and the participants' status. In the NTSB corpus, every decision has been taken collectively by Board members and as a result they are written from an exclusive *we* standpoint. In the multinational corpus, 24 samples are written in the first person singular, from an '*I*- perspective' and only six use *we*. Two judgments from the United Kingdom are impersonal, and another two (from Hong Kong and New Zealand) maintain a dual tone (7, my emphasis) owing to the coexistence of *we* and *I* in different parts of the text and with different functions. *I* is not only a marker of opinion and responsibility but a discourse-structuring device that advances argumentative stages or informs of the points to be touched upon, while *we* accompanies readers across the reasoning process. Impersonality is attained through *abstract rhetors* (Thompson/Thetela 1995), which are signalling nouns (in this legal context mainly designating collectives, institutional entities, or procedures, elements and outcomes of the judicial decision) that perform a deictic function and relieve the author of agency as inanimate subjects of human actions (8, italics and underlining mine).

(7) *I* shall presently deal in greater detail with these reasons but before doing so, *I* would like to set out the relevant background and also identify the Applicant's approach in the court below. (DISCOURSE-STRUCTURING) [...]
I agree for the reasons given by *my* Lord the Chief Judge that the appeal should be dismissed. (OPINION MARKING) [...]
Of course, as *we* have seen, the relevant decision of the Respondent in December 2004 was only made after he had further consulted representatives of ECASS (see paragraph 18(6) above). (ARGUMENTATIVE GUIDANCE)
[High Court of the Hong Kong Special Administrative Region Court of Appeal, CACV 324/2005]

(8) *The Tribunal* <u>finds</u> that the Applicant was unfairly dismissed.
[Employment Appeal Tribunal, 58 Victoria Embankment-London EC4Y ODS. Appeal No. EAT/1049/97] (COLLECTIVE)

Surprisingly, in their expression of stance the NTSB and the multinational courts boost or emphasize their statements roughly in equal measure (see Table 4), but differ largely in their use of hedges and attitudinals. The multinational frequency of hedges trebles that of the NTSB, and the occurrence of expressions of attitude in multinational decisions nearly doubles the NTSB figure. We may wonder whether the NTSB boosts more to leave an imprint of firm authority, given that it issues vital safety recommendations but, as I mentioned before, has no enforcement power. This may be a plausible interpretation of why the presence of certainty boosters (e.g. *clearly*, *conclusively*, *demonstrate*, *prove*, *failed to*, etc.), which infuse the decision with a certain dogmatism, is greater than that of boosters of frequency (e.g. *always*, *never*, etc.) and degree (e.g. *completely*, *totally*, *wholly*, etc.).

Stance marker	*NTSB*	*Multinational corpus*
Hedges	3.4	11.1
Boosters	2.6	2.4
Attitudinals	5.8	10.4

Table 4. Relative frequencies of stance markers in both corpora (per 1,000 tokens).

Among the various kinds of hedges (i.e. of frequency/scope, degree, quantity, certainty, and source or attribution), the ones most profusely used are those of quantity (yielding comparable frequencies for the NTSB and multinational corpora – respectively of 2.2 and 2.7 per 1,000 tokens) and certainty, which in the multinational corpus are three times as many (6.5 per 1,000 tokens). The bulk of occurrences corresponds to the modals *may* and *could*, followed by *can* and *might*, all of which are used in the successive hypotheses and arguments along the lines of reasoning within the analysis.

As to attitudinal expressions, the occurrence of disjuncts (e.g. *(un)fortunately*, *curiously*, *interestingly*, etc. as sentence starters or in mid-position between commas) is negligible. Relevance markers of the type *important*, *significant*, *crucial*, etc., *I/we note/insist/emphasize*, or pseudoclefts[12] with diverse functions (9, my emphasis), are ten times more common in the multinational corpus, maybe because of their bi-functionality: they are 'fuzzy' markers that blend the expression of stance with metadiscursive guidance, and may be considered glosses of sorts as they discriminate between essential and subsidiary information.

(9) *What I have to decide is whether* this obligation involved a duty to give reasons for his decision. In my opinion it did. *[High Court of Ireland. Manorcastle Ltd. v Commission for Aviation Regulation. High Court Record Number: 2008 1049 SP]* (Focus)

A less dramatic imbalance (5.9 items per 1,000 tokens in the multinational corpus and 3.0 in NTSB decisions) is observed in the recourse to attitudinals of authority through modal and pseudo-modal verbs. In both corpora *must*, *should* and *will* rank first, *shall* occupies an inter-

12 Seemingly they are an idiolectal feature of the South African Court.

mediate position, and *have to* and *be to* are the least used. Evaluative expressions (of procedures and the appellant's behaviour) undergo equivalent patterns in each corpus, with a marginally higher use by the NTSB (2.7 versus 2.3 items per 1,000 tokens), although multinational judgments offer more variety (e.g. *strange*, *odd*, *faulty*, *sloppy*, etc.). The NTSB is not so precise and restricts evaluation to the criticism of former hearings and appellant performances (e.g. *improperly*, *appropriately*, *erroneously*, *diligently*, *wrong*, *well*, *properly*, *correct*, etc.) and to the self-praise of its analyses (10, emphasis added), particularly with the adjectives and adverbs *reasonably*, *(in) detail / detailed*, *carefully*, *meticulous(ly)*, and *thoroughly*.

(10) *We carefully examined* the record and find no basis for overturning the law judge's finding that in the event of an engine failure respondent could not have made an emergency. *[NTSB Order No. EA-5619]*

To conclude, how the appellant is referred to is also a revealing indicator of stance. Table 5 highlights the NTSB's liking for simplicity (it prefers the term *respondent* over the more complicated French loan *plaintiff* and the ambiguous *defendant*)[13] and for the assignment of fixed names (and implicitly of fine-grained roles)[14] to the participants. Multinational judgments, on the contrary, are more prone to use those two names (excepting the courts of British Columbia, Isle of Man and United Kingdom for *plaintiff* and British Columbia and United Kingdom for *defendant*). *Applicant* is not used by Australia and Singapore, and only very sporadically by Singapore and South Africa. *Appellant* is not used by South Africa, very little by Hong Kong, Ireland, Isle of Man and Singapore, but massively by Australia, New Zealand and the United Kingdom. *Complainant* is adopted in New Zealand, by a few NTSB decisions, and appears in one sample from the United King-

13 Its varying meanings according to the type of case may lead to confusion: while in civil cases the plaintiff is the person bringing the lawsuit and the defendant is the person being sued, in criminal cases where a charge is field by the Government (there is no plaintiff), the defendant is the person who has been charged.

14 Note that the different names denote distinct nuances of the same action: *appeal, apply, defend, petition, complain, claim, respond.*

dom. *Claimant* abounds in the Isle of Man's documents and is employed once by Alberta and South Africa. *Respondent* is not used by the Isle of Man and barely by Australia, South Africa and Singapore.

Name	*NTSB*	*Multinational corpus*
Appellant	4	290
Appellee	0	0
Applicant	52	190
Defendant	1	*601*
Petitioner	5	1
Plaintiff	2	*506*
Complainant	15	5
Claimant	0	32
Respondent	*918*	358

Table 5. Raw frequencies of legal names for the appellant.

Obviously, each court has its tradition and preferences, and these may affect the readability and comprehension of the document if they are not consistently adopted. Let us not forget that consistency is precisely the basis of the NTSB's branding.

3.3. Embedded engagement

Insertions of subsidiary narratives within the matrix case story may take place in the *body of text* and/or the *paratext* (i.e. footnotes and appended materials, like the full transcripts of previous hearings). In the NTSB corpus there are 51 embeddings across 17 documents (half of the samples), 41% of which are pre-decisional (i.e. they complement the factual background of the case and the procedural history) and 59% are placed in the decision proper. Pre-decisional embeddings tend to be more informative than cogent, while in-decision ones are essentially persuasive, attempting to justify the verdict. Regardless of their location, embeddings always mark points of inflection: prior to the decision/analysis they determine whether there has been rule violation or an issue for resolution exists (by introducing voices of judges or legal references), and complete the factual picture by highlighting plural testimonies before informing of the judge's initial decision, left for readers to guess, and thus building up a certain 'suspense'.

Inside the analysis, coincident polyphonic testimonies, NTSB case antecedents, and references to legal literature climactically pave the way for the final verdict and serve to justify it. But all this is not exclusive of NTSB judgments, since the multinational corpus does contain a larger inventory of instances; what is distinctive is its use of *free indirect speech* – the fusion of paraphrase and direct quotation – as reporting mode, which exerts an intermediate degree of narrative control (11, my emphasis).

(11) As to the lack of qualification, the law judge *noted, "it's* the Administrator's policy that any revocation is a lack of qualification." Oral Initial Decision at 103. The law judge *found "there's* not a lack of qualification shown by a preponderance of the evidence... but *I am* obligated to find that there was a violation, as alleged, of the regulation FAR 61.15(d), in that there were three motorvehicle actions." Id. at 107. *[NTSB Order No. EA-5629]*

The other peculiarity of NTSB embeddings is their handling of footnotes, very scant in the multinational corpus (only two samples from New Zealand use them, with a total of 22 cases). Like relevance markers, footnotes are multi-purpose devices that span the thin line between stance and engagement: their superscripts are at one time directive and endophoric, and the note itself organises discourse (i.e. sets apart additional information that otherwise would disrupt linearity) and acts as a gloss. Table 6 lists the functions fulfilled in my corpora.

Function	*NTSB*	*Multinational*
Definition or clarification	11 *(3.8%)*	–
Expansion or explanation of factual background	9 *(3.2%)*	1 *(4,5%)*
Summary or explanation of procedural facts	77 *(27.2%)*	–
Transcripts of previous hearings or briefs	15 *(5.3%)*	–
Justification of law application	10 *(3.5%)*	–
In-document endophorics	7 *(2.8%)*	3 *(13,6%)*
Explicit directives	49 *(17.3%)*	3 *(13.6%)*
In-document textual information	16 *(5.6%)*	–
Law references	162 *(57.2%)*	15 *(68.2%)*

Table 6. Raw frequencies and percentages of footnote functions in both corpora.

Six caveats should be borne in mind in relation to these functions:

1) As footnotes in general (and in-text endophorics in particular) are inevitably directive, I have called 'explicit directives' those instances containing an imperative (*see* in all cases) (12).
2) Within law references, straightforward case citations (13) hold the biggest proportion (see Figure 2), but other functions, although less directly, also cite previous proceedings and somehow overlap (e.g. the transcripts of hearings and briefs, the explanation of procedural facts (Example 4), and the justification of law application).
3) In-document endophorics (14) send the reader to parts of the text, whereas in-document textual information (15) anticipates that the court transcript of the previous hearing is attached.
4) Law mentions (16) provide references of rules and regulations, law paraphrases (17) summarize what the rule/regulation or principle, and law quotations (18) insert excerpts.
5) The justification of law application is personal, written from an 'exclusive *we*' perspective (19).
6) In the NTSB corpus, many of the footnotes (a total of 283) are multifunctional (that is, there are function overlaps), which prevents the percentages given in the table from being constitutive of the whole.

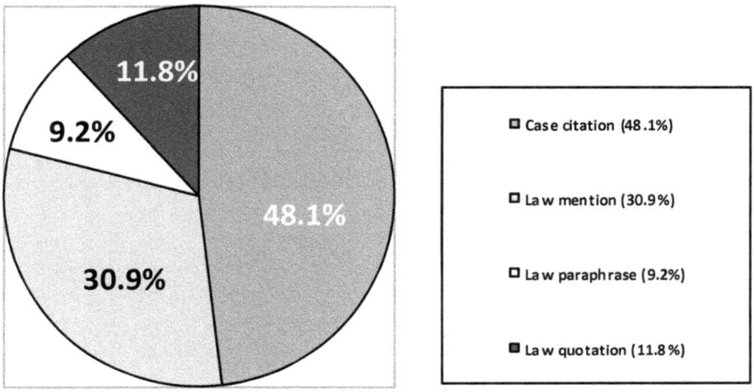

Figure 2. Percentages of law reference types.

(12) [2]*See Administrator v. Hooper*. 6 NTSB 559 (1988). *[NTSB Order No. EA-5630]*

(13) [9]*Administrator v. Haddock*, NTSB Order No. EA-5596 (2011) *[NTSB Order No. 5616]*

(14) [28]*Supra* note 18. *[NTSB Order No. 5641]*

(15) [1]A copy of the oral initial decision is attached. *[NTSB Order No. 5629]*

(16) [15]FAA Order 2150.3B, Appendix B, Figure B-3-h(1)(b). *[NTSB Order No. 5613]*

(17) [2] Section 91.13(a) prohibits careless or reckless aircraft operations so as to endanger the life or property of another. *[NTSB Order No. 5625]*

(18) [2]Section 91.7(a) provides, "[n]o person may operate a civil aircraft unless it is in an airworthy condition." *[NTSB Order No. 5635]*

(19) [8]While we decline to depart from our jurisprudence on the timeliness of filings, it is apparent respondent's interests were not well served by his attorney in this case. *[NTSB Order No. 5617]*

In light of their profusion and adaptable functions, paratextual embeddings could be envisaged as *meeting spaces* for lay and expert readers, where didactic glossing and specialized knowledge converge. Their engaging power is such that the pages of some NTSB case appeals are equally divided into body of text and footnotes, as navigation through the former may require technical and legal expertise. The value of NTSB paratext is then both ideational and pragmatic.

4. Concluding remarks

We have seen that NTSB decisions, influenced by the unique role of the Board as court of appeals, the mixed nature of their broad readership, and the current U.S. legal framework as to institutional transparency (FOIA), are highly engaged with lay readers. This engagement, however, does not diminish their proximity bonds with the expert communities of practice (aeronautical and legal) that generate the texts, but manage instead to conciliate *accessibility* and *informativeness* through a series of choices.

Indeed, case appeals are made accessible online, although they do not incorporate some digital affordances (e.g. hyperlinks) that would enrich the narrative, neither do they abridge the content to increase reader-friendliness, or filter the information resorting to 'reporters' (other than the judges) who recapitulate it and sign the document at the end, as do the Singapore judgments. Together with a web-based dissemination, the NTSB pursues *intelligibility* through *explicitness* and *memorability.* These two properties do not lean so much on conventional metadiscourse but on *rhetorical organization* (i.e. on a stable, ritualistic format) and a *storytelling quality* that, unlike the rigid structure of numbered paragraphs, permits the insertion of subordinate narratives.

These tangential stories raise the *level of disclosure* with their extra detail and introduce *multivocality,* making the case account more informative and the reporting more democratic, which in turn impinges on explicitness and memorability. Court dialogues, quotes, and legal references create an intertext that finds room either in the body of the opinion or in the paratext, the latter basically composed of footnotes and appended transcripts of former hearings.

NTSB decisions, in short, undermine the ingrained view of legal texts as impersonal and uncommitted: their didacticism and reader-considerateness (fundamentally structural) and idiosyncrasies (i.e. paratextual use, legal lexis, structural format, free indirect reporting, typographic emphases and delayed authorship) turn them into alternative models of engagement.

Acknowledgments

My deepest thanks to Juan Antonio Plaza Rubio (Investigator-Coordinator at CIAIAC-Spanish Commission for the Investigation of Civil Aviation Accidents and Incidents) and Jorge Juan Rodríguez Valero (CIAIAC Secretary).

References

Alcaraz Varó, Enrique 1994. *El Inglés Jurídico: Textos y Documentos.* Barcelona: Ariel.

Alcaraz Varó, Enrique / Mateo Martínez, José / Yus Ramos, Francisco (eds) 2007. *Las Lenguas profesionales y Académicas.* Barcelona: Ariel-IULMA.

Anthony, Laurence 2007. *AntConc 3.2.1w.* <http://www.antlab.sci.waseda.ac.jp/software.html>

Bhatia, Vijay K. / Candlin, Christopher N. / Gotti, Maurizio (eds) 2003. *Legal Discourse in Multilingual and Multicultural Contexts: Arbitration Texts in Europe.* Bern: Peter Lang.

Bhatia, Vijay K. / Candlin, Christopher N. / Engberg, Jan (eds) 2008. *Legal Discourse across Cultures and Systems.* Hong Kong: Hong Kong University Press.

Borja Albí, Anabel 2007. Los Géneros Jurídicos. In Alcaraz Varó/ Mateo Martínez/Yus Ramos (eds), 141-153.

Breeze, Ruth 2011. Disciplinary Values in Legal Discourse: A Corpus Study. *Ibérica* 21, 93-115.

Breeze, Ruth 2013. Traversing Legal Narratives. In Gotti, Maurizio / Sancho Guinda, Carmen (eds) *Narratives in Academic and Professional Genres.* Bern: Peter Lang, 343-362.

Brooks, Peter 1996. The Law as Narrative and Rhetoric. In Brooks/ Gewirtz (eds), 14-22.

Brooks, Peter / Gewirtz, Paul (eds) 1995. *Law's Stories.* New Haven and London: Yale University Press

Buscetti, Stefania 2006. Tag Questions in Courtroom Discourse. In Flowerdew, John / Gotti, Maurizio (eds) *Studies in Specialized Discourse.* Bern: Peter Lang, 209-238.

Campos Pardillos, Miguel Ángel 2007. El Lenguaje de las Ciencias Jurídicas: Nuevos Retos y Nuevas Visiones. In Alcaraz Varó/ Mateo Martínez / Yus Ramos (eds), 155-165.

Candlin, Christopher N. / Bhatia, Vijay K. / Jensen, Christian H 2002. Developing Legal Writing Materials for English Second Language Learners: Problems and Perspectives. *English for Specific Purposes* 21, 299-320.

Charnock, Ross 2008. When *May* Means *Must:* Deontic Modality in English Statute Construction. In Salkie, Raphael / Busuttil, Pierre / van der Auwora, Johan (eds) *Modality in English. Theory and Description.* Berlin: Mouton de Gruyter, 177-198.

Clinton, Robert N. 1992. *Introduction to Reading & Briefing Cases and Outlining.* <http://robert-clinton.com/wordpress/wp-content /uploads/2008/02/brief>

Díaz Rafael, Gema (2008). *Descubrir el Derecho Aeronáutico.* Madrid: AENA.

Frade, Celina 2002. The Legal Cooperative Principle: An Essay on the Cooperative Nature of Contractual Transactions. *International Journal for the Semiotics of Law* 15, 337-343.

Gewirtz, Paul 1996. Narrative and Rhetoric in the Law. In Brooks/ Gewirtz (eds), 2-13.

Gotti, Maurizio 2007. Legal Discourse in Multilingual and Multicultural Contexts. In Kredens, Krzysztof / Gozdz-Roszkowski, Stanislaw (eds) *Language and the Law: International Outlooks*. Frankfurt am Main: Peter Lang, 21-33.

Gotti, Maurizio 2011a. Identity Traits in Legal Texts. In Baccolini, Raffaella / Chiaro, Delia / Rundle, Christopher / Whitsitt, Sam (eds) *Minding the Gap. Studies in Linguistic and Cultural Exchange for Rosa Maria Bollettieri Bosinelli*. Bologna: Bononia University Press, 287-298.

Gotti, Maurizio 2011b. Exercising Power and Control in Arbitration Proceedings. *International Journal for the Semiotics of Law* 24, 179-193.

Gotti, Maurizio 2011c. Litigational Influence on Arbitration Discourse. *World Englishes* 30/1, 81-91.

Gotti, Maurizio / Williams, Christopher (eds) 2010. *Legal Discourse across Languages and Cultures*. Bern: Peter Lang.

Hollander, John 1996. Legal Rhetoric. In Brooks/Gewirtz (eds), 176-186.

Hyland, Ken 2005a. *Metadiscourse. Exploring Interaction in Writing*. London: Continuum.

Hyland, Ken. 2005b. Stance and Engagement: a Model of Interaction in Academic Discourse. *Discourse Studies* 7/2, 173-192.

Hyland, Ken 2010. Constructing Proximity: Relating to Readers in Popular and Professional Science. *Journal of English for Academic Purposes* 9/2, 116-127.

Johnstone, Barbara 1987. 'He Says... so I said': Verb Tense Alternation and Narrative Depictions of Authority in American English. *Linguistics* 25, 33-52.

Kerr, Orin S. 2005. How to Read a Judicial Opinion: A Guide for New Law Students. <http://euro.ecom.cmu.edu/program/law/08-732/Courts/howtoreadv2.pdf>

Labov, William / Waletzky, Joshua 1967. Narrative Analysis: Oral Versions of Personal Experience. In Helm, June (ed) *Essays on the Verbal and Visual Arts*. Seattle: University of Washington Press, 12-44.

López Samaniego, Anna / Tarandilla, Raquel 2012. Análisis Contrastivo de la Formulación de Recomendaciones en Dos Géneros Jurídicos. *Ibérica* 23, 65-88.

Mazzi, Davide 2007a. *The Linguistic Study of Judicial Argumentation. Theoretical Pespectives, Analytical Insights.* Modena: Il Fiorino.

Mazzi, Davide 2007b. The Rhetoric of Judicial Texts: The Interplay of Reported Argumentation and the Judge's Argumentative Voice. In Garzone, Giuliana / Sarangi, Srikant (eds) *Discourse, Ideology, and Specialized Communication.* Bern: Peter Lang, 379-400.

Mazzi, Davide 2008. The Construction of Argumentation in Judicial Texts. Combining a Genre and a Corpus Perspective. *Argumentation* 21, 21-38.

NTSB Case Decisions Database. <http://www.ntsb.gov/legal/o_n_o/query.aspx>

NTSB Website. <http://www.ntsb.gov/>

Pascual, Esther 2006. Questions in Legal Monologues: Fictive Interaction as Argumentative Strategy in a Murder Trial. *Text & Talk* 263, 383-402.

Pavličková, Eva 2010. Legal Writing in Light of Grice's Cooperative Principle. In Kačmárová, Alena (ed) *English Matters II: A Collection of Papers by the Department of English Language and Literature.* Prešov: Faculty of Humanities and Natural Sciences.<http://www.pulib.sk/elpub2/FF/Kacmarova2/pdf_doc/pavlickova.pdf>

Riley, Alison 1991. *English for Law.* London: Macmillan.

Russsell, Frances / Locke, Christine 1992. *English Law and Language. An Introduction for Students of English.* London: Cassell.

Sala, Michele 2010. Interrogative Forms as Professional Identity Markers in Legal Research Articles. In Garzone, Giuliana / Archibald, James (eds) *Discourse, Identities and Roles in Specialized Communication.* Bern: Peter Lang, 301-320.

Takahashi, Hiroshi 2009. Modality in L2 Legal Writing: A Functional Analysis. *Language Research Bulletin* 24 < http://web.icu.ac.jp/lrb/volume-24.html>

Tessuto, Girolamo 2012. *Investigating Legal Genres in Academic and*

Professional Contexts. Newcastle upon Tyne: Cambridge Scholars Publishing.

Thompson, Geoff / Thetela, Puleng 1995. The Sound of One Hand Clapping: the Management of Interaction in Academic Discourse. *Text* 15/1, 103-127.

University of British Columbia 2008. *Introduction to Reading and Briefing a Case*. <http://www.law.ubc.ca/files/pdf/current/jd/lrw/Case_Brief_example.pdf>

U.S. Courts's website on 'Review of Agency Decisions' 2013. <http://cdn.ca9.uscourts.gov/datastore/uploads/guides/stand_of_review/IV_Review_AD.html>

Vass, Holly 2004. Socio-Cognitive Aspects of Hedging in two legal Discourses. *Ibérica* 7, 125-141.

Vázquez, Ignacio / Giner, Diana 2009. Authoritative Intervention and (In)directness in Legal Discourse. A Genre-Based Study of Judgments and Arbitration Awards. *XXVII AESLA International Conference*. Universidad de Castilla-La Mancha, 26-28 March.

Volokh, Eugene 2007. *Academic Legal Writing: Law Review Articles, Student Notes, Seminar Papers, and Getting on Law Review*. New York: Foundation Press.

Wagner, Anne / Cacciaguidi-Fahy, Sophie (eds) 2008. *Obscurity and Clarity in the Law. Prospects and Challenges*. Aldershot, Hampshire: Ashgate.

West's Encyclopedia of American Law [2]2008. *The Free Dictionary-legal Dictionary*. <http://legal-dictionary.thefreedictionary.com/judgment>

Multinational corpus

Alberta, Canada

- Citation: Rural Aviation Corp. (Appellant) v Dave's Field Service Ltd. (Respondent). In the Court of Queen's Bench of Alberta, Judicial District of Edmonton. Action No. 9703 22771
- Citation: Airco Aircraft Charters Ltd. v. Edmonton Regional Airports Authority, 2010 ABCA 36. In the Court of Queen's Bench of Alberta, Judicial District of Edmonton. Docket: 1003-0226-AC

- Citation: Aero Aviation Inc. v. Dac Aviation International Ltée, 2010 ABQB 577. In the Court of Queen's Bench of Alberta, Judicial District of Calgary. Docket: 0701 05196
- Citation: R. v. Khorfan, 2011 ABPC 84. In the Court of Queen's Bench of Alberta, Judicial District of Calgary. Docket: 100109263P10101
- Citation: R. v. Servisair Inc., 2012 ABPC 63. In the Court of Queen's Bench of Alberta, Judicial District of Calgary. Docket: 101522241P10101-0102
- Citation: Durunna v. Air Canada, 2013 ABPC 31. In the Court of Queen's Bench of Alberta, Judicial District of Edmonton. Docket: P1290301793
- Citation: Edmonton Flying Club v Edmonton Regional Airports Authority, 2013 ABCA 91. In the Court of Queen's Bench of Alberta, Judicial District of Edmonton. Docket: 1203-0262-AC; 1203-0263-AC

Australia (District Court South Wales)

- Medium Neutral Citation: Noel CAMPBELL v Rodney Victor HAY [2013] NSWDC 11 File Numbers: DC 2010/120631

British Columbia, Canada

- Citation: VIH Aviation Group Lyd. V. CHCH Helicopter LLC, 2012. BCCA 125. Docket: CA038970

Hong Kong

- Cathay Pacific Airways Flight Attendants Union v. The Director-General of Civil Aviation [2007] HKCA 118; [2007] 2 HKLRD 668; [2007] 2 HKC 393; CACV324/2005 (23 March 2007)
- Kwok Kam Ming v. China Airlines Ltd [2008] HKCA 424; [2009] 3 HKC 11; CACV412/2007 (28 October 2008)

Ireland

- Judgment Title: Manorcastle Ltd v Commission for Aviation Regulation. High Court Record Number: 2008 1049 SP
- Judgment Title: Ryanair Ltd v Commission for Aviation Regulation. High Court Record Number: 2008 421 SP
- Judgment Title: Ryanair Ltd v Terravision London Finance Ltd. High Court Record Number: 2010 208 S
- Judgment Title: Flightlease (Ire.) Ltd (In Voluntary Liquidation) & Cos Act High Court Record Number: 2006 60 COS
- Judgment Title: Hennessey v Aer Lingus Ltd. High Court Record Number: 2009 33 CA
- Judgment Title: Transportstyrelsen v Ryanair Limited. High Court Record Number: 2009 3691 S

Isle of Man

- Title: Castle Aviation v Manhattan Aviation. Case reference SCP 1210 (2010)

New Zealand

- Air New Zealand Ltd V David McAlister CA CA216/07 30 July 2008 [2008] NZCA 264

- Paul Maxwell Jones V Civil Aviation Authority CA CA717/2008 11 June 2009 CA717/2008 [2009] NZCA 240
- Air National Corporate Limited (Plaintiff) V Aiveo Holdings Limited (First Defendant) and Bonner William Bylsma (Second Defendant) CIV-2011-404-001187 [2012] NZHC 2258
- Air Chathams Limited & Anor v Civil Aviation Authority of New Zealand & Anor, [2003, HC CP 146/98]

Singapore

- Brinkerhoff Maritime Drilling Corp and Another v PT Airfast Services Indonesia and Another Appeal [1992] 2 SLR 776; [1992] SGCA 45
- Ang Ming Chuang v Singapore Airlines Ltd (Civil Aeronautics Administration, Third Party) [2005] 1 SLR 409; [2004] SGHC 263
- Civil Aeronautics Administration v Singapore Airlines Ltd [2004] 1 SLR 570; [2004] SGCA 3

South Africa

- Welkom Municipality (Appellant) V J P MASUREIK & H G HERMAN (1st Respondents) t/a LOTUS CORPORATION K J DAVIDSON (2nd Respondent) CASE NO. 412/1995 The Supreme Court of Appeal OF South Africa
- Olga Alexseevna Denissova N.O. (Plaintiff) V Heyns Helicopters (PTY) LTD (Defendant). CASE NO: 5875/02 High Court of South Africa, Cape of Good Hope Provincial Division
- Charter Hi (PTY) Limited (First Plaintiff), Haw & Inglis (PTY) Limited (Second Plaintiff), Haw & Inglis (Third Plaintiff) and The Minister Of Transport (Defendant) CASE NO: 35719/99 High Court of South Africa, Transvaal Provincial Division
- ZSSVN Syndicate (Plaintiff) V 43 Air School (PTY) Ltd (Defendant) and Stephen David Onions (Third Party) CASE NO. 1066/05 High Court of South Africa, Eastern Cape Division

United Kingdom

- Captain B L Friend (Appellant) v Civil Aviation Authority (Respondents), Employment Appeal Tribunal, 58 Victoria Embankment, London EC4Y 0DS Appeal No. EAT/915/94
- Aviation & Airport Services Ltd. (Appellant) v Mr C Harris (Respondent), Employment Appeal Tribunal, 58 Victoria Embankment, London EC4Y 0DS Appeal No. EAT/1049/97
- John Hoyte (Appellant) v Information Commissioner (Respondent) and The Civil Aviation Authority (Additional Party), Heard at Field House, London, EC4 Information Tribunal Appeal No. EA/2007/0101
- Civil aviation Authority (Appellant) v Information Commissioner (Respondent) and Malcolm Kirkaldie (Additional Party) Information Tribunal Appeal Number: EA/2009/0033
- British Airways plc (Respondents) v Williams (Appellant) and others. On appeal from: A2/2008/0632 [2010] UKSC 16

CHRISTOPHER WILLIAMS

Interpersonality in Legislative Drafting Guides and Manuals: the Case of the Scottish Government Publication *Plain Language and Legislation*

My aim in this chapter is to analyse how "the interpersonal component of texts (i.e. the ways in which the writers project themselves and their audience in the discourse)" (Lorés-Sanz/Mur-Dueñas/Lafuente-Millán (2010c: 1) plays a role in the way legislative drafting guides and manuals are written. Within the realm of legal discourse, legislative drafting guides and manuals constitute a subgenre of their own. For the purposes of this chapter I distinguish between legislative drafting *manuals*, which tend to be exhaustive in covering a wide range of technical points in considerable detail, and legislative drafting *guides* which tend to be shorter in length and are not usually meant to be as exhaustive in scope. Referring to legislative drafting manuals, Cormacain (2013: 205) affirms that:

> There is no common definition of legislative drafting manuals to which all jurisdictions conform. At a very general level, the most that can be said is that a legislative drafting manual is a manual on how to draft legislation. Beyond this broad statement, jurisdictions go their own ways. Manuals are generally prepared by the centralised drafting unit or by those with responsibility for the quality of legislation within a jurisdiction. The manual can be a single document or it can be spread across multiple documents dealing with different aspects of the legislative process.

Manuals tend to be 'jurisdiction specific' (Cormacain 2013: 206), are principally written for fellow drafters, and will largely be of little interest to non-experts, whereas guides may be written not only for fellow drafters but also for readers who may have little knowledge of the workings of the law. There will inevitably be cases where the boundary between manual and guide is blurred, as is the case of the

Government of Canada Privy Council Office (2001) *Guide to Making Federal Acts and Regulations,* which never calls itself a manual, but at over 200 pages of detailed technical instructions it has all the features of a manual rather than a guide. On the other hand the Australian Government Office of Parliamentary Counsel (2013) *Plain English Manual* (first published in 1993) calls itself a manual despite being only 41 pages in all.

Legislative drafting manuals tend to be found in much of the English-speaking world, particularly among the various States of the United States of America, as well as Australia, New Zealand and Canada. As Cormacain (2013: 206) observes, the UK constitutes an exception in this regard, though a recent publication from the Office of the Parliamentary Counsel (United Kingdom) (2013) entitled *Legislative Guidance* is far more exhaustive in scope than any of the previous guides published within the UK to date, and at 103 pages hovers on the borderline between guide and manual. The Scottish Government publication *Plain Language and Legislation* (2006) defines itself as a 'booklet' and undoubtedly comes within the category of guides rather than manuals.

However, legislative drafting guides and legislative drafting manuals clearly have many features in common, including those inter-discursive elements which can be found in user guides as a whole where impersonal technical information is interspersed with (generally simple) instructions frequently conveyed by means of imperatives aimed directly at the reader. One obvious difference with respect to most technical user guides (e.g. on how a DVD player operates) is the greater degree of contextualization of the information and instructions that can generally be found in legal drafting guides and manuals. This is a reflection of the complexity – and essentially social nature – of the legislative process where a large number of people tend to be involved in the various stages of preparation of a legislative text which, in turn, may impact on the lives of the community at large.

The subgenre of legislative drafting guides and manuals will clearly differ in some respects from other related subgenres from the legal sphere which involve the conveying of instructions, notably jury instructions, where we can also find a wide variety of texts available, ranging from highly detailed and technical advice – aimed above all at other legal professionals rather than laypersons – relating to the various facets of regulating jury service, as in Illinois Courts (2013), to informative online leaflets for non-experts requiring basic information about what jury service entails, as in Howell (2012). The writers of legislative drafting manuals and guides are not necessarily bound to provide any basic information and may assume that their addressees are perfectly *au fait* with the intricacies of the legislative drafting process. However, it is worth underlining that, as with legislative drafting guides and manuals, the influence of plain language principles has often proved to be decisive in terms of prioritizing clarity of expression (see, for example, Utah State Courts 2013).

I go on to explore the questions of authorship and of readership in relation to legal drafting guides and manuals. I observe that, when specifying authorship, it is not unusual to find that such guides and manuals mention only the drafting body that prepared the text (or, as is frequently the case with manuals, the latest version of it) without naming the individual members of the team. As for readership, unlike user guides or manuals on how to use some electronic device where the readers are the direct beneficiaries of the instructions provided, it could be argued that the beneficiaries of legislative drafting guides and manuals are not only actual or potential legislative drafters – who are essentially providing a service to the public by drawing up a legally binding text – but also legal professionals who may subsequently need to consult the drafted texts, as well as the general public whose lives may be positively or adversely affected by a law and even by the way it has been drafted.

These days most legislative drafting guides and manuals are designed to be read online. Hence an awareness of having to appeal to – or at least acknowledge the existence of – a potentially much wider readership than just drafters or interested legal professionals may affect the type of interpersonality strategies employed by those preparing online guides and manuals. In particular, the multimodal aspect of online communication may influence our ways of perceiving the roles of 'writer/speaker' and 'reader/listener' within this particular subgenre. However, given that drafting legislation is a highly specialist activity requiring an expert knowledge of the way laws are structured, the scope for producing guides or manuals that might appeal to a non-specialist Internet-savvy readership is rather limited, especially in the case of manuals stretching to several hundred pages. It is likely that only a very tiny percentage of readers will ever read a manual in its entirety, but that is hardly likely to dishearten the authors of such texts, because their overriding aim in writing them lies elsewhere, as we shall see.

For the purposes of this chapter I have compiled a small corpus of 22 drafting guides and manuals (taking length as my main criterion, I would define eight of these as guides and 14 as manuals) written in English from Australia, Canada, Ireland, New Zealand, the United Kingdom and the United States of America as well as from international organizations such as the European Union, the Food and Agriculture Organization and the International Labour Organization. The texts vary enormously in length, the shortest being merely a few pages, the longest stretching to 684 pages. For reasons of space, in this chapter I do not intend to provide a corpus-based statistical analysis: my aim, rather, is to provide first a general overview of the question of interpersonality in relation to this particular subgenre and then take one particular text and analyse it in detail.

In Section 2 I examine the interpersonal features to be found in the online booklet *Plain Language and Legislation* published by the Scottish Government in 2006. I observe that although the Scottish booklet is written in a style that largely conforms to standard drafting guides written in English elsewhere, it also contains certain traits that endow this piece of prose with a specific blend of interpersonal features, some of which contribute in giving it a distinct Scottish 'personality', such as the Scottish accent of the synthetic female reader of the audio version of the booklet. My conclusions are contained in Section 3.

1. Characteristics of legislative drafting guides and manuals and the role of interpersonality

In general terms, legislative drafting guides and manuals come within the broader category of user guides and manuals where the aim is to provide practical instructions about how to do things. Clearly, the purpose of writing a legislative drafting guide or manual is very different from the vast majority of 'how to' guides or manuals, be they instructions about how to use a vehicle or electrical appliance correctly, or how to apply for a government grant, plan a garden or embroider a tablecloth. Moreover, even within the subgenre of legislative drafting guides and manuals, we can find a variety of approaches to the subject which stretch from those which are of a more strictly technical nature to those which are more discursive and provide information and insights regarding the social and legal context in which the drafting process occurs. The majority of legislative drafting guides and manuals fall somewhere between the two, providing above all technical advice on how to draft legislation, but also placing that advice within a wider framework which is generally outlined in the introductory part of the manual. The proportion of text devoted to illustrating the wider framework rather than providing technical 'how to' advice is generally greater in guides rather than it is in manuals.

Most legislative drafting guides and manuals are produced by teams of drafters working for bodies such as legislative counsel or offices for parliamentary counsel. Some texts – generally guides rather than manuals – may be the work of individuals who have considerable experience as drafters and wish to pass on their knowledge and expertise to others in a specific area of legislative drafting, e.g. Rosenbaum (2007). For the purposes of this chapter, and for the sake of uniformity, I only take into consideration drafting guides and manuals that have been published by institutions that draft laws, be they federal, national or international. This is in no way to belittle the huge amount of excellent work that has been done over the years by drafting practitioners, legal professionals and academics, as well as associations and journals such as *Clarity*, *The Loophole*, *Statute Law Review* or *International Journal of Legislative Drafting and Law Reform*, offering advice and insights relating to legislative drafting, some of which take the form of legal drafting guides, such as Butt/Castle (2006), or examine specific aspects of legislative drafting manuals, e.g. Cormacain (2013). I will clearly be referring to some of these more academically-inclined works in my attempt to delineate the issue of interpersonality in relation to legislative drafting guides and manuals.

The debate surrounding the drafting of legislative texts has been particularly intense in recent years also because of the current state of flux of legal English where calls for modernization of legal language, coming above all from the plain language movement, have led to a series of changes being introduced in the sphere of drafting (for an overview see, for example, Asprey 2010; Williams 2011). A further impetus for effectuating such changes has been the diffusion of information technology which has made the need to publicize and regularly update drafting practices appear more urgent. Moreover, technological advances in the fields of formatting and editing texts in general have made the task of compiling or updating drafting guides and manuals less daunting than it used to be.

1.1. The question of authorship

Hyland (2005: 181) rightly observes that "writers cannot avoid projecting an impression of themselves and how they stand in relation to their arguments, their discipline, and their readers". Admittedly, Hyland was referring to academic writing, but the same holds true even in the seemingly more 'impersonal' realm of legal drafting guides and manuals. As regards the interpersonal qualities of legal drafting guides and manuals, one preliminary question that requires answering is who the authors are and whether they are explicitly mentioned by name. Here lies one of the major differences – in terms of interpersonality – with respect to academic journals, the written genre that would seem to be the most widely studied so far from the interpersonal perspective (see, for example, Hyland/Tse 2004; Hyland

2005, 2010; Kuhi 2010; Lorés-Sanz/Mur-Dueñas/Lafuente-Millán 2010a, 2010b; Dustadsigh/Kuhi 2012). Explicitating authorship in academic journals is a key feature, one might even say the *raison d'être*, of academic publishing, which plays a pivotal role in determining the career paths of academic scholars: one wonders how many scholars would bother publishing if they knew their names were not going to appear in print! Legal drafting guides and manuals, on the other hand, tend not to mention by name the author(s) of the guide or manual in question.

Plain Language and Legislation (2006) represents a case where the authors are not mentioned by name. All we are told in this regard is that "The Office of the Scottish Parliamentary Counsel have prepared this booklet about the use of plain language in legislation" (The Scottish Government 2006), but we are not told who its members were then or are now. Indeed, a collective reference to the drafting body responsible for preparing the guide or manual is quite common in such cases, e.g.:

(1) This guidance has been produced by the Drafting Techniques Group of the Office of the Parliamentary Counsel ('OPC'). (Office of the Parliamentary Counsel (United Kingdom) 2013: i)

(2) Prepared by the Staff of the Texas Legislative Council. (Texas Legislative Council Manual 2013: i)

(3) This pamphlet has been prepared by the office of the code reviser as a guide for the preparation of bills for the Washington legislature. (Washington State Legislature / Statute Law Committee 2013).

However, in the last case, at the end of the Preface we do find a list of the names of the nine people who contributed to writing the 'pamphlet' and their respective roles within the Office of the Code Reviser: Code Reviser, Deputy Code Reviser, Senior Assistant Code Revisers, Assistant Code Revisers, and Indexer (Washington State Legislature / Statute Law Committee 2013).

The Massachusetts House and Senate Counsel manual constitutes an interesting case. The 2010 manual (the 6th edition available since it was first published) opens in the form of a letter addressed to a generic 'Legislative Drafter', specifies that the manual has been prepared by the House and Senate Counsel, and is signed ('Sincerely') by two senior members of the Counsel (Massachusetts House and Senate Counsel 2010):

(4) Dear Legislative Drafter:
The House and Senate Counsel have prepared this manual to help legislative lawyers and other staff who are drafting or reviewing bills for the Massachusetts General Court. We hope you will find it useful.
Its purpose is to promote uniformity in drafting style, and to make the resulting statutes clear, simple and easy to understand and use. This manual is not a substitute for advice and drafting assistance from the House and Senate Counsel. Rather, we hope it will encourage you to call or visit our offices for further help. We welcome any corrections, suggestions for improvement and other comments.
Sincerely,
Alice E. Moore
David Namet
Counsel to the Senate Acting Counsel to the House

If we look at the 3rd edition of the Massachusetts Senate (2003) manual, we find the wording of the letter is almost identical, but this time it is signed by the then Counsel to the Senate, David E. Sullivan. This highlights a second major difference with respect to the interpersonal features of academic journals in terms of the purpose of writing and the role of the author(s): in most cases the author of a legal drafting guide or manual – who will generally be part of a team – makes no claim to being original or to creating a distinctive authorial voice. He/she may feel perfectly entitled to copy large parts of previous editions of the text even if he/she was in no way involved in producing previous editions. Some guides and manuals may explicitly acknowledge their debt to other drafting manuals and textbooks, as does Oregon Legislative Counsel (2012: iii) in the 16th edition of its *Bill Drafting Manual* (the first edition appeared in 1958):

(5) In preparing this manual, we have drawn upon manuals of other states and on textbooks. Reed Dickerson's outstanding textbooks *Legislative Drafting* (1954) and *The Fundamentals of Legal Drafting* (1965) were especially helpful. Extensive parts of this manual have also been derived from the *Form and Style Manual for Legislative Measures*, published by the Publication

> Services staff of the Legislative Counsel's office. We gratefully acknowledge our debt to all of these sources.

Indeed, the very concept of authorship – with its connotations of creativity and originality – seems to be somewhat out of place when referring to the persons involved in the preparation of legal drafting guides and manuals, particularly if they are part of a body such as a legislative counsel. Referring to academic writing, Hyland (2010: 117) affirms that "the process of writing involves *creating* a text that we assume the reader will recognise" (my italics); in the field of legal drafting guides and manuals it would probably be more accurate to say that in most cases the process of writing involves *preparing* a text.

However, if we stray outside the realm of legal drafting guides and manuals prepared by teams working for particular bodies such as legislative counsels and examine legal drafting guides written by individuals for a wider audience – albeit published by an organization such as FAO – then the picture may be rather different. For example, Rosenbaum (2007: 2) offers a much more personalized view of legislative drafting and tries to engage the reader also by underlining his own prejudices and shortcomings:

(6) Every drafter has style preferences and prejudices. I will disclose a few of mine. First, in the debate between the 'plain language' school and the 'precision' school, I lean towards plain language. The precision school says that capturing policy exactly is more important than capturing it in simple language. That may be true, but it is not impossible to be precise with simple language; it is just difficult. If you cannot be both precise and simple, by all means be precise, but strive to be both. Second and more idiosyncratically, computer programming theory has influenced my philosophy of drafting. This is admittedly odd. Human languages are far more complex and prone to ambiguity than computer languages. Writing an algorithm for a computer is not the same as writing rules for people. And I don't claim to understand computer-programming theory particularly well.

Nevertheless, most legislative drafting guides and manuals tend to convey the opinions of the drafting team taken as a whole rather than of individuals, hence the frequent recourse in some – but by no means all – guides and manuals to the personal pronoun *we* and to the possessive adjective *our*, as in New Zealand Parliamentary Counsel Office (2009: 35):

(7) Our practice is to regard the phrase 'take into account' as imposing a stricter requirement than 'have regard to'. We generally use 'take into account' if the intention is to require the decision-maker to address each matter and give it some weight.

1.2. The question of readership

Legislative drafting guides and manuals – particularly those which give little contextual information – tend to be written essentially for a relatively select readership of professionals who are either already involved in drafting legally binding texts or who might become involved in or be affected by such activities in the future. The targeted readership is generally made explicit at the beginning of the text:

(8) Prepared primarily for use by staff members of the Legislative Counsel's office. (Oregon Legislative Counsel 2012: ii)

(9) It is designed for members of OPC who are drafting Bills to be considered in Parliament. (Office of the Parliamentary Counsel (United Kingdom) 2013: i)

(10) The purpose of this manual is to assist persons who have had little or no drafting experience as well as to provide a reference and explanatory material to more sophisticated legislative drafters. (Massachusetts House and Senate Counsel 2010)

(11) The main audience for this Guide consists of officials in the Government of Canada who are involved in the law-making process and who have responsibility for one or more of the following activities:
• developing policy to be implemented by legislation,
• supporting a Minister in obtaining Cabinet approval to draft legislation,
• participating in the drafting of legislation,
• managing legislative projects. (Government of Canada Privy Council Office 2001: 1).

Evidently, despite the relatively small number of potential readers, the preparation – and in some cases the regular updating – of such guides and manuals is considered to be a worthwhile exercise. This is ultimately because of the importance that the law plays in society in general, hence the constant need to ensure that legally binding texts do the job they are meant to do as efficiently as possible. This in turn entails that drafters working for the same organization should follow the same set of rules so as to guarantee uniformity of style and intent. Each body that produces legally binding texts, which may range from a local council to a federal state or a multilingual international organization such as the European Union, will have its own conventions and ingrained habits which will inevitably be to some extent specific to that particular body.

Given that the underlying purpose of guides and manuals is to advise readers about how to do something, directives – which "instruct the reader to perform an action or to see things in a way determined by the writer" (Hyland 2005: 184) – obviously play a key role. Legislative drafting guides and manuals tend to differ from other user guides such as operating instructions for electrical appliances or cookery books in terms of the frequency of recurrence of the imperative form. The imperative tends to be massively used, especially in operating instructions where the author is normally the anonymous 'voice' of the company or corporation, devoid of any individual personality, and the reader is addressed as *you*, as in Pioneer Corporation (2013: 53):

(12) Check the power cord once in a while. When you find it damaged, ask your nearest PIONEER authorized service center or your dealer for a replacement.

Also in cooking recipes the imperative is widely used, but writers tend to engage their readers by alternating instructions with overtly emotive and evaluative language, as in Oliver (2014):

(13) First things first: remove the stalks from the aubergines, slice them up into 1cm thick slices, and put to one side. Whether you're using a griddle pan or a barbecue, get it really hot. [...] You can use the same method substituting courgettes or fennel for the aubergines – both are delicious. But do try making it with aubergines – you'll love it!

Some legal drafting guides and manuals would appear to use imperative forms almost as frequently, though the general tendency is to vary the ways in which instructions can be conveyed, for example by alternating with the deontic modal auxiliary *should*, as in New Zealand Parliamentary Counsel Office (2009: 16):

(14) Avoid terms for occupations or activities that are gender-specific. In particular, 'chairman' should not be used.

As I have pointed out elsewhere (Williams 2002), simply because of the way English is structured, within the context of instructions imperatives often tend to appear as more 'personal' and more overtly aimed at the addressee than they do in a language such as Italian which has two different types of imperative which can either be conveyed in the second person singular (or plural) when giving instructions to a specific person (or specific persons) or in the infinitive form when giving instructions more generically.

As mentioned earlier, another general feature concerning the author/reader relationship in legal drafting guides and manuals is that, even if they are written as a coherent whole, the authors probably do not expect their readers to read the text from start to finish. The text is meant to be above all a guide that will assist the reader in coping with the difficulties of drafting laws, and the reader will therefore tend to select those sections of greatest difficulty or interest, ignoring other sections.

Some legal drafting guides and manuals tend to address their readers using the second person *you*, as if all readers were actually drafters, as in Australia Parliamentary Counsel (2013a: 5):

(15) If you come across an apparently 'gender-specific' expression in existing legislation, you should discuss the matter with your instructors, or with the head drafter, before deciding to replace it.

Others prefer to keep to a more impersonal style by referring to the drafter in the third person, as in Florida Senate (2009: 22):

(16) The drafter should construct each sentence so that its meaning does not depend upon punctuation. If this is not possible, the punctuation used should

> not cast doubt on the meaning of the provision. Generally, a well-constructed sentence is not difficult to punctuate properly. If the drafter has trouble punctuating a sentence correctly, he or she should rewrite the sentence.

We will return to the topics of authorship and readership in Section 2.

2. Interpersonality and the Scottish Government publication *Plain Language and Legislation*

2.1. An overview of the booklet

This online 'booklet', published in March 2006 comprises a total of 49 pages (13,689 words) and is divided into four chapters, respectively, 'What is plain language?', 'Drafting legislation in plain language', 'International comparisons' and 'Plain language techniques'. It should be borne in mind that the Scottish Parliament had only been set up in 1998, so this publication by the Office of the Scottish Parliamentary Counsel can be seen as an attempt to assert an identity that differed from its counterpart in Westminster, as is explicitly acknowledged in Chapter 2 (The Scottish Government 2006: 8):

> (17) The establishment of the Scottish Parliament has presented an opportunity for divergence in the style of Scottish legislation and it has been noticed that Acts of the Scottish Parliament seem to be remarkably short and succinct compared with legislation enacted at Westminster albeit that factors other than drafters drawing on the civilian traditions of Scots law may be at least partly responsible for this shift.

It was written not only with fellow drafters in mind but also for a wider readership of interested laypersons, with three out of four chapters devoted to explaining the importance, history and ethos of using plain language in legislative drafting. It is as much a statement of commitment to a particular style of drafting as it is a guide to drafters about how to deal with specifically technical issues, rather like the *Plain English Manual* of the Australian Government Office of

Parliamentary Counsel 2013 [1993]. As I pointed out in Williams (2009), at the time of its publication the Scottish online booklet was probably the most advanced within the UK in terms of its commitment to plain language (see also Williams 2011), though it does acknowledge the importance of the Tax Law Rewrite Project set up in Westminster in the mid-1990s to rewrite the 6,000 pages of the UK's tax legislation (see Williams 2007). In recent years, however, Westminster's Office of the Parliamentary Counsel has openly endorsed its commitment to plain language, culminating in the publication in December 2013 of its *Drafting Guidance*. On the contrary, the Scottish publication has not been updated since it came out in 2006.

2.2. Interpersonal features of the booklet and the question of authorship and readership

As was mentioned earlier, the authors of the online booklet are not specified by name but merely as the Office of the Scottish Parliamentary Counsel. This impersonal approach is further enhanced by the fact that they refer to themselves as *they* rather than *we*, as in The Scottish Government (2006: 8):

(18) The Counsel in that office are responsible for drafting Bills for the Scottish Executive. They are committed to drafting legislation in plain language.

This contrasts with the more personal approach conveyed by the use of *we* adopted, for example, by the Australian Government Office of Parliamentary Counsel (2013), as was noted in Section 1, Moreover, as I mentioned earlier, the reader is explicitly acknowledged in the Australian Government Office of Parliamentary Counsel (2013) as if he or she were a legislative drafter, whereas in the Scottish online booklet there are no cases in which the reader is addressed directly by means of *you* or even as *the reader*. There are several references to *the drafter* or *drafters* where the authors refer to a broad professional category rather than directly acknowledging the reader as a potential drafter, as in The Scottish Government (2006: 17-18):

(19) Drafters will always need to frame legislation robustly enough to allow it to withstand the intense scrutiny of legal challenge. [...] Using plain language helps the drafter to create clear, unambiguous law.

However, the imperative – the use of which would seem to imply, at least in theory, that the reader is seen as a drafter whose 'presence' as addressee is directly acknowledged – is frequently adopted in the text, particularly in Chapter Four on plain language techniques, as in The Scottish Government (2006: 37):

(20) Take care with punctuation but try not to place too much reliance on it. Consider restructuring a provision if a change in punctuation can alter its meaning.

Generally speaking, though, there are few engagement markers in the text. There is only one question in the text, namely the heading of the first chapter 'What is plain language?', a trait common to informative leaflets where the question and answer structure is adopted to create a more informal, user-friendly format that facilitates the reader's comprehension.

On the other hand, the booklet is rich in attitude markers, boosters and hedges, thus illustrating the authors' concerted attempts to persuade the readers of the validity of their argument, in particular in terms of portraying the adoption of plain language in legislative drafting in a positive light. Here are three examples illustrating, respectively, an attitude marker, a booster and a hedge (The Scottish Government 2006: 17, 4-5, and 10 respectively: my italics):

(21) [Drafters] should *ideally* try to ensure that [legislation] is incapable of being misconstrued, even in bad faith.

(22) But plain language does not involve using 'poor' English. And it is *definitely* not a pidgin.

(23) *Perhaps* the main advantage of plain language is that describing certain concepts in simpler ways will increase the likelihood of them being understood.

Explicitly evaluative terms and expressions abound throughout the text (e.g. *remarkably short and succinct*, *highly intricate*, *particularly sensitive*, *is arguably better suited*) though we can also find many cases where ideas are expressed as if they were logical facts rather than opinions, as in The Scottish Government (2006: 4 and 8 respectively):

(24) The purpose of legislation is not to entertain or captivate its readers so drafters should not be concerned as to whether their audience enjoys reading their product. It is more important that statutes be easy to read and understand – goals which using plain language can help to achieve.

(25) Although Scots common law has much more in common with continental civilian tradition than its English counterpart the fact that responsibility for legislating for Scotland lay with the Westminster Parliament for almost 3 centuries means that the degree of precision in Scottish Acts reflects that which appears in Acts which apply to other parts of the UK (not least because many Acts apply to the UK as a whole).

The booklet represents a good case of the dilemma facing all legislative drafters as is outlined by Cormacain (2013: 208-210), i.e. on the one hand the need for consistency and clear guidelines that can be used systematically, while on the other there is explicit recognition that, even in the relatively hidebound realm of the law, language is constantly changing and needs to be updated, as is acknowledged in The Scottish Government (2006: 11):

(26) Drafters can usually devise innovative ways of restating or referring to established rules or concepts which will make them more understandable to the modern day reader but will not change their meaning. But there is always a risk associated with change – there is often much to be said for the continued use of words with a well established legal meaning and any difference in the wording of a law will be analysed closely.

Hence the balance between boosters and hedges in the text: the authors are eager to persuade their readers that their endorsement of plain language is justified and that using plain language techniques will have a positive effect on legislative drafting, but they do not wish to 'sell' their idea too aggressively or underplay some of the more controversial aspects associated with the adoption of plain language.

One feature of this online booklet which, to the best of my knowledge, is unique with respect to the other legislative drafting manuals and guides I have come across so far, is the possibility of listening to the text being read by a synthetic female voice with an unmistakably Scottish accent by clicking on the 'Listen' link on the website. This inevitably widens up the traditional concept of readership of legislative manuals and guides by providing the element of 'listenership', though it is unlikely that anyone would persevere in listening to the text for any length of time, given the rather unnatural intonation and flow of the computerized spoken text. However, the overall impact of this aural dimension on the reader/listener is likely to be one of curiosity and approval, partly because of the novelty of being able to listen to a type of text that is not normally considered as 'natural' listening material unlike, say, stories or the news, and partly because of the speaker's Scottish accent which pleasantly highlights the national identity factor.

Finally, as was noted earlier, this text was first published in 2006 but has since remained unchanged. Given the necessity of regularly updating information in online communication, it is likely that this 'age factor' will increasingly be perceived in negative terms by potential readers who will soon start to see the booklet as a piece of recent history rather than as a document that is at the cutting edge of what is happening in the legislative drafting world.

3. Conclusions

As we have seen, the online booklet published by the Scottish Government can clearly be defined as a guide rather than a manual. Its interpersonal features are not, on the whole, so different from those found in other guides and manuals relating to legislative drafting, with the possible exception of the general lack of direct or indirect references to the reader. In other respects, however, the text is authored in a relatively engaging manner with the aim of persuading the reader that the adoption of plain language principles can only have a positive effect on the way laws are drafted. The Scottish identity aspect is present at given moments in the text but can hardly be said to be foregrounded to any significant extent. The authors are more concerned with underlining the specificity of the Scottish legal system and promoting a drafting style based on plain language principles than with making a broader political statement. As I mentioned earlier, the text would seem to be aimed as much at the interested layperson as it is for fellow drafters.

Taking a wider perspective and comparing this particular sub-genre with other areas where interpersonality has been analysed in detail, in particular in the sphere of academic discourse, it would seem that the categories employed, for example, by Hyland (2005, 2010) and Hyland and Tse (2004) to identify the interpersonal features of academic writing can also be usefully adopted for legislative drafting guides and manuals. Obviously, the frequency of directive features such as the use of imperatives, and more in general of deontic rather than epistemic modality, will tend to be much greater in guides and manuals than in academic texts. As I have said, because of the way imperatives are conveyed in English, the outward effect on the reader may appear to be one of being directly addressed and strongly advised to behave in a particular way.

However, as a more general point, it is interesting to note that, despite the often highly technical nature of the subject-matter, which might be superficially dismissed by an outsider as boringly dry and impersonal, in actual fact the authors of such texts are often engaged in a complex act of persuasion in convincing the reader not only of their competence in a highly specialist field but also of the correctness of their position vis-à-vis the adoption of particular drafting techniques. In this respect academics and the writers of legislative drafting guides and manuals would seem to have much in common, even if their underlying aims in writing are quite different, one major difference being, as was outlined briefly in Section 1, that authors of legislative drafting guides and manuals are not generally interested in originality or in creating a unique 'space' for themselves, unlike most academics whose cognitive framework when writing – either collaboratively or individually – is commonly based on the CARS model first outlined by Swales (1990).

This chapter is meant to represent nothing more than an initial overview of the question of interpersonality in relation to legislative drafting guides and manuals, together with an illustration of some of the interpersonal features appertaining to one specific text. There is undoubtedly considerable scope for further research in this field. Possible avenues of exploration include corpus-based statistical studies based, for example, on Hyland's (2005: 175) interactional metadiscourse categories, also in terms of the differences in interpersonal strategies adopted by writers of drafting guides as opposed to writers of drafting manuals.

From a diachronic perspective it could be worthwhile verifying whether legislative drafting manuals today are less prescriptive than they used to be – Xanthaki (2010: 111, note 12) speaks of "their regrettable past as a series of commands" – and how interpersonal strategies may have evolved accordingly over time. Another potentially fruitful line of research could be that of comparing the extent to which this particular subgenre has adapted (or has not adapted, as the case may be) its interpersonal strategies to the digital world of online communication with respect to other subgenres in the legal sphere such as jury instructions, law-related blogs, online law-related journals, or websites offering legal advice.

References

Asprey, Michèle M. 2010. *Plain Language for Lawyers*. Annandale, NSW: Federation Press.

Butt, Peter / Castle, Richard 2006. *Modern Legal Drafting: A Guide to*

Using Clearer Language. Cambridge: Cambridge University Press.

Cormacain, Ronan 2013. An Empirical Study of the Usefulness of Legislative Drafting Manuals. *The Theory and Practice of Legislation* 1/2, 205-225.

Dustadsigh, Zahra / Kuhi, Davud 2012. *Diachronic Evolution of Metadiscourse in Academic Writing: A Novel Approach to the Issue of Interpersonality*. Saarbrücken: Lap Lambert.

Hyland, Ken 2005. Stance and Engagement: A Model of Interaction in Academic Discourse. *Discourse Studies* 7/2, 173-192.

Hyland, Ken 2010. Constructing Proximity: Relating to Readers in Popular and Professional Science. *Journal of English for Academic Purposes* 9/2, 116-127.

Hyland, Ken / Tse, Polly 2004. Metadiscourse in Academic Writing: A Reappraisal. *Applied Linguistics* 25/2, 156-177.

Kuhi, David 2010. *Interpersonal Resources in Academic Discourse: Research Genres vs. Instructional Genres*. Saarbrücken: Lap Lambert.

Lorés-Sanz, Rosa / Mur-Dueñas, Pilar / Lafuente-Millán, Enrique (eds) 2010a. *Interpersonality*. Special issue of *Journal of English for Academic Purposes* 9/2.

Lorés-Sanz, Rosa / Mur-Dueñas, Pilar / Lafuente-Millán, Enrique (eds) 2010b. *Constructing Interpersonality: Multiple Perspectives on Written Academic Genres*. Newcastle upon Tyne: Cambridge Scholars.

Lorés-Sanz, Rosa / Mur-Dueñas, Pilar / Lafuente-Millán, Enrique 2010c. Introduction. In Lorés-Sanz/Mur-Dueñas/Lafuente-Millán (eds, 2010b), 1-10.

Swales, John 1990. *Genre Analysis*. Cambridge: Cambridge University Press.

Williams, Christopher 2002. Non-progressive Aspect in English in Commentaries and Demonstrations Using the Present Tense. *Journal of Pragmatics* 34/9, 1235-1256.

Williams, Christopher 2007. Crossovers in Legal Cultures in Westminster and Edinburgh: Some Recent Changes in the Language of the Law. *ESP Across Cultures* 4, 101-118.

Williams, Christopher 2009. Scottish Parliament and Plain Language Legal Drafting. In Šarčević, Susan (ed.) *Legal Language in Action: Translation, Terminology, Drafting and Procedural Issues*. Zagreb: Globus, 301-312.

Williams, Christopher 2011. Legal English and Plain language: An Update. *ESP Across Cultures* 8, 139-151.

Xanthaki, Helen 2010. Drafting Manuals and Quality in Legislation: Positive Contribution towards Certainty in the Law or Impediment to the Necessity for Dynamism of rules? *Legisprudence* 4/2, 111-128.

Primary sources

Australian Government Office of Parliamentary Counsel 2013 [1993]. *Plain English Manual*. <http://www.opc.gov.au/about/docs/Plain_English.pdf>.

Australia Parliamentary Counsel 2013a. Drafting Direction No. 2.1: English usage, gender-specific and gender-neutral language, grammar, punctuation and spelling. <http://www.opc.gov.au/about/docs/drafting_series/DD2.1.pdf>.

Australia Parliamentary Counsel 2013b. Drafting Direction No. 2.2: Use of various expressions in draft legislation. <http://www.opc.gov.au/about/docs/drafting_series/DD2.2.pdf>.

Colorado General Assembly 2009. Colorado Legislative Drafting Manual. <http://colorado.state.co.us/gov_dir/leg_dir/olls/LDM/OLLS_Drafting_Manual.pdf>.

European Commission's Directorate-General for Translation 2013. English Style Guide. A handbook for authors and translators in the European Commission. < http://www.fjfhs.eu/esg/>.

European Communities 2003. Joint Practical Guide of the European Parliament, the Council and the Commission for persons involved in the drafting of legislation within the Community institutions. <http://eur-lex.europa.eu/en/techleg/pdf/ en.pdf>.

Florida Senate 2009. Manual for Drafting Legislation. <http://www.flsenate.gov/PublishedContent/ADMINISTRATIVEPUBLICATIONS/Manual-for Drafting%20-Final.pdf>.

Government of Canada Privy Council Office [2]2001. *Guide to Making Federal Acts and Regulations*. <http://www.pco- bcp.gc.ca/docs/information/publications/legislation/pdf-eng.pdf>.

Howell, David 2012. Courtroom Advice. The Rules of Jury Service. <http://www.courtroomadvice.co.uk/rules-of-jury-service.html>.

Illinois Courts 2013. Illinois Pattern Jury Instruction – Criminal. <http://www.state.il.us/court/circuitcourt/CriminalJuryInstructions/default.asp>.

International Labour Office 2006. Manual for drafting ILO instruments. <http://www.ilo.org/public/english/bureau/leg/download/man.pdf>.

Ireland Revenue Legislation Services 2007. Guide to the legislative process. <http://www.revenue.ie/en/about/publications/legislative-process.pdf>.

Massachusetts House and Senate Counsel [5]2010. *Legislative and Research Drafting Manual*. <http://archives.lib.state.ma.us/bitstream/handle/2452/47796/ocn549554381.pdf?sequence=1>.

Massachusetts Senate [3]2003. *Legislative and Research Drafting Manual*. <https://www.google.it/?gfe_rd=cr&ei=U0vJUunUMsWP_AbQv4DQBw#q=%222003%22+house+and+senate+manual+massachusetts>.

New Zealand Parliamentary Counsel Office 2009. Principles of Clear Drafting. <http://www.pco.parliament.govt.nz/assets/Uploads/pdf/clear-drafting.pdf>.

Office of the Parliamentary Counsel (United Kingdom) 2013. *Drafting Guidance*. <https://www.gov.uk/government/uploads/system/uploads/attachment_data/file/265753/OPC_Drafting_Guidance_Dec_2013.pdf>.

Oliver, Jamie 2014. Recipe of the day: Aubergine Parmigiana. <http://www.jamieoliver.com/recipes/vegetables-recipes/aubergine-parmigiana-melanzane-alla-parmigiana>.

Oregon Legislative Counsel 2012. *Bill Drafting Manual*. <www.lc.state.or.us/pdfs/*draftingmanual.pdf*>.

Pioneer Corporation 2013. Pioneer Elite DVD Player DV 05 Operating Instructions. <http://www.pioneerelectronics.com/pio/pe/images/portal/cit_11221/140981220DV-05%20OPERATING%20INSTRUCTIONS.pdf>.

Rosenbaum, Kenneth L. 2007. Legislative Drafting Guide: A Practitioner's View. A resource of people working on international technical assistance projects. *FAO Legal Papers Online* 64, 1-43. <http://www.fao.org/fileadmin/user_upload/legal/docs/lpo64.pdf>.

Texas Legislative Council 2013. *Drafting Manual*. <www.tlc.state.*tx.us/legal/dm/draftingmanual.pdf*>.

The Scottish Government 2006. Plain Language and Legislation. <http://www.scotland.gov.uk/Publications/2006/02/17093804/0>.

Utah State Courts 2013. Guidelines for Drafting Plain-Language Jury Instructions. <http://www.utcourts.gov/committees/muji/guideline%20summary.pdf>.

Washington State Legislature/ Statute Law Committee 2013. *Bill Drafting Guide*. <http://www.leg.wa.gov/CodeReviser/Pages/bill_drafting_guide.aspx>.

IGNACIO VÁZQUEZ-ORTA

Exploring the Interplay Between Discursive and Professional Practices in Domain Name Arbitration Awards[1]

1. Introduction

The interpersonal dimension in professional communication has been approached from different analytical perspectives, such as stance (Biber/Finegan 1989; Conrad/Biber 2000; Biber 2006), evaluation (Hunston 2000; Hunston/Thompson 2000a, 2000b), appraisal (Martin/White 2005), metadiscourse (Hyland 1996, 1998; Ädel 2006; Hyland/Sancho Guinda 2012) or voice (Matsuda/Tardy 2007) among others. It is now widely accepted that specialized discourse is conditioned by the writer-reader relationship. This relationship can be adequately explored by the umbrella concept of 'interpersonality', which we understand as the complex interplay of writers and readers as projected in the text, as well as how this projection is influenced by and influences the writers' position in relation to their own and others' texts. Interpersonality is here understood as a generative metaphor, a view of professional writing as writer-reader and writer-text interaction. This metaphor, together with the Bakhtinian notions of dialogism and heteroglossic diversity, can help to facilitate a critical discussion of the way in which arbitrators get engaged in a dialogue

1 This research has been carried out within the framework of the project entitled InterLAE (Interpersonalidad en el Lenguaje Académico Escrito/Interpersonality in Written Academic Language), financially supported by local and national authorities (*Diputación General de Aragón* (Group H21) and *Ministerio de Educación y Ciencia* (FFI2009-009792 (subprograma FILO).

with the parties going for arbitration and with a wider professional community of practice.

Arbitration is increasingly considered as an efficient, economical and effective alternative to litigation in order to solve legal conflicts. *Litigation* can be defined as a civil action brought before a court, where the party initiating the action seeks a legal or equitable remedy. Arbitration, on the other hand, is included in the group of alternative dispute resolution (ADR) methods of solving disputes, together with *conciliation* and *mediation*. Companies and individuals are increasingly turning to ADR as the means to resolve their disputes, as a faster and less costly alternative to going to court. In litigation, judges are not selected by the parties but rather play the traditional legal role of adjudicator and exert their control over the substance of the process and the process itself. Litigation is carried out according to the law. Arbitration provides an alternative to the courts for the resolution of disputes, both domestically and internationally, and it is a mechanism which is recognised and supported by the laws of most developed and developing nations. In arbitration, the parties themselves design their method of dispute resolution, choose the ground rules and agree to be bound by the decision of the arbitrator. In the case of future disputes arising under a contract, the parties insert an arbitration clause in the relevant contract. Arbitration lies, then, somewhere between mediation and litigation.

One of the critical moments of litigation and arbitration practice is the issuing of a judgment by a judge and of an arbitral award by the arbitrator or panel of arbitrators. Arbitral awards have been selected here for being the final expression of arbitrators' legal professional practice. They emerge as the outcome of the processes of arbitration and they represent the most crucial document where arbitrators have to defend their viewpoints strongly in order to make their decisions appear fair and well-grounded and, therefore, gain credibility. Those arbitral resolutions are called administrative panel decisions.

There are three prominent characteristics that feature in those texts: *authoritativeness, interpersonal way of reasoning* and *use of legalese*. In this chapter I study the interpersonal rhetoric of WIPO (World Intellectual Property Organisation) domain name arbitration awards in English by focussing on these three aspects, which are illustrated in a textual analysis of a sample of arbitration awards taken from the WIPO website (<http://www.wipo.int/amc/en/>).

Section 1 of the chapter looks at interpersonality as a generative metaphor, that is, a re-description of authors' writing through 'seeing as', that is, looking at the awards as a result of a dialogic process. It also offers a comprehensive definition of the interpersonal features examined. To arrive at this definition, certain cognitive factors are addressed, including the relationship between derivation of meaning and shared linguistic and extra-linguistic knowledge. This entails relating production and interpretation of features of interpersonality to commonly-held views on human cognition, including the theory that categories are structured by prototype as well as schema (Taylor 1995). In addition, production and interpretation of the interpersonal features are related to certain social factors, such as desire for acceptance by a determined community of practice. Thus, the link between interpersonal features and the fulfilment of both macro-level and micro-level expectations are discussed. Section 2 deals with the discursive practices of the professional discourse of domain name arbitration. Section 3 brings evidence for the textual analysis of arbitration awards. Section 4 draws some conclusions of the previous analysis.

1.1. Interpersonality as a generative metaphor

Metaphor is a normal feature of language, not simply an embellishing literary figure. It is difficult to isolate it for study, however, partly because it operates at many different linguistic 'levels' (itself a metaphor): at the grammatical level, at word level, at sentence/utterance/text levels, and at the level of the context and underlying concept of a discourse. According to Lakoff and Johnson (1980: 3), "our ordinary conceptual system, in terms of which we both think and act, is fundamentally metaphorical in nature".

The English word *metaphor* is derived from the Greek *meta pherein* [carry across], indicating the importation of understanding or insight from one sphere of experience to another. If metaphor is then broadly, but usefully, described as "experiencing or understanding something in terms of something else" or "seeing as" (Schön 1979: 24), it can be observed that this principle informs a great many aspects of linguistic activity,[2] and cognitive activity in general. Metaphors, especially conventionalized metaphors, are a mode of dealing with experience that pervades our cognition; and they are so pervasive that we tend to overlook them and accept the views they present as 'literal', natural and non-negotiable. Metaphor is central to the task of accounting for our perspectives on the world: how we think about things, make sense of reality, and set the problems we later try to solve. In this sense, 'metaphor' refers both to a certain kind of product – a perspective or frame, a way of looking at things – and to a certain kind of process – a process by which new perspectives on the world come into existence. In this chapter 'interpersonality' is used as a generative metaphor, in which there is a process of *meta pherein* or 'carrying over' of frames or perspectives from one domain of experience to another. Under the umbrella term 'interpersonality' we see the writing process as a dialogic process, as the interplay of writers and readers projected in the text.

Traditionally, professional writing has been regarded as the objective report of facts derived from the correct application of normal and neutral procedures (conduit metaphor). However, following social construction theories, there is more to professional writing than merely using words to represent an external objective piece of data. Reality is considered to be constructed socially, as nature has no language of its own in which it can speak to us (Toulmin 1972), and therefore there is no secure means of distinguishing between objective observation and subjective inference. Schön's (1979) discussion of generative metaphor, mainly in the context of social policy, begins by observing that such metaphors regularly arise as part of the normal process of problem setting:

---

2 Rumelhart (1979) assigns a crucial role to metaphor in the acquisition of language, in which learners use a kind of metaphorical extension in applying old words to new situations and objects. The creative rule-formation and lexical innovation of children acquiring a language demonstrate the generative principle of metaphor at work.

> Problem settings are mediated [...] by stories people tell about troublesome situations – stories in which they describe what is wrong and what needs fixing. When we examine the problem-setting stories, it becomes apparent that the framing of problems often depends upon metaphors underlying the stories, which generate problem setting and set the directions of problem solving. One of the most pervasive stories about social services, for example, diagnoses the problem as 'fragmentation' and prescribes 'coordination' as the remedy. But services seen as fragmented might be seen, alternatively, as autonomous. Fragmented services become problematic when they are seen as the shattering of a prior integration. The services are seen something like a vase that was once whole and now is broken. [...] Under the spell of metaphor, it appears obvious that fragmentation is bad and coordination, good. But this sense of obviousness depends very much on the metaphor remaining tacit [...]. We can spell out the metaphor, elaborate the assumptions which flow from it, and examine their appropriateness in the present situation. (Schön 1979: 156)

Identification and analysis of generative metaphor is therefore a useful tool in making unexpressed assumptions explicit, and it underlies the analytical methodology used in this chapter.

2. Genres and the discursive practices of professional discourse

Genres are conventionalized discursive actions, in which participant individuals or institutions have shared perceptions of communicative purposes. They also share the constraints operating on their construction, interpretation and conditions of use. In this sense, genres are socially constructed, interpreted and used in specific, social, institutional and professional contexts, and have their own identity. The analysis of domain name arbitration discourse we are pursuing here focuses on the discursive construction and interpretation of a professional genre (administrative panel decision) in the context of a specific professional practice, that of arbitrators working for the World Intellectual Property Organisation (WIPO).

2.1. Domain name arbitrators' professional practice

In this chapter, arbitral awards have been selected for being the most representative expressions of arbitrators´ professional practice. My hypothesis is that, in arbitration awards writing practice, authors use different strategies in order to achieve their purposes, and I will argue that those strategies are constrained by the interpersonal factors that play a decisive role in arbitrators' professional practice. Domain name arbitration awards are normally referred to as 'domain name administrative decisions'; later on, we will see that the name makes a difference and why it does make a difference.

With the advent of Internet as a global-multimedia system, companies register domain names that are associated with their trademarks in order to use them as business identifiers or virtual adverts. Yet there are occasions when trademarks have been registered fist by third parties unconnected to the business. As the registration of domain names is almost a fully automated online process following a first-come, first-served principle, firms have seen their trademarks tarnished by cyberpiracy. According to the International Chamber of Commerce, companies have reached to lose over 25 billion dollars a year worldwide to brand and trademark abuse online.

Specially oriented to protect Internet addresses from cyberpiracy, firms have found in Domain Name Arbitration an effective method to solve disputes concerning conflictive Internet addresses. Domain Name Arbitration is an alternative dispute resolution process, in which one or more panelists of the World Intellectual Property Organization (WIPO) make a binding decision over the legitimacy of a domain. WIPO Domain Name Arbitration deals with domain name abusive registration and cyberpiracy. The WIPO created the WIPO Arbitration and Mediation Centre in 1994 to solve disputes concerning domain names. The centre monitors the overall integrity and fairness of WIPO arbitration procedures. Two parties are distinguished, the *Claimant* and the *Respondent.* According to WIPO arbitration Rules (article 1), the Claimant is the party initiating an arbitration process and therefore responsible for transmitting the request for Arbitration to the Centre and the Respondent. On the other hand, the Respondent is, not only the Party against which the arbitration process is initiated, but the Party that will reply and counter-claim to the particulars indicated in the Statement of Claim.

The Rules clearly state that any person or entity may initiate an administrative proceeding by submitting a complaint in accordance with the Policy and these Rules to any Provider approved by ICANN.[3] In order to do that, the Complainant has to describe, in accordance with the Policy, the grounds on which the complaint is made including, in particular,

1. the manner in which the domain name(s) is/are identical or confusingly similar to a trademark or service mark in which the Complainant has rights;
2. why the Respondent (domain name holder) should be considered as having no rights or legitimate interests in respect of the domain name(s) that is/are the subject of the complaint;
3. why the domain name(s) should be considered as having been registered and being used in bad faith.

The administrative process is described as follows:

> (a) The Panel shall conduct the administrative proceeding in such manner as it considers appropriate in accordance with the Policy and these Rules.
> (b) In all cases, the Panel shall ensure that the Parties are treated with equality and that each Party is given a fair opportunity to present its case.
> (c) The Panel shall ensure that the administrative proceeding takes place with due expedition. It may, at the request of a Party or on its own motion, extend, in exceptional cases, a period of time fixed by these Rules or by the Panel.
> (d) The Panel shall determine the admissibility, relevance, materiality and weight of the evidence.
> (e) A Panel shall decide a request by a Party to consolidate multiple domain name disputes in accordance with the Policy and these Rules.

---

3 ICANN stands for Internet Corporation for Assigned Names and Numbers. Since 1998, ICANN has assumed its responsibility from the U.S. Department of Commerce to regulate the root domain name from which all domain names emerge. ICANN has developed the concept of accredited registrars, organizations to which ICANN has delegated limited responsibility for the sale and administration of parts of the domain name hierarchy.

2.2. Panel decision

A Panel will decide a complaint on the basis of the statements and documents submitted and in accordance with the Policy, these Rules and any rules and principles of law that it deems applicable. The Panel's decision is in writing, provides the reasons on which it is based, indicates the date on which it was rendered and identifies the name(s) of the Panelist(s). The panel decision is the final outcome of the dispute resolution process and that is the reason why we have chosen this particular genre.

In a recent interpretation of genre analysis (Bhatia 2004), the relationship between text and context has been revisited, and context has been assigned a more important role, redefining genre as:

> a configuration of text-internal and text-external resources, thus highlighting two kinds of relationships involving texts and contexts. Interrelationships within and across texts focusing primarily on text-internal properties are viewed as intertextual in nature, whereas interactions within and across genres involving primarily text-external resources may be viewed as interdiscursive in nature. (Bhatia 2004: 391)

The central argument here will be that the complex nature of the discourse of domain name arbitration, as it is manifested in the panelists' administrative decisions, is the result of the interplay of their writers and readers as projected in the text, taking also into account that this projection is influenced by and influences the writers' position in relation to their own and others' texts. Our hypothesis here is based on a Bakhtinian view of language as being inherently dialogic. This notion of dialogism is one of the basic tenets underlying the account of professional writing as writer-reader and writer-text interaction included in the generative metaphor of interpersonality.

3. Textual analysis

Domain name arbitration discourse constitutes identifiable linguistic practices, which make it specific, but at the same time it shows links with the professional discourse of law, the discourse of litigation, and bureaucratic discourse. When examining final decisions in WIPO arbitration, we will consider different interpersonal aspects in the final three structural elements that have been proposed as a generic structure of this genre (*Parties' Contentions, Discussion and Findings* and *Decision*). The generic structure of final decisions in WIPO arbitration is parallel to Maley's (1985) generic structure of judgments, and these are the five structural elements we propose for WIPO decisions:

1. Identifying the parties and Procedural History
2. Summary of facts
3. Parties' Contentions
4. Discussion and Findings
5. Decision

The 'Parties' Contentions' move is the first move I consider for analysis, as it is the first carrier of legal reasoning. The two previous moves have a purely descriptive function. The 'Parties' Contentions' and the 'Discussion and Findings' together with the 'Decision' are the most argumentative parts of the administrative panel decision. Here I explore the nature and function of interdiscursivity on these three moves as they are central to the understanding of this professional genre.

Legal reasoning (providing the reasons on which panel decisions are based) has been described as an attempt to engage in dialogue with the purpose to persuade (Goodrich 1986). The strategy of persuasion appropriate for legal writing requires concise, clear, complete and logical explanation and argument. It requires a clear statement of issue, a complete discussion of relevant factors, and a logical analysis of points leading to a conclusion. In this presentation legal reasoning enters into two kinds of dialogue:

1. The first mediates between the writer's text and other related texts (Policy, these Rules, and any rules and principles of law that it deems applicable), between the writer's position and al-

ternative positions; in this respect, both intertextuality and interdiscursivity are present for different purposes. There is a continuous reference to the Policy Manual and the Rules regulating the administrative proceedings. Both documents are a wonderful source of bureaucratic language. The discourse of arbitration is fully colonised by this bureaucratic style of administrative discourse.

2. The second kind is not about alternative positions, but a dialogue about degrees of ideational and interpersonal meanings. Reader solidarity with the writer's position is assumed, but at the same time a space for reader alignment is created through scaling meanings, up and down. ('Graduation'[4] is the semantic resource for this kind of dialogue). In this chapter I leave out this aspect altogether, and I focus on the first one only.

Our basic assumption to carry out the textual analysis is that all structural elements of an award are highly dialogic. There is dialogue with other texts, where alternative meanings are attributed to external voices (extra-vocalisation). There is dialogue about alternative meanings where the alternatives are inscribed in the writer's own words, and there is dialogue about degrees of experimental and interpersonal meanings. These dialogues unfold throughout the administrative panel decision: facts are not 'found', but are socially constructed. This Bakhtinian notion of dialogism also underlies the system of engagement (White 2003; Martin/White 2005), an analytical framework which has been developed in recent years within Systemic Functional Linguistics, and some of whose metalanguage can very usefully be employed to facilitate a discussion of the interpersonal features of administrative decision from a dialogistic perspective. Central to engagement is the Bakhtinian notion of heteroglossic diversity, the

4 Graduation is a resource for legal reasoning to negotiate legal issues, rules, categories, precedents and facts. It is constructed as either/or choices (typology of graduation). Graduation is also a resource to negotiate degrees of meaning (topology of graduation). With respect to legal reasoning, graduation makes it possible to frame legal issues as matters of degree. Graduation does not make new meanings, but allows writer and reader to enter into a dialogue about the degree of experiential and interpersonal meanings.

notion that there always exists a variety of alternative positions one might take up with respect to a single phenomenon. The system of engagement is a systematic semantic map of the different ways in which 'heteroglossic diversity' might be handled in discourse. There is a delicate balance here between 'monoglossic' utterances assuming reader alignment and 'heteroglossic' utterances acknowledging alternative positions. For instance, are the possible views of others *acknowledged* or *ignored*? If acknowledged, are they *embraced* (through dialogically *expansive* wording) or *dismissed* (through dialogically *contractive* wordings? If embraced, how are the alternative views embraced? And, if dismissed, how is the dismissal done?

From the many categories of heteroglossic engagement identified by White (2003), the following, in my opinion, are particularly useful as we develop a dialogic account of authority in domain name arbitration. Panelists are bound to make a pronouncement, so they construct their decisions little by little as they take a stance on the different issues of the dispute, using either dialogically expansive strategies or dialogically contractive strategies.

3.1. Dialogically expansive strategies

With these categories panelists acknowledge the existence of viewpoints/positions that are different from those that they are forwarding in their text, and also embrace the viability of these diverse viewpoints, and therefore expand the potential for dialogue. Panelists acknowledge the existence of such a multiplicity of viewpoints using dialogic utterances and position themselves as participating members of a wider community of practice. Those strategies are most prominent in the 'Parties' contentions' and 'Discussion and Findings' sections of the decision. Focusing specifically on sites of heteroglossic engagement in panelists' writing, those sections can be read as sites of dialogue on two levels: a) between the panelist and the parties; b) between the panelist and the wider disciplinary community of practice. How this level of dialogicity operates can be illustrated with a number of extracts from the 'Parties' contentions' move of the administrative panel decisions under scrutiny. For instance, in Case D2007-

0477 (Borges, S.A., Tanio SAU v James English), the panel gives voice to both parties as if trying to show that the writer's participation in the dialogue of a wider community of practice. All the extracts address the matter at issue and touch on the three criteria established by WIPO regulations: identical or confusingly similar, rights of legitimate interests and bad faith. In the text, the panellist gives voice to the Complainant and seems to fully support his position:

(1) The Respondent acquired the disputed domain name, even though he has no relevant trademark. The Complainant's trademark has become famous in Spain and other countries. The disputed domain name is identical to the Complainant's BORGES mark. The fame of that trademark increases the likelihood of confusion. (WIPO D2007-0477: 3).

About rights and legitimate interests of the parties, the panel finds that:

(2) there is no doubt about the Complainant's legitimate rights, but there is no less doubt about the lack of the Respondent's rights or legitimate interests. The Complainant emphasizes in this connection its heavy investment in marketing associated with its mark [...]. The objective of the registration appears to have been to profit from the disputed domain name by selling it, or to take advantage of the Complainant's well-known trademark, to confuse and divert internet users to the Respondent's website or other sponsored links for commercial gain and to the detriment of the Complainant. (WIPO D2007-0477: 3)

Again, the panelist seems to support the Complainant's position. However, in the next paragraph, the panel seems to be of the opposite opinion:

(3) The Respondent has rights and legitimate interests in the disputed domain name. The Respondent is an avid reader of the author José Luis Borges. The Respondent intends to use the disputed domain name in connection with a website relating to that famous author. (WIPO D2007-0477: 4)

Concerning good faith,

(4) there is no doubt that most consumers would immediately identify the 'Borges' name and relate it to the Complainant. The Complainant markets its

> products extensively, and has agents in over 100 countries. The Complainant vigorously defends its intellectual property rights. Its BORGES mark is registered on the principal register of the USPTO. The first use of its mark in commerce in the United States of America was in 1983 [...] The Complainant also has a strong presence on the Internet, such that it was (among other circumstances) impossible that the Respondent was not aware of it. (WIPO D2007-0477: 12)

Again, the panelist' argument is in line with the Claimant's way of arguing his case.

Respondent's voice may be identical or confusingly similar:

(5) The disputed domain name is not identical to the Complainant's trademark. That mark is a word and design mark. Previous administrative panels have found that disputed domain names are not identical to word and design marks. (For example, MAHA Maschinenbrau Haldenwang Gmbh & Co. KG v. Deepak Rajani). (WIPO D2000-1816: 6)

Here the panelist seems to take the Respondent's position and refers to a previous administrative decision backing that position.

As regards rights or legitimate interests, the Respondent has rights or legitimate interests in the disputed domain name. The Respondent is an avid fan of the author Jorge Luis Borges. The Respondent intends to use the disputed domain name in connection with a website relating to that famous author. Indeed, the Respondent provided various evidence of his interest in the author, including as a student of Spanish, photographs of his collection of Borges' works, and emails with another – who also provided a declaration relating to this case – concerning the author.

The Complainant has wholly missed the point of the 'no rights or legitimate interests' element of the Policy. In the words of a previous panel, the Complainant appears to believe that:

(6) because its marks are famous and the Respondent knows of them, the Respondent could never have rights or legitimate interests in respect of domain names that wholly or partially incorporate those marks. Stated that broadly, the argument must be mistaken, for the entire point of the second element of the test is that it is quite possible for two, or even many, persons or entities to have rights or legitimate interests in respect of the same domain name. This

element of the Policy is designed to weed out such cases […]. (FMR Corp. v. Native American Warrior Society, Lamar Sneed, Lamar Sneede, WIPO D2004-0978: 4)

As regards bad faith:

(7) The Respondent did not register the disputed domain name in bad faith. The Respondent had no actual knowledge of the Complainant. None of the advertising provided as evidence by the Complainant was published in the United States of America, and so would not have been accessible to the Respondent. There is insufficient evidence to show that the Respondent registered the disputed domain name in bad faith, in any of the circumstances set out in paragraph 4(b) of the Policy. (WIPO D2004-0978: 5)

In these examples, engagement works both to meet readers' expectations of inclusion and to rhetorically position them by capturing their attention and focusing them on key issues. Basically, engagement features are important as they offer insights into writers' perceptions of audience and into the ways that the current text is aligned with other texts (Bakhtin 1986). In other words, writers address an audience by drawing on their knowledge of earlier texts to shape writing so that readers will recognize intertextuality between texts.

3.2. Dialogically contractive strategies

When panelists reach this stage, they start sounding more forceful. 'Discussion and Findings' is the move where panelists start setting up their argumentative rhythm by embracing or dismissing the different arguments that were put forward by the parties. The writing of this section of the award is constrained both by the Policy and by Rules and Regulations (bureaucratic discourse), because Rules instruct the Panel as to the principles they have to use in determining the dispute.[5]

5 "A Panel shall decide a complaint on the basis of the statements and documents submitted in accordance with the Policy, these Rules, and any Rules and principles of law that it deems applicable" (paragraph 15 (a) of the Rules)". "Paragraph 4 (a) of the Policy requires a Complainant to prove that: a) the domain name is identical or confusingly similar to a name, trademark or

Once the parties themselves have argued their cases, panelists construct their arguments in their own words and warn that certain contentions were only the parties' contentions. With these strategies in mind, panelists acknowledge viewpoints contrary to the one being forwarded, but do so in a way that dismisses them as less viable (White 2003). Because one particular position is being privileged over its alternatives, the dialogic potential is contracted.

3.2.1. Identical or confusingly similar

(8) The Panel finds that the disputed domain name is virtually identical to the registered trademark in which the Complainant has rights. The Complainant provided substantial evidence of those registered rights. (WIPO D2007-0477: 6)

Here the Panelist backs the Complainant's position, but he admits the Respondent's argument that the disputed domain name is not identical or confusingly similar, since the disputed domain name only includes the word element of the Complainant's mark, and this mark is a word and device mark, rather than simply a word mark. However, he contradicts this argument and admits that, in this case, the dominant textual elements of the Complainant's mark are the word 'Borges', which is prominently displayed over a device. In many of the Complainant's marks, no other text appears together with device. It is self-evident therefore that the disputed domain name is identical to that dominant element of those marks. The complainant succeeds on this first element under the Policy.

3.2.2. Rights or legitimate interests

The Panel finds that the Respondent has presented substantial and plausible evidence of his rights or legitimate interests in the disputed domain name:

---

service mark in which the complainant has rights; b) the Respondent has no rights or legitimate interests in respect of the domain name; c) the domain name has been registered or subsequently used in bad faith".

(9) The respondent claims and provides evidence that he has an amateur interest in the author Jose Luis Borges, For this purpose, the Respondent includes evidence of having obtained the disputed domain name recently, having a collection of works by the author and having discussed the author's works with others. The Respondent provided a declaration also attesting to these and other things, as well as indicating that his intention is to use the disputed domain name for a website relating to the author Jorge Luis Borges. There is no evidence that the Respondent acquired the disputed domain name for commercial gain to misleadingly divert consumers or to tarnish the Complainant's trademark. [...] For all these reasons, the Panel finds that the Respondent has established a legitimate interest in the disputed domain name. It follows that the Complainant has not established a case under this second element of the Policy. (WIPO D2007-0477: 6-7)

3.2.3. Bad faith

It is interesting to note here how the strict regulation of the WIPO's Policy conditions the way in which this panelist solves the case; in spite of the fact that he admits that it is not necessary to make it explicit that the Complainant made his case in bad faith, he does make it explicit in order to prove that he has applied the three criteria and therefore has complied with the Policy:

(10) Because of the Panel's finding above, it is not strictly necessary for it to consider whether the Complainant has made its case under this element of the Policy. Nevertheless, the Panel notes that it would also not find that the disputed domain name was registered and used by the Respondent in bad faith. (WIPO D2007-0477: 8)

3.3. Heteroglossically disengaged strategies

The final part of the decision is normally very brief and very authoritative, as can be seen in the following examples:

(11) For all the foregoing reasons, the Complaint is denied as is the allegation of reverse domain name hijacking (WIPO D2007-0477).

(12) For the foregoing reasons, in accordance with paragraph 4 (i) of the Policy and 15 of the Rules, the Panel orders that the disputed domain names 'Swa-

> rovski-onlinecheap.com' and 'swarovskioulet-online.com' be transferred to the Complainant. (WIPO D2013-0399)

Administrative panel decisions are authoritative texts that are presumed to be a clear and complete expression of the communicative intentions of their makers. By authoritative legal texts we mean those that create, modify, or terminate a legally recognized state of affairs. In many ways, these texts constitute what Austin (1962) might have called *written performatives* or what lawyers often refer to as *operative*, and this is particularly visible in the Decision move.

4. Conclusions

In this chapter I have investigated the 'integrity' of WIPO domain name arbitration practices as they are reflected in the final outcome of domain name disputes. I have identified three features especially prominent in those texts: their authoritativeness, their way of reasoning and legalese. The first two features lead us to conclude that the discourse of domain name arbitration has been influenced by the discourse and practices of litigation (all WIPO panelists have to be professional lawyers) and by the bureaucratic discourse of WIPO. The panelists' stance is very authoritative in these texts: they either deny the complaint or they order that a certain domain name be transferred to the Complainants.

I have also proposed and demonstrated that one fruitful way of exploring authority in administrative domain name decisions is to see them as being the product of two kinds of interpersonal moves: a) the assertion of panelists' voice and b) the locating of that voice within the ongoing or past 'conversations' of their discipline. This dialogic account of authority is intended to extend, not to supplant, existing approaches to the study of this phenomenon. It will thus be noticed that the ideas raised here are compatible with the work already done in the areas of attribution and intertextuality (Thomson/Ye 1991; Fairclough 1992; Hunston 1995; Groom 2000). But, as Casanave (2002) has pointed out, the way in which a phenomenon is framed for discussion impacts on how we understand it. My exploration of authority through the lens of dialogism is an attempt to frame these issues in a new way, and to offer researchers a conceptually integrated and accessible approach to the study of authority in professional writing.

The second feature (bureaucratic way of reasoning) proves that the WIPO Mediation and Arbitration Center leaves panelists very little room for manoeuver. All the decisions have to take into account the Policy, Rules and Supplemental Rules, using the three criteria mentioned (Identical or confusingly similar, Rights or legitimate interests, Bad faith). Legalese is present throughout all sections: *Claimant and Respondent, hereinafter, whereby*, expressions such as *it is the claimant who has the burden of proof.* The result is that domain name arbitration has in fact become an administrative process of adjudication, rather than an arbitration process. The balance is most of the time on the Complainant's side, which is the party that pays the fees to the Center.

All in all, we could conclude that, with the limitation of the scarcity of data presented here, all my findings point out in one direction: the discourse of domain name arbitration has been colonized, both by litigation discourse and by the bureaucratic practices of the WIPO Mediation and Arbitration Center.

References

Ädel, Annelie 2006. *Metadiscourse in L1 and L2 English*. Amsterdam: John Benjamins.

Austin, John L. 1955. *How To Do Things With Words*. The William James Lectures delivered at Harvard University. Ed. James Opie Urmson. Oxford: Clarendon.

Austin, John L. [2]1975. *How to Do Things With Words*. James Opie Urmson / Marina Sbisà. Cambridge: Harvard University Press.

Bakhtin, Mikhail M. 1986 *Speech Genres and Other Late Essays*. University of Texas Press.

Bhatia, Vijay K. 2004. *Worlds of Written Discourse*. London: Continuum.

Biber, Douglas / Edward Finegan. 1989. *Sociolinguistic Perspectives on Register*. Oxford: Oxford University Press.

Biber, Douglas 2006. *University Language: A Corpus-based Study of Spoken and Written Registers*. Amsterdam: John Benjamins.

Casanave, Christine Pearson. 2002. *Writing Games: Multicultural Case Studies of Academic Literacy Practices in Higher Education*. Hillsdale, N.J.: Erlbaum.

Conrad, Susan / Douglas Biber 2000. Adverbial Marking of Stance in Speech and Writing. In Hunston/Thompson (eds), 56-73.

Dirven, René / Johan Vanparys (eds) 1995. *Current Approaches to the Lexicon*. Berlin: Peter Lang.

Fairclough, Norman. 1992. *Discourse and Social Change*. Cambridge: Polity.

Goodrich, Peter 1986. *Reading the Law: A Critical Introduction to Legal Method and Techniques*. Oxford: Blackwell.

Groom, Nicholas. 2000. Attribution and Averral Revisited: Three Perspectives on Manifest Intertextuality in Academic Writing. In Thompson, Paul (ed.) *Patterns and Perspectives: Insights for EAP Writing Practice*. Reading: University of Reading, 15-26.

Hunston, Susan 1995. A Corpus Study of Some English Verbs of Attribution. *Functions of Language* 2/2, 133-158.

Hunston, Susan 2000. Evaluation and the Planes of Discourse: Status and Value in Persuasive Texts. In Hunston/Thompson (eds), 176-207.

Hunston, Susan / Thompson, Geoffrey (eds) 2000a. *Evaluation in Text. Authorial Stance and the Construction of Discourse*. Oxford: Oxford University Press.

Hunston, Susan / Thompson, Geoffrey 2000b. Evaluation: An Introduction. In Hunston/Thompson (eds), 1-27.

Hyland, Ken 1996. Writing without Conviction: Hedging in Science Research Articles. *Applied Linguistics* 17/4, 433-54.

Hyland, Ken 1998. *Hedging in Scientific Research Articles*. Amsterdam: Benjamins.

Hyland, Ken / Sancho Guinda, Carmen (eds) 2012. *Stance and Voice in Written Academic Genres*. Basingstoke: Palgrave MacMillan.

Lakoff, George / Johnson, Mark 1980. *Metaphors we Live By.* Chicago: University of Chicago Press.

Martin, James.R. / White, Peter R. 2005. *The Language of Evaluation. Appraisal in English.* Basingstoke: Palgrave MacMillan.

Matsuda, Paul Kei / Tardy, Christine M. 2007. Voice in Academic Writing: The Rhetorical Construction of Author Identity in Blind Manuscript Review *English for Specific Purposes* 26/2, 235-249.

Maley, Yon. 1985. Judicial Discourse: The Case of Legal Judgment. In J.E. Clark (ed.) *The Cultivated Australian.* Hamburg: Buske, 159-175.

Ortony, Andrew (ed.) 1979, ^{2}1995. *Metaphor and Thought.* Cambridge: Cambridge University Press.

Rumelhart , David E. 1979. Some Problems with the Notion of Literal Meaning. In Ortony (ed.), 71-83.

Sadock, Jerrold M. 1979. Figurative Speech and Linguistics. In Ortony (ed.), 38-57.

Schön, Donald A. 1979. Generative Metaphor: A Perspective on Problem-Setting in Social Policy. In Ortony (ed.), 124-151.

Taylor, John R. 1995. Approaches to Word Meaning: The Network Model (Langacker) and the Two-level Model (Bierwisch) in Comparison. In Dirven/Vanparys (eds), 4-26.

Thomson, Geoff / Ye, Yiyun 1991. Evaluation in the Reporting Verbs Used in Academic Papers. *Applied Linguistics* 12, 365-382.

Toulmin, Stephen.1972. *Human Understanding: The Collective Use and Evolution of Concepts*. Oxford: Clarendon Press.

White, Peter 2003. Beyond Modality and Hedging: A Dialogic View of the Language of Intersubjective Stance. *Text* 23/2, 259-84.

Ismael Arinas Pellón

Interpersonal Patent Relations: Persuasion Pointers to Novelty, Creativity, and Ownership in U.S. Patent Property Claiming

1. Introduction

Formally, patents are written for a convenient fictional audience: a person having an ordinary skill in the art (PHOSITA). In practice, lawyers such as Roberts (2007: 6-9) consider that patents are drafted for two broad adversarial audiences: the *validity people* and the *infringement people*. The first group has to be persuaded that each patent application is useful, new, and non-obvious or, in other words, valid intellectual property. The second group has to be dissuaded from commercially trespassing some exclusive ownership. Validity people double-check that patent applications describe patentable matter, that they describe this matter sufficiently for the PHOSITA, and that these descriptions are clear and supported. Infringement people are interested in knowing how much property is covered by an issued patent. Patentees may want to either control the acts of licensees or prevent the competitive activities of competitors through patents.

With the help of a POS-tagged sub-corpus of 401 U.S. patents, I will show how the interpersonal metafunction serves the persuasion strategies that patent drafters use to overcome the objections of the validity and infringement people. The identification of an unsolved problem serves to demonstrate novelty and creativity, while stance markers as well as metadiscourse are used to evaluate the deficiencies of prior art. Additionally, intertextuality is both required by patent law and an awareness of the appropriate tenor in patents. And finally, vagueness in patents plays a strategic role in the writer/reader relationship. For example, *-ble* adjectives and de-adjectival adverbs are employed to deter competitors from engineering around valid patents and, thus, claim as much property as possible.

The chapter begins with an introduction to the U.S. patent genre and its context. The next section presents the literature available on this genre, mostly for U.S. patents, and is followed by a description of my research data. The ensuing section demarcates the interpersonal features analyzed, as well as the approaches used for this purpose. The chapter concludes both with an explanation of the role of interpersonality in the patent obtention process and the proposal of further lines of interpersonality research in the patent genre.

2. United States patents in a nutshell

Article 1, Section 8, Clause 8 of the United States Constitution acknowledges the right of authors and inventors to intellectual property. The first U.S. patent was issued to Samuel Hopkins in 1790 and by the end of 2014 the total number of patents granted is expected to reach 9 million. With over 400,000 applications and more than 200,000 grants per year, the patenting process in the U.S. currently requires 7,935[1] examiners, five offices[2], and approximately two years until a final decision is communicated to the applicants.[3]

Although the Leahy-Smith American Invents Act, signed by President Barack Obama on September 16, 2011,[4] changed the U.S. patenting system from a first-to-invent to a first-to-file process in line with the rest of the world, there are still significant differences with other major patenting systems. One of these peculiarities regards what can be patented. Patentable matter at the United States Patent and Trademark Office (USPTO) is grouped under three categories: *utility* patents, *plant* patents, and *design* patents. These categories are divided

1 USPTO Performance and Accountability Report for Fiscal Year 2012, page 10. <http://www.uspto.gov/about/stratplan/ar/USPTOFY2012PAR.pdf>.

2 <http://www.uspto.gov/about/locations/index.jsp>.

3 Page 3 of the Performance and Accountability Report for Fiscal Year 2012.

4 <http://www.uspto.gov/aia_implementation/20110916-pub-l112-29.pdf>.

into more than 400 classes and around 160,000 sub-classes (USPTO: 2012: 1-3).

Utility patents include devices, compositions of matter, and methods to manufacture them. Interestingly, software and fiscal strategies to pay less tax (U.S. Patent Class 705/36T) were admitted as patentable matter by considering them business methods. Although business method patents are very controversial (Jaffe/Lerner 2004, Bessen/Meurer 2008, Vee 2010), only Class 705/36T patents (fiscal strategies) have been withdrawn as patentable matter with the Leahy-Smith Act. Another idiosyncratic interpretation of what constitutes patentable inventions is exemplified by the U.S. Supreme Court's acceptance in 1980 (Diamond v. Chakrabarty, 447 U.S. 303, 206 USPQ 193)[5] of microorganisms produced by genetic engineering as a type of composition of matter. A later Supreme Court ruling (June 13th, 2013 Association of Molecular Pathology v. Myriad Genetics)[6] reinterprets Diamond v. Chakrabarty and restricts the patenting of DNA to cases where synthetic genetic material produces alternative effects to those caused by natural DNA. Plant patents were introduced by the Patent Act of 1930 and cover new botanical varieties that have been asexually reproduced. The European Union, for example, grants an alternative protection to plant varieties under what is known as *claim plant breeders' rights* or *plant variety rights*. Design patents relate to the external appearance of an article and are only granted for a period of 14 years from the date of application. Other countries, (India, Japan, Canada, etc.) offer an alternative protection through the category of *industrial designs*.

U.S. patent examiners verify that at least some features of the invention submitted to consideration are new in relation to prior art (35 USC § 102), that the new features are not obvious modifications (35 USC § 103) for a person having an ordinary skill in the art (PHOSITA), that the invention is useful (USC 35 § 101), and that all this is communicated sufficiently as well as clearly. Essentially, U.S. patent applications resort partially to interpersonal features to persuade patent examiners of the novelty, non-obviousness, and usefulness of the invention seeking intellectual protection. Furthermore,

5 <http://digital-law-online.info/cases/206PQ193.htm>.
6 <http://www.supremecourt.gov/opinions/12pdf/12-398_1b7d.pdf>.

subtle interpersonality strategies aim to reduce competitors' chances of finding unprotected gaps in the property claimed by the patentees (Zaby/Heger 2013). Bazerman (1997) tells us that patents are macro-speech acts that 'constitute value' or more bluntly said: a way of transforming your ideas into money (Bazerman 1994). This transformation process requires initially persuading patent examiners of the novelty, non-obviousness, and utility of an invention. Nevertheless, the process may extend beyond the patent grant as other stakeholders may want to contest the validity of granted intellectual property. In that case, court judges are the audience that needs to be persuaded of the felicity of a contested patent.

3. Previous research on the patent genre

In comparison to other research genres such as journal articles, patents have received little and fragmented attention from scholars in linguistics. As a consequence, interpersonality in patents remains an unexploited line of research. The existing research on patents has focused on the following aspects: diachronic studies of scientific discourse, description of the genre for translation purposes, contrastive studies between language pairs, legal research from a linguistic perspective, and genre analysis. The available literature on *diachronic studies* of *scientific discourse in patents* is restricted to two authors: Charles Bazerman and Katherine T. Durak. Bazerman's (1999) seminal work includes U.S. patents among a collection of other genres involved in the process of transforming an idea into profitable property. This work is the culmination of some previous research (Bazerman 1993, 1994, 1997, 1998). Bazerman (1999) has proposed we should consider patents as a macro-speech act of request whose success fixes both a property and a description of an innovation. Durack 1997, 2003) has studied patents from a feminist point of view (looking at the difficulties for certain published artifacts to become patentable matter at the beginning of the 20th century. She has also presented the untapped research opportunities that U.S. patents offer within the field of technical communication both from a diachronic and a synchronic point of view (Durack 2001, 2004). In addition, she has analyzed how the presentation of tacit knowledge in patents changed after the elimination of the requirement of submitting models along with patent applications. Finally, Durack (2006) has looked at the historical role that patents have played in the transfer of technical knowledge in comparison to the peer review system and the publication of journal articles.

The literature devoted to the linguistic description of patents for translation purposes follows two main lines that are relevant for this study: (a) the *description of U.S. patents*; and (b) *the description of British patents*. There is another line of research which tangentially concerns my research: descriptions of patents in other languages (German, Italian, French, Spanish). This last trend either deals with descriptions of the document or presents contrastive studies between pairs of languages. There are very few authors who have specifically described U.S. patents for translators or from a translator's point of view. These descriptions tend to provide some basic background information about patents, describe their heading-structure, and provide some basic linguistic information about lexis and phraseology for translation purposes (Gläser 1979, 1990, 1998; Frobert-Adamo 2000; Mayor Serrano *et al.* 2008). Cross (2006) describes the types of U.S. patent translations according to the goals of these translations, but his comments are not only applicable to U.S. patents. Göpferich (1995) describes the heading structure and basic features of the British patents, which have evolved along different linguistic and legal conventions from those in the United States (Cole 2006). Again, Göpferich (1998) writes some general comments about patents as a translation genre and introduces some differences between the British and North American patent document structures. In a more restricted approach, Meraw (1993) provides the basic structure of British and U.S. patent claims and indicates how to use it when translating patent claims into English.

I mention here some of the contrastive studies between language pairs to illustrate the range of research that has evolved from this approach. Japanese-English is the most required pair for patent translations in the United States,[7] whose most typical translation problems into American English are mentioned by Vitek (2007) and other authors, such as Carroll (2007) or Stein (1993). Carroll provides useful clues on the skills required for translating Japanese, German, French, Italian, or Spanish language patents into U.S. patent applications, and Stein carries out a contrastive analysis of nominal groups in French and German patents. In relation to Italian and German patents and user manuals, Hempel (2004) pinpoints some aspects worth a further contrastive research for translation purposes and Härtinger (2009, 2010a, 2010b) has studied the adequacy of translation memories for the job of translating between German and Spanish patents. Finally, although focused on German patents, Schamlu (1985), Liu (1988), and Wittman (1990) provide valuable insights on the rhetoric strategies in German that can be applied to the contrastive research of U.S. patents.

Very few lawyers have approached U.S. patents from an interdisciplinary approach that combines legal and linguistic views. Osenga (2006, 2011a, 2011b, 2012) advocates the inclusion of syntax, semantics, and pragmatics among the repertoire of techniques used by jurists for the interpretation of patent claims. She considers the use of dictionaries to verify the meanings of terms as a naïve strategy that obviates the important pragmatic aspects involved in the writing conventions of patent applications. Feldman (2009) essentially intends to promote a policy of clearer patent drafting by using a language that is not exclusive to patent attorneys and scientists. She particularly refers to Lakoff's hypothesis that, in order to understand a metaphor, both the emitters and the receivers of a message must share not only experiences but also the linguistic devices used to create the metaphor. In other words, to interpret some of the metaphorical language in patents, judges and juries would need to share both the legal experience and conventions that patent attorneys display in their word choices. She proposes that the language of patents should avoid isolation from *common discourse* or the language use of non-experts (Feldman 2009). Naturally, those authors who have specifically developed books for teaching the intricacies of patent application drafting have also speci-

7 The USPTO reports 85,184 utility patent applications from Japan in 2011. <http://www.uspto.gov/web/offices/ac/ido/oeip/taf/appl_yr.htm>.

fically addressed the peculiarities of *patentese* (Cole 2006, Roberts 2007, Slusky 2007).

Genre analysis applied to the synchronic study of U.S. patents also seems to be a neglected field of research. Aragonés Lumeras (2007, 2008a, 2008b, 2009) has used genre analysis as a research strategy to solve translation problems and to characterize the sub-genre of patent abstracts in Chinese, English, French, and Spanish. The corpus that she has used for her study does not contain only U.S. patent abstracts, but also examples from other English-speaking patent offices. This methodology, which may be suitable in the case of patent abstracts, is not adequate for whole patents as the linguistic conventions, laws, and communities of practice that use them are somewhat different. A more recent genre study on U.S. patents is the corpus exploration conducted by Lin/Hsieh (2010a, 2010b, 2011). This is a good example of the pitfalls of approaching a genre through the statistical analysis of its vocabulary isolated from the understanding of its purpose, audience, and the standard practices that shape it as a communication tool within a community of professionals. More recently, Lamberg (2013) has written her master's thesis on the generic features of patents based on a corpus of European patents.

Myers performed an ethnographic study of the process of patent writing (1995) and a rhetorical analysis on the strategic use of vagueness in the patent document (1996).[8] In the same research tradition, Reyman, a rhetorician, has teamed up with Burk, a lawyer, to develop a multidisciplinary research project seeing patents as a genre. Apart from the slides, video podcast, and summary of their presentation at the Intellectual Property Scholars Conference in 2007,[9] Burk and Reyman (2013) covered the formal structure of patent documents and stressed the intertextual nature of this genre.

A more specific study of the move structure of U.S. patents is Arinas Pellón's (2010). This line of research was followed by an exploratory study of description strategies in patents (Arinas Pellón/

---

8 This strategic use of vagueness is further analyzed by Zaby/Heger (2013) from an economics point of view.

9 <http://www.law.depaul.edu/centers_institutes/ciplit/ipsc/schedule.asp>. Professor Reyman confirmed personally that for the moment there is no other materials available.

Sancho Guinda 2010), an overall analysis of metaphors in patents (Sancho Guinda/Arinas Pellón 2011) and two papers on the use of vagueness in U.S. patents (Engberg/Arinas Pellón 2011; Arinas Pellón 2012). Engberg/Arinas Pellón (2011) compares the use of vagueness in U.S. legislation, contracts, and patents to see their degree of similarity. Arinas Pellón (2012) offers a detailed analysis of the vagueness strategies in patents according to Channell's (1994) classification of vague language, and Sancho Guinda (2012) establishes the key role of metadiscourse in achieving flexibility within U.S. patent texts.

4. Corpus data

Within U.S. patents, the rhetorical move that most depends for its communicative success on the interpersonal metafunction of language is the one *determining gaps in the prior art* (Arinas Pellón 2010), whereby patent applicants convince the PHOSITA of the utility and novelty of their invention. Therefore, from a corpus of 401 utility patents granted between 1999 and 2009 I have extracted a sub-corpus that includes only the excerpts corresponding to this rhetorical move. In future references, I will either use the expression *Gaps in Prior Art Patent Corpus* or its equivalent acronym *GPAPC.*[10] I have used two different concordancers for the purposes of this analysis: AntConc 3.2.4w[11] and TXM Platform.[12] The first one provides the keywords in both corpora and the second one is used for the rest of the analysis. For the keyword extraction, my reference corpus was the British National Corpus, which consists of 100 million words. The keyword measurement used was the *log-likelihood.* Table 1 presents the corpus general statistics as provided by TXM Platform. This software pack includes characters such as commas, parentheses, etc. in its definition of tokens.

---

10 The tokens in this corpus represent 15.33% of those in the main full-patent corpus and the types 40.5%.

11 <http://www.antlab.sci.waseda.ac.jp/software/antconc3.2.4w.exe>.

12 <http://sourceforge.net/projects/txm/?source=dlp>.

Number of documents	401
Tokens	443,380
Tokens excluding non-alphabetic characters	229,133
Types	12,722
Types excluding non-alphabetic characters	11,717
Types disregarding letter case	10,472
Type/Token Ratio (TTR)	4.57%
Token/Type Ratio	21.88
Average tokens per document	571.4
Hapax Legomena	3,158 (30.15% of all types)

Table 1. GPAPC statistics provided by TXM Platform.

By looking at TXM's initial wordlist, we can see that hyphenated strings (*high-speed*, *cylinder-by-cylinder*, *DC-to-DC*, *N-*), strings with an apostrophe (*driver'*, *user'*, *ao'*), strings of numbers or numbers and letters (*12s2*, *475Li*, *Z2241*, *YL-VAC14*, *6-membered*, *4-carboxyben-zaldehyde*), symbols or punctuation marks (\, &, ?, >, #) and strings of mixed letter cases (*AlGaAs*, *pH*) are recognized as separate types. After making the query on TXM *[word="[A-Za-z]*"]*, I obtained all the tokens (229,133) and types (11,717) that contain exclusively alphabetic characters. But this new list still regards as separate types instances of the same word with different letter case (*the*, *The*, *THE*). By performing the search *[word="[A-Z]*"]* (5,406 tokens and 1,245 types), I obtained all the strings in the corpus containing at least one capital letter. I could deduct the resulting 1,245 types from the 10,540 types of only alphabetical-string tokens, nevertheless a very little number of types only occur in my corpus containing some capitals (e.g., *Ta*, *TA* but no occurrences of *ta*). Many other tokens containing only one capital letter are hapax legomena (3,158 tokens or 30.15% of all the hapax legomena) so identifying this variant is not enough to calculate the number of total repeated types. Moreover, words with an apostrophe are treated as separate tokens from those without apostrophe (e.g.: *driver* and *driver'* are different types for TXM). And finally, TXM considers hyphenated strings different from unhyphenated and whitespace-separated versions (for example, *voltage-controlled* is seen as a different token from both *voltage* and *controlled* while other concordancers would always separate the two strings to the sides of the hyphen and count them with their corresponding tokens). These token-counting procedures point to subtle differences in the token definitions used by the different concordancing tools.

5. Interpersonality strategies in U.S. patents

As mentioned in Section 3, interpersonality in patents remains an untapped source of research. The classification of different interpersonality strategies is a controversial issue (Ädel 2005, Sanderson 2008, Ädel/Mauranen 2010), therefore, I will refer here to all the interpersonality strategies that I have found in patents, but only describe in some detail those that are related to persuading both the *validity people* and the *infringement people* of the novelty and non-obviousness of a patent, I will further discuss some interpersonal language that is aimed at claiming as much property as possible. The drafters of a patent application must write their specification with a strong awareness of tenor. They select both terminological and stylistic strategies that have proven to be effective in previous patent applications. This effectiveness depends, on the one hand, on patent examiners and court judges, who play the role of gatekeepers. On the other, on competitors and licensees, who seek to invalidate totally or partially the property rights of the patent holders. The subjective presence of the drafters in patents becomes evident when they identify shortcomings in the prior art that point to the novelty and non-obviousness of their invention. In doing so, patent applicants draft a text for a selected audience (Martin/White 2005) and use those structural, content, and phraseological standards established by the law (Bazerman 1994).

One such standard is the strategic use of vagueness. Myers (1996), Arinas Pellón (2012) and Zaby/Heger (2013) document it in U.S. patents for influencing the behavior of competitors, for disclosing only a convenient amount of information, for a persuasive use of language, and for self-protection in case of error. In previous research (2012) I have provided a detailed description of the use of vagueness in patents, but for the purposes of this chapter, I will confine my analysis to some instances of vagueness related to *property claiming, stance* (Biber/Finnegan 1989; Hyland 2005b, 2009; Biber 2006) or *appraisal* (Martin/White 2005), *metalanguage* (Ädel 2005; Hyland 2005a; Ädel/Mauranen 2010), and *intertextuality* (Bazerman 2004).

Roberts (2007), as an experienced patent lawyer, recommends patent drafters to claim the inventions as they would be found on the shop shelves. That is, to avoid drafting the patent in such a way that it is only infringed when the invention is switched on or in use. He proposes to describe moving parts of inventions with de-verbal adjectives containing the suffix *-ble*. Table 2 shows all the relevant adjectives in my corpus plus their less convenient alternative.

activatable (6) ➔ activated	magnetizable (2) ➔ magnetized
adaptable (1) ➔ adapted	mountable (1) ➔ mounted
adjustable (22) ➔ adjusted	movable/moveable (34) ➔ moving
attachable (1) ➔ attached	operable (28) ➔ operating
changeable (1) ➔ changed	oscillatable (2) ➔ oscillating
collapsible (7) ➔ collapsed	positionable (2) ➔ positioned
connectable (2) ➔ connecting	retrofittable (1) ➔ retrofitted
controllable (6) ➔ controlled	reversible (4) ➔ reversed
crosslinkable (2) ➔ crosslinking	rotatable (9) ➔ rotating
curable (2) ➔ cured	saturable (7) ➔ saturated
deactivatable (3) ➔ deactivated	separable (1) ➔ separated
decodable (3) ➔ decoded	shearable (5) ➔ sheared
detachable (18)➔ detached	shiftable (2) ➔ shifting
displaceable (3) ➔ displaced	steerable (1) ➔ steering
exchangeable (2) ➔ exchanged	submersible (1) ➔ submersed
expandable (6) ➔ expanding	swappable (1) ➔ swapped
inflatable (2) ➔ inflated	switchable (1) ➔ switched
interchangeable (6) ➔ interchanged	tunable (3) ➔ tuned
interlockable (2) ➔ interloking	variable (105) ➔ variating
lockable (4) ➔ locking	wearable (2) ➔ wearing

Table 2: Adjectives with the suffix *-ble* (with corpus frequency) versus their problematic alternatives.

Example (1), from a real patent, illustrates how the use of adjectives from Table 2 describes inventions *on the shelf*, while (2) shows an alternative problematic draft for the same description (my italics):

(1) The construction involves a device utilizing galvanometer theory where a *movable coil* rotates to an angle where the torque and a spring force are in equilibrium, [...]. (U.S. Patent 5,966,009)

(2) The construction involves a device utilizing galvanometer theory where a *moving coil* rotates to an angle where the torque and a spring force are in equilibrium, [...].

The GPAPC mainly contains references to prior patents as a means to highlight defects or lacks in existing inventions, so the use of these adjectives is an example of interdiscursivity as they are actually quotes from prior art. Interdiscursivity in patents has a clear interpersonal function. Of the six techniques of interpersonal representation that Bazerman (2004) proposes, U.S. patents apply these three:

- mentioning of prior art in the form of other patents, journal articles or other relevant references;
- using a recognizable phraseology as well as terminology typically related to this genre and its community of practice;
- evaluating the prior art mentioned to pinpoint deficiencies and property gaps.

The first use of interdiscursivity is required by the law. Title 37 Code of Federal Regulations § 1.56 (a) states that:

> Each individual associated with the filing and prosecution of a patent application has [...] a duty to disclose to the Office all information known to that individual to be material to patentability.

The final version of the patent text also includes the additional prior art references that the patent examiners have found during the prosecution process. Arinas Pellón (2010) has studied the prototypical phraseology found in U.S. patents and has found that it can be used to identify a rhetorical move that determines gaps in the prior art. The GPAPC displays the use of a very limited range of section sub-headings identifying this rhetorical move[13] (see examples 3, 4, and 5), as well as collocations that are typical of the move (see Tables 3 and 4).

13 Although some patents will show no subheadings after the main heading 'Description'.

(3) Background Art / BACKGROUND ART (16 occurrences)

(4) (THE) BACKGROUND OF THE INVENTION (64 occurrences)

(5) Prior Art / Discussion of Prior Art / Description of Related Art / Description of (the) Prior Art (13 occurrences)

Disclosed	in the prior art
Found	
Known	
Offered	
Proposed	
Uncovered	

Table 3. Verb collocations with 'in the prior art'.

[...] advantages	of the invention	[...] is/are (also) described
[...] aspect[s]		[...] is/are explained
[...] background		[...] may be
[...] component		[...] may have
[...] compositions		[...] is/are to detect
[...] description		
[...] design		[...] is/are to disclose
[...] development[s]		
[...] embodiment[s]		[...] is/are to furnish
[...] essence		
[...] feature		[...] is/are to measure
[...] novel features		
[...] field		[...] is/are to prevent
[...] idea		
[...] limits		[...] is/are to propose
[...] methods		
[...] object		[...] is/are to provide
[...] objective[s]		
[...] refinement		[...] is/are to reduce
[...] scope		
[...] subject-matter		[...] makes/make provision
[...] virtue		

Table 4. Collocations of 'of the invention'.

Interdiscursivity through evaluation in U.S. patents is a central strategy in persuading the PHOSITA that the invention is remedying some unsolved problem or deficiency in the prior art, thus overlapping with the expression of stance, evaluation or appraisal. Ädel (2005) and Sanderson (2008) state that *metadiscourse* concerns reflexive linguistic expressions about the text itself or the writer's persona, while *evaluation* is the expression of the writer's stance towards something mentioned in the text. Other authors (Hyland 2010) do not make this distinction and consider metadiscourse as the choice of strategies used by writers to purposefully structure their texts, interact with readers, and indicate their standpoint regarding both what they write and their audience. Nevertheless, both views agree on the interpersonal effects of linguistic elements used for organizing a text, showing the writer's visibility, or evaluating what is being said. I will focus here on the features aimed at showing the PHOSITA the lacks in prior art inventions and the non-obviousness of the proposed new patent.

As a starting point and to search for stance markers in my corpus I have used three sources: Martin and White's (2005) sophisticated classification of evaluative language, and Biber's (2006) and Hyland's (2005a) corpus-based lists of interpersonal language used in the academia. Cautioned by Ädel and Mauranen's (2010) indication as to the interpersonal view of metadiscourse,[14] I have focused on appraisal or stance markers, checking carefully the contexts in which they are found. Biber (2006) starts his list of stance markers with modal verbs. In my corpus only *can* (996 occurrences; *cannot* 94) and *may* (589 occurrences) appear in the keyword list. They both appear mainly in contexts where they either point to a potential deficiency in prior art, a problem to be solved (examples 6 and 7), or an improvement resulting from the patentable invention (examples 8 and 9). Other modal verbs are significantly less frequent (*will*, 269 occurrences; *must*, 196; *would*, 156; *could*, 77; *might*, 20; *shall*, 1; and *have to*, 23) and only *will*, *would*, *could*, and *might* are used in relation with problems in prior art.

14 These authors note that researchers approaching metadiscourse from a broad definition tend to consider all the retrieved instances of metadiscursive lemmas and words interpersonal per se.

(6) Additionally, a creeping movement of the vehicle *can be excluded* and it *can be accelerated* immediately when releasing the brakes quickly and actuating the gas pedal quickly, [...]. (U.S. Patent 6,634,247)

(7) Such lower cetene levels *may undesirably* reduce the compression ignition quality of the internal combustion engine thereby potentially causing the engine to misfire during cold starting or cold running conditions. (U.S. Pat. 6,763,807)

(8) It *can prove particularly beneficial* to arrange one gear input shaft as a hollow shaft around the other gear input shaft. (U.S. Pat. 6,634,247)

(9) The air brakes utilize air lines which *may easily be connected* to the air brakes of a tractor. (U.S. Pat. 6,652,042)

Adjectives with the *-a/ible* suffix (119 with a total of 927 occurrences, excluding those mentioned in Table 2) are with few exceptions absent from the keyword list, but they are clearly used to show the advantages of the proposed invention (*desirable*, 111 occurrences; *favorable*, 9; *objectionable*, 3; *preferable*, 12; *reasonable*, 7; *reliable*, 19; *suitable*, 41; *susceptible*, 6; *valuable*, 3; *(non-)viable*, 6; *vulnerable*, 4). Among the adverbs marking stance and evaluation of both prior art examples and the patent described, those in Table 5 are the only ones appearing in the keyword list of the GPAPC. *Particularly* has a preference to collocate with adjectives, *typically* with verbs, and *preferably* is less selective in the company it keeps.

Particularly	*Typically*	*Preferably*
particularly beneficial 17	typically provide 8	is preferably + verb / adjective 13
particularly preferred 7	typically includes 6	are preferably + verb 5
particularly advantageous 3	typically comprises 5	be preferably + verb 3
particularly difficult 3	typically include 5	used preferably+ prep. phrase 1
particularly true 3	typically used 4	preferably + noun phrase 22
particularly useful 3	typically made 3	preferably + prep. phrase 12
particularly high 2	typically needed 3	
particularly relevant 2	typically positioned 3	
particularly simple 2	typically required 3	
particularly suitable2	typically uses 3	
particularly anti-soil 1	typically applied 2	
particularly compact 1	typically comprise 2	
particularly desirable 1	typically consist 2	

particularly efficacious 1 particularly great 1 particularly harsh1 particularly important 1 particularly intriguing 1 particularly legible 1 particularly many 1 particularly noticeable 1 particularly objectionable 1 particularly prevalent 1 particularly resistant 1 particularly sensitive 1 particularly susceptible 1	typically equipped 2 typically experiences 2 typically located 2 typically passes 2 typically require 2 typically requires 2 typically utilized 2 + 54 additional singular co-occurrences with verbs	

Table 5. Collocations for keyword adverbs marking stance.

The variety in the range of problems, lacks, and deficiencies in prior art is varied because each technology presents its distinctive technical features, and this heterogeneity calls for a wide variety of adjectives, adverbs, verbs, and nouns to describe the virtues and deficiencies of inventions. Table 6 displays 56 examples of hapax legomena adjectives, adverbs, verbs, nouns used to convey to the reader the defects of prior art. These do not appear in my keyword list due to their very low frequency. Similar results can be seen for adjectives (43 types), nouns (20 types), verbs (15 types), and adverbs (13 types) with the negative prefix *in/im/il/ir-* with frequencies ranging from 20 to 1 occurrences.

unacceptably	undesirability	unloading	unspecified
unaided	undetected	unmanned	unsprung
unaltered	undistorted	unmodified	unsteerable
unavailable	unequal	unmoved	unsubstantiated
unavoidable	unevenly	unnaturally	unsynchronized
unbalance	unfettered	unpredictable	untrained
uncertainty	unfortunately	unprotected	untwist
unclassified	unfriendly	unpublished	unused
uncoated	unintended	unrepaired	unwarranted
uncomfortably	unkempt	unrestricted	unwieldy
uncompressed	unknown	unsaturated	unworkable
uncontrollably	unlatched	unsaturation	unworked
uncritical	unlikely	unscrewing	

Table 6. Stance markers with the *-un* prefix.

Hyland (2005a) includes self-mention of the author as an interpersonality device. We can also add personal pronouns, possessive pronouns, and possessive adjectives mentioning the second and third persons as means of interaction with the readership. Table 7 shows that patents are not characterized by the use of these words, probably because the genre focuses on the invention and not the inventor. In fact, most of them appear as negative keywords (statistically far less frequent than expected in comparison with the reference corpus). The third person instances are almost exclusively plural. The third person singular references (see Table 7) address the users of the invention.

1st person singular	*2nd person singular/ plural*	*3rd person singular*
I – 1	You – 2	He – 7
Me – 0	Your – 0	She – 3
My – 0	Yours – 0	Him – 1
Mine – 0		Her – 6
		His – 22
		Hers – 0
1st person plural		*3rd person plural*
We – 7		They – 160
Us – 10		Them – 53
Our – 5		Their – 127
Ours - 0		Theirs – 0

Table 7. Occurrences of pronouns and possessives.

6. Conclusion

Interpersonality in U.S. patents not only is a sign of belonging to a community of practice, but also a standard persuasive resource to justify the need for an invention and its originality. Additionally, by being aware of tenor, patent drafters describe their invention in a way that claims as much intellectual property as possible. This is achieved by a combination of intertextuality, vague stance and appraisal markers, and textual metadiscourse. Patents persuade the gatekeepers (patent examiners or judges) of their novelty and non-obviousness through a blend of technical data and interpersonal strategies. Essentially, the interpersonal features displayed by U.S. patents are three: an explicit mention of prior art, the evaluation of this prior art to pinpoint existing deficiencies and property gaps, and the use of both terminology and phraseology which are typical of the genre. Evaluation, when aimed at underscoring the advantages of the invention, mainly recurs to the use of *-a/ible* adjectives. The use of personal pronouns is anecdotic as the genre focuses on the invention and not the inventor.

The wide range of technical fields covered by U.S. patents introduces many evaluative adjectives and adverbs. This has shown one of the limitations of using corpus keyword lists and frequency lists when analyzing stance and evaluation in multidisciplinary genres. Adjectives and adverbs used for evaluation may be discipline-dependent and thus occur as hapax legomena in a wide range of options. An analysis of the collocates of technical terms will provide a more reliable picture of how patent drafters evaluate prior art. Patents offer a wide range of further research possibilities regarding their use of the interpersonal metafunction in comparison to other coexisting genres. For example, a comparative study of interpersonal metalanguage in research articles, project proposals, and patents would shed light on how research writers may interrelate differently with different readers belonging to co-working communities of practice.

References

Ädel, Annelie 2005. On the Boundaries between Evaluation and Metadiscourse. In Tognini-Bonelli, Elena / Del Lungo Camiciotti, Gabriella (eds) *Strategies in Academic Discourse*. Amsterdam: John Benjamins, 153-162.

Ädel, Annelie / Mauranen, Anna 2010. Metadiscourse: Diverse and Divided Perspectives. *Nordic Journal of English Studies* 9/2, 1-11.

Aragonés Lumeras, Maite 2007. Translating Patents: Translative Strategies. *Proceedings of 48th ATA Anual Conference*, 30th October-3rd November, 327-334.

Aragonés Lumeras, Maite 2008a. *La contextualización de la patente.* <http://ns5.freeheberg.com/~maite/contextualizacion_de_la%20 patente-puntoycoma.htm>.

Aragonés Lumeras, Maite 2008b. Convenciones formales de patentes. In *Puntoycoma, 109.* <http://ec.europa.eu/translation/bulletins/ puntoycoma/109/pyc1093_es.htm>.

Aragonés Lumeras, Maite 2009. *Estudio descriptivo multilingüe del resumen de patente: aspectos contextuales y retóricos.* Bern: Peter Lang.

Arinas Pellón, Ismael 2010. How Does a Patent Move? Genre Analysis Has Something to Say about It. In Gotti, Maurizio / Williams, Christopher (eds) *Legal Discourse across Languages and Cultures*. Bern: Peter Lang, 313-334.

Arinas Pellón, Ismael 2012. How Vague can your Patent Be? Vagueness Strategies in U.S. Patents. *Hermes – Journal of Language and Communication in Business* 48, 55-74.

Arinas Pellón, Ismael / Sancho Guinda, Carmen 2010. Descriptive Strategies in U.S. Patents. In Heine, Carmen / Enberg, Jan (eds) *Reconceptualizing LSP. Online proceedings of the XVII European LSP Symposium 2009.* Aarhus. <http://bcom.au.dk/file admin/www.asb.dk/isek/pellon_sancho-guinda.pdf>.

Bazerman, Charles 2004. Intertextuality: How Texts Rely on Other Texts. In Bazerman, Charles / Prior, Paul (eds) *What Writing Does and How it Does it: An Introduction to Analyzing Texts and Textual Practices*. Mahwah, NJ: Erlbaum, 83-96.

Bazerman, Charles 1999. *The Languages of Edison's Light.* Cambridge, Massachusetts: The MIT Press.

Bazerman, Charles 1998. Emerging Perspectives on the Many Dimensions of Scientific Discourse. In Martin, James R. / Veel, Robert (eds) *Reading Science: Critical and Functional Perspectives of Discourses of Science.* London: Routledge, 15-30.

Bazerman, Charles 1997. Performatives Constituting Value: the Case of Patents. In Gunnarson, Britt-Louise / Linell, Per / Nordberg,

Bengt (eds) *The Construction of Professional Discourse*. London: Longman, 42-53.

Bazerman, Charles 1994. Systems of Genres and the Enactment of Social Intentions. In Freedman, Aviva / Medway, Peter (eds) *Genre and the New Rethoric*. London: Taylor & Francis, 79-101.

Bazerman, Charles, 1993. Patent Realities: Legally Stabilized Texts and Market Indeterminacies. In Hultberg, John (ed.) *The Narrative Construction of the Anxious Object: Papers from the 4S/ EASST Conference*. Göteborg: University of Göteborg, 5-12.

Bessen, James / Meurer, Michael J. 2008. *Patent Failure: How Judges, Bureaucrats, and Lawyers Put Innovatiors at Risk*. Princeton, NJ: Princeton University Press.

Biber, Douglas 2006. *University Language: A Corpus-Based Study of Spoken and Written Registers*. Amsterdam: John Benjamins.

Biber, Douglas / Finegan, Edward 1988. Adverbial Stance Types in English. *Discourse Processes* 11/1, 1-34.

Biber, Douglas / Finegan, Edward (1986). Styles of Stance in English: Lexical and Grammatical Marking of Evidentiality and Affect. *Text* 9/1, 93-124.

Carroll, Alison (ed.) 2007. *The Patent Translator's Handbook*. Alexandria, VA: American Translators Association.

Channell, Joanna 1994. *Vague Language*. Oxford: Oxford University Press.

Cole, Paul 2006. *Fundamentals of Patent Drafting*. London: The Chartered Institute of Patent Attorneys.

Cross, Martin 2006. Types of Patent Translation. In *The ATA Chronicle*, June, 13-15.

Durack, Katherine T. 2006. Technology Transfer and Patents: Implications for the Production of Scientific Knowledge. *Technical Communication Quarterly* 15/3, 315-328.

Durack, Katherine T. 2004. Tacit Knowledge in Patent Applications: Observations on the Value of Models to Early US Patent Office Practice and Potential Implications for the 21st Century. *World Patent Information* 26, 131-136.

Durack, Katherine T. 2003. Instructions as 'Inventions': When the Patent Meets the Prose. In Kynell-Hunt, Teresa / Savage, Gerald J. (eds) *Power and Legitimacy in Technical Communication. Vol.*

I: The Historical and Contemporary Struggle for Professional Status. Amityville, NY: Baywood, 15-37.

Durack, Katherine T. 2001. Research Opportunities in the US Patent Record. *Journal of Business Technical Communication* 15/4, 490-510.

Durack, Katherine T. 1997. Patterns for Success: a Lesson in Usable Design from U.S. Patent Records. In Technical Communication 44/1, 37-51.

Engberg, Jan / Arinas Pellón, Ismael 2011. The Secret to Legal Foretelling: Generic and Inter-Generic Aspects of Vagueness in Contracts, Patents and Regulations. *International Journal of English Studies* 11/1, 55-73.

Feldman, Robin 2009. Plain Language Patents. *Texas Intellectual Property Law Journal* 17/2, 289-304.

Frobert-Adamo, Monique 2000. Influence of Linguistic Patterns on the Transfer of Strategic Information: A Diachronic Study of the Rhetoric of Patent Applications in the United States. In Hager, Peter J. / Schreiber, Howard Jeffrey (eds) *Managing Global Communication in Science and Technology.* New York: Wiley & Sons, 153-178.

Gläser, Rosemarie 1998. Fachtextsorten der Techniksprachen: die Patentschrift. In Hoffman, Lothar / Kalverkämper, Hartwig / Wiegand, Herbert Ernst (eds) *Fachsprachen: ein internationales Handbuch zur Fachsprachenforschung und Terminologiewissenschaft*, Vol. I. Berlín: Mouton de Gruyter, 556-562.

Gläser, Rosemarie 1990. *Fachtextsorten im Englischen.* Tübingen: Gunter Narr.

Gläser, Rosemarie 1979. *Fachstile des Englischen.* Leipzig: Enzyklopädie.

Göpferich, Susanne 1998. Patentschriften. In Snell-Hornby, Mary / Hönig, Hans G. / Kußmaul, Paul / Schmitt, Peter A. (eds) *Handbuch Translation.* Tübingen: Stauffenburg, 222-225.

Göpferich, Susanne 1995. *Textsorten in Naturwissenchaften und Technik: Pragmatische Typologie – Kontrastierung – Translation.* Tübingen: Gunter Narr.

Härtinger, Heribert 2010a. Textsortentypische Phraseologismen und Formulierungsmuster in Europäischen Patentschriften: Kulturspezifik, Typen, Translatorisches Management. *Trans-Kom* 3/2, 209-238.

Härtinger, Heribert 2010b. Zur Maschinenunterstützten Übersetzung von Patentschriften: der Stellenwert der Internen Rekurrenz. *Fachsprachen* 32/1-2, 18-39.

Härtinger, Heribert 2009. Textsortenbezogene Linguistische Untersuchungen zum Einsatz von Translation-Memory-Systemen an einen Korpus Deutscher und Spanischer Patentschriften. *Journal for Language Technology and Computational Linguistics* 24/3, 87-112.

Hempel, Karl Gerhard 2004. La Traduzione Tecnica Italiano-Tedesco: Brevetti e Manuali d'Uso. In Cusato, Domenico / Iaria, Domenica / Palermo, Maria R. (eds) *Atti del III Convegno Internazionale Interdisciplinare su Testo, Metodo, Elaborazione elettronica.* Messina: Andrea Lippolis, 269-304.

Hyland, Ken 2010. Metadiscourse: Mapping Interactions in Academic Writing. *Nordic Journal of English Studies* 9/2, 25-143.

Hyland, Ken 2005a. *Metadiscourse: Exploring Interaction in Writing.* London: Continuum.

Hyland, Ken 2005b. Stance and Engagement: a Model of Interaction in Academic Discourse. *Discourse Studies* 7/2, 173-192.

Jaffe, Adam B. / Lerner, Josh 2004. *Innovation and its Discontents: How our Broken Patent System is Endangering Innovation and Progress and What to Do about It.* Princeton, N.J.: Princeton University Press.

Lamberg, Jaana 2013. *Genre Features of Patent Applications.* Master's Thesis. Helsinki: Helsinki University.

Lin, Darren Hsin-Hung / Hsieh, Shelley Ching-Yu 2011. Characteristics of Independent Claim: A Corpus-Linguistic Approach to Contemporary English Patents. *Computational Linguistics and Chinese Language Processing* 16/3-4, 77-106.

Lin, Darren Hsin-Hung / Hsieh, Shelley Ching-Yu 2010a. Collocation Features of Independent Claim in U.S. Patent Documents: Information Retrieval from LexisNexis. In *Proceedings of the 22nd Conference on Computational Linguistics and Speech Processing (ROCLING 2010)*, 296-310.

Lin, Darren Hsin-Hung / Hsieh, Shelley Ching-Yu 2010b. The Specialized Vocabulary of Modern Patent Language: Semantic Associations in Patent Lexis. In *PACLIC 24 Proceedings, Poster Papers*, 417-424.

Liu, Yong-Dong 1988. *Fachsprachliche Zeige- und Verweisungsstrukturen in Patentschriften*. München: Iudicium.

Martin, James / White, Peter R.R. 2005. *The Language of Evaluation: Appraisal in English*. New York: Palgrave Macmillan.

Mayor Serrano, Mª Blanca / Gallardo San Salvador, Natividad / Gómez de Enterría Sánchez, Josefa 2008. Aspectos Textuales de la Patente. *Translation Journal* 12/2.

Meraw, Leonard J. 1993. Patent Claim Translation. In Wright, Sue Ellen / Wright, Leland Jr. (eds) *Scientific and Technical Translation*. Amsterdam: John Benjamins, 109-119.

Myers, Greg 1996. Strategic Vagueness in Academic Writing. In Ventola, Eija / Mauranen, Anna (eds) *Academic Writing: Intercultural and Textual Issues*. Amsterdam: John Benjamins, 3-18.

Myers, Greg 1995. From Discovery to Invention: The Writing and Rewriting of Two Patents. *Social Studies of Science* 25/1, 57-105.

Osenga, Kristen 2012. The Shape of Things to Come: What we can Learn from Patent Claim Length. *Santa Clara Computer & High Technology Law Journal* 28/3, 617-656.

Osenga, Kristen 2011a. A Penguin's Defense of the Doctrine of Equivalents: Applying Cognitive Linguistics to Patent Law. *New York University Journal of Law & Liberty* 6, 313-358.

Osenga, Kristen 2011b. Cooperative Patent Prosecution: Viewing Patents through a Pragmatics Lens. *St. John's Law Review* 85/1. 115-175.

Osenga, Kristen 2006. Linguistics and Patent Claim Construction. *Rutgers Law Journal* 38/1, 61-108.

Roberts, Gwilym 2007. *EIPR: A Practical Guide to Drafting Patents*. London: Sweet & Maxwell.

Sancho Guinda, Carmen 2012. Flexibility Features in Patent Writing. *Ibérica* 24, 185-210.

Sancho Guinda, Carmen / Ismael Arinas Pellón. 2011. How Patent can Patents Be? Exploring the Impact of Figurative Language on the Engineering Patents Genre. *Review of Cognitive Linguistics* 9/1, 179-197.

Sanderson, Tamsin 2008. *Corpus, Culture, Discourse*. Tübingen: Gunter Narr.

Schamlu, Mariam 1985. *Patentschriften – Patentwesen. Eine Argumentationstheoretische Analyse der Textsorte Patentschrift am Beispiel der Patentschriften zu Lehrmitteln, Studien Deutsch Band 1*. München: Iudicium.

Slusky, Ronald D. 2007. *Invention Analysis and Claiming: A Patent Lawyer's Guide*. Chicago: American Bar Association.

Stein, Achim 1993. *Nominalgruppen in Patentschriften. Komposita und Prädikative Nominalisierungen im Deutsch-Französischen Vergleich*. Tübingen: Niemeyer.

Teubert, Wolfgang 2005. Evaluation and its Discontents. In Tognini-Bonelli, Elena / Del Lungo Camiciotti, Gabriella (eds) *Strategies in Academic Discourse*. Amsterdam: John Benjamins, 187-204.

USPTO 2012. *Overview of the U.S. Patent Classification System (USPC)*.<http://www.uspto.gov/patents/resources/classification/overview.pdf>.

USPTO, Office of Classification Support 2012. *U.S. Patent Classification System*. <http://www.uspto.gov/web/patents/classification/ uspcindex/front_page_preface.pdf>.

Vee, Annette (2010). Carving up the Commons: How Software Patents are Impacting our Digital Composition Environments. *Computers and Composition* 27/3, 179-192.

Vitek, Steve Vlasta 2007. Linguistic Problems with Translation of Japanese Patents to English. *Translation Journal* 11/2. <http://translationjournal.net/journal/40patents.htm>.

Wittmann, Alfred 1990. Die Fachsprache des Patentwesens. In *MDÜ. Mitteilungsblatt für Dolmetscher und Übersetzer* 36/5, 11-17.

Zaby, Aleksandra K. / Heger, Diana 2013. *The Strategic Use of Fuzziness in Patent Specifications*. Discussion Paper No. 13-043. Mannheim: Zentrum für Europäische Wirtschaftsforschung. <http://ftp.zew.de/pub/zew-docs/dp/dp13043.pdf>.

Interactions between legal experts and lay people

RUTH BREEZE

The Discursive Construction of Professional Relationships through the Legal Letter of Advice

The letter of advice is a pivotal genre in the legal profession. In practical terms, it is the standard document for conducting written communications with clients, and it is the medium through which potential legal cases are first clarified with clients and colleagues, and the routes open for legal action are mapped out. It is transactional, in that it is organised to achieve particular goals beyond the text itself, and it is relational, in that it both assumes and projects relationships between the sender and the addressee, and possibly with other parties. Like other types of transactional letter, the letter of advice is embedded in a dialogic relationship: the writer has already received information from the client, and has to discuss and return it indicating possible courses of action for the client to take. This is reflected in the structure of the letter itself: the lawyer first acknowledges the client's query, reformulates his/her problem to align it with the frameworks of the law, proposing possible interpretations or solutions, and finally resubmits the matter to the client with indications as to what actions can be taken, since the client has to make the final decision as to how to proceed. However, it is important to note that the relationship between lawyer and client is also subtly constructed and maintained through the skilled management of the linguistic resources used at each stage of the text. In particular, the lawyer uses relational features to project an appropriately authoritative professional identity and offer a suitable client role. Resources of hedging and (occasionally) boosting are also applied judiciously to safeguard the lawyer's professional reputation by delimiting the scope of what is certain and what is contingent. At the same time, a specific repertoire of lexical choices is used to establish a professional tone. In all this, it can be seen that the lawyer steers both the client and the proceedings towards what is legally possible and/or expedient, through a process of discursive alignment.

Learning to construct and maintain professional relationships through texts of this kind is a vital part of becoming a fully-fledged member of the legal discourse community. Nonetheless, the abundant published material on this topic suggests that this presents a challenging task, even for young professionals whose first language is English. For the growing body of lawyers from other language backgrounds, who have often been trained in different legal cultures, writing such letters often poses considerable difficulty. This chapter discusses the legal letter of advice in terms of relational features (Hyland 2005), drawing also on genre theory (Bhatia 2004) and appraisal theory (Martin/White 2005), building on an empirical analysis of legal advice letters gathered from textbooks and professsional sources. First, I discuss the nature of the professional relationships and transactions reflected in and constructed through the letter of advice, providing an initial explanation of the letter in the light of genre theory and move analysis (Askehave/Swales 2001; Bhatia 2004). I then move on to analyse the letters in greater detail, considering the writer's stance and use of relational resources at each stage in the text. Finally, I use this analysis to develop guidelines for novice L2 legal writers.

1. Introduction

One consequence of globalization is that members of the legal profession all over the world have had to learn to cope with an increasing volume of work involving parties in or from more than one country. It is now practically essential for European or Asian commercial lawyers to be able to operate professionally in English, and to be familiar with the written genres that constitute the basic tools of the English-speaking legal profession, such as the letter of intent, the contract, the in-house memorandum, the letter of advice and the legal opinion.

However, even the most straightforward of these may cause difficulties to young lawyers whose first language is not English, and who have been trained in a completely different legal culture where such documents may be constructed quite differently, or may rarely be used. Even the basic letter of advice to a client may pose difficulties to trainees from cultures where advice is rarely written down, or the written style adopted by professionals is greatly at variance with that used in English. In this chapter, I consider the legal letter of advice as a genre which is embedded in a specific social context, that of the English-speaking legal profession and its relationships with clients. I look at the way in which lawyers steer their relationship with their client through such letters, and try to make visible the inner workings of the discourse of the letter of advice in order to develop guidelines that can be useful for non-native English writers.

The letter of advice is a key legal genre that fulfils important interpersonal functions despite its apparently impersonal features. There are two major reasons supporting this statement: first, the organisation of the text provides a systematic way of relating the facts of the case to the cognitive framework of the law, and of building a professional relationship between the lawyer and the client that may lead to future action. Second, through use of relational devices, epistemic modulation and specific lexical choices, the lawyer reinforces his/her professional role, narrowing down the range of possible actions, delimiting the responsibilities, and setting the discursive tone of the relationship.

It is generally accepted that the moves in professional texts are characterised not only by discursive purposes, but also by the use of different linguistic resources, which can be investigated using corpus tools (Biber *et al.* 2007). However, rather than quantifying all the items that might hold clues to the different interactional approaches adopted (Kanoksilapatham 2007; Biber *et al.* 2007), the present study focuses specifically on three areas of language that are particularly significant in interpersonal terms: the use of personal pronouns, hedging and boosting, and choice of adjectives. As I have already advanced, these are first quantified in each move using corpus tools, and are then examined in context in order to determine their pragmatic functions and find pedagogical applications.

2. The structural framework

In terms of organisation, the letter of advice bears a strong resemblance to other legal genres. In its overall rhetorical structure, it shows the imprint of the well-known 'IRAC' structure that underpins much legal analysis, from law school exercises to high court judgments (Calleros 2002: 73). The 'IRAC' structure, which is a staple of legal training in common-law countries, provides a logical, organised way of approaching what is intrinsically a complex task. Basically, it means that legal analysis should begin by identifying the Issue. It is then usual to state the Rule and explain the Application of the rule to the case at hand. The process ends with a Conclusion. Although this may seem something of an oversimplification, it is a time-honoured heuristic means to help lawyers organize their analysis, which inevitably shapes their approach to many different areas of work. The letter of advice is no exception, but we should note that its structure also has to make room for other elements. On a practical level, we could say that it needs to make space for elements such as facts, disclaimers, and so on, and all this needs to be sandwiched inside a specific interpersonal framework made up by the first and last paragraphs of the letter. Viewed from the perspective of engagement analysis (Martin/White 2005), the writer needs to reposition the essentially theoretical analysis provided through the IRAC structure within an ongoing dialogue, situating it within a framework that is geared towards action.

If we analyse the genre moves (Swales 1981, 1990) of a typical legal letter of advice, our results will produce the structure detailed in Table 1 (names changed and sections shortened). In most examples, the sections of the letter are identified with headings (Issues, Facts, Analysis, Conclusions), which are presented in bold and may be numbered. For reasons of clarity, lengthy letters of advice may also include a 'brief answer' or 'executive summary' move between moves 1 and 2, in which the writer's main conclusions are synthesised before the full analytical procedure is set out. It should be noted that aspects such as the heading, salutation and closing are obligatory structural elements, but cannot truly be described as moves (Shaw 2008).

Heading	Re: Bone Ltd.'s possible breach of contract on the Crown project.
Salutation	Dear Mr. Devonport
Move 1: state issue	You have asked us to advise you concerning whether Bone Ltd. breached the contract with your company, Devonport Ltd., by using Snark roofing tiles instead of Tronder tiles when building Crown Hotel, and whether you should sue Bone Ltd. for breach of contract.
Move 2a: state facts (optional Move 2b: disclaimer)	The advice in this letter is premised on the following facts. You contracted Bone Ltd. to build Crown Hotel in June 2012. The construction plans clearly state that Tronder tiles were to be used throughout. [...] Should this summary of the facts prove to be incomplete or incorrect, you should not rely on the advice provided here without first consulting us.
Move 3: analyse case by identifying rules and applying them to the facts	The construction contract plainly states that Bone Ltd. were to use Tronder tiles, and Bone Ltd. admit that they used Snark. Bone Ltd. has therefore breached the contract. However, the legal question is whether this breach is material, that is, whether it is so substantial that it deprives Devonport Ltd. of the primary benefit it was to receive from the contract.[...] In this case, Bone's breach is probably not material, because Snark tiles are generally regarded as equal to Tronder tiles in terms of quality, durability and aesthetic appearance. [...]
Move 4a: summarize conclusion Move 4b: offer advice Move 4c: indicate future actions	In summary, Bone certainly breached the contract, but a court would probably find that this breach was not material. It does not seem advisable to proceed to file a suit. However, you may wish to call in an impartial expert to determine what damage, if any, the use of Snark tiles has caused.
Move 5: indicate willingness to continue professional relation-ship and arrange next contact	Please do not hesitate to contact me if you have any questions about this matter, or if any new issues arise.
Closing	Sincerely,
Signature	Camilla Crawford for Crawford, Crabtree and Snitch

Table 1. Move structure for letter of advice, illustrated with example.

This move structure provides an interactional framework which allows the lawyer to seek confirmation of the issue and the facts, to apply rules or principles to those facts, to propose solutions, either by recommending a course of action or by explaining the options and remitting the responsibility for the decision to the client, and to offer to take further action. The lawyer thus receives information, reworks it professionally, and sends it back in a new form for the client to make the ultimate choice. It is as though the lawyer exercises his/her professional skills on the material prima that he/she has been given, shaping it in line with the structures available, and then handing it over to the giver with an idea as to what is next to be done with it. As we shall see in the next section, the way language is used in each move of the letter reinforces the different roles of the writer and the addressee, as the lawyer subtly leads the client through a discursive routine in which dependency and responsibility are unequally apportioned.

3. Building and shaping relationships

In their discursive construction of professional identity, writers tend to take care as to how much they themselves are obviously present in the text. A text with large numbers of first person pronouns is generally regarded as being 'personal' in a way that a text mainly written using impersonal forms such as passives and nominalised verbs is not (Potter 1996). This is not to say that a text without personal pronouns is necessarily more objective than one in which the first person abounds: it is just that the agency of the writer is rendered invisible (Hyland 2002). On the other hand, a text with many personal pronouns is not necessarily 'personal' in the usual sense, because the *I* or *we* of the text is not the personal *I* or *we* of informal conversation, but is instead associated with the projection of a professional identity. The verbs associated with such first person pronouns contribute greatly to the picture of what the writer is overtly doing. However, there are also other devices through which writers build their textual personae. The degree of hedging and boosting in the text, in addition to any purely epistemic functions, may be used to accept or evade responsibility for what the writer is saying (Hyland 1999, 2005). The lexical choices made also help the writer to align him/herself with particular values and social expectations, contributing to the creation of the discoursal self (Ivanic 1998) and the discoursal other – who can be seen in the case of legal writing to be specifically professional discoursal selves and others. In what follows, we shall see how the lawyer, through pronominal use, hedges and boosters and lexical choices, constructs a particular professional self and other. We will thus observe how the constraints on this relationship are shaped by the exigencies of the professional context, and how the letter itself perpetuates the discourse system within which such relationships operate.

3.1. Textual roles of I, we *and* you

The role of personal pronouns has attracted considerable research attention within applied linguistics, although there is no definitive theory that can account for all their uses. In Hyland's (2005) highly influential model of stance and engagement, use of the first person is grouped as an aspect of stance, whereas second person pronouns are classed as an aspect of engagement. Although there are arguments for maintaining this division in academic genres, where second person pronouns are mainly used for rhetorical effect, it might be more appropriate to group together the use of first and second person pronouns in the case of highly dialogic genres like the transactional letter. Here, the relationship between the writer (*I, we*) and the addressee (*you*) constitutes the letter's very reason for existing, and provides the backbone onto which the thematic components of the letter are articulated. The relationship between *I/we* and *you* runs along the axis of such letters, and through it information is conveyed, actions attributed and responsibilities clarified. Table 2 shows the distribution of the pronouns *I/we* and *you* across the five moves of the letters in this corpus.

	I	*we*	*you*
Move 1 (issue)	30	17	54
Move 2 (facts)	7	7	100
Move 3 (analysis)	35	39	133
Move 4 (conc./advise/act)	24	18	32
Move 5 (next contact)	37	5	39

Table 2. Distribution of personal pronouns across moves.

In the rest of this section, I shall consider in more detail the writer/lawyer and reader/client roles expressed through personal pronouns in the advice letter. The pronouns *I* and *we* are both frequent in this corpus, although it should be noted that *we* is more common in the handbooks for L1 writers than in the L2 textbook examples, which often use *I*. Regarding their position and role in the move structure, *I* and *we* are found throughout the letters, but their functions vary through the different moves.

In moves 1 and 2, first person pronouns are mainly confined to conventional formulae, such as for the metatextual functions that the writer is performing in moves 2a and 2b, as in the following two examples:

(1) In formulating our advice on this matter, we have analysed the following questions.

(2) Should these facts prove to be incorrect or incomplete, we must ask you to contact us at your earliest convenience.

Moves 1 and 2 are extremely important in the interactional structure of the letter, because it is here that the writer establishes the consensual account of the issue and facts with the client which is necessary in order to ground the analysis and advice that follow. It can be observed that the writer effectively pre-fabricates this consensus in his/her account of the issue and facts, and then holds them up for the reader's approval in the disclaimer (move 2b). The lawyer thereby maintains fundamental control of the discourse, but also provides a mechanism which allows leeway to the client and protection for the lawyer.

Regarding the choice of *I* or *we*, it should be noted that in both the examples from the L1 handbooks and the authentic letters, *we* is generally used to express the notion that the writer represents the law-firm as an institution, thus conveying greater authority and reducing the degree of personal responsibility (Pennycook 1994; Hyland 2001):

(3) We act on behalf of Lightbown and Spooner Ltd. regarding protection and enforcement of the company's intellectual property rights.

With precisely this function of conveying the professional view of the lawfirm, *we* appears again with a greater density in moves 3 and 4 (submoves a and b), where it mainly co-occurs with verbs expressing the speech acts of advising, recommending and warning, and with reporting verbs like *summarise* or *conclude*:

(4) We therefore recommend that you take no further action without consulting us.

However, in move 4c, we again find use of *I* as well as *we*, in combination with action verbs like *draft*, *take steps*, *file* and so on. In some letters, there is a marked shift from *we*, as the dispenser of advice who takes responsibility for what is recommended, to *I* as the performer of actions, who undertakes concrete tasks like drafting complaints or filing returns:

(5) In order for us to succeed in a claim against the supermarket, we must advise you that it will be necessary to prove that the inspection system used by the supermarket was inadequate [...] I will now write to the supermarket to obtain the accident book entry.

Although our corpus contains some instances of 'inclusive *we*' (Hyland 1999) that indicate that the addressee is also implied, such examples are far from common:

(6) The purpose of this letter is to summarise the issues we discussed and outline the steps that need to be taken.

While the use of *I* and *we* establishes a professional persona for the lawyer, the use of *you* sets up a role for the client that he/she is expected to accept. The letters of advice in this corpus had a high density of *you* pronouns, particularly in moves 2 and 3. In reality, the facts (move 2) are frequently framed as that rare phenomenon, a story told in the second person:

(7) You were in the store doing your weekly shopping. You walked round the corner from the meat counter into the aisle containing detergents, and you slipped on something on the floor.

The *you* narrative of fact is interesting in two ways. First, it must present a story with which the client can identify. And second, it begins to align the events of the case with possible legal categories, so that the *you* subject is eased into the role of 'injured party' which he or she will be understood as in legal terms. As the narrative here is purified of anecdotal detail, what remains is the bare story, the essential facts which may – or may not – come to match with the interpretations available under the law.

Although *you* often figures prominently in move 2 (facts), it is also extremely common in move 3 (analysis), which revisits the facts in some detail, draws out their possible legal implications, and tentatively reidentifies the client in terms of legal categories:

(8) You may inadvertently have breached the contract by […].

Moves 3 and 4 also contain *you* as the subject of possible future legal action. When this is the case, there is an emphasis that it is the client, not the lawyer, who will take the responsibility for such action. Interestingly, the modal verb often used to open this possibility is *may*, which has strong legal connotations of permission and therefore almost suggests that the laywer is allowing his/her client to take this particular action (Belotti 2010):

(9) You may wish to sue the breaching party.

Similarly, *you* may sometimes be the subject of actions that are recommended by the lawyer in move 4c. Again, the responsibility for carrying out the real action is also left with the client. Use of the modal *may* leaves the responsibility with the client, although the action is discursively validated by the lawyer, while use of *must* both stresses the lawyer's authority and indicates that he/she accepts some of the responsibility for the action:

(10) You must first inform the tenant that the sum is overdue.

You is also often the object of verbs of advising (see above), as in the following typical example:

(11) We therefore advise you to wait until further evidence can be obtained.

Table 3 shows the most typical verbs with *I/we* and *you* subjects across the five moves of the letter.

	I / we	*You*
1	write, give advice, advise, provide advice	ask for advice, inform, ask, request, ask for information,
2 a b		verbs of action (narrative of fact) not rely, inform, contact
3	Advise	may / may not / must legal verbs of action (sue, terminate, etc.)
4 a b c	summarise, outline, explain, inform propose, suggest, recommend, warn, support, believe, conclude, be quite confident, attach, research, make arrangements, take steps, draft, weigh up	have the right, may, must legal verbs of action: not accept, refuse, agree, be aware, file make decision, submit, pay, authorise, inform, consult, file, notify
5	await, assure	contact, call, write, indicate

Table 3. Verbs found with *I / we* and *you* subjects.

What is perhaps most striking about the high incidence of personal pronouns *I*, *we* and, particularly, *you*, in these texts is the way that the letters manage to be intensely interactional without being personal in the usual sense. As we have seen, *I* and *we* are generally vested with professional authority, while *you* is constructed as a person who has asked for guidance. Yet *I* and *we* often leave the main decision as to what is to be done to the client, so responsibility for future actions often resides with *you*. This unequal discursive relationship, which bears a certain resemblance to that found in other types of professional interaction, cannot be accounted for in terms of the pronominal system alone. In the next section, In what follows, I shall look at other factors which help to anchor the professional identities of both writer and addressee and set the parameters of the relationship.

3.2. Asserting truth and leaving room for doubt

One essential aspect of a writer's stance is the way he/she uses the resources of hedging and boosting. Hedges are not common in this sample of letters, and degrees of uncertainty are mainly expressed through modal verbs rather than adverbs or adjectival constructions. The frequent *if* constructions, particularly first conditionals with *will* or *may*, might be construed as being related to the phenomenon of hedging, since they are used to limit the probability, possibility or advisability of some event to a particular set of circumstances. Boosters are even less common than hedges, and both phenomena are unevenly distributed across moves. Table 4 shows the distribution of modals and *if* across the five moves.

	if	*will*	*would*	*could*	*may*
Move 1	2	5	4	0	0
Move 2	1	2	0	1	0
Move 3	52	31	21	13	10
Move 4	11	12	9	3	1
Move 5	14	10	6	3	0

Table 4. *If* and modal verbs in the five moves.

In particular, it is noticeable that moves 1 and 2 contain very few hedges, while in moves 3 and 4 there is some hedging as regards future actions and outcomes. I shall examine the use of hedging, and the occasional instances of boosting, in more detail.

In moves 1 and 2, what is sought is maximum clarity and maximum certainty. The salient circumstances of the case are stripped of inconsequential detail and reduced to basic facts, often told using discourse markers that indicate chronological order (*first, later, then*), and occasionally, causal relationships (*therefore, due to*). Hedging is mostly absent, precisely because the function of these moves is to establish what is really known (and not what may perhaps be the case).

Move 3 contains no hedges when stating rules or precedents. The lawyer has been consulted for his/her professional expertise, and so it is definitely not appropriate for him/her to say that the contract "might not commit you to a definite term of employment" or that a particular law "could mean that you have to pay a fine". After all, the lawyer has been hired for his/her professional advice because he/she is supposed to be an expert in the law and to know what the law means. Thus lawyers express certainty when they are talking about points that are certain, such as what a contract states or what the law provides. Hedging does occasionally appear when the writer is weighing up the likelihood of a particular future outcome ("the breaching party could claim", "it is unlikely that the judge would find", "we may be reasonably certain that the company will not sue").

However, move 3 often does have a somewhat tentative air to it, partly because of the high frequency of *if* constructions (especially first conditionals with *will* and conditionals with *may*: "if you wrongly withhold payment, you may yourself be liable"). The *if* construction enables the lawyer to set out the possibilities or options with maximum clarity. This serves to establish limits and demarcate concepts. This is not a hedge in the general sense of the term, but it is a way of indicating where the lines are drawn, so that the client can perceive how matters stand with regard to the particular case at hand, and whether or not the issue is clear-cut. Thus the lawyer does not write "the breach may be material", which is open to doubt, but rather states when the breach is or is not regarded as material in legal terms:

(12) The breach is material if it is so substantial that it robs the party of the primary benefit expected from the contract.

Move 4 often offers a tentative summary (move 4a) through which the lawyer uses hedging to protect him/herself from the consequences of an inaccurate prediction ("in short, a court would probably find"). Since the principal function of this letter is to provide advice, the advice is then given (move 4b), but may also be hedged, either by use of modal verbs ("the judge may find"), some variation on the theme of likelihood ("the court will probably rule"), or in some stronger form when the lawyer considers that a particular step entails a grave risk ("it would be risky to file a suit", "you would have difficulty proving"). The few boosters encountered in these letters are also found in the recommendations section ("I strongly recommend you to settle the bill without delay"). It must be underlined that the final stage of move 4 (move 4c), namely to indicate future action, is usually not hedged. Where the decision is left to the client, this is again made clear using *if* constructions ("if you indicate that you wish to proceed, I will draft the complaint"). The instances of *may* and *could* found in this move express optional actions recommended by the lawyer to the client ("in the meantime, you could also").

Hedging is thus mainly found when talking about the future, and its function seems chiefly to be to avoid commitment: predictions of outcome are often hedged, as are recommendations for further action. Boosters are uncommon in this corpus, and are also associated with recommendations. There is thus a notable difference between the type of hedging (and boosting) encountered in legal letters, which is used to modulate the advisability of taking an action or the probability of success in court, and the hedging and boosting found in, say, academic writing, where hedging and boosting are used to attenuate or strengthen truth claims within the paradigm of moving gradually closer to the truth. In legal letters of advice, hedging fulfils a significant professional function, protecting the lawyer from the consequences of particular actions and maintaining a certain distance from the client's final decision.

3.3. Maintaining a professional tone

Two devices by which writers can modulate the tone of the text and convey their attitude to what they are discussing are evaluative adjectives and adverbial attitude markers (Hyland 1999). Here we shall look first at the adjectives that occur in these letters, and then at the adverbials. The type and distribution of adjectives within the letters both embody and project the professional values of the writers but these adjectives are rarely descriptive – in the recital of facts (move 2) and the analysis of the case (move 3) unless the information they convey is pertinent to the case:

(13) The impact of the vehicle made a large hole in the garage door.

The facts are thus told and discussed without the type of embellishment with detail that might characterise conversational or media narrative, and actually most of the adjectives found in this corpus are evaluative rather than descriptive. Within the move structure, by far the greatest number of adjectives in this corpus are found in the summary/advice moves (move 4a and 4b), where their main function is to evaluate the different options and their likely outcomes:

(14) In short, although the idea of suing the breaching party immediately may seem attractive, it would probably be wiser to try to settle out of court.

Interestingly, if we analyse the evaluative adjectives from move 4 in the light of the Appraisal framework (Martin/White 2005), they almost all fall within the category of appreciation. For example, the frequent adjectives *important* and *significant* used to describe facts, arguments or points can both be classified as belonging to the area of "appreciation: reaction: impact", because they are the writer's assessment of the impact of a particular fact or point on the development of the case. Other frequent adjectives often used in combination with recommended courses of action could be classified as "appreciation: quality: positive", such as *advantageous, attractive, safe, wise*, which indicate that the writer wishes to ascribe a positive quality to a particular action. Finally, the third subtype of appreciation that is frequently represented is "appreciation: composition: balance and complexity": arguments or scenarios were described positively as *clear* or *plain*, or negatively as *misleading*.

What is striking about these patterns is not so much the presence of adjectives of appreciation, as the absence of other types of evaluative adjective. These writers hardly ever apply adjectives from the range of 'affect' or 'judgement'. This is an essential feature of the persona created in the letter. Not only is the writer concerned to be unemotive, placing people and events in terms of factual events and legal relationships. The writer also refrains from judging people, and chooses instead to state facts and assess the wisdom/correctness/ appropriacy of people's actions. The writer is therefore highly unlikely to say that "Bayer is a bad worker", but is careful to state that "Bayer arrived late for work seventeen times in the month of November", or "Jones may have acted imprudently". In this way, the writer maintains a professional tone and sets the parameters of his/her relationship with the client and the other parties. The lawyer assumes a critical, knowledgeable voice, using adjectives belonging to the category of appreciation to convey a sense of distance and objectivity (see Breeze 2012).

Adverbs such as *unfortunately* and *hopefully* also play a role in setting the tone of the text and building common cause with the reader. In this corpus, such instances were rare, but when they occur, the purpose of forging a bond with the reader is clear:

(15) You are understandably concerned about this situation and wish to know what options are open to you.

In short, the letters appear to make regular use of a specific and limited range of evaluative adjectives, particularly when weighing up future actions and their likely consequences. In this, the lawyer both projects a persona that is prudent and judicious, and protects him/ herself from the possible consequences of a wrong prediction. On the other hand, in his/her appraisal of different arguments, he/she is mainly concerned with grading importance and with assessing the coherence of arguments or explanations.

3.4. Defining professional voices

The issue of knowing when to hedge and when not, when to appraise and when not, and how strongly writers should express themselves, is a matter of professional judgement. Legal writers need to know which voice to use, and in which move. On the basis of the study of hedging, boosting and evaluative language outlined above, three distinct voices can be identified in these letters, each of which appears to instantiate a different evaluative key (Martin/White 2005: 164):

- An 'informer' voice, in which the writer states the facts and says what the law is. The informer voice is confident of what it says and does not hedge. Because the informer voice predominates, it sets the authoritative tone of the letter. As much of the content as possible is conveyed in the informer voice.
- An 'appraiser' voice, in which the writer evaluates different arguments and actions and makes tentative predictions about what is likely to happen. The appraiser voice uses modality and adjectives to assess how convincing the arguments are, how sensible a particular course of action might be, or how likely a particular outcome is. The appraiser often hedges these propositions. The appraiser voice speaks with an appropriately measured professional tone and is used to assess arguments and courses of action. It is not used to talk about things that are certain (the informer voice is used for this), or to judge people (none of the voices does this).
- A 'directive' voice, in which the writer asks the client for confirmation that the facts are correct, or tells the client what he/she needs to do next. When using the directive voice, the writer makes courteous use of imperatives.

The informer voice prevails in moves 1 and 2, although the directive voice appears if there is a disclaimer at the end of move 2. The informer voice also plays the major role in move 3. Here, however, the appraiser voice is also brought into play: once the informer has stated what is known, the appraiser can evaluate the situation and offer suggestions. Move 4 begins by informing, then appraises as appropriate, and ends with intentions or instructions which may contain the use of directives. Move 5 is generally a conventional indication of willingness to continue professional relations. It should be borne in mind that all the voices are highly relational, directed from *I* or *we* to *you* in what amounts to one encounter within the ongoing professional dialogue between the laywer and his/her client.

Within the relational structure of the letter, these voices offer the reader a specific subject position: the informer and the directive voice are categorical, leaving no room for manoeuvre; but the appraiser voice operates more subtly, persuading the reader to share a particular view of the situation, but also suggesting that the responsibility for accepting that view ultimately lies with the reader.

4. Developing guidelines

On the basis of the move structure and interpersonal elements analysed above, the following table was designed for use with L2 law students. The interactional purpose of each move is identified (the writer is *I/we*, the client is *you*).

Move	Interactional purpose What I must do. (*What I say to you.*)
1	I state the issue. (*I say what you asked me.*) *Inform.*
2 a	I state the facts neutrally, using simple past and present tenses, without judging the people or conveying emotional reactions. (*I tell you what happened and what you did.*) *Inform.*
b	I ask for confirmation of this account, sometimes using a disclaimer. (*I ask you to confirm that these facts are true.*) *Direct.*

3	I explain the rule, say how it applies to the facts. (*This is the rule. This is how it applies to the facts.) Inform.* I must explain what different things the client can do, and the likely outcome of each. (*You can do this. If you do this, this may happen.*) *Inform. Appraise.*
4 a	I summarize the main ideas from move 3. (*In short, this is my analysis of your situation.*) *Inform.*
b	I evaluate the possible courses of action and make predictions about what their outcomes are likely to be. I take care not to commit myself unless I am certain. (*This is the best thing for you to do. If you do this, this is likely to happen. You must make the decision.*) *Appraise.*
c	I say what must be done next. (*This is what happens next. You must do this, and I will do this.*) *Inform. Direct.*
5	I offer to answer any question the client has. (*If you need more information, you should contact me.*)

Table 5. Interpersonal structure of moves in the legal letter of advice.

5. Conclusions

We have seen that the relationship between lawyer and client is subtly constructed and maintained through the skilled management of the linguistic resources used at each stage of the text. As in other types of legal text, these letters are characterised by an inherent imbalance, since the writer dispenses advice, offers choices, indicates obligations, and so on, while the reader is constructed as a compliant recipient of information and recommendations. At the same time, we should not forget that in this case the ultimate responsibility for the next step is often handed back to the client, which entails greater freedom and greater risk for him/her, and reduced responsibility for the lawyer. There would seem to be nothing intrinsically sinister or unjust about this imbalance because, after all, the client has consulted the lawyer precisely in order to receive expert advice. Having said this, it is interesting that this expert-client relationship is further shaped and modulated in the course of the letter, as the client's experiences, concerns and aspirations are aligned with the framework offered by the law and appraised in the light of the lawyer's professional experience.

In particular, the lawyer uses relational features to project an appropriate authoritative yet judicious professional identity, dispense expert knowledge and build a consensual understanding of the facts and issues. Also, he/she extends a role to the client in which the real situation he/she has experienced is reformulated in terms of legal roles and relationships. Resources of hedging are also applied judiciously to safeguard the lawyer's professional reputation by delimiting the scope of what is certain and what is contingent – and simultaneously, a specific repertoire of lexical choices is used to establish a professional tone. In all this, it can be seen that the lawyer steers both the client and the proceedings towards what is legally possible and/or expedient, through a process of discursive alignment. The guidelines provided in the fourth section of this chapter are intended to go some way towards making this process visible for lawyers from non-Anglo-American legal cultures.

References

Askehave, Inger / Swales, John 2001. Genre Identification and Communicative Purpose: A Problem and a Possible Solution. *Applied Linguistics* 22/2, 195-212.

Belotti, Ulisse 2010. Unequal Discourse and the Role of Modality. In Evangelisti Allori, Paola / Garzone, Giuliana (eds) *Discourse, Identities and Genres in Corporate Communication*. Bern: Peter Lang, 283-302.

Bhatia, Vijay K. 2004. *Worlds of Written Discourse*. London: Continuum.

Biber, Douglas / Connor, Ulla / Upton, Thomas 2007. Identifying and Analyzing Rhetorical Moves in Philanthropic Discourse. In Biber, Douglas / Connor, Ulla / Upton, Thomas (eds) *Discourse on the Move*. Amsterdam: John Benjamins, 43-72.

Breeze, Ruth 2012. Appraisal Analysis of Dissenting and Concurring Opinions. In Bhatia, Vijay K. / Candlin, Christopher / Gotti, Maurizio (eds) *Discourse and Practice in International Commercial Arbitration: Issues, Challenges and Prospects*. Farnham: Ashgate, 113-128.

Calleros, Charles 2002. *Legal Method and Writing*. New York: Aspen.

Hyland, Ken 1999. Disciplinary Discourses: Writer Stance in Research Articles. In Candlin, Christopher / Hyland, Ken (eds) *Writing: Texts, Processes and Practices*. London: Longman, 99-121.

Hyland, Ken 2001. Humble Servants of the Discipline: Self-mention in Research Articles. *English for Specific Purposes* 20/3, 207-226.

Hyland, Ken 2002. Authority and Invisibility: Authorial Identity in Academic Writing. *Journal of Pragmatics* 34, 1091-1112.

Hyland, Ken 2005. Stance and Engagement: A Model of Interaction in Academic Discourse. *Discourse Studies* 7/2, 173-192.

Ivanic, Rosalind 1998. *Writing and Identity. The Discoursal Construction of Identity in Academic Writing*. Amsterdam: John Benjamins.

Kanoksilapatham, Budsaba 2007. Rhetorical Moves in Biochemistry Research Articles. In Biber, Douglas / Connor, Ulla / Upton, Thomas (eds) *Discourse on the Move*. Amsterdam: John Benjamins, 73-119.

Martin, James / White, Peter 2005. *The Language of Evaluation. Appraisal in English*. London: Palgrave Macmillan.

Pennycook, Alistair 1994. The Politics of Pronouns. *ELT Journal* 48/2, 173-8.

Potter, Jonathan 1996. *Representing Reality*. London: Sage.

Shaw, Philip 2008. Purpose and Other Paradigmatic Similarities as Criteria for Genre Analysis: The Case of '419 Scam' Emails. In Gotti, Maurizio / Gillaerts, Paul (eds) *Genre Variation in Business Letters*. Bern: Peter Lang, 257-281.

Swales, John 1981. *Aspects of Article Introductions*. Birmingham: University of Aston Language Studies Unit.

Swales, John 1990. *Genre Analysis*. Cambridge: Cambridge University Press.

Source of letters used for corpus

Brieger, Nick / Kosta, Joanna 2008. *Success with ILEC*. Oxford: Summertown.
Brown, Gillian / Rice, Sally 2007. *Professional English in Use*. Cambridge: Cambridge University Press.
Calleros, Charles 2002. *Legal Method and Writing*. New York: Aspen.
Cambridge ESOL 2006. *ILEC Handbook for Teachers*. Cambridge: Cambridge ESOL.
Chartrand, Marcella / Millar, Catherine / Wiltshire, Edward 1997. *English for Company and Contract Law*. London: Sweet and Maxwell.
Haigh, Rupert 2006. *The Oxford Handbook of Legal Correspondence*. Oxford: Oxford University Press.
Krois-Lindner, Amy 2006, 2010. *International Legal English*. Cambridge: Cambridge University Press.
Krois-Lindner, Amy / Firth, Matt / Translegal 2008, 2009. *Introduction to International Legal English*. Cambridge: Cambridge University Press.
Schulz, Nancy / Sirico, Louis 2004. *Legal Writing and Other Lawyering Skills*. Newark, NJ: Matthew Bender.

MAURIZIO GOTTI

Interpersonality in Mediation Discourse

In the last few decades Alternative Dispute Resolution (ADR) has become more and more common as an alternative to litigation for settling disputes without resorting to ordinary justice. Many factors have inspired the origin and spread of these alternative procedures, basically relying on the desire to provide a new tool to defend the rights of all those subjects that, mainly for economic reasons, could not afford long and expensive court proceedings. In certain countries, the fundamental reason was substantially the crisis of ordinary justice that was not able to provide effective and timely solutions to disputes. In general, the slow and time-consuming development of court cases and the elevated costs of traditional justice have led disputants to rely on alternative systems deemed to be more economical, faster and more efficient.

Mediation – together with arbitration and conciliation – is a typical example of ADR. This process has proved to be very successful and is now employed in many countries, where it has become an integral part of the judicial system (cf. Berger 2006). Indeed, as it implies a negotiated agreement between the parties, mediation has become a very attractive ADR option. In this procedure agreement is reached by the parties through the work of a neutral party, the mediator, who helps them analyze the true interests involved in the dispute. He/she also identifies the differences implied in the parties' respective positions, leading them towards a resolution of the dispute without imposing any decision.

In the last few years greater and greater emphasis has been laid on the mediator's mastery of the interpersonal features of the process (cf. Bush/Folger 1994; Folger/Bush 1994, 1996). While previously (e.g. Kressel/Pruitt 1989) the stress was put on the ability of mediators to deal with their cases as a problem-solving task, carefully and objectively assessing facts and circumstances in terms of problems to be solved, more recently greater attention has been devoted to the parties' emotions and feelings and the complex interaction and relationship generated in the mediation session(s). Mediators are encouraged to focus on what goes on in the room as the 'here and now' – particularly the specific statements of the parties – is what matters most for the solution of a mediation case.

1. Aims and method

Drawing on documentary data, this chapter investigates the main interpersonal strategies adopted in mediation discourse as it is shaped by its community of practice. The analysis of oral transcripts from three procedures taking place both in a traditional setting and online[1] is used to illustrate the negotiation techniques employed by mediators in the accomplishment of their professional aims. The main focus of the chapter is on the realization and distribution of interpersonal features as they appear in various moves and steps of a typical mediation process.

The analysis of interpersonality features will mainly focus on the tactics adopted by the various parties involved in the dispute

1 The online mediation sessions analysed here took place during a self-running simulation of the CAN-WINSM conferencing system and are used by Resolution Forum Inc. (<http://www.resolutionforum.org/>) as part of the training materials employed in the courses required for qualification as an Impartial Third Party in the state of Texas. The traditional international mediation process took place in Munich, and was reconstructed, recorded, filmed and transcribed for educational purposes. The video entitled *Resolution through Mediation: Solving a Complex International Business Problem* was prepared by INTA (<http://www.inta.org/Mediation/Pages/AboutADRand Mediation.aspx>) with the aim of assisting not only trainers of mediation and negotiation skills, but also disputants (and their advisors) preparing themselves for an assisted settlement negotiation. A synopsis of the three cases is presented in the Appendix.

resolution process and how these tactics are constructed in mediation discourse so as to reflect the way participants orient themselves to them. From the methodological point of view, emphasis will be given to the stance (or 'footing' in Goffman's 1979 terms) adopted by participants to orient themselves to others and thus frame the production of their utterances in their interactions. Indeed, as pointed out by Goffman, the description of interactions cannot be limited to a dyadic, speaker-hearer perspective, but should consider a variety of ways people behave in encounters, adopting different attitudes in relation to what they say.

Another important construct which lies at the basis of our analysis is that of 'face' (Goffman 1955), that is "the public self-image that every member of a society wants to claim for himself/herself" (Brown/Levinson 1978: 66). Facework can either be positive or negative: positive facework refers to the need a person feels for appreciation and approval, inclusion, and respect, which is expressed in interactions by means of such speech acts as compliments and promises. Negative facework reflects instead the degree to which a person protects his/her own freedom and privacy from interference. Effective mediators are very careful in identifying and meeting the different face needs of their disputants and adopt appropriate strategies to address them to their advantage.

As Brown and Levinson (1978) have shown, speech acts may be more or less face-threatening. Direct speech acts are seen as posing the highest threat to the parties' face, while indirect speech acts are considered the least threatening and hence the politest verbal acts. The use of speech acts has relevant consequences for the outcome of the mediation process, since when the parties' faces are threatened, there is greater tendency to withhold important information. The more indirect their approach, the less threatening the mediators will be seen by the disputing parties, and the more trustworthy and credible they will be perceived as being.

Ng (1999) has identified four main facework strategies applied to the mediation process:

1. *Face-Assertion* (or *Self-Positive Face*), which meets the need to defend and protect one's desire for inclusion and association. In mediation, parties display this concern to mediators by trying

not to appear too nasty or stubborn in their demands and by showing a reasonable and compromising attitude towards the negotiated offers.

2. *Face-Giving* (or *Other Positive-Face*), which makes it possible to signal respect for the other person's need for freedom, space and dissociation. This strategy is particularly used by mediators, who are keen to include both parties in the mediation process, assuring disputant equality and showing appreciation for the parties' positive spirit of cooperation.
3. *Face-Restoration* (or *Self Negative-Face*), which is meant to guarantee the possibility to give oneself freedom and space to protect oneself from another's infringement on one's autonomy. The preservation of one's own face may concern important decisions in the mediation process, affecting, for example, the amount and depth of information parties wish to disclose and how cooperative they want to be.
4. *Face-Saving* (or *Other Negative-Face*), which enables a party to signal respect for the other person's need for freedom, space and dissociation. This strategy may be visible whenever the mediator suggests a caucus session to protect one of the parties' autonomy and thus avoid the disclosing of information that might embarrass the other person.

Such strategies are very frequent in mediation, as will be shown by several examples found in the processes examined in this chapter. The analysis will mainly rely on the generic structure of a common procedure (cf. Gotti 2013), which can be summed up in the following sequence of moves and steps (to use Swales' 1990 well-established terms):

1. The opening move
    1.1. Introducing participants
    1.2. Specifying mediator's role
    1.3. Assuring confidentiality
    1.4. Seeking confirmation of the mediation process
2. Presenting the case
    2.1. Asking the parties to present their positions
    2.2. Asking each party to summarize the other party's positions

    2.3. Ascertaining the parties' main goals
3. Working towards a solution
    3.1. Asking for solutions
    3.2. Coping with conflicts
    3.3. Interacting in private sessions
    3.4. Dealing with emotional outbursts
    3.5. Facilitating consensus
4. The ending move
    4.1. Ensuring that the parties are well aware of the agreement terms
    4.2. Asking the parties to sign the final form

2. Establishing a neutral role

The aim of the first move of the mediation process is to introduce the mediator and give a clear presentation of the role that he/she is to perform, highlighting in particular his/her neutrality and his/her task as a settlement facilitator, not as a judge/decision-maker. This simple introductory move achieves a number of goals, because in laying out these points, the mediator:

1. Starts building a trusting relationship with each of the parties by being balanced, non-positional, open, honest, competent and positive;
2. Educates by explaining mediation goals and procedures and prepares the parties, who may be unfamiliar with the process, for what will occur, in order to avoid surprises;
3. Demonstrates competence by showing command of the process and neutrality regarding its outcome; this helps in developing the parties' trust in the mediator's abilities.

In the first step of the opening move the mediator begins the process by introducing himself, welcoming the parties, and highlighting key aspects of the mediation process. More specifically, the mediator ensures that everyone at the table is properly introduced and their capacities are known:

(1) M1[2]: Good morning hum, ladies and gentlemen, I'm happy that you're here in Munich, I hope that you had a good trip to Munich. Would you please introduce yourselves shortly?
[M1 looks towards W and P]
W: I'm Peter Tchaikovsky, President and CEO of Wonderbrandski in Russia, leading manufacturer and marketer of the alcohol products.
P: hum, I'm Alex Pushkin, I'm Peter's attorney.
[M1 looks towards A]
A: My name is D.D. Kruze. I'm President of Alcopops Inc. based in Chicago.
S: I'm here as council for Alcopops. (2:18-2:51)

This introductory phase conveys an atmosphere of minor formality and greater cooperation compared to litigation taking place in court. This difference is confirmed by certain conversational conventions, such as greetings or enquiries about well-being, which are omitted in court (Jackson 1995: 413) but used in a mediation hearing, though they are kept very brief. Indeed, although the setting and atmosphere of the mediation proceedings are more friendly than in court, they remain formal, as the mediator fears that an informal attitude might reduce the degree of detachment required by the situation and thus hinder his/her willingness to show great independence and impartiality.

In Step 2 the mediator specifies his/her neutrality and role as a settlement facilitator, not as a judge/decision-maker but as someone neutral and uninvolved,[3] by whom the parties have agreed to be guided. However, in order to be successful in his/her task, this person has to gain the parties' respect and trust. This need for trust and

2 M1: traditional mediator / A: D.D. Kruze, President of Alcopops Inc. / P: Alex Pushkin, Tchaikovsky's attorney / S: Mush Striver, council for Alcopops / W: Peter Tchaikovsky, CEO of Wonderbrandski.

3 In spite of the fact that neutrality is commonly considered a key component of mediation, the issue of strict neutrality has been called into question by several scholars (e.g. Bernard *et al.* 1984, Cobb/Rifkin 1991, Rifkin *et al* 1991, Kolb/Kressel 1994, Dyck 2000).

confidence explains why the first move of the mediation process is always devoted to a clear presentation of the role that the mediator is to perform:

(2) M1: Very well, thank you. My name is hum Peter Müller, I'm from Munich, Germany and hum I'm your mediator. I would like to introduce you very briefly into the mediation process. I'm not a judge and I'm not an arbitrator, so actually you are negotiating and I don't decide anything. I would prefer to have a joint session first, where we exchange hum the items we would like to discuss. (2:52-3:24)

As can be seen, besides adopting a self-labelling strategy (Heisterkamp 2006) by means of which he defines himself as an unbiased party, the mediator then strengthens this strategy by providing his own description of the mediation process, emphasizing the high degree of neutrality required on his part. In doing this, the mediator adopts a first-person pronominal choice so as to reduce social distance and thus sound less face-threatening and mitigate the imposition deriving from his request for cooperation. The mediator then reminds participants that the process will be confidential, and furthermore that he will not disclose to the other party any information identified by a party as confidential.

In the fourth step of the opening move, although the participants have previously exchanged working papers and are probably familiar with the mediation process, the mediator makes sure that the parties are aware of the rules of the procedure, and then asks the disputants to confirm their willingness to engage in the mediation process:

(3) M2[4]: All right, I believe we now have everyone present. Since you are familiar with our experience and qualifications, I will not go through those items with you again. Also, Janet and I understand you are both satisfied that we have no conflicts of interest that would diminish our neutrality as co-mediators in this matter. Is that correct?

T: Yes, we accept you as mediators.

R: We have present the President from R and Billy Bob Gibbs an expert engineer in land slides. We also have R lead counsel and co-counsel.

4 M2: mediator of Online Mediation 1 / T: Texas Department of Transportation / R: Roadbuilder.

M2: We assume from your quick responses that you are both agreeable to our serving as your mediators today. We also assume you have both read, agreed to, and signed the mediation agreement and that you have made the commitments of good faith negotiation, confidentiality, and willingness to stay with us that are set forth in that writing. Is that correct?

T: Yes.

R: Your assumptions are correct. Signed, sealed and delivered.

M2: Thank you. Mediation is a voluntary process through which people can tell their stories and talk about the issues with which they are concerned. We don't take sides or make decisions for you. Our role is to help you tell your story and explore ways to work out this situation. (16:39-16:46)

3. Evaluating positions and expectations

In the first step of the second move the mediator asks the parties to briefly present their positions. However, the mediator's interest is not in the mere detailed reconstruction of the facts but mainly in finding out how the parties feel about them:

(4) M2: Since we have received your written position papers, we are generally familiar with your respective legal positions in this matter. Therefore, we do not believe it would be productive to ask you to repeat all the facts you have given us in those papers. However, it would probably be helpful if you could summarize the issues as you see them. Because R's expert, Billy Bob Gibbs, is present, perhaps he would be willing to list R's main contentions?

R: We recognize that there have been some oversights made by both parties in this unfortunate situation. We believe that there were many problems some of which were the following: […] These are the most pressing issues we feel need to be addressed.

M2: Thank you, R. Now, I wonder if T would give us a very brief idea of their main position?

T: Thank you for your comments. Please allow us to respond to them in order. First, we agree the contract was liberally enforced; we do not agree the terms were not specific. Second, the worksite condition was different because of the change in season that occurred while R was delaying the start of the project. Third, the slope and drainage problem was a seasonal problem, not a design defect. Fourth, the irregular weather conditions would not have been a problem if construction had begun in the time specified in the contract. (16:48:27-17:08:07)

By asking the parties to speak first, the mediator accomplishes several objectives at once:

- The parties feel active in handling their own interests;
- Each side gets to focus on the other side's legal position;
- The legal issues are explained, and put on the table early, rather than being left unexpressed for possible interference later.

In the next step the mediator invites each side to summarize the position of the other. This has the effect of simultaneously forcing everyone to focus on the other side's case and of reducing the likelihood of misunderstandings as everyone feels that they have been heard and understood. In doing so also other objectives are accomplished:

- The parties can reflect on the positions of the other side, thereby also instinctively evaluating their own positions from another angle;
- By focusing on the other side's legal position, both parties realize that there is some credible argument on both sides.

In this way the mediator tries to get the case onto the relational path and away from strict legal rights and interpretations of the dispute. To favour this process of 'clearing the ground', the mediator summarizes the legal positions of the parties and asks them to confirm the plain facts as they have been reported. To stress his/her neutral position, the mediator frequently uses tentative verbs and hedging expressions when reporting the facts (*"we understand that", "it also appears", "may depend", "it seems"*). Although his/her report is totally neutral, it does not avoid mentioning the controversial points still open; the fact that these points are presented in a very objective way, however, represents a useful starting point for the following phase of the mediation process:

(5) M2: Summarizing your respective views, we understand that T feels that R's delay in getting started was the primary cause of the many problems

> experienced, and that R attributes the cause to the design problems and to the different worksite conditions. It also appears from your position papers that clarification of the facts may depend upon the testimony of a person who is not currently available. So, it seems, we have some difference in our recollections and some uncertainty about the facts? (17:08)

This move is also meant to verify what result the parties expect from the mediation process. Since parties may be reluctant to disclose information that weakens their own insistence on positions, the mediator must often dig for such information and will typically start such inquiry with open-ended questions. The questions typically used by mediators include: "*What do I need to know to understand this matter?*" or "*What do you hope to get out of this course of action?*" and "*What is your goal in this mediation?*" This practice assures the mediator's firm understanding of the main expectations of each party and allows for the channels of communication to be opened by recognizing that not all information is confidential.

In the next move the mediator tries to get the parties to come to an agreement by focusing on concrete evidence and preventing any venting up of emotions. He/she repeatedly and specifically asks for solutions, ideas and suggestions to force the two parties to work together towards common ground. He/she also underlines any cooperative behaviour of the parties with appreciative expressions such as *"Good for both of you!", "Now we are getting well down the road"*:

(6) M2: R, do you have any specific suggestions about how the people of Texas could have their new road at no extra cost to the taxpayers?
R: Is T amenable to discussing completion of the contract with R?
T: On behalf of the taxpayers of Texas, we are willing to entertain any consideration of compromise.
M2: Good for both of you! Now we are getting well down the road, thanks to your mutual cooperative attitudes. Perhaps we are ready for some specific ideas to resolve the matter. R, do you have any ideas to share?
M2: While we await R's reply, let me ask T if it has any ideas how this matter might be resolved? (17:20-17:28)

The quotation above shows an example of the adoption of face assertion by one of the parties when he says that they "are willing to entertain any consideration of compromise", thus highlighting their reasonable attitude. The mention of the word *compromise* immediately sparks off a very positive reaction on the part of the mediators, who are quick to seize this opportunity for a possible resolution of the conflict.

It is interesting to note that, in order to underline the parties' cooperative behaviour, the mediators make a change in footing by shifting their perspective from the use of exclusive-*we* (*"we understand that*", quotation 5) expressing a personal viewpoint, to inclusive-*we* (*"Now we are getting well down the road", "Perhaps we are ready for some specific ideas to resolve the matter"*, quotation 6) so as to promote the adoption of a collective viewpoint. As they envisage some points of agreement that can be reached by both disputing parties, the mediators decide to adopt an inclusive strategy in order to suggest that a unitary perspective will be beneficial to all. The adoption of this collective stance does not hinder the mediators' neutral attitude, as no bias is shown to either disputant since their shift of footing does not affiliate or disaffiliate them with one specific party.

Besides producing evaluative statements about the positions of the disputants, a further strategy employed by one of the online mediators to get the parties to reach an agreement is to make them aware of the costs of a possible legal action:

(7) M2: Let's discuss for a minute what is likely to happen if you decide that legal action is your best alternative at this point. R, could you give us an estimate of your trial and appellate costs if you proceed with legal action? (17:14)

This move is made to lead the parties to consider whether they intend to collaborate in the mediation or not and how economically favourable a mediated solution is. The mediator must often use this move to help the parties to keep their feet on the ground and to accept that their legal position is not so strong as they think it is.

4. Coping with conflicts

When the parties present their cases, they often assert that the other side is at fault, accusing them of unfair behaviour:

(8) A: They are trying to elevate their cheap, bad vodka by trading on our goodwill and I think that's bad faith.
W: No, no, no I think they don't understand the alcohol market and I think they're crazy.
P and W: [They speak to each other in Russian, gesticulating]
A: How can you say we don't understand the alcohol market? Alcopops is one of the largest sellers of alcohol. Much bigger than Wonderbrandski, I might add.
[Overlapping voices]
A: [repeatedly pointing at W] We are here because your company deliberately traded on our goodwill and acted in bad faith. If you ask me, they are nothing less than cheap pirates!
W: Now stop, please stop that, Mr Müller. Stop. I don't want
[Overlapping voices]
M1: Hum, yes
[Overlapping voices]
W: If she uses this word again, I [pause] I go out of this room. Out of this mediation [gesticulating].
[Overlapping voices]
A: […] bad faith
M1: Ladies and gentlemen, I
[Overlapping voices]
M1: I very well understand that you are upset.
P: We didn't want to do it in the first place
[Overlapping voices]
M1: I understand that the feelings are running high, so I, hum, propose that we, hum, adjourn into a private session […] (9:07-10:05)

As can be seen in the quotation above, the mediator allows the outburst to take place. By listening patiently without interrupting, he expressly acknowledges the anger being shown, and then offers a justification that both parties can accept for this outburst, making it no one's fault ("*I very well understand that you are upset. I understand that the feelings are running high. So I propose that we adjourn into a private session*"). He thus prevents further polarization that could have disrupted settlement efforts by calmly asserting his control over the process. Moreover, in doing so he is able to maintain impartiality by acknowledging the feelings of the party seeking face-restoration, but also reminding that party that all participants have an equal opportunity to share their perspectives.

Dividing the two parties and dealing with each of them in private is a frequent strategy adopted by the mediator when the conflict becomes too bitter. Particularly when parties are concerned with face-saving, the use of caucuses is the best technique. Private sessions enable each side to meet alone with the mediator to disclose facts, concerns, interests, limitations and offers that they would not ordinarily reveal to an opponent, which explains why at the opening of this step the mediator is particularly keen to reassure the parties about confidentiality. Without certainty about the confidentiality of disclosures made in private sessions, parties would be reluctant to share information and the mediator's task of perceiving underlying interests and shaping value-added outcomes would be made much more difficult. Indeed, trust in the mediator and in the confidentiality of information shared is vital to the success of mediation:

(9) M1: I would like to confirm that everything we say is confidential unless you authorize me to tell it to the other side. (10:20-10:25)

In private sessions, the mediator can ask his or her questions very openly, framing them in such a way as to require the parties to explain their point of view, and not just simply say 'yes' or 'no'. For example, the mediator asks questions requiring lengthy explanations such as the following: "*So what do you think about the complaints Alcopops has*?" (11:02) or: "*I need to know more. What are your real intentions in Russia*?" (15:16). With this format, the mediator is able to maintain total neutrality on party positions throughout the mediation process without expressing any value judgments on the party's answers or opinions. The form of the question, focusing on a broad topic, also allows the speakers to respond as they see fit without the mediator narrowing or targeting the question on any particular aspect of the issue.

Moreover, the mediator takes great pains, through questioning and through demonstrations of empathy, to ensure that all participants feel that they have been heard and understood. This technique helps develop the crucial sense of trust that participants must place in the mediator if mediation is to be successful. The mediator often punctuates his/her remarks with phrases such as *Yes... I understand... I know... I see...*:

(10) P: Yes, if they introduce it in Russian market, it will be a disaster. But don't tell it to anybody, ok?
M1: I understand. (12:32-12:38)

Mediators show great interest in what the parties say. To underline their active listening they empathetically acknowledge understanding without expressing any evaluation. A nod of the head as a person is speaking or a short verbal response assures a party that they have been heard. For instance, the traditional mediator depicted in the video shows that he is an active listener not only by acknowledging his interlocutor's utterances ("*I understand...*", "*Yes, I see...*") but also by prodding for more information, as when he says to Alcopops' counsel: "*Yes I clearly understand, you know? But I need to know more. I mean, what are your real interests in Russia? Why do you now do the big launch?*" (15:18-15:23)

Periodically, the mediator summarizes the parties' priorities or concerns. This technique allows him/her to test his/her comprehension and permits the client to adjust any misunderstandings. It also gives the party immediate assurance of having been heard and understood. In the video, for example, the mediator says to Mr. Tchaikovsky: "*If I understood right, you have the luxury Zenitskaya, the super-premium Spartakskaya and you have the premium Dynamoskaya...*" (13:26-13:34) thus showing his knowledge of the Wonderbranski portfolio.

5. Dealing with emotional outbursts

Emotional outbursts can occur for a number of reasons, particularly in victim-offender mediations, where the factual situation is often extremely complex but of little importance because the true issues are emotional (Hilll 2000). Outbursts are commonly related to the parties' frustration at not being heard or understood, and to their having a belief that there is not just a legal but a moral basis for their own convictions. These emotional moments are considered a fundamental aspect of mediation proceedings:

> For many participants, mediation is about the 'venting' of feelings and emotions that they would be unable to express in a more formal setting such as a courtroom. The opportunity to tell one's version of the case directly to the opposing party and to express accompanying emotions can be cathartic for mediation participants. (Eisen 1998: 1323)

The techniques commonly used by the mediator in these situations are either to recognize the emotion (*"I sense that you are angry (or sad, etc.)"*) or probe to find the reasons underlying the positions (*"I would like to understand better the reasons why you feel that..."*). In trying to cope with emotional outbursts, mediators attempt both to empathize with the frustrated party and at the same time to identify and isolate the issue which can be later dealt with, and, hopefully, resolved. It could be remarked nonetheless that emotions sometimes have a strong impact on the participants and are difficult to manage. In the following quotation, for example, the discussion becomes very heated, with the two parties quarrelling bitterly with each other and the arbitrator clearly encountering great difficulties in calming down the participants:

(11) M3[5]: Tom, it sounds like you felt that you were clear about what the apartment had to offer. Can you tell us what your concerns are now?

B: Well, she's trying to hold us responsible for other people's actions. No one's happy about what happened, but she wants us to pay for a shrink. That's ridiculous. Half this neighborhood needs a shrink. But it's really not possible to discuss this, she just starts screaming at me whenever I try.

M3: Tom, can you tell us more about what you mean about Rhonda holding you responsible for others' actions?

---

5 M3: mediator of Online Mediation 2 / B: Tom Benson / D: Rhonda McDonald.

B: The guy who jumped her in the garage. This is a high crime area, and those things happen. It's happened to me.
M3: Tom, sounds like you had been willing to discuss these matters. Could you talk about what you'd like to communicate about this?
D: First, it is a blatant falsehood that I was NEVER told that there was security in this building. His exact words to me were: "the apartment management retains a 24-hour security guard and the apartments would soon be fitted with deadbolt locks". And the issue concerning the psychiatrist was something that was on advice of my private doctor. I don't need a shrink. I need a little more security personally since the apartments have failed to provide it physically.
B: We're trying to make things safer for all our tenants, but it's really a money issue. The rents here are pretty low, and it's not cheap. (17:35-17:43)

The parties' angry feelings often lead them to ignore the rules of regular turn-taking and to respond immediately, instead of waiting for their turn. Moreover, their emotional urge makes them forget about the basic convention of mediation, which requires that each speaker should address the mediator and not the other party directly:

(12) B: Every time I try to talk to her about what happened she gets hysterical and tries to blame me for all her problems.
M3: Rhonda, sounds like you are mostly concerned with issues of safety and how Tom has communicated with you when your concerns have not been addressed. Is this right?
D: What attempts have you made to talk to me? That's a very sexist statement to claim that I get 'hysterical'!
B: I thought we were supposed to talk to the mediator. (17:20-17:23)

The mounting feeling of frustration experienced by the parties and the growing dissatisfaction about the outcome of the mediation case are clearly expressed by one of the participants:

(13) B: This keeps getting into an argument which I can do at home so how is this mediation any different? (17:44:06)

To put an end to this highly aggressive situation, the mediator may give one of the parties an 'assignment' (to write a possible solution to the dispute); in the meanwhile he/she will negotiate with the other party. During the private session the mediator can thus continue his/her negotiating activity, further uncovering the parties' interests and helping them determine their real priorities. As interests, concerns and priorities are sought, mediators may need to seek clarification or more details of the information offered to assure full understanding. In private sessions, in fact, mediators can question the parties directly to discover further information that may be useful for the achievement of a potential solution designed to satisfy as many interests of both parties as possible. Through the use of appropriate questions, the mediator can certainly guide the parties to observe their contradictions and reformulate their views according to those perceptions:

(14) M3: Rhonda, it's pretty clear that it doesn't matter to Tom if you leave or not and he is willing to let you out of the lease and give you security and last month's rent back. He has acknowledged that you have legitimate safety concerns. But he has indicated being unwilling to give you other compensation, pay for counseling, or get other security measures in place before three months from now. What options do you realistically have? Would you prefer to move out? If you stay, do you have any creative ideas to help Tom change his mind?

D: I need my expenses paid! I've sacrificed so much! My school work, my job, I have no alternatives. I am lucky to be alive, and people want to quibble over money. If I stay, I will pay for my own security and not pay two months' rent. Or if I move, I want all my money back. He lied, he put me at risk, and I have to suffer the consequences forever! If I don't get this help, I'll never get on with my life! His attempts are not clear enough, and not good enough essentially. (18:29:02-18:32:52)

By means of these inquiries the mediator is able to go well beyond legal positions such as liability, damage and remedies, and extend to personal or emotional interests, allowing the parties to bring to the surface their face-saving needs:

(15) M3: Rhonda, you clearly want more compensation for your experiences which he contributed to and you want more understanding from him. We are happy to talk with him about these things and see what is possible. While we speak with him, can you think a little bit about what your choices are IF he doesn't end up agreeing to more. (18:36)

As can be seen in this quotation, when one of the participants brings forward her demands in an angry and emotional way, the mediator decides to report the request focusing on matters instead of emotions. In this way, he is able to reframe disputant face-threats by restating disputant criticisms of another into the expression of a possible solution. In paraphrasing previous utterances, mediators do not always display strict neutrality but sometimes employ 'selective facilitation' (Greatbatch/Dingwall 1989), a conversational process meant to facilitate discussions regarding favoured resolution options. As has been shown, this technique of restating and summarizing what a disputant advocates employing 'selective facilitation' is an important strategy used by mediators, which turns out to be not at all neutral as in this way "they can manipulate the substantive character of a discussion and push disputants toward settlements they might not ordinarily accept" (Jacobs 2002: 1414).

6. Facilitating consensus

During the discussion, mediators and participants are seen proposing possible solutions for consideration. These proposals generally aim to satisfy both sides to some degree. They are an amalgam of creative solutions, information and party interests. During the whole process mediators probe the feelings of the disputants and seek to establish viable options, so that – when they assume the moment is appropriate for it – they convey proposals, usually party-generated, in the form of hypothetical suggestions (phrased by the mediator as "*What if ...?*" or "*Suppose ...?*"). For example, in the mediation cases analysed here, as well as formulating many proposals and hypothetical suggestions, the mediator constantly asks for ideas from the parties to solve the conflict, using tentative expressions (highlighted in the following quotations):

(16) M2: T, *would you consider* splitting the cost of the consultant *if you were able to* otherwise resolve this without litigation and possible insolvency? (17:50)

(17) M2: *I wonder if it might be helpful* to have the consultant concentrate on the extra cost R would incur by reason of the site conditions. As you may recall, that was to be the focal point of the mini-trial we were to consider if an agreement could not be negotiated. *Perhaps, if* you both had faith in the neutral consultant, that would give you a common point for deciding how much is due R at this point. T, *would that be* an appropriate function for the consultant? (17:59:12)

Also, the various proposals formulated in private sessions are here reported to the other party to see if they meet with his/her approval:

(18) M3: Tom, thanks for waiting. We asked you a while ago about how you would like to be approached in the future by Rhonda. A second question for you then is given both of your concerns about how the safety issue is resolved, what is your response to the following suggestion from Rhonda. She offers to put in her own security system in lieu of paying two months' rent.

B: A little while ago she said that she wants a $9.95 lock from Walmart, so two months seems too much. We'll agree to one month's rent plus $20. And if she wants to use it for a lock, that's fine. She can consider the month's rent as us saying we're sorry about what happened to you, even though it wasn't our fault.

M3: Tom, sounds like we are getting close to building an agreement and have some offers on the table to work with. Why don't we bring you both together. (18:39-18:45)

When the mediator believes that a party's proposal would be totally unacceptable to the other party and could not form the basis for an agreement, he reframes the proposal into acceptable terms that could become part of a settlement. In the video, the mediator hears Wonderbrandski's threat: "*If they still launch KYK HIGH OCTANE in Russia we will keep and fight for this PICO BELLO OCTAVE to the end!*" (22:40-22:48) and reframes it a few minutes later more usefully as: "*Ah, OK, so you would be happy with HIGH OCTANE as long as you are doing the distribution*?" (26:04-26:08). This reformulation results in making less of an imposition upon the other disputant's face and thus proves to be not only an ideational alteration in the text but also an interpersonal one.

When common consent has been reached, the mediator ensures that the parties are well aware of the agreement terms before the participants are asked to sign the final form. Rather than listing all commitments by one party and then those of the other, the mediator prefers to phrase the components of the agreement in a balanced fashion with one concession offset by the other side's concession. This balancing helps underscore the mutual advantages in the agreement and allows mutual face saving by showing concessions on both sides:

(19) M2: Good. Thanks, once again, for your cooperative attitudes in this matter. It appears to me that you should be able to get this resolved this evening. As I understand your respective wishes, you would like the consultant to make an inspection of the jobsite and give you his estimates regarding R's additional costs for completing the work within the time specifications of T, and once that cost has been determined, R will receive periodic payments during the work, which will prevent its pending bankruptcy. This way, Texas gets its highway at less cost than it would take for a new contractor to come in and complete the work. Is this about what you have so far agreed? (18:06)

In the last move the mediator also ensures that parties will sign a memorandum of agreement before leaving the session:

(20) M1: Ok, so maybe I'll shortly repeat the major hum points we have [parties nod]. So you will drop the stripes of the bottle [looking at W] and get rid of the two-tone […]

[…]

M1: Ok, perfect. So I wrote this down and I then would like you two to sign the agreement and everything else is taken to the lawyers. So, thank you very much. I'm very happy, I guess we have a good solution and well, I hope you will have some progress in the future, maybe together, and hum, hopefully very successful. (36:26-37:09)

This phase also has a relevant role in terms of interpersonality. As Katsh, Rifkin and Gaitenby rightly assert:

> The agreement process in traditional mediation not only expresses the substantive terms of the settlement but also serves as a ceremonial moment in the mediation process. When the parties shake hands, sign an agreement, and get congratulated personally by the mediator, there is both symbolic as well as substantive closure to a mediation. (Katsh/Rifkin/Gaitenby 2000: 716)

7. Conclusion

The analysis carried out in this chapter has enabled us to highlight the main negotiation strategies commonly adopted by mediators to help parties to listen and understand concerns, empathize with each other, vent feelings and confront emotions. We have seen that in order to be effective, mediators need to be aware of the disputants' different face needs as well as of their expectations and adopt appropriate discursive strategies such as questioning, reporting, rephrasing, summarizing, shifting in footing and turn-taking control. By providing summaries and reports of the parties' positions with a different stance or an appropriate shift of footing, mediators are able not only to clarify arguments and give their desired direction to the discussion, but also indirectly to make arguments and advocate standpoints without overtly taking over the responsibilities for advocacy or decision-making, which are instead apparently left with the disputants so as to guarantee an appearance of neutrality.

Moreover, in order to overcome the mistrust and the disagreements of the parties, mediators also adopt various psychological techniques that allow them to interpret the participants' nonverbal language as well as their attitudes, their emotions and their immediate reactions. By alternating between analysing issues in private sessions and discussing them in the 'conference room', mediators are able to maintain confidentiality in the procedure and guarantee privacy in the negotiation process. As has been shown, in order to be successful in their function, mediators need not only high competence in the use of these negotiation strategies, but also full mastery of the discursive skills required and of the generic forms typical of this procedure.

References

Berger, Klaus Peter 2006. *Private Dispute Resolution in International Business: Negotiation, Mediation, Arbitration.* The Hague: Kluwer Law International.

Bernard, Sydney / Folger, Joseph / Weingarten, Helen / Zumeta, Zena 1984. The Neutral Mediator: Value Dilemmas in Divorce Mediation. *Mediation Quarterly* 4, 61-74.

Brown, Penelope / Levinson, Stephen 1978. Universals in Language Usage: Politeness Phenomena. In Goody, Esther (ed.) *Questions and Politeness: Strategies in Social Interaction.* Cambridge: Cambridge University Press, 256-289.

Bush, Robert / Folger, Joseph 1994. *The Promise of Mediation.* San Francisco: Jossey-Bass.

Cobb, Sara / Rifkin, Janet 1991. Practice and Paradox: Deconstructing Neutrality in Mediation. *Law and Social Inquiry* 161, 35-62.

Dyck, David 2000. The Mediator as Nonviolent Advocate: Revisiting the Question of Mediator Neutrality. *Mediation Quarterly* 18, 129-149.

Eisen, Joel B. 1998. Are we Ready for Mediation in Cyberspace? *Brigham Young University Law Review.* <http://www.highbeam.com/doc/1P3-38788128.html>.

Folger, Joseph / Bush, Robert 1994. Ideology, Orientations to Conflict and Mediation Discourse. In Folger, Joseph / Jones, Tricia (eds) *New Directions in Mediation.* London: Sage, 3-25.

Folger, Joseph / Bush, Robert 1996. Transformative Mediation and Third-Party Intervention: Ten Hallmarks of a Transformative Approach to Practice. *Mediation Quarterly* 13/4, 263-278.

Goffman, Erving 1979. Footing. *Semiotica* 25, 1-29.

Goffman, Erving 1955. On Face-work: An Analysis of Ritual Elements in Social Interaction. *Psychiatry: Journal for the Study of International Processes* 18, 213-231.

Gotti, Maurizio 2013. Investigating the Generic Structure of Mediation Processes. In Johannesson, Nils-Lennart / Melchers, Gunnel / Björkman, Beyza (eds) *Of Butterflies and Birds, of*

Dialects and Genres: Essays in Honour of Philip Shaw. Stockholm: Acta Universitatis Stockholmiensis, 61-76.

Greatbatch, David / Dingwall, Robert 1989. Selective Facilitation: Some Preliminary Observations on a Strategy Used by Divorce Mediators. *Law & Society Review* 23, 613-641.

Heisterkamp, Brian L. 2006. Conversational Displays of Mediator Neutrality in a Court-based Program. *Journal of Pragmatics* 38, 2051-2064.

Hill, Richard 2000. Common Points and Differences among Different Types of Mediation. *The Arbitration and Dispute Resolution Law Journal* 9, 95-106.

Jackson, Bernard S. 1995. *Making Sense in Law*. Liverpool: Deborah Charles Publications.

Jacobs, Scott 2002. Maintaining Neutrality in Dispute Mediation: Managing Disagreement while Managing not to Disagree. *Journal of Pragmatics* 34, 1403-1426.

Katsh, Ethan / Rifkin, Janet / Gaitenby, Alan 2000. E-Commerce, E-Disputes, and E-Dispute Resolution: In the Shadow of 'eBay Law'. *Ohio State Journal on Dispute Resolution* 15/3, 705-734.

Kolb, Deborah / Kressel, Kenneth 1994. The Realities of Making Talk Work. In Kolb, Deborah (Ed.) *When Talk Works: Profiles of Mediators*. San Francisco: Jossey-Bass Publishers, 459-461.

Kressel, Kenneth / Pruitt, Dean 1989. *Mediation Research: The Process and Effectiveness of Third-party Intervention*. San Francisco: Jossey-Bass.

Ng, John 1999. The Four Faces of Face: Implications for Mediation. Paper presented on 28 March 1999 at the 2nd Mediation Conference at the National University of Singapore. Retrieved on April 13, 2013 from <http://www.mediate.com/articles/the_four_faces_of_face.cfm>.

Rifkin, Janet / Miller, Jonathan / Cobb, Sara 1991. Toward a New Discourse for Mediator: A Critique of Neutrality. *Mediation Quarterly* 9, 151-164.

Swales, John M. 1990. *Genre Analysis*. Cambridge: Cambridge University Press.

Appendix

Wonderbrandski A/O vs. Alcopops Inc (Traditional Mediation)

A dispute has arisen between two of the largest alcoholic beverage companies in the world. Wonderbrandski A/O is a Russian vodka producer. One of its brands is PICO BELLO, a potato-based vodka. Wonderbrandski's President is the entrepreneur Peter Tchaikovsky. Alcopops Inc is a Chicago-based beverage alcohol marketing company. It sells KYK, a rye vodka, internationally. Until recently, Alcopops had no presence in Russia except in Moscow Airport Duty Free, where small quantities of KYK CLASSIC had been available for several years. Alcopops' President is D.D. Kruze, a well-known business leader. In 1992, by a brief exchange of letters, Alcopops granted Wonderbrandski a non-exclusive, royalty-free license to use its 8-sided bottle design in Russia on any of Wonderbrandski's alcoholic beverages. Wonderbrandski never made use of the license because 8-sided bottles were costly; nevertheless, the licence was never terminated. Alcopops recently met with Vladivod, a leading former State-run distillery based in the Russian Far East, with a view to appointing Vladivod as Russian distributor of all three variants of KYK vodka. A deal was agreed verbally but not yet signed. Wonderbrandski then precipitously re-launched its PICO BELLO OCTAVE vodka in an 8-sided bottle and in trade dress that Alcopops considers makes it look like KYK OCTANE. Alcopops filed a complaint with the Russian Anti-Monopoly Committee claiming unfair competition by Wonderbrandski. Wonderbrandski, in response, argues that (a) they own the trademark OCTAVE in Russia and consider Alcopops' use of OCTANE a violation of Wonderbrandski's Russian trademark, and (b) Wonderbrandski has a license from Alcopops itself to use an 8-sided bottle.

Roadbuilder vs. Transportation Department (Online Mediation 1)

The Texas Department of Transportation decided to construct a new road over a rough, mountainous area in West Texas. The work was to be performed under two separate $25 million fixed-price contracts. A number of highway construction firms participated in the bidding process, among them Roadbuilder, Inc. of Newark, New Jersey, which was awarded both contracts because of its lowest combined bid. Roadbuilder was delayed in commencing the work, and ran into delays and additional expenses due to encountering unexpected rock outcrops and inclement weather. In February 1997, Roadbuilder notified the Department of its additional expenses incurred in the work and refused to proceed further until these expenses were reimbursed. In early March 1997, the State notified Roadbuilder that it was terminating the contract because of Roadbuilder's failure to perform.

Rhonda McDonald vs. Easy Living Apartments (Online Mediation 2)

Rhonda McDonald is a law student. She works all day and takes night classes. She was looking for a place to live and looked at Easy Living Apartments as a possible solution. She spoke with Mr. Benson, the unit manager, because safety was her main concern since this building is located in a high-crime and high-risk area. She was assured that the building had 24-hour security guards and deadbolt locks on all the doors and only after that assurance did she move in. She had made repeated attempts to follow up on the locks and security guards but at all times her inquiries were dismissed. A few weeks ago, on the way from her car to the apartment, she was grabbed by a man and threatened to keep quiet. She was barely able to escape and make it into her apartment and the neighbours called the police. Easy Living Apartments refuse to be held responsible for what happened and believe nothing was said concerning security when Rhonda McDonald first visited the building.

PATRIZIA ANESA

The Realization of Interpersonality Features in Jury Instructions

A jury trial is intrinsically based on the interaction between participants displaying different levels of knowledge and expertise in relation to legal issues. Indeed, crucial to the idea of having lay jurors as triers of fact is the presupposition that a cross-societal representation of citizens will make a just decision, based on the application of the law which is given to them and drawing on the concept of collective wisdom.

In light of the concept of knowledge asymmetry in jury communication (cf. Anesa 2012, Anesa/Kastberg 2012), this chapter aims to reach a better understanding of the dynamics underlying the interaction between experts and laypeople in a specific part of a jury trial, namely the jury instruction phase. More specifically, the case analyzed here is the US civil trial by jury between the SCO Group, Inc. and Novell, Inc. (Case No. 2:04-CV-139TS). Drawing on authentic data, I will analyse jury instructions in order to observe the emergence of interpersonality features in the interaction between the judge and the jurors involved, focusing on different levels of analysis (pragmatic, textual, syntactic and lexical).

After a brief presentation of the role played by jury trials within the American legal system, I will discuss the functions of jury instructions by describing, in particular, their pragmatic aspects. The following section will focus on the concept of interpersonality in legal discourse, while the analytical part will observe instances of interpersonality as well as impersonality features in pre-instructions and final instructions.

1. Jury trials in the US

In modern democracies, trials are generally considered the prototypical procedure for the realization of justice. However, the percentage of cases that are terminated by trial in the US has decreased in recent years as a higher number of cases are terminated before pre-trial in a variety of judicial fora. In this respect, Figure 1[1] shows data referring to civil trials in US district courts:

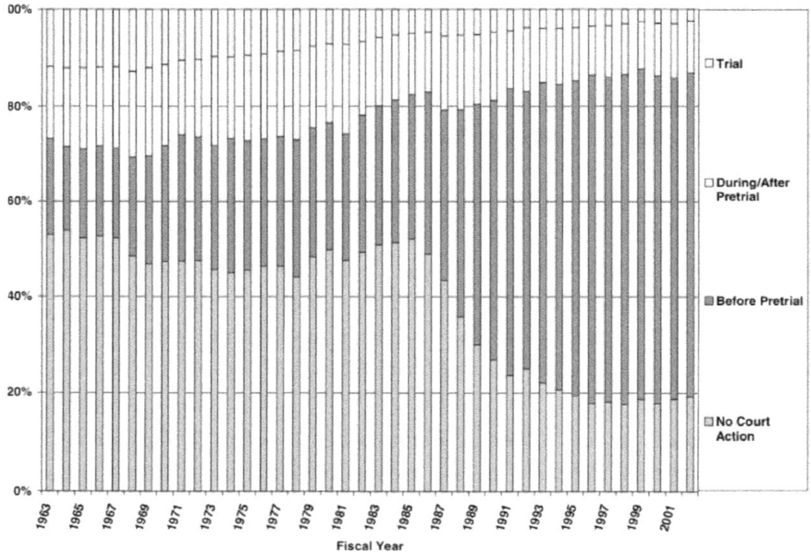

Figure 1. Percentage of civil cases terminating at each stage, U.S. district courts, 1963-2002 (Galanter 2004: 483).

The process of counting trials is particularly complicated as it not simple to determine exactly what procedures should be defined as trials, or when a trial should be counted, i.e. in which phase of the proceedings (see Kritzer 2013). However, Figure 1 shows an indication of the decreasing number of trials in the last decades. Moreover, recent

1 State-of-the-States Survey of Jury Improvement Efforts (April 2007), National Center for State Courts.

studies show that the year 2010 also saw a sharp increase in terminations before trial. Among the different factors determining this decline, it is generally agreed that the number of trials taking place in courts is affected by IDR (Internal Dispute Resolution) and ADR (Alternative Dispute Resolution) procedures.

Even though the decrease in the number of trials in US district courts has led several commentators to talk about the death or the disappearance of trials, this form of dispute resolution has traditionally been one of the tenets of the American legal system. In particular, it has been stated that more 90 percent of all jury trials in the world take place in the US (Graham 2009: 4). As Figure 2 shows, the decrease of trials has been marked predominantly by the decrease of bench trials:

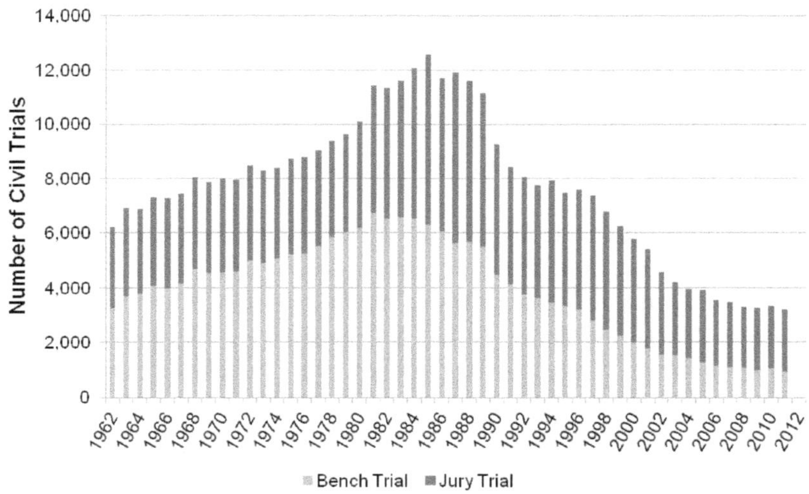

Figure 2. Civil Trials from AO Table C4 (Administrative Office of the United States Courts) (Kritzer 2013: 420).

The idea of a declining use of jury trials is not new, to the extent that as early as 1928 Moley talked about the 'vanishing jury trial'. However, jury trials remain an intrinsic part of the American justice system and have an important impact also from a cultural and social point of view. Every year a large number of citizens come (directly or indirectly) into contact with some phases of a jury trial. For example, according to the National Center for State Courts[2] in the US, the number of people summoned each year for jury service is approximately 32 million and the estimated number of jurors impaneled is 1.5 million (Graham 2009: 6).

2. Pragmatic aspects of jury instructions

2.1. Speech acts and legal language

The law is "the arena of speech acts par excellence", argues Fletcher (2003: 85). An in-depth analysis of the concept of speech acts (e.g. Austin 1962, Searle 1969, 1975) would go beyond the scope of this study, but their application can offer a deeper understanding of potential categorizations related to the concept of legal language (see *inter alia* Danet 1980).

Austin theorized the notion of *performative* (Austin 1962) and used it in connection with the term *operative*, the latter being used more specifically in legal contexts. In some initial work on speech acts (Austin 1962), utterances would fall into two different categories, namely *performatives* and *constatives*, but the distinction was not maintained in later works, as Austin argued that it was ultimately not defensible. It is interesting to note that Hart (1994) also relates the Austinian interpretation of *performative* utterances to the notion of *operative* utterances.

An influential distinction was then made between the three oft-quoted different aspects that utterances may display: *locutionary* (the physical utterance of what is literally said), *illocutionary* (the work an utterance accomplishes in a specific context), and *perlocutionary* (the effect on the hearer) (Austin 1962). More precisely, Austin's prelimi-

2 State-of-the-States Survey of Jury Improvement Efforts (April 2007), National Center for State Courts.

nary taxonomy of illocutionary acts included the following five categories (Austin 1962):

- *Verdictives*: acts which deliver a finding or a judgment (e.g. acquit).
- *Exercitives*: acts that consist of giving a decision for or against a course of action (e.g. sentence).
- *Commissives*: acts of committing the speaker to a course of action (e.g. declaring one's intention).
- *Behabitatives*: expressions of attitudes toward the conduct, fortunes or attitudes of others (e.g. apologizing).
- *Expositives*: acts of expounding of views, conducting of arguments, and clarifying (e.g. denying).

Further typologies of speech acts have subsequently been developed (see in particular Ohmann 1972, Fraser 1974a, 1974b, Searle 1975). Although I will not enter into a retrospective analysis of the various interpretations offered, speech act theory is particularly relevant to the understanding of the functional nature of legal texts, in that it shows that speech acts do not simply describe legal propositions but assume a fundamental constitutive function.

In particular, Searle (1975) offers an influential taxonomy of illocutionary acts and identifies *representatives*, *directives*, *commissives*, *expressives*, and *declarations*, plus an additional subclass, *representative declarations*. These categories may also be applied specifically to the study of legal language (Danet 1980) in order to identify the primary illocutionary point of different types of legal texts. Blurred contours of categories are inevitable, but they may be described as follows (Searle 1975):

- *Representatives*: the main purpose of these acts is to "commit the speaker (in varying degrees) to something's being the case, to the truth of the expressed proposition" (Searle 1975: 354). The degrees of commitment vary from weak cases such as hypothesizing to strong cases such as solemnly swearing. Examples include testifying, swearing, asserting, claiming and stating.
- *Directives*: they are seen as attempts "by the speaker to get the hearer to do something" (Searle 1975: 355). In these cases like-

wise, the degree of attempt may vary from weak cases such as suggesting something be done, to strong cases such as commanding something be done. Other examples are requesting, praying, permitting and advising. Questions are also defined as directives because in Searle's view they constitute "attempts to get the hearer to perform a speech act" (1975: 356). Galdia remarks that statutes, as well as legal texts on different hierarchical levels such as ordinances and decrees, are typically directives (Galdia 2009: 149). Moreover, in courtroom contexts, subpoenas, jury instructions, and appeals, amongst others, may all be seen as directives.

- *Commissives*: they are defined as those acts whose illocutionary point "is to commit the speaker (again in varying degrees) to some future course of action" (Searle 1975: 356). Typical legal examples of this category are represented by documents found in private law, such as contracts and agreements, and wills. Similarly, guarantees, pledges, and promises of different kinds would fall within the category.
- *Expressives*: these express a psychological state in the speaker regarding a state of affairs that the expressive refers to or presupposes. Expressives neither represent (as representatives do) nor coerce (as commissives do) reality; they take it for granted, and the truth of the proposition is presupposed (Searle 1975: 357). Typical expressives are thanking, congratulating, welcoming, deploring, but the category comprises a wide range of acts, from forgiving to blaming, from absolving to condemning. However, texts may be related to different speech acts and, for instance, a constitutional preamble may include commissives as well as expressives (see Galdia 2009: 149).
- *Declarations*: the illocutionary point of this class lies in the possibility of determining a change in reality if the act is performed successfully; one example of this concept is the idea that "if I successfully perform the act of marrying you, then you are married" (Searle 1975: 358). In legal contexts, such acts include, for instance, objections, sentences, and appellate opinions (see Danet 1980: 460).

The distinction between these categories is often blurred. For instance, Searle also identifies a subcategory defined as *representative declarations*. In this case, the two categories (representatives and declarations) cannot be separated because "in certain institutional situations we not only ascertain the facts but we need an authority to lay down a decision as to what the facts are after the fact-finding procedure has been gone through" (Searle 1975: 360). With specific reference to the legal sphere, indictments, confessions, pleas of guilty/not guilty, and verdicts could be defined as representative declarations (Danet 1980: 460). More specifically, a representative declaration involves a truth claim (because of its representative character), but it also transcends it (in that it is a declaration). For example, if the jury declares the defendant guilty, for legal purposes he is guilty (even if he is actually innocent). In this situation an appeal can result in a different representative declaration which replaces the previous one, or it may simply confirm the previous ('erroneous') representative declaration (Searle 1975: 360-361).

2.2. The functional nature of jury instructions

In terms of speech acts, as has been mentioned, jury instructions are predominantly directives as the court clearly instructs the jurors about the behavior they must assume. By adopting a related but different perspective, legal texts may also be categorized according to their functional nature. Focusing in particular on written legal documents, Tiersma (1999a: 139) suggests a division into three main groups:

1. *Operative legal documents*, which aim principally at the creation or the modification of legal relations. This category includes, for instance, statutes, contracts, wills, etc, which, from a linguistic perspective, assume a performative function. Austin (1962: 6) illustrates the concepts of 'performative' as indicating that "the issuing of the utterance is the performing of an action". Interestingly, Austin takes into consideration the adjective 'operative' as somehow related to 'performative', but with the former actually being a "technical term [...] used strictly by lawyers" (Austin 1962: 6).

2. *Expository documents*: they aim to explain the law and assume, therefore, an expository function. They include, for instance, schoolbooks, professional manuals, letters to clients, etc.
3. *Persuasive documents*: these display a persuasive function. Typical examples are the briefs submitted to courts.

These distinctions are not always clear-cut, but they may be useful in identifying the main features of different texts. In particular, Tiersma (1999a: 141) points out that "[g]enerally speaking, operative documents have by far the most legalese, as compared to persuasive and expository documents". In this respect, he also argues: "it is highly ironic that documents with the most legalese (like contracts, wills, deeds, and statutes) are also most likely to be read by clients and directly affect their interests" (Tiersma 1999a: 141). Following this categorization, jury instructions seem to assume a hybrid function. Instructions about the development of the trial or about the law to be applied may be seen as expository in that informative, explanatory and descriptive tools are utilized in order to effectively present the law to the jurors. However, the instructional phase also imposes rules on the conduct of the jurors, assuming operative contours.

Working along the same lines, but adopting different functional criteria, Šarčević presents another valuable classification and, in particular, distinguishes between *prescriptive* and *descriptive* texts (Šarčević 2000: 9). The former are normative instruments, such as laws, rules, codes, contracts and treaties, whereas the latter include different text types, such as articles and textbooks, which are generally written by legal scholars. It is interesting to point out that their authority varies according to the legal system and, for instance, in Civil Law countries the opinion of legal scholars contributes significantly to the definition of legal concepts (Šarčević 2000: 9). Between these two categories, it is also possible to identify hybrid texts, which include both prescriptive and descriptive elements. We can place instructions along this continuum since they assume a predominantly prescriptive role but at the same time have a descriptive approach.

More specifically, as regards prescriptive texts, Williams (2005: 64) identifies two distinctive functions: a *communicative* one (the message conveyed by prescriptive texts is generally addressed to a multiplicity of receivers) and a *pragmatic* one. From a pragmatic point of view, it is plausible to assume that instructions should be easily comprehended by the people they address, who are not legal experts. On the other hand, it is difficult to imagine that jury instructions could be written in such a way as to be immediately understood by all laypeople. The debate remains open and supporters of the Plain English Movement[3] often stress the paradox that lies behind the complexity of legal language and the fact that it mainly affects ordinary people.

2.3. Jury instructions and the Plain English movement

The intricacy of legal English often represents a challenge for the lay public. Tortuous syntax and archaic vocabulary are only some of the factors determining incomprehensibility and members of the legal profession may tend to perpetuate the linguistic and conceptual complexities they are trained in. Professionals often justify this approach with the idea that it is impossible to make sudden and significant changes to a set of traditional linguistic routines and practices that have acquired a consolidated and clear meaning over the centuries.

The concern about the accessibility of legal language on the part of laypeople emerges clearly in jury trials, as the correct comprehension of instructions is at the basis of a just and fair trial. Issues linked to the comprehensibility of jury instructions have received considerable consideration (see *inter alia* Conley 2000, Ellsworth/Reifman 2000, Heffer 2008), and in recent years, particular attention has been devoted to the process of redrafting instructions in order to render them more concrete, understandable and simple (see Tiersma 1993, 1999b, Tiersma/Curtis 2008).

The gradual affirmation of the Plain English movement has clearly affected the linguistic, textual and pragmatic features of different text-types. While the initial focus was on contractual language, various kinds of documents have gradually undergone this process of

3 For a further reflection on the use of Plain English in legal texts see *inter alia* Flesch (1979), Martineau (1991), Steinberg (1991), Garner (2001), Wydick (2005).

simplification. Jury instructions are no exception and, for instance, several US States now adopt pattern jury instructions that are based on the principles of Plain English. Tradition notwithstanding, evolution is inevitable in any system. Indeed, it is now generally accepted that this linguistic simplification is not a cause of inaccuracy in that clarity and precision, as well as simplicity and accuracy, are not necessarily mutually exclusive.

3. Interpersonality in jury instructions

Courtroom communication is highly conventionalized and standardized. This holds true even for spoken interaction (see *inter alia* Gibbons 1994, 2003, Heffer 2005) and is evident in written communication. Texts such as jury instructions, which are written and meant to be read, often display static and conservative features. The high level of institutionalization of the texts delivered may lead one to think that a uniformly impersonal style is used, in that the presentation of the duties of the jurors should not be subject to interpretative issues. Courts tend to make use of pattern jury instructions that are theoretically universally applicable to all cases (with some adaptations). Therefore, intuitively, interpersonal references may be quite limited and positioned within an abstract perspective. However, the need to adopt Plain English in drafting these instructions may also lead to the emergence of more interpersonal features and the use of a more concrete and case-specific approach.

Pattern instructions have traditionally been drafted by legal experts with two main objectives in mind: firstly, to reduce costs and time related to writing instructions anew for each case; and secondly, to limit the room for potential erroneous instructions which would lead to an appeal or reversal. Instructions in Plain English have generally been drafted in collaboration with linguists and communication specialists in order to render the texts more easily understandable for a heterogeneous lay audience. The ultimate attempt is to optimize jury performance in the application of such instructions, starting from the assumption that understanding instructions is the *sine qua non* for their correct and consistent application.

Instructions may be seen as hybrid texts for a variety of reasons. First, in terms of mode, we are dealing with written texts that are read orally to the jury and the written texts may be integrated with comments offered by the judges. Jurors can also rely on a written copy of the instructions, as well as their own notes, when in the deliberation room. What emerges is a form of coexistence and interdependence between the written and the spoken mode.

Secondly, the target is also hybrid. The manifested target is the jury, but the ultimate target is often represented by appellate judges, and instructions have to respect the principle that they must submit the issues and applicable law to the jury fairly and adequately. Guidelines for the use of Plain English in drafting jury instructions insist on the necessity to keep in mind that the audience consists of both lay people and experts. However, the tension between the need for a clear and simple style and the need to conform to standard rules and practices is evident.

Thirdly, in terms of style, the formality of written legal texts may be accompanied by more informal comments on the part of the judge.

Jury instructions seem to constantly move along different continua, such as:

- Written and spoken discourse
- General applicability and specificity
- Vagueness and precision
- Formality and informality
- Impersonality and interpersonality

Interpersonality may be intended as any form of interaction or communication which aims to create relationships among participants (Sudweeks/Simoff 1999). Therefore, interpersonality in communication may be seen as inevitable, following the well-known principle that we cannot not communicate. More specifically, it may also be argued that interpersonality is related to any verbal, para-verbal or non-verbal interaction between participants, which inevitably creates, redefines and affects the relationship between them. Focusing on impersonality in academic language, Hyland (2002: 1095) notes that "impersonality is seen as a defining feature of expository writing as it embodies the positivist assumption that academic research is purely empirical and objective". Similarly, impersonality in legal texts seems to convey the idea that the law is not applied subjectively and arbitrarily, but according to clear and uniform criteria.

Rather than a mere syntactic choice, 'impersonality' can be intended as the opposite pragmatic realization of agency (Yamamoto 2006), given that an impersonal construct does not theoretically express the agent manifestly. The legal sphere is apparently the pantheon of impersonality as, by definition, laws should be applied identically to all citizens regardless of their individual characteristics. The analytical section will focus on the process of delivering jury instructions. Particular attention is devoted to the interaction between the participants (namely, the judge and the jurors) in such a constrained and institutionalized context, and more specifically to the communicative realization of interpersonality features within the event.

4. Analysis

4.1. The case

The analysis is based on the well-known civil trial between the SCO Group, Inc. (plaintiff) and Novell, Inc. (defendant). The trial started in March, 2010, before the Honorable Ted Stewart (District of Utah, Central Division, Case no. 2:04-CV-139TS). The entire *SCO vs Novell* case was based largely on the interpretation of the APA (Asset Purchase Agreement) between the SCO Group (previously Santa Cruz Operation) and Novell. SCO claimed the rights to the Unix code and accused Novell of slander of title in 2004. After a series of events in 2005, Novell filed a counter-suit accusing SCO of slander of title, breach of contract, failure to remit royalties and failure to conduct audit obligations. Numerous developments in the lawsuit battle followed. Before the case was appealed to the Tenth Circuit, Judge Kimball ruled that Novell was the sole owner of the Unix and UnixWare Copyrights. The last event of this extended legal battle was the trial on remand for copyright issues, which started on March 8, 2010. The jury trial took place before Judge Ted Stewart in the district of Utah. At the end of the trial the jury returned a unanimous verdict in favor of Novell, and the decision was also affirmed by the Court of Appeals. For the purpose of this chapter, and for the sake of clarity and consistency, only the jury instruction phase of the trial on remand will be analyzed.

4.2. Jury instructions in SCO vs Novell

Following Heffer (2008: 47-52), the expression 'jury instruction' can be intended as a series of processes through which the jurors are instructed upon issues such as the development of the trial, the applicable law, and the conduct to be assumed (Jonakait 2003: 198-199). Instead, the definition 'jury instructions' generally refers to the texts that are read to the jurors in the instruction phase. Such texts may also be made available to the jurors in the jury room to be used as reference during deliberations.

It has been argued that the comprehension of instructions may be affected by the moment at which instructions are delivered. Giving instructions solely before deliberation has been compared to "telling jurors to watch a baseball game and decide who won without telling them what the rules are until the end of the game" (Schwarzer 1991: 583). Instead, preliminary instructions (also called initial or pre-instructions) given before opening statements may help the jurors to frame the information they are exposed to in a more meaningful way and may facilitate jurors' understanding.

In *SCO vs Novell* the preliminary jury instructions were delivered on March 8, 2010, when the trial started and final instructions were read on March 26.

4.2.1. Preliminary instructions: addressing the participants

Jury instructions are generally introduced by a sort of preamble, in order to clarify what the purpose of this phase is. The introductory remarks metadiscursively emphasize the primary objectives of this phase:

(1) THE COURT: *Ladies and gentlemen*, what we're now going to do is I'm going to give *you* some brief instructions that are intended to outline for *you* how *you* are to conduct *yourselves* as jurors during the course of trial and also to give *you* some indication of what will transpire during the trial.

The conventionalized nature of legal language leads to the use of the typical opening 'Ladies and gentlemen' to attract the jurors' attention. Subsequently, the judge usually addresses the jurors using the listener-inclusive pronoun *you*. The use of a more abstract and less direct form, such as *the jurors*, is generally less communicatively effective. In terms of personalization strategies, the use of *you*, as a tendency, allows a higher level of involvement on the part of the listeners.

Subsequently, the judge highlights the importance of the juror's function for the outcome of a trial, and this is in line with the need to make the jurors aware of the crucial role they play:

(2) You, and you alone, are the judges of the facts. You will then have to apply to those facts the law as *the Court* will give it to you. You must follow that law whether you agree with it or not.

In this case he uses the impersonal expression *the Court*. This is a conventionalized and standardized approach and it is considered a form of respect towards the function of the court. Abstaining from the use of a first-person perspective does not mean complying with a formalist ideology that denies the personal role of the judge. Instead, it suggests that the Court is a supra-personal institution, whose role and function are independent of a judge's individual attitudes. The third-person perspective comes from the traditional legal heritage and was typical of jury instructions before the use of Plain English in these texts. As Tiersma states: "Lawyers and judges have a tendency to avoid using personal pronouns, especially *I* and *you*. Thus, older jury instructions almost always started with the phrase *the court instructs the jury*" (Tiersma 2005: 9).

The following instruction is also characterized by a high level of abstractness and all-inclusiveness. Referring to the participants as *the jurors* and *the Court* instead of *you* and *I* may be seen as to privilege generality and impersonality rather than specificity and directness:

(3) Justice through trial by jury must always depend upon the willingness of *each individual juror* to seek the truth as to the facts from the same evidence presented to *all the jurors* and to arrive at a verdict by applying the same rules of law as given in the instructions of *the Court*.

Moreover, the third person narration in legal texts generally enhances an idea of impartiality and authoritativeness (Williams 2004: 114). In the case analyzed here, the entire instruction phase is based on an alternation between the expression of principles in abstract terms with the participants referred to as third parties, as if it was a story told by an omniscient narrator, and a more direct approach.

4.2.2. Explanatory approaches

Some legal principles and concepts are presented to the jurors trying to adopt a very schematic, simple and clear approach. For example, what constitutes evidence is described in the following excerpt:

(4) Certain things are not evidence and must not be considered by you. I will list them for you now. First, statements, arguments and questions by lawyers are not evidence. Second, objections to questions are not evidence. […] Third, testimony that the Court has excluded or told you to disregard is not evidence and must not be considered. And, fourth, anything you may have seen or heard outside of the courtroom is not evidence and must be disregarded. You are to decide this case solely on the evidence presented here in the courtroom.

It has often been noted that the way in which instructions are delivered can be adapted, simplified and structured in a more effective way, but the texts have to respect and illustrate the law without modifying, altering or omitting parts of it. Therefore, the law has to be stated, despite the difficulties connected to its application. The example above is based on a paratactic construction with a list of elements that should not be considered evidence. Numbering the elements of this list contributes to clarity, and so does the repetition of the notion that each of these elements is not evidence. This reiteration may appear redundant but helps to convey transparency, avoid misunderstanding and is deemed to facilitate the acquisition and the recalling of the concept that is being illustrated.

Defining evidence is particularly important for the outcome of the trial. Criticism towards the jury system has often been based on the fact that non-evidentiary factors are taken into account during the decision making process and a large extant body of research confirms that limiting instructions may be difficult or impossible to apply on the part of the jurors (Lieberman *et al.* 2009). The third element listed in Example 4 appears particularly incongruous as disregarding information on command is not cognitively possible. In this case the abstract principle is at odds with the real possibility of applying it. Indeed, the theory of ironic process of mental control (e.g., Wegner 1994) suggests that an effort of mental control includes both a conscious search for the desired mental state and an unconscious one for indications of failure in the control process. Thus, monitoring processes check if the thought is absent from consciousness. Therefore, ironically, mental suppression may lead to an increased accessibility of the unwanted thought.

The judge then illustrates the nature of the trial in question:

(5) This is a civil case. Plaintiff has the burden of proving its case by *what is called* the preponderance of the evidence. *That means* plaintiff has to produce evidence which, considered in the light of all the facts, leads you to believe that what plaintiff claims is more likely true than not. *To put it differently, if you were to put plaintiff's and defendant's evidence on opposite sides of the scales*, plaintiff would have to make the scales tip somewhat on its side. If plaintiff fails to meet this burden, the verdict must be for defendant.

The use of definitions, reformulations and paraphrases is constant and metadiscursive code glosses such as 'what is called', 'that means' 'to put it differently' are used in an attempt to improve clarity. Analogical and hypothetical constructions are also used in order to translate abstract legal principles into more concrete images ('if you were to put plaintiff and defendant on opposite sides of the scales'). The use of common nouns to refer to the role assumed by the participants (plaintiff, defendant) is common in pattern jury instructions, especially in the initial part of the instruction phase. It has been suggested that the use of the specific names of the parties (e.g. SCO and Novell) may help the jurors to understand the situation in more concrete terms. A more specific approach is used in subsequent passages, whereas the beginning of the instruction phase is based on more general and abstract definitions, in order to introduce the basic principles of the trial from a more general perspective.

While introducing issues related to the concept of reasonable doubt, the judge tries to create a higher level of involvement thanks to references to possible experiences the jurors might have found themselves in:

(6) Those of you who have sat on criminal cases will have heard of proof beyond a reasonable doubt. That requirement does not apply to a civil case and you should therefore put it out of your mind.

As intertextuality is cognitively unavoidable, it is unlikely that, while listening to or reading a text, jurors may be able to ignore any reference to a related text they are familiar with. No text exists in isolation and the knowledge of a text or part of it is inevitably linked to a myriad of other texts from which it cannot be cognitively excluded.

Then the judge instructs the jurors about the conduct to be assumed during the trial, and he stresses importance of this point for the just and fair development of the trial. The cataphoric reference also creates expectation and stimulates attention:

(7) Next, a few words about your conduct as jurors. I want you to pay particular attention to what I am about to say to you.

The organization of the text regarding the conduct of the jurors is very clear and schematic, and signaling devices help the jurors to follow the logical reasoning behind it:

(8) *First*, I instruct you that during the trial you are not to discuss the case with anyone, including fellow jurors, or permit anyone to discuss it with you. Until

> you retire to the jury room at the end of the case to deliberate on your verdict, you simply are not to talk about this case. I will stress that means family, friends, neighbors, strangers on the street. You just simply are not to discuss the case. *Second*, […]

The same concept is reformulated and reiterated several times ('you are not to discuss the case', 'you simply are not to talk about this case', 'you just simply are not to discuss the case'). The level of simplicity is high in order to highlight that the interpretation of the instruction should not be problematic as the linguistic formulation is linear and based on common, everyday terms.

One of the aspects characterizing (especially written) legal English is the use of passive constructions (Jackson 1995: 119-120). Williams points out that approximately one quarter of all finite verbal constructions in prescriptive legal texts written in English take the passive form (Williams 2004: 228). Passive structures determine an impersonal style of writing (Šarčević 2000: 177), which is typical of legal texts. However, the instructions analyzed here show a predominant use of active forms. Exponents of the Plain English movement have often criticized the excessive use of passives (e.g. Asprey 2003: 102-103) and, in this respect, the instructions delivered seem in line with Plain Language criteria.

4.2.3. Final instructions

The final phase of the jury instruction process is represented by the reading of the final jury instructions of the applicable law. In *SCO vs Novell* final instructions were read on March 26, 2010. Before reading the text, the judge gives a short preamble and reminds the jurors that they will be provided with a written copy:

> (9) Good morning, ladies and gentlemen. Let me begin by reassuring you that a copy of the instructions that I'm about to read to you will go with you into the jury room, so I do not expect you to memorize this as I go through it.

Some scholars suggest that providing jurors with a written copy of the court's instructions facilitates jury understanding (see Hastie *et al.* 1983's seminal work).

Subsequently, the judge makes a precise comment on the note-taking process:

(10) During the trial I have permitted you to take notes. Many courts do not permit note-taking by jurors. And as instructed at the beginning of trial, a word of caution is in order. There is always a tendency to attach undue importance to matters which one has written down. [...] Your notes are not evidence, and are by no means a complete outline of the proceeding or list of the highlights of the trial. Above all, your memory should be your greatest asset when it comes to deliberating and rendering a decision in this case.

As has been shown, the instruction phase is based on the fluctuation between the written and the spoken mode and may therefore be seen as hybrid in terms of modality. First of all, the texts are read to the jurors and such texts are complemented with extra oral comments when the judge considers it necessary. Moreover, in the deliberation room the jurors have the written instructions with them for their own reference.

When preliminary instructions are given, jurors are not yet given notepads to take notes, but they are instructed that note-taking is possible ('Jurors are allowed to take notes during the trial'). Even though jurors are then instructed not to base their judgment on their notes, this is cognitively complicated as writers themselves generally assign a certain level of credibility to their own notes. Ideally, all these texts (the original instructions, the judge's comments and the juror's notes) should be perfectly consistent and there should be no discrepancy, but they inevitably display different textual and pragmatic characteristics.

In this final phase of the jury instruction process the names of the parties are used instead of abstract definitions such as *plaintiff* or *defendant*:

(11) The claim of *Novell* that *SCO* slandered *Novell*'s title is no longer before you and will not be decided by you. Do not concern yourselves with this development and do not speculate about it. *SCO* has the burden of proving its claim by a preponderance of the evidence.

As has been shown, in other cases general terms such as *plaintiff* and *defendant* are used, thus giving the text a high level of abstractness, but at the same time of all-inclusiveness. Even though these two terms are not highly complex and the jurors should presumably know exactly the roles assumed by the different participants, the use of proper nouns to refer to the parties enhances clarity and avoids ambiguity. Even though depersonalization may be used for strategic reasons, a clear and consistent identification of the parties is important. Specific names are helpful in order to frame the role of each participant and to render the instruction more case-specific.

Final instructions also state the law that is applicable to the case. The applicable law cannot be easily reformulated without affecting its accuracy and precision. Thus, the explanation of some legal principles is characterized by linguistic complexity, especially from a lexical point of view, and the use of legal jargon seems inescapable:

(12) In this particular *civil case*, one of the elements of the *claim* made by SCO, the showing of *constitutional malice*, has a different *burden of proof* called *clear and convincing evidence*. That means that SCO has a higher *burden* than preponderance of the evidence, but it does not require *proof beyond a reasonable doubt*.

The legal concepts to be applied are explained through definitions, but the judge does not generally make use of analogical thinking, figurative language, exemplifications or other explanatory tools in order not to violate the conventions of a correct and precise instruction.

The judge also makes use of endophoric references, which should contribute to the cohesion and coherence of the text:

(13) Clear and convincing evidence leaves no substantial doubt in your mind that the constitutional malice is highly probable, as previously explained in Instruction No. 13.

In this case, having the written text is extremely important for the jurors in order to be able to refer to the correct instruction.

It has often been argued that, when dealing with the instructions related to the applicable law, jurors either ignore it or are extremely confused by it (Diamond/Murphy/Rose 2012). The law/facts dichotomy is a fundamental construct of a jury trial in that the court determines the law and juries determine the facts. However, the process of applying the law lies in the hands of the jury. In this respect, it should be noted that, historically, American juries were not generally instructed in the law before the nineteenth century. Indeed, it was assumed that they could derive the law autonomously (Millon 1993: 137). Therefore, originally the role of the jury was twofold: to determine the facts as well as the law to be applied. As early as 1939 DeWolfe Howe noted that the jury's authority was gradually being restricted, and its role has subsequently been reduced to that of triers of facts (Rubenstein 2006).

5. Conclusions

Starting from the assumption that effective communication among the participants is essential for the adequate development of a jury trial, this analysis has focused on spoken interaction in court, and in particular on the delivery of jury instructions. Particular attention has been devoted to the communication dynamics that emerge between the judge and the jurors within the specific constraints imposed by the legal and procedural framework.

Jury instructions have two primary objectives: "achieving legal accuracy and effectively conveying information to jurors" (Severance/Loftus 1982: 155). The former aspect cannot be overlooked as a jury verdict may be the subject of appeal in a higher court if there is a claim of error in the jury instructions. On the other hand, it is clear that these texts should also effectively provide jurors with the tools to execute their task in a correct and just way. Consequently, these two objectives are inevitably at odds.

Pattern jury instructions that display a universal applicability to all cases (with the necessary specific adaptations) are widespread and the high level of standardization of the texts delivered may lead us to conclude that a decidedly impersonal style is inevitably used. On the other hand, the need to adopt Plain English to communicate with lay juries also determines the emergence of interpersonal features, which aim to maintain a high level of attention and involvement on the part of the jurors and help the court to manage the tension between abstractness and concreteness, as well as between generality and specificity. For example, the choices adopted to address the participants show an alternation between abstract expressions such as *the Court* and *the jurors* and direct personal pronouns such as *I* and *you*. The impersonal approach is deemed suitable especially when referring to generalizable rules and principles. By contrast, the pronoun *I* is used by the court in order to create a clearer link between the concrete figure of the Judge presiding a specific trial and the jurors. A constant use of a third person perspective may seem more impersonal and sound like a reference to a more abstract situation rather than to the current case in question. Similarly, in order to define the parties, the instructions analyzed make use of both general definitions (e.g. *plaintiff*, *defendant*) and their specific names.

In 1973 Friedman defined jury instructions as "stereotyped, antiseptic statements of abstract rules" (Friedman 1973: 155). A certain level of impersonality and abstractness remains as it is traditionally typical of legal discourse. However, in comparison with other legal texts, instructions seem to display a less significant use of impersonal constructions, such as passives, and a clear attempt to avoid excessively intricate syntactic patterns. A clear organizational structure is generally adopted, including, for example, the use of numbered lists. This approach is in line with the assumption that simplification in terms of lexical and syntactic choices and textual features can improve jurors' understanding (Tiersma 1993). On the other hand, even though instructions are aimed for laypeople and should theoretically avoid the use of legal jargon, instructing the jury about the applicable law is particularly complex, as the importance of legal accuracy cannot be overestimated. Therefore, final instructions show a higher level of complexity and impersonality when dealing with the applicable law.

In the light of the concept of knowledge asymmetry in jury communication (cf. Anesa 2012), using clear, comprehensible and effective instructions is fundamental in order to allow the jury to execute its task fairly and justly. It has often been suggested that instructions should be tailored and customized to the individual case, for instance, including the names of parties instead of general definitions. This choice is often adopted in the case analyzed here even though it coexists with a more abstract approach, especially in the delivery of initial instructions.

References

Anesa, Patrizia 2012. *Jury Trials and the Popularization of Legal Language: A Discourse Analytical Approach.* Bern: Peter Lang.

Anesa, Patrizia / Kastberg, Peter 2012. On Some Communicatively Salient Complexities of Knowledge Asymmetries in a Jury Trial. *Text & Talk* 32/1, 1-19.

Asprey, Michèle [3]2003. *Plain Language for Lawyers.* Annandale, NSW: The Federation Press.

Austin, John L. 1962. *How to Do Things with Words.* Oxford: Clarendon.

Conley, John 2000. Epilogue: A Legal and Cultural Commentary on the Psychology of Juror Instructions. *Psychology, Public Policy, and Law* 6, 822-831.

Danet, Brenda 1980. Language in the Legal Process. *Law and Society Review* 14/3, 445-564.

DeWolfe Howe, Mark 1939. Juries as Judges of Criminal Law. *Harvard Law Review* 52, 582-616.

Diamond, Shari Seidman / Murphy, Beth / Rose, Mary R. 2012. The 'Kettleful of Law' in Real Jury Deliberations: Successes, Failures, and Next Steps. *Northwestern University Law Review* 106/4, 1537-1608.

Ellsworth, Phoebe C. / Reifman, Alan 2000. Juror Comprehension and Public Policy: Perceived Problems and Proposed Solutions. *Psychology, Public Policy, and Law* 6, 788-821.

Flesch, Rudolf 1979. *How to Write Plain English: A Book for Lawyers and Consumers.* New York: Harper and Row.

Fletcher, George 2003. Law. In Smith, Barry (ed.) *John Searle*. Cambridge: Cambridge University Press, 85-101.

Fraser, Bruce 1974a. An Analysis of Vernacular Performative Verbs. In Shuy, Roger / Bailey, Charles-James N. (eds) *Towards Tomorrow's Linguistics*. Washington: Georgetown University Press, 139-58.

Fraser, Bruce 1974b. An Examination of the Performative Analysis. *Papers in Linguistics* 7, 1-40.

Friedman, Lawrence 1973. *A History of American Law*. New York: Simon and Schuster.

Galanter, Marc 2004. The Vanishing Trial: An Examination of Trials and Related Matters in Federal and State Courts. *Journal of Empirical Legal Studies* 1/3, 459-570.

Galdia, Marcus 2009. *Legal Linguistics*. Frankfurt a.M.: Peter Lang.

Garner, Bryan A. 2001. *Legal Writing in Plain English*. Chicago: University of Chicago Press.

Gibbons, John 1994. *Language and the Law*. Longman: London.

Gibbons, John 2003. *Forensic Linguistics: An Introduction to Language in the Justice System*. Oxford: Blackwell.

Graham, Fred 2009. American Juries. *eJournal USA* 14/7, 4-6.

Hart, Herbert L. A. [2]1994. *The Concept of Law*. Oxford: Clarendon.

Hastie, Reid / Penrod, Steven D. / Pennington, Nancy 1983. *Inside the Jury*. Cambridge, Mass.: Harvard University Press.

Heffer, Chris 2005. *The Language of Jury Trial: A Corpus-aided Analysis of Legal-Lay Discourse*. Basingstoke: Palgrave Macmillan.

Heffer, Chris 2008. The Language and Communication of Jury Instructions. In Gibbons, John / Turell, Teresa (eds) *Dimensions of Forensic Linguistics*. Amsterdam: John Benjamins, 47-65.

Hyland, Ken 2002. Authority and Invisibility: Authorial Identity in Academic Writing. *Journal of Pragmatics* 34, 1091-1112.

Jackson, Bernard 1995. *Making Sense in Law: Linguistic, Psychological, and Semiotic Perspectives*. Liverpool: Deborah Charles.

Jonakait, Randolph N. 2003. *American Jury System*. New Haven, CT: Yale University Press.

Kritzer, Herbert M. 2013. The Trials and Tribulations of Counting 'Trials'. *DePaul Law Review* 63, 415-441.

Lieberman, Joel D. / Arndt, Jamie / Vess, Matthew 2009. Inadmissible Evidence and Pretrial Publicity: The Effects (and Ineffectiveness) of Admonitions to Disregard. In Lieberman, Joel D. / Krauss, Daniel A. (eds) *Jury Psychology: Social Aspects of Trial Processes*. Abingdon: Ashgate, 67-98.

Martineau, Robert 1991. *Drafting Legislation and Rules in Plain English*. St. Paul, Minn.: West Publishing Co.

Millon, David 1993. Juries, Judges, and Democracy. *Law & Social Inquiry* 18, 135-164.

Moley, Raymond 1928. The Vanishing Jury. *Southern California Law Review* 2, 97-127.

Ohmann, Richard 1972. Instrumental Style: Notes on the Theory of Speech as Action. In Kachru, Braj B. / Stahlke, Herbert F. W. (eds) *Current Trends in Stylistics*. Edmonton, Ill.: Linguistic Research, 115-141.

Rubenstein, Arie M. 2006. Verdicts of Consciousness: Nullification and the Modern Jury Trial. *Columbia Law Review* 106, 959-60.

Šarčević, Susan 2000. *New Approach to Legal Translation*. The Hague: Kluver Law International.

Schwarzer, William W. 1991. Reforming Jury Trials. *Federal Rules Decisions*, vol. 132. St. Paul: West, 575-96.

Searle, John R. 1969. *Speech Acts. An Essay in the Philosophy of Language*. New York: Oxford University Press.

Searle, John R. 1975. A Taxonomy of Illocutionary Acts. In Gunderson, Keith (ed.) *Language, Mind, and Knowledge*. Minneapolis: University of Minnesota Press, 344-69.

Severance, Laurence J. / Loftus, Elizabeth F. 1982. Improving the Ability of Jurors to Comprehend and Apply Criminal Jury Instructions. *Law & Society Review* 17/1, 153-198.

Steinberg, Edwin R. 1991. *Plain English: Principles and Practice*. Detroit: Wayne State University Press.

Sudweeks, Fay / Simoff, Simeon J. 1999. Complementary Explorative Data Analysis: The Reconciliation of Quantitative and Qualitative Principles. In Jones, Steve (ed.) *Doing Internet Research – Critical Issues and Methods for Examining the Net*. London: Sage, 29-56.

Tiersma, Peter 1993. Reforming the Language of Jury Instructions. *Hofstra Law Review* 22, 37-78.

Tiersma, Peter 1999a. *Legal Language*. Chicago: The University of Chicago Press.

Tiersma, Peter 1999b. Jury Instructions in the New Millennium. *Court Review* 36/2, 28-36.

Tiersma, Peter 2005. Communicating with Juries: How to Draft More Understandable Jury Instruction. *The Scribes Journal of Legal Writing* 10, 1-54.

Tiersma, Peter / Curtis, Matthew 2008. Testing the Comprehensibility of Jury Instructions. *Journal of Court Innovation* 1, 231-261.

Wegner, Daniel M. 1994. Ironic Processes of Mental Control. *Psychological Review* 101, 34-52.

Williams, Christopher 2004. Legal English and Plain Language: an Introduction. *ESP Across Cultures* 1, 113-124.

Williams, Christopher 2005. *Traditions and Change in Legal English*. Bern: Peter Lang.

Wydick, Richard C. ^{5}2005. *Plain English for Lawyers*. Durham, N.C.: Carolina Academic Press.

Yamamoto, Mutsumi 2006. *Agency and Impersonality: Their Linguistic and Cultural Manifestations*. Amsterdam: Benjamins.

ISABEL CORONA

The Management of Conflict: Arbitration in Corporate E-releases

1. Introduction

Corporate communication is generally concerned with construing and projecting the company's identity and image. Both are realized through their discursive practices by means of the communicative resources they have at their disposal. Corporate communication is addressed to four main target groups: employees, investors, customers and the wider audience. The texts and genres produced by corporations vary according to who the audience will be. As Breeze (2013) contends, we can approach corporate communication from the perspective of who these texts and genres are intended for, and thus foregrounding 'the dialogic purpose of discourse' (Breeze 2013: 25). Press releases are discursive events that are at the centre of corporate life. Attached to day-to-day professional practices and corporate decisions, they act as carriers of image, identity and values and thus are particularly associated with the media and the wider audience. Furthermore, their communicative function has been profusely studied and in general terms there is the widely accepted assumption that these texts are a hybrid genre (Bhatia 1995, 2004) that incorporates different discourses, mostly informative and promotional. However, the precise motives and purposes underlying a particular press release can vary substantially.

The texts which are the object of study in this chapter comply with the principles of genre construction and description: they are communicative artefacts that represent the textual articulation of social processes and, as such, they are reproduced, adapted and transformed; they develop as an 'embedded social process', one which "concomitantly both shapes and reflects organizational attitudes and behaviours" (Swales/Rogers 1995: 225).

The social process here is arbitration, a mechanism or legal device for the resolution of commercial disputes between corporations. Arbitration is largely preferred to litigation because it is supposed to be more flexible, speedy, economic and private. However, corporations are legally or ethically bound to disclosure of arbitration when they are listed in financial markets, when they are dealing with a purchaser (Denoix de Saint Marc 2003) or when the law applies the principle of public interest. In those cases the company's duty is to provide shareholders or prospective purchasers with information that may impact the value of the company. They may publicise the case at several critical moments during the process of arbitration: at the filing, during the procedures, or when the award, that is, the final ruling, is communicated by the arbitral tribunal. The channel of immediate communication is the e-press release.

These public announcements by the corporations dealing with arbitration processes are a professional practice carried out by public relations personnel or press officers within the corporations, but also, given the nature of the subject-matter, by the corporation's legal counsel. These texts are critical sites of engagement of corporate commitments and community expectations with a considerable risk of damage to the company's reputation and consequently of a high impact in the corporations' financial results.

This study seeks to explore how these specific texts are constructed not only to inform shareholders and the general public, building a positive image of the company, but also, and more importantly, to naturalise their stance in the argumentation of the conflict, lead the audience to see 'the truth' from their perspective and thus minimise the negative impact. How does the legal conflict, that is, the propositional content of the press releases dealing with arbitration, affect the genre? How does the voice of each corporation position itself with respect to the audience and to the other party, particularly if we consider that these public announcements construe a sequence of discursive events within a single process, that of an arbitration procedure?

In order to answer these questions, I draw on two theoretical concepts: *genre* and *interpersonality*. When approaching genre, I share the widely assumed view of genre as typified rhetorical action (Miller 1994) and a goal-oriented configuration of meanings (Martin 1992). The present study draws in particular on Critical Genre Analysis as proposed by Bhatia (2004, 2008) who adopts a multiperspective methodology that includes professional culture, professional practices, discursive practices, genres and, ultimately, texts with the purpose of describing and explaining professional discourse.

I understand interpersonality as an umbrella term that serves to include, as Mur-Dueñas *et al.* (2010: 83) summarise, "the complex interplay of the writer and their readership as projected in the text, as well as how this projection is influenced and influences the writer's position in relation to their own texts and the texts of others". The study of interpersonality has been carried out following several frameworks, such as metadiscourse, stance, voice, evaluation or appraisal, all of them accounting for the grammatical resources and the rhetorical strategies employed to bring about the authors' communicative objectives. The present analysis applies the Appraisal Theory framework (Martin/Rose 2003; Martin/White 2005) and in particular its development of Engagement, as it explores the social dialogic resources that "position the speaker/writer with respect to the value position being advanced and with respect to potential responses to that value position" (Martin/White 2005: 36). Engagement brings together the strategies deployed by corporations to represent themselves, their identity and image, their position towards the conflict and their audience, which includes stakeholders, journalists and the wider audience. This framework will be applied to explore the dialogistic positioning of the companies and, importantly, to unveil the monoglossic or heteroglossic character of their standing. The Engagement framework will assist in determining the rhetorical resources by which corporations negotiate their point of view and establish a dialogue with the audience – and between themselves – in the arbitration process through the genre of the press release.

The analytical work is based on previous studies which have dealt with a corpus of over 70 corporate press releases from fifteen different international commercial arbitration cases between corporations (Corona 2011a, 2011b, 2012, 2013) and takes them as a point of departure to focus on the entire process of one single case, from the origin of the dispute, in 2010, to the final award, in November 2013. The reason for the choice lies, first, in its completeness and hence in the possibilities this offers for the analysis of the textual behaviour of both corporations along the whole procedure. Secondly, in the major agents: the case involved two well-known multinational corporations with strong identity and image, Starbucks – one of the 'World's 10 Most Admired' companies, according to *Fortune*'s 2013 List – and Kraft Foods.

The present study takes a three-dimensional perspective on interpersonality: as individual, social and dialogic voice (Tardy 2012). As individual voice, because it construes the identity and image of the corporation; as social voice, because it is determined by genre, as the discursive means to accomplish the social occasion of arbitration, and as dialogic voice, because the multiple addressees play a key role in the construction of this manifestation of the press release genre.

To better understand the contextual factors affecting these texts, it is necessary to consider them not as isolated products, but as a chain of communicative events dealing with a very specific social situation: a legal conflict made public. It is for this reason that the next section explains this social situation and summarises the arbitration case, that is, the data. Section 3 tackles the question of the genre of the press release, exploring its internal features as instantiated in the data, and the external factors affecting the texts, namely, the pragmatic role of confidentiality in the case under study. Then section 4 focuses on the analysis of interpersonality, that is, on the particular dialogistic resources found in this text type. The chapter closes with some final remarks.

2. The Kraft Foods *v* Starbucks case

The reconstruction of the dispute has been possible through the information provided by the press releases, the financial reports of the companies at their quarterly filings and the numerous news reports published during the three-year dispute. Starbucks started its business with one store in Seattle (USA) in 1971. More than forty years later, with more than 19,000 stores in 62 countries, it is probably the world's largest coffee chain. In 1998, Kraft Foods, the North America's largest food company, signed an agreement with Starbucks to distribute its packaged coffee to grocery stores. In August 2010, Starbucks made an offer to buy Kraft out of the agreement, which Kraft rejected, arguing that the offer was below fair market value. In October, Starbucks told Kraft in a letter that it was in material breach of the contract. On November 4 Kraft responded in a similar fashion denying the breaches; a few hours later Starbucks made the dispute public at its earnings call. On November 29 Kraft initiated arbitration proceedings in Chicago, arguing that Starbucks could not end the agreement unilaterally. Their standpoints could be summarised as follows: while Starbucks accused Kraft of breach of the agreement, Kraft denied any breach and claimed compensation if Starbucks wanted them out of their shared business.

A few days after the filing Kraft sought a preliminary injunction in a district court to prevent Starbucks from taking back the business while in arbitration. It was denied shortly afterwards, a denial subsequently affirmed by the Appellate Court. From then, end of February 2011, to the final award, in November 2013, there were no public announcements from any of the two corporations. Starbucks took full control of the business in March 2011. The private hearing, an obligatory and private step of the arbitral procedure in which the parties present arguments and evidence in support of their respective cases, was held in July 2012, and was not communicated about, although news reports on the pending arbitration case did not cease to appear. The issue was in fact to determine how much money the loser should pay to the winner, and how that would affect their financial results and future earnings. For financial analysts, it was clear that the payment of the settlement, whoever won the case, would harm the losing company's bottom line. Starbucks had claimed damages of up to $62.9 million while Kraft claimed damages of up to $2.9 billion, plus attorney fees. Eventually, the arbitrator ruled in favour of Kraft, the award stating that Starbucks had to pay $2.23 billion in damages plus $527 million for interest and legal fees. In after-hours trading on that day, shares of the winner rose 3 percent while Starbucks's fell 1.5 percent.

During the three-year process both corporations issued six press releases each, twelve in total, dealing with the dispute, all of them made available on the corporations' websites (<www.Kraftfoods company.com>, <http://news.starbucks.com/news>). The total number of words devoted to the issue is quite similar: 1,742 by Starbucks and 1,991 by Kraft. On average, Starbucks's press releases contained 290.3 words and Kraft's 331.8 words. This estimation, however, is misleading, because in fact the number of words of each press release depends on the contextual situation: a response to a previous release by the other company, a new development in the arbitration case, or the preliminary injunction process; the event that prompts the press release signals the need to be more or less explanatory, and hence the number of words varies substantially (see Table 1).

Phases	*Date*	*Starbucks (S) Headlines*	*No. words*	*Kraft (K) Headlines*	*No. words*
Phase 1: Dispute is made public	4 Nov 2010	(S1) *Statement: Update on Starbucks Consumer Packaged Goods Business*	90	(K1) *Kraft Foods Statement regarding Starbucks Agreement*	94
		(S2) *Statement: Response to Kraft's Statement Regarding Starbucks Consumer Packaged Goods Business*	73		
Phase 2: Filing for arbitration	29 Nov 2010	(S3) *Starbucks Comments on Media Reports Regarding Termination of Contract with Kraft Foods*	350	(K2) *Kraft Foods Challenges Starbucks Attempt to Terminate Strategic Partnership*	278
Phase 3: Preliminary injunction	6 Dec 2010	(S4) *Starbucks Response to Kraft Foods Recent Actions*	138	(K3) *Kraft Foods Seeks Preliminary Injunction Against Starbucks*	779
Phase 4: The case in District and Appellate Courts	23 Dec 2010	(S5) *Starbucks Comments on District Court Conference with Kraft*	572		
	28 Jan			(K4) *Court Denies Kraft Foods' Request*	260

	2011			*For Preliminary Injunction*	
	25 Feb 2011			(K5) *U.S. Appellate Court Denies Kraft Foods' Request For Reversal*	253
Phase 5: Final award	12 Nov 2013	(S6) *Starbucks concludes Packaged Coffee Dispute with Kraft*	519	(K6) *Arbitration Ends Coffee Contract Dispute*	327

Table 1. The press releases issued by Starbucks and Kraft on the dispute between 2010 and 2013.

The dynamics of these public announcements can be best understood if we organise them chronologically, in terms of phases, that is, according to the events that prompted the corporations to have their say. The five phases identified are set out in Table 1. However, it is necessary to clarify that the initial press releases are the first generic manifestations of some events that occurred earlier, which could be grouped under the label 'Phase 0': the prior buyout offer by Starbucks, Kraft's rejection and Starbucks's letter alleging breach of contract, all of them apparently having taken place privately. The issuing of the press releases had Kraft as initiator of the exchange in four occasions, Starbucks in two. The phases developed as follows:

- *Phase 1: The disagreement is made public.* After the quarterly financial results calls of both companies, held on the same day, three press releases are issued within hours. Starbucks issues an 'update' press release in which it announces to the media that a month earlier it had communicated Kraft its intention to end the contract. Another one from Kraft follows, 'clarifying' the situation; that is, that the contract is 'perpetual' and that, if Starbucks wants to leave, it must compensate Kraft. Then a second by Starbucks, in which it disagrees with Kraft's 'mischaracterization' of the contract and refers covertly to arbitration, not mentioned as such, but as a "specific mechanism within the agreement for the resolution of disputes."
- *Phase 2: Kraft initiates arbitration.* Starbucks issues a long press release arguing its position, allegedly mischaracterised by

Kraft and the media, and 'notes' again that "there are binding dispute resolution procedures under the agreement". Later that day, Kraft announces its filing for arbitration.

- *Phase 3: Kraft requests preliminary injunction* in the district court and Starbucks responds, strongly disapproving of Kraft's action and reaffirming its position and 'transition' plans.
- *Phase 4: The dispute goes to court.* After the hearing to discuss the injunction at the District Court, Starbucks issues a long press release. Kraft will only come on stage days later, to communicate the denial by the District Court and also when the Appellate Court affirmed the denial.
- *Phase 5: The arbitrator renders the final award* and both companies issue their respective press releases.

3. The arbitration press release

The overall communicative purpose of a corporate press release is to publish news about the company and to present the company in as favourable a light as possible. These texts on good news tend to adopt the generic structure of news reports and thus serve as pre-cooked texts to be used by journalists in their institutions. Jacobs (1999a, 1999b) was the first to identify and describe a series of linguistic resources that were characteristic features of press releases, which he named, due to their rhetoric functionality, as 'pre-formulating strategies', that is, texts that were aimed at producing prefabricated news reports in order to facilitate the job of journalists, who were to 'reuse' those texts for media consumption. At a text-organizational level, these strategies are powerful headlines, leads to summarise the piece of news, information about the company at the end of the text and contact details. At a micro level, three linguistic resources were found to be pervasive: a) the use of pseudo-quotes – to evaluate the facts –, b) the use of third-person reference – to take the journalist's perspective and reinforce the tellability of the information released by the corporation –, and c) the use of past tense – used instead of present tense to talk about events that had not taken place yet.

More recent research has further explored this path. From the identification of moves as consisting of just ^Announcement ^Development ^Comment and ^Contact details (McLaren/Gurău 2005), further explorations have identified a whole range of moves that reflect the flexibility of press releases, which adapt to their specific, situated communicative purposes, and show the presence of many discourses – informational, promotional, legal or other (Corona 2011a, 2012) – which has reinforced the view of this text type as a hybrid genre, or, as Catenaccio (2008: 10) puts it, a 'rhetorical embodiment', or even, as Lassen (2006) argues, to question its genre status at length.

Similarly, ethnographic research (van Hout *et al.* 2011) of the 'metapragmatic features' (Jacobs 1999b), that is, the pre-formulating devices deployed in press releases and their actual functionality in the newsrooms, has also thrown new light on their use and validity (Sleurs/Jacobs 2005; Pander Maat 2008; van Hout/Jacobs 2008). Recent exploration into the writing practices of public relations firms has shown that corporate press releases are created by templates – visual frameworks – where texts are inserted, and by what these authors term 'boilerplate', which refers to the content, usually reused, sometimes just by updating facts and figures (Jones *et al.* 2012). These findings, together with the pervasive deployment of positive lexis to refer to the company's accomplishments and future actions or expectations, lead us to consider whether these strategies, by dint of their almost formulaic nature and their widespread use, have ceased to be communicatively effective. In fact, According to Hickey (2008), "the press release is the least loved document in the media universe" (some journalists referring to them as 'spam'), however its influence and benefits for the corporations are certainly expanding.

In the case under study, we can see in Table 2 the application of the typical strategic devices, at a linguistic and generic level. Kraft sticks to them in all the press releases, while Starbucks has a more selective application (see Table 1 for its peculiar way of headlining the texts, as 'Comments', or 'Response'). Apart from the classic pieces 'About the corporation' and the 'Forward-looking Statement', in previous explorations into the generic organization of arbitration press releases (Corona 2012) it became clear that the structure of these texts is closer to the move structure of legal cases, as identified by Bhatia (1993). Three of the devices (see Table 2) are only used by Starbucks in the last press release (S6), to announce the arbitral final decision (dealt with in section 4).

Pre-formulating strategies	*Starbucks*	*Kraft*
Informative headline	no	yes
Lead	no	yes
'About the corporation'	yes	yes
'Forward-looking Statement'	only in S6	yes
Contact details	yes	yes
Use of past tense	only in S6	yes
Use of pseudo-quotation	only in S6	yes
Use of third-person reference	yes	yes

Table 2. Deployment of pre-formulating strategies.

As for third-person reference, a pragmatic resource that is also exploited in corporate discourse to reinforce the objectiveness of the information released by the corporation, it is also present in both by using the name of the company ('Kraft is', or 'Starbucks has') but it undergoes a clear transformation as events unfold and the dialogue between the parties becomes more and more aggressive and confrontational, a circumstance that deserves more detailed analysis.

3.1. First-person reference and 'egocentrism'

There is a referential switch, from third- to first-person pronouns and first-person possessive determiners (see Table 3 for their occurrence).

First-person reference	*we*	*I*	*our*	*our (mutual/shared)*	*us*	*Total*
Starbucks	20	1	23	5	1	50
Kraft	14	0	11	3	2	30

Table 3. First-person reference formulations and their occurrence.

However, the use of first-person reference is not a 'solidarity building' resource, or an inclusive pronoun *we* or an inclusive possessive determiner *our*. The eight cases of apparently 'inclusive' *our* found in the texts – five for Starbucks and three for Kraft – refer to their mutual 'agreement', the issue under dispute, or to their shared 'customers', likely to be affected by the situation. This out-of-the-ordinary situation, to a certain extent, lends weight to the fact that these texts are an ongoing dialogue between the parties: an *I v. them* structure. Here, first-person reference is not the 'classic rhetorical device for fostering affiliation' of corporate discourse (Swales/Rogers 1995: 231), or a reflection of 'democratic ideals of equality', as Breeze (2013) shows to be the case in other corporate genres. Kraft and Starbucks consciously choose to adopt explicit 'authorial identity' (Hyland 2005), emphasizing the 'egocentric' nature (Jacobs 1999b: 220) of their communiqués, as they need to project how they stand in relation to their arguments:

(1) *We* are confident in *our* position and look forward to presenting the facts before the arbitrator.(K2)

Furthermore, exclusive self-mention (Lorés Sanz 2011) increases its explicit presence – to the detriment of the expected 'objective' third-person reference, as their exchanges harden in tone and show a need to reinforce their positions, even more so in the more conflicting moments. Their development, according to the phase of the arbitration procedure they are involved in, is set out in Table 4.

Phase	*First-person reference*	
	Starbucks	*Kraft*
1. Dispute is made public	0	0
	8	
2. Initiation of arbitration	0	2
3. Preliminary injunction	9	5
4. District and Appellate Courts	11	
		7
		9
5. Final award	22	7
Total references	50	30

Table 4. First-person reference development according to the arbitration phase.

Kraft uses this referential choice more profusely when they are denied the preliminary injunction. Starbucks's display of first person is fully developed in the last press release, after the final award has been rendered. The twofold purpose of third-person reference, meeting the requirements of news writing while at the same time trying to look more objective, is completely overlooked when bad news threatens the company's public image. Pragmatic demands clash with the objective standards of the press. The surge to reinforce their position and their perspective on the negative events sweeps away press release writing conventions. Even the all-inclusive, institutional *we* is superseded by the exclusive, defensive *we*. We could argue that corporate disclosure discourse becomes even more 'egocentric' as the crucial communicative purpose for corporations is to legitimate their actions, that is, to defend themselves.

3.2. The pragmatics of the principle of confidentiality

In arbitration proceedings privacy has traditionally referred to the fact that only parties to the arbitration may attend arbitral hearings, while confidentiality implies a legal obligation to avoid public disclosure of the existence of the arbitration, or its subject matter, the evidence, the documents or the award, all of which can be considered as sensitive information. As to laws and regulations, in the United States, where the arbitration case under study was filed, neither the Federal Arbitration Act nor the Uniform Arbitration Act imposes a confidentiality obligation on the parties. The American Arbitration Association requires the arbitrators, not the parties, to maintain the confidentiality of the arbitration proceedings and the awards. The legal counsel of corporations usually advise parties to incorporate express confidentiality provisions in their arbitration clause, as appears to have been the case in our data. However, the public-interest exception is clear when companies and financial institutions require by law to divulge information that could affect their share value. As Stevens (2000) argues, a company could find itself "under a positive duty to provide certain information about its activities to its shareholders, especially regarding its involvement in a process the outcome of which could perhaps significantly affect its share value."

Corporations are aware of this weakness of the arbitration system. The existing loophole allows parties to circumvent, make a selective use, or otherwise avoid confidentiality altogether. Prior research in this area (Corona 2011a, 2011b, 2013) has revealed different motives: to put pressure on the other party, to defend themselves, to promote themselves, to justify their decisions or even, when the case is expected to go against their interests, to make the process last longer.

Whatever the hidden agenda of some corporations with respect to their pragmatic use of the confidentiality principle, to disclose sensitive information, or, to put it bluntly, to wash their dirty linen in public, is not a desirable scenario. It is a challenging task and a reality that corporations are reluctant to accept because of the consequences it may have for their present and future developments. Conflict management means taking action when conflict hits. The communicative goal of the corporations is to minimise damage and convince stakeholders and the public in general that operations are as normal as possible. Crandall *et al.* (2009) clarify the situation when they distinguish two interconnected crisis landscapes: internal and external. The former refers to the management of primary stakeholders and the latter mainly to negative media coverage. One of the most important challenges of conflict management is to manage communication effectively and display the adequate 'damage control' procedures with the media.

In the present case, there is a recurrent situation of gradual disclosure, which, not surprisingly, starts with a gate-keeping attitude of not willing to give information about an issue deemed private. The first exchange displays identical formulations from both companies:

(2) Starbucks intends to keep the discussions with Kraft private and will not be providing further details or comments at this time. (S1)

(3) Kraft Foods intends to keep the discussions with Starbucks private and will not be providing further details or comments at this time. (K1)

The third press release of the day – the second by Starbucks – insists on the private character of their confrontation:

(4) It has been, and continues to be, our intention to keep these conversations private. (S2)

McIntyre (2010) exposed this apparent contradiction in his news report in *The Daily Finance* the following day:

> So, apparently, each side intends to keep the details private, but that claim is somewhat undercut by the fact that they both posted their comments in the press release sections of their corporate websites, for all to see. The feuding companies are clearly hoping to get some sympathy from customers and the press.

It is precisely that 'sympathy from customers and the press' that will motivate the evolution of their prior gate-keeping attitude towards an increasingly open strategy, albeit arguing that it is the other party's inappropriate disclosure to the media, or the media themselves that pushes them to open up. The headline of the third press release issued by Starbucks pinpoints this 'external' circumstance:

(5) Starbucks Comments on Media Reports Regarding Termination of Contract with Kraft Foods. (S3)

Again, in the fifth press release, after a full argumentation of its position in the dispute, Starbucks ends the text with the following coda:

(6) Starbucks looks forward to the opportunity to have our side of the argument heard fairly and without Kraft's misleading media spin being applied to the facts of the case. (S4)

In the last press release, in which Starbucks announces that it has lost the arbitration case, privacy comes again to play its pragmatic role:

(7) The details of the arbitrator's decision are confidential and Starbucks respects the privacy of the arbitration process so the company will not be sharing additional details from the ruling or the proceedings. (S6)

Between the first and the last references to confidentiality, ten press releases were issued. How these texts were interpersonally construed is explained in the following sections.

4. Managing conflict: dialogism and monoglossia

I take Bakhtin's (1981, 2000) perspective that any text, any verbal utterance is part of a dialogue. As Bakhtin (2000: 93) contends, "[U]nless one accounts for the speaker's attitude toward the *other* and his utterances (existing or anticipated), one can understand neither the genre nor the style of speech" (italics as in original). This dialogistic perspective is clearly instantiated in the press releases dealing with arbitration, where the texts have a special sense of understanding of their readers. As the legal counsel of each corporation will try to convince the arbitrator of the 'merits of their case', the press releases issued during an arbitration process will have the same communicative purpose. As a logical consequence, here as in the legal arena, corporations stand against each other. In arbitration press releases, Bakhtin's (2000: 94) notion of addressivity, "the quality of turning to someone", is crucial. They are written in reaction to prior texts and events, seeking to reinforce their position, or to undermine or attack particular assertions from the other party. There lies the key issue in this type of texts, as we can see a real exchange of viewpoints taking place between them. The point here is to know how they present their value position, either as authoritative, one that "demands our unconditional allegiance" (Bakhtin 1981: 343), or as one that can be questioned, resisted or rejected, but that will have to persuade us. Here lies "the struggle and dialogic interrelationship" (Bakhtin 1981: 342) between authoritative – monoglossic – discourse, where the writer "presents the current proposition as one which has no dialogistic alternatives" (Martin/White 2005: 99), and persuasive – heteroglossic – discourse, which may have other competing views and allows for alternatives, that is, it is presented as one of a range of possible options.

The analysis applies Appraisal Theory (Martin/Rose 2003; Martin/White 2005) and its development of the subsystem of Engagement as a framework to analyse the rhetorical resources by which each corporation construed its position in the arbitration process in order to align their audience. Engagement is the technical term used to identify the resources that "introduce additional voices in the discourse" (Martin/Rose 2003: 54), where the key issue is whether the texts choose one or more voices, that is, if they are monoglossic or heteroglossic. In heteroglossic terms, in order to identify the meanings associated with a particular dialogistic positioning, Martin and White (2005) distinguish two orientations, namely 'contractive' dialogue and 'expansive' dialogue, respectively restricting or opening up dialogic alternatives. These two orientations are in turn subdivided into two different types of resources according to their dialogistic functionality. Thus, within the subsystem of dialogic expansion, the value *entertain* refers to those locutions that may hold or consider other alternatives, while the value *attribution* refers to the positioning being grounded in an external voice. Dialogic contraction differentiates between *disclaim*, for those locutions expressing disagreement or rejection of dialogic alternatives, and *proclaim*, for those locutions expressing confrontation, challenge or exclusion of dialogic alternatives. The engagement system, briefly explained here, is set out in Figure 1. The linguistic realisations of engagement values are lexico-grammatically diverse. Hence, and following Martin and White (2005), I refer to them more generally as formulations.

Dialogue	*Category*	*Examples from the press releases*
Expansive	Entertain	(S2) *We believe it unfortunate that Kraft ...* (K4) *We avidly believe this case justifies an injunction ...*
	Attribute	(S5) *Kraft has claimed that it has grown Starbucks business ...* (K3) *Starbucks unilaterally and unjustifiably declared ...*
Contractive	Disclaim	(S3) *there was never any improvement in Kraft's performance* (K3) [the contract] *has no expiration day*
	Proclaim	(S5) *Kraft's own senior executives have acknowledged Kraft's neglect ...* (K2) *Starbucks has recognized and acknowledged Kraft's role ...*

Figure 1. Dialogic expansion and contraction (Martin/White 2005).

The summary of the occurrence of the four values in the twelve texts (Table 5) has shown fairly similar rhetorical strategies in both groups.

Press releases	*Dialogistic expansion*		*Dialogistic contraction*		*Total*
	Entertain	*Attribute*	*Disclaim*	*Proclaim*	
Starbucks 1-6	8	3	9	6	*26*
Kraft 1-6	8	4	14	4	*30*
Total per value	*16*	*7*	*23*	*10*	*56*

Table 5. Dialogic expansion and contraction formulations.

The total number of formulations expressing dialogic values is practically the same, 26 and 30, and with fairly equal distribution regarding each parameter, 11 and 12 instantiations each group for dialogic expansion, and 15 dialogic contraction formulations by Starbucks, 18 by Kraft. Table 6 presents the data for the development of dialogic formulations of the categories and subcategories of the engagement system in the twelve texts, summing the total number of formulations. Texts are identified by their order of publication and are also grouped according to the different phase of the arbitration process.

Phases	*Press releases*	*Dialogistic expansion*		*Dialogistic contraction*	
		Entertain	*Attribute*	*Disclaim*	*Proclaim*
1. Dispute is made public	S1	–	–	–	–
	K1	–	–	–	–
	S2	2	–	–	–
2. Filing for arbitration	K2	2	1	–	1
	S3	1	1	5	2
3. Preliminary injunction	K3	2	3	8	2
	S4	1	1	–	–
4. District and Appellate Courts	S5	3	1	4	4
	K4	2	–	4	1
	K5	1	–	2	–
5. Final award	K6	1	–	–	–
	S6	1	–	–	–
Total Starbucks *(S1-S6): 26*		*8*	*3*	*9*	*6*
Total Kraft *(K1-K6): 30*		*8*	*4*	*14*	*4*

Table 6. Occurrence of dialogic expansion and contraction formulations in the texts.

4.1. Monoglossia

The first exchange of press releases, Phase 1, shows total absence of dialogic instantiations because there is no dialogue, but a monoglossic turn-taking, each party asserting their position. The first press release, described by Starbucks as an 'update', makes public a past event that appears not to be new information for Kraft:

(8) A month ago Starbucks informed Kraft of its intention to *end* that distribution arrangement.(S1)

It is an intertextual reference to previous exchanges. The dialogue had started via different modes and media. However, Kraft had claimed 'ignorance' when reviewing its quarterly results at a conference call for investors, and later on the same day Starbucks produces the press release to counterclaim: the truth of the matter is that Kraft knew of Starbucks intentions. Kraft, in this turn-taking, responds with another monoglossic proposition: the 'agreement is perpetual':

(9) Kraft Foods' agreement with Starbucks regarding the sale of packaged coffee in grocery stores and other channels *is perpetual*. (K1)

This bare assertion acts as a counterargument and, with the inclusion of the adverb *importantly* to lend weight to its arguments, Kraft goes on to supply the facts to support their value position:

(10) Importantly, if Starbucks decides to exit its relationship with Kraft Foods, the agreement requires Starbucks to pay Kraft Foods the fair market value of the business plus, in certain instances, a premium. (K1)

This is the key issue of the dispute: Starbucks was not satisfied with the way Kraft distributed its packaged coffee and would try to convince the audience (and the arbitrator) of its right to exit the agreement freely. Kraft, on its part, will not accept it so willingly, and will argue that the agreement includes its rights to get compensation. In other words, Kraft challenges Starbucks's termination of the contract. The core of the dispute is thus whether the agreement has been breached – in which case Kraft has nothing to complain about – or not, in which case Kraft must have compensation. The communicative goal of Starbucks's press releases is to demonstrate that Kraft has breached the agreement, while Kraft's is the opposite. These opposing views are going to build the overall dialogue of the remaining ten press releases. The following subsections will show the results of the analyses of the dialogic resources put to use by the two corporations.

4.2. Dialogic expansion

Dialogic expansion choices for both groups of press releases are very similar (Table 6). Formulations of the *entertain* subcategory belong to two types of locutions: mental verbs with attributive projection of the type *we consider*, *we believe* + evaluative proposition:

(11) We *believe* that an injunction is unnecessary because there is no "irreparable harm" to Kraft (S5)

The second type refers to deontic modality with *must* or *could* as instantiations:

(12) Starbucks *must compensate* Kraft for the fair market value of the business (K3)

Although arguing that something *must* be the case may sound rather assertive, according to Martin and Rose (2003: 50), "modality acknowledges alternative voices around a suggestion or claim", opening up a space for negotiation.

Taking the *attribution* parameter into account, we must consider first that, as complying with the rhetorical conventions of press releases, these texts use reporting verbs for self-attribution, as in

(13) As we *said* in our earnings call, we will ensure that our mutual customers remain well-served. (S2)

or as in the following case, where a switch from third- to first-person reference occurs in mid-sentence:

(14) *Starbucks* has repeatedly *said* that *we* have terminated our agreement. (S4)

These frequent instantiations have not been considered as expansive dialogue. Attribution in this framework refers to "those formulations which disassociate the proposition from the text's internal authorial voice by attributing it to some external source" (Martin/White 2005: 111) and thus engaging interactively with it. Locutions of the dialogic expansion of *attribution* are scarce in both groups of press releases, and all the cases that have been identified are used to report what the other party has expressed publicly in previous press releases, or in the media, or elsewhere. They do not include other external voices. This strong intertextuality is seen to fulfil two distinct rhetorical functions, namely, either to counter argue the other party's position, or to demonstrate that, in fact, they 'agreed', reinforcing their own point of view, that is, backing up the authorial voice's standing on a given issue. The former is expressed through reporting verbs that explicitly imply distance or separation from the internal voice, as in

(15) Kraft has *claimed* that it has grown Starbucks business when, in fact, any recent gains have been due directly to Starbucks ongoing innovation in the packaged coffee space and overall coffee market price increases. (S5)

or by means of other indicators that clearly signal where they stand with respect to the attributed material. In the following case, with two strongly evaluative adverbials:

(16) Starbucks *unilaterally and unjustifiably declared* in public statements the agreement's termination (K2)

The second strategy consists of using attribution to lend support to an argument. In the following example, Kraft exposes Starbucks's explicit endorsement to the proposition expressed by the internal voice:

(17) Starbucks *praised* Kraft's role in building a 'highly profitable' CPG business, *citing* Kraft's 'world-class' capabilities in manufacturing, research and development, marketing and distribution. (K3)

Although this type of attribution falls within the heteroglossic category, we could reasonably say that the attitudinal assessment is monoglossic in that it categorically aligns with the internal voice's value position. Kraft is trying to invalidate Starbucks arguments of a breach of the agreement which are based on "Kraft's failure".

4.3. Dialogic contraction

Dialogically contractive meanings are those which "are directed towards excluding certain dialogic alternatives from any subsequent communicative interaction or at least towards constraining the scope of these alternatives" (Martin/White 2005: 116). Those 'excluding' meanings fall under the category of *disclaim*, and include denials, that is, the use of negative clauses to reject other alternatives:

(18) Kraft *did not meet* its responsibilities. (S3)

Denials place the internal voice in relation to the opposing one, that is, the other company. It is considered dialogic because it invokes two voices. As Martin and Rose (2003: 49) explain, it is "a voice acknowledged but denied".

The second set of *disclaim* resources are counterarguments ('counter', in Martin and White's (2005) terminology), by which the alternative proposition is supplanted by means of concessive constructions. The interesting aspect to pinpoint in the use of counter expectations in these texts is that they are not used for supplanting other alternatives, but to reinforce the authorial voice:

(19) Starbucks raised these issues with Kraft, *but* there was *never* any improvement in Kraft's performance. (S3)

Starbucks states that it acted as it should, but according to Kraft it did not. Here there is a double display of disclaiming resources, the concessive conjunction *but*, and the negative adverbial *never*.

Also included in this area is what Martin and Rose (2003) describe as 'continuatives', another set of resources for adjusting expectations, and which also help relate the proposition to the preceding move in the ongoing dialogue:

(20) Without proof of material breach, Starbucks *only* legitimate termination mechanism is to pay Kraft fair market value for the business. (K4)

Denial is used by Kraft in two press releases – not answered by Starbucks – after the injunction is rejected by both the district and the appellate courts. Kraft needs to clarify the audience that the arbitration proceedings continue and the process is not affected by the downside news, to which markets are very sensitive. By means of negative clauses, Kraft is pre-empting the affirmative possibility:

(21) That arbitration process will continue over the next several months and is *not affected by* today's Court decision. (K4)

The analysis of the occurrence of contractive dialogue formulations has revealed that they are more numerous than those of dialogic expansion, with formulations of *disclaim* being the most frequent dialogic resource used, with 23 instantiations, 9 by Starbucks and 14 by Kraft.

Proclaim, the second category within dialogic contraction, refers to those formulations which "act to limit the scope of dialogistic alternatives in the ongoing colloquy" (Martin/White 2005: 121). They are less frequent, with 6 cases in Starbucks's texts and 4 in Kraft's. In fact, they mostly occur in combination with other dialogistic resources, showing their argumentative nature. In the following examples, *proclaim* overlaps with *attribution*, with a communicative purpose similar to the one explained in example (17) that of lending support to the internal voice:

(22) Over the years, Starbucks *has recognized and acknowledged* Kraft's role in building Starbucks presence in grocery stores. (K2)

More complex is Kraft's argumentation in the following paragraph, where it presents a development of *attribution* (*allegation*) + *disclaim* (deny) + *proclaim* (agree: *of course*) + *disclaim* (counterargument: *But*) + *disclaim* (deny) + *disclaim* (deny):

(23) Their latest *allegation* is that *Kraft is not assisting* in the 'transition plan' that they launched on their own. *Of course*, we would cooperate in a transition, if there were a valid termination. *But* that's the point; *there hasn't been.* For them to complain about this *makes no sense*. (K3)

Attribution is used by Kraft to report a claim by Starbucks, namely, that Kraft "is not assisting". The second part of the argument starts with conditioned concurrence, to directly deny the condition and consequently Starbucks's argument.

Similar argumentation is used repeatedly by both companies, with the rhetorical pair *disclaim* (counterargument *when*) + *proclaim* (pronounce *in fact*) following a bare assertion (*Kraft is seeking the injunction*):

(24) Kraft is seeking the injunction to stop Starbucks from proceeding as if the agreement has been terminated, *when, in fact*, the contract is still in force.(K3)

The same combination, introduced by *attribution*:

(25) Kraft has *claimed* that it has grown Starbucks business *when, in fact*, any recent gains have been due directly to Starbucks ongoing innovation in the packaged coffee space and overall coffee market price increases.(S5)

Again, in (26), showing the structure *disclaim* (counterargument *while*) + *proclaim* (*acknowledge*) + *entertain* (*believe*):

(26) *While* we've always *acknowledged* that there are certain legal hurdles for obtaining a preliminary injunction, *we avidly believe* this case justifies an injunction and will argue that point vigorously on appeal. (K4)

Also, with the structure *disclaim* (counterargument *while*) + *attribute* (*state*) + entertain (*could be repaired*) + *disclaim* (deny):

(27) *while stating* that the damage could be repaired, *made no clear attempt* to do so. (S5)

The numerous examples found in the texts present a clear similarity with legal reasoning. The deployment of mainly contractive dialogistic resources resembles a recent development in legal argumentation, described as the pragma-dialectical approach (Feteris/Kloosterhuis 2013), which assumes that argumentation occurs in the context of a difference of opinion about the applicability of a legal rule in a concrete case where the structure is one of an exchange of arguments for and against each other's position, or, as Feteris and Kloosterhuis (2013: 17) explain, "a rational discussion in which a protagonist defends a standpoint against the anticipated or actual reactions of a critical antagonist". In our case, the 'legal rule' applicable to the dispute is the business contract between the parties, the arguments for and against, the fulfilment – or breach – of this agreement and hence the right for compensation.

4.4. Damage control: 'When things get rough, the rough get going'

If going through arbitration is certainly not a pleasant situation, a ruling which is contrary to the company's expectations is even more difficult to manage. Usually, corporations face the negative outcome in the public sphere by producing very short press releases which take one of the following positions: either challenging the award or accepting it without further comments, and then either alleging confidentiality or just expressing their will to leave the event behind. Two examples will illustrate both combinations. The first one was issued by Nike, after an 'unfavourable ruling' against its subsidiary Converse:

(28) "We disagree with the ruling and will exercise our legal right to challenge both the award and the amount of damages," said NIKE, Inc. General Counsel Jim Carter. Standard confidentiality provisions in the arbitration rules forbid the company from commenting on the substance of the ruling.[1]

The alternative position is exemplified in the following press release issued by Eventim, who filed for arbitration against Live Nation in 2010, and was rendered an adverse award in 2013:

---

1 'Arbitration court decides on CTS EVENTIM / Live Nation case'. <http://nikeinc.com/news/unfavorable-arbitration-ruling-involving-converse-subsidiary>.

(29) The management board of CTS EVENTIM AG is disappointed but will accept the ruling without further comments. It is important, after 3 years duration of proceedings,[2] that Eventim is able to fully concentrate on its operational business again.[3]

In the case under study, shortly after Starbucks reported, in its fourth quarter results, that 2013 had been the best year in its 42-year history, with a profit of 63 cents per share, the bad news was made known: Starbucks had lost the case and had to pay its former distribution partner Kraft for everything, legal fees included. The impact of the award resulted in a loss of 1.64 per share. How did one of the world's most admired companies, according to *Fortune*, position itself then? Starbucks's last press release – the longest of the series – changed its communicative purpose. Not surprisingly, it includes the entire strategic devices mentioned earlier (see section 3). Furthermore, Starbucks adds to the discourse of legitimation that has characterised the whole process, the discourse of reassurance towards investors. First, Starbucks reaffirms its position, both with respect to Kraft's performance and to their 'right' to exit the agreement:

(30) We believe Kraft did not deliver on its responsibilities to our brand under the agreement, the performance of the business suffered as a result, and that we had a right to terminate the agreement without payment to Kraft. (S6)

The company supports its argument by highlighting the benefits of its decision. In-house distribution of its packaged-coffee business has improved performance in terms of 'growth' and 'health' of the organization since then:

---

2 As in the case studied here, many arbitration proceedings take much longer than this mechanism is expected to. Reed (2010) echoed a study carried out by the Paris-based Corporate Counsel International Arbitration Group (CCIAG, <http://www.cciag.com>), which found that "100% of the corporate counsel participants believe that international arbitration "takes too long" (with 56% of those surveyed strongly agreeing).

3 'Unfavorable arbitration ruling involving converse subsidiary'. <http://www.eventim.de/obj/media/en/relations/press/2013/130612-AdHoc-Live-Nation-Urteil-english.pdf>.

(31) The results over the past two and a half years *clearly demonstrate* that Starbucks at-home coffee portfolio is significantly healthier than it was before we assumed direct control from Kraft in 2011. (S6)

Next comes the thorny issue of damages, i.e. the financial consequence of the adverse award, which is the truly negative factor that is most likely to impact shareholders. This is anticipated and naturally turned into a positive message with a bare assertion:

(32) The amount awarded reflects the value of our at-home coffee business. (S6)

And, more importantly, also anticipating shareholders' reactions, there is no problem in that payment, expressed with another bare assertion:

(33) We have adequate liquidity both in the form of cash on hand and available borrowing capacity to fund the payment. (S6)

Starbucks's last text signals the end of the dialogue with Kraft to turn to shareholders as preferential addressees, trying to control a situation that would most certainly damage the company's image, identity and future prospects.

5. Concluding remarks

We have observed that when the propositional meanings of the press releases deal with arbitration, we find a very specific contextual setting, where the genre is required to change in specific ways. The rhetorical actions to be accomplished in the texts produced by the two corporations are fairly similar and thus we can definitely recognise relevant similarities in both groups of texts. The social situation is one of vulnerability for the corporations: the companies' reputation and the investors' confidence may be at stake; a situation of conflict emerges and thus the rhetorical needs vary. The positive entourage that characterises press releases, to the point of self-promotion and total absence of negative language, is drastically modified. They no longer focus on positive egocentrism, but a new, preferential rhetorical need emerges: that of self-defence. By means of dialogistic resources, the discourse of legitimation opens up a new perspective in press releases. They need to argue the legitimacy of their (re)actions against the other party's (re)actions. The surge to provide their grounds and motivations against the reasons of the other creates the necessary social conditions for this type of legal argumentation. The arguments for justification and hence for legitimation build a different text type which takes from legal genres its pragma-dialectical argumentative structure.

Are generic resources useful in case of conflict? Do the pre-formulating strategies serve the specific communicative purpose of these texts? The texts reveal a number of dialogistic features of specific rhetorical significance, as they revolve around fostering allegiance in an *us v. them* rhetorical confrontation. Whatever the conventions genres are constrained by, genres are dynamic and adapt themselves to the new and ever changing social situations. The press releases of arbitration adapt to the rhetorical situation, varying the generic form and the discourses embedded in it. We find here another example of Bhatia's (2004) notion of 'genre integrity' and of the 'hybrid nature' of genres, that is, how genres borrow discourse strategies originating from other genres. The propositional content influences its form, but it does not appear to create functional tension. The genre can 'accept' the new communicative purposes without modifying the social frame in which it is created. The genre is not *in conflict* (Bhatia 2002), it just seeks other rhetorical resources to *manage* context.

References

Bakhtin, Mikhail M. 1981. *The Dialogic Imagination*. Austin: University of Texas Press.

Bakhtin, Mikhail M. 2000. The Problem of Speech Genres. In Duff, David (ed.) *Modern Genre Theory*. Harlow: Pearson, 82-97.

Bhatia, Vijay K. 1993. *Analysing Genre. Language Use in Professional Settings*. London: Longman.

Bhatia, Vijay K. 1995. Genre-mixing in Professional Communication: The Case of 'Private Intentions' v. 'Socially Recognised Purposes'. In Bruthiaux, Paul / Boswood, Tim / Du Babcock, Bertha (eds) *Explorations in English for Professional Communication.* Hong Kong: City University of Hong Kong, 1-19.

Bhatia, Vijay K. 2002. Genres in Conflict. In Trosborg, Anna (ed.) *Analysing Professional Genres.* Amsterdam: Benjamins, 147-161.

Bhatia, Vijay K. 2004. *Worlds of Written Discourse: A Genre-Based View*. London: Continuum.

Bhatia, Vijay K. 2008. Towards Critical Genre Analysis. In Bhatia, Vijay K. / Flowerdew, John / Jones, Rodney H. (eds) *Advances in Discourse Studies.* London: Routledge, 166-17.

Breeze, Ruth 2013. *Corporate Discourse*. London: Bloomsbury.

Catenaccio, Paola 2008. Press Releases as a Hybrid Genre: Addressing the Informative/Promotional Conundrum. *Pragmatics* 18/1, 9-31.

Corona, Isabel 2011a. Arbitration Recontextualized. *World Englishes* 30/1, 129-140.

Corona, Isabel 2011b. Confidentiality at Risk: The Interdiscursive Construction of International Commercial Arbitration. *Discourse & Communication* 5/4, 355-374.

Corona, Isabel 2012. Confidentiality vs Publicity: The Impact of International Arbitration in the Media. In Bhatia, Vijay K. / Candlin, Christopher N. / Gotti, Maurizio (eds) *Discourse and Practice in International Commercial Arbitration: Issues, Challenges and Prospects.* London: Ashgate, 283-297.

Corona, Isabel 2013. Arbitration across Genres: from 'Private Resolution' to 'Public War". In Tessuto, Girolamo / Williams, Christopher (eds) *Language in the Negotiation of Justice: Contexts, Issues and Applications.* London: Ashgate, 79-102.

Crandall, William R. / Parnell, John A. / Spillan, John E. 2009. *Crisis Management in the New Strategy Landscape.* London: Sage.

Denoix de Saint Marc, Valéry 2003. Confidentiality of Arbitration and the Obligation to Disclose Information on Listed Companies or

During Due Diligence Investigations. *Journal of International Arbitration* 20/2, 211-216.

Feteris, Eveline / Kloosterhuis, Harm 2013. Law and Argumentation Theory. Theoretical Approaches to Legal Justification. <http://papers.ssrn.com/sol3/papers.cfm?abstract_id=2283092>.

Hickey, Matt 2008. The Evolution of the Press Release. <http://techcrunch.com/2008/05/11/the-evolution-of-the-press-release>.

Hyland, Ken 2005. Stance and Engagement: A Model of Interaction in Academic Discourse. *Discourse Studies* 7/2, 173-192.

Jacobs, Geert 1999a. *Preformulating the News*. Amsterdam: Benjamins.

Jacobs, Geert 1999b. Self-reference in Press Releases. *Journal of Pragmatics* 31, 219-242.

Jones, Rodney H. / Bhatia, Vijay K. / Bremner, Stephen / Peirson-Smith, Anne 2012. Creative Collaboration in the Public Relations Industry. In Jones, Rodney (ed.) *Discourse and Creativity.* Harlow: Pearson, 93-108.

Lassen, Inger 2006. Is the Press Release a Genre? A Study of Form and Content. *Discourse and Communication* 8/4, 503-530.

Lorés Sanz, Rosa 2011. The Construction of the Author's Voice in Academic Writing: the Interplay of Cultural and Disciplinary Factors. *Text & Talk* 31/2, 173-193.

Martin, James R. 1992. *English Text: System and Structure*. Amsterdam: Benjamins.

Martin, James R. / Rose, David 2003. *Working with Discourse. Meaning beyond the Clause.* London: Continuum.

Martin, James R. / White, Peter R. R. 2005. *The Language of Evaluation: Appraisal in English*. London: Palgrave.

McIntyre, Douglas 2010. The Coffee Wars: Starbucks Tries to Fire Kraft. *The Daily Finance* (5 Nov 2010). <http://www.dailyfinance.com/2010/11/05/starbucks-Kraft>.

McLaren, Yvonne / Gurau, Calin 2005. Characterising the Genre of the Corporate Press Release, *LSP & Professional Communication* 5/1, 10-30.

Miller, Carolyn R. 1994. Genre as Social Action. In Freedman, Aviva / Medway, Peter (eds) *Genre and the New Rhetoric*. New York: Taylor & Francis, 23-42.

Mur-Dueñas, Pilar / Lorés-Sanz, Rosa / Lafuente-Millán, Enrique 2010. Editorial. In Mur-Dueñas, Pilar / Lorés-Sanz, Rosa / Lafuente-Millán, Enrique (eds.) *Interpersonality in Written Academic Discourse. Journal of English for Academic Purposes* 9/2, 83-85.

Pander Maat, Henk 2008. Editing and Genre Conflict: How Newspaper Journalists Clarify and Neutralize Press Release Copy. *Pragmatics* 18/1, 87-113.

Reed, Lucy 2010. Corporate Criticism on International Arbitration. <http://kluwerarbitrationblog.com/blog/2010/07/16/more-on-corporate-criticism-of-international-arbitration>.

Sleurs, Kim / Jacobs, Geert 2005. Beyond Preformulation: an Ethnographic Perspective on Press Releases. *Journal of Pragmatics* 37/8, 1251-1273.

Stevens, Margrete 2000. Confidentiality Revisited. *News from ICSID* 2/1. <www.worldbank.org/icsid/news/n-17-1-2.htm>.

Swales, John M. / Rogers, Priscilla S. 1995. Discourse and the Projection of Corporate Culture: the Mission Statement. *Discourse & Society* 6/2, 223-242.

Tardy, Christine M. 2012. Current Conceptions of Voice. In Hyland, Ken / Sancho Guinda, Carmen (eds) *Stance and Voice in Written Academic Genres*. London: Palgrave Macmillan, 34-48.

Van Hout, Tom / Jacobs, Geert 2008. News Production Theory and Practice: Fieldwork Notes of Power, Interaction and Agency. *Pragmatics* 18/1, 59-85.

Van Hout, Tom / Pander Maat, Henk / De Preter, Wim 2011. Writing from News Source: The Case of Apple TV. *Journal of Pragmatics* 43, 1876-1889.

Notes on Contributors

PATRIZIA ANESA holds a PhD in English Studies from the University of Verona. She is a member of the Research Centre on Specialized Discourse (CERLIS) at the University of Bergamo, and teaches English Language and Translation at the same university. Her research interests lie mostly in the area of specialized discourse, with particular reference to legal language and courtroom communication. She also cooperates with a number of international organizations and institutions as a consultant in the field of Discourse, Conversation and Frame Analysis.

ISMAEL ARINAS PELLÓN lectures in English and Spanish for specific purposes at the Universidad Politécnica de Madrid (UPM), Spain. He has also developed online Business English courses for CEPADE (the online branch of UPM) and Universidad Nacional de Educación a Distancia (UNED), Spain. His research interests include the use of corpora as learning tools by students, the analysis of multidisciplinary genres such as patents, and the linguistic mechanisms used to communicate innovation. He is currently involved in the development of an ontology based on the prototypical phraseology of the US patent genre.

VIJAY K. BHATIA has recently retired as Professor from the City University of Hong Kong. His research interests include applied Genre Analysis of professional discourse, including legal, business, newspaper, and advertising genres; ESP and Professional Communication (Theory and Practice); simplification of legal and other public documents; cross-cultural and disciplinary variation in professional discourses. He has widely published in international journals. His work on genre analysis includes two books, *Analysing Genre: Language Use in Professional Settings* (1993) and *Worlds of Written Discourse: A Genre-based View* (2004).

RUTH BREEZE has a PhD in Language Education and has researched and published widely in the area of Discourse Analysis applied to media language and specialised discourse, focusing particularly on the field of legal English. Her most recent books are *Corporate Discourse* (Bloomsbury Academic, 2013) and *Rethinking Academic Writing Pedagogy for the European University* (Rodopi, 2012). She is Head of the Institute of Modern Languages at the University of Navarra, and a member of the GradUN Research Group in the *Instituto Cultura y Sociedad.*

ISABEL CORONA (PhD) is a Lecturer in English Philology at the Universidad de Zaragoza, Spain. She participated in the international project 'International Commercial Arbitration Practices: A Discourse Analytical Study'. Her publications in this research area include 'Arbitration Recontextualized' (*World Englishes*); 'Confidentiality at Risk: The Interdiscursive Construction of International Commercial Arbitration' (*Discourse & Communication*); 'Confidentiality vs Publicity: The Impact of International Arbitration in the Media' (in V.K. Bhatia/ C.N. Candlin/M. Gotti (eds) *Discourse and Practice in International Commercial Arbitration: Issues, Challenges and Prospects*, Ashgate 2012). Her main research interests are genre analysis, media discourse analysis, and English as a Lingua Franca (ELF). She is a member of the research group InterLAE (<www.interlae.com>).

MAURIZIO GOTTI is Professor of English Language and Translation, Head of the Department of Foreign Languages, Literatures and Communication, and Director of the Research Centre on Specialized Languages (CERLIS) at the University of Bergamo. His main research areas are the features and origins of specialized discourse (*Robert Boyle and the Language of Science,* 1996; *Specialized Discourse: Linguistic Features and Changing Conventions*, 2003; *Investigating Specialized Discourse*, ³2011). He is also interested in English syntax and English lexicology and lexicography, with particular regard to specialized terminology and canting. He is a member of the Editorial Board of national and international journals, and edits the *Linguistic Insights* series for Peter Lang.

CHRISTOPH A. HAFNER is an Assistant Professor in the Department of English at the City University of Hong Kong. He teaches a range of courses in discipline specific English and digital literacies at both undergraduate and postgraduate levels. His research interests include academic and professional literacy, digital literacies, and legal discourse. In addition to his other publications, he has co-authored a book (with Rodney H. Jones) entitled *Understanding Digital Literacies: A Practical Introduction* (2012).

DAVIDE MAZZI is a researcher in English Language and Translation at the University of Modena and Reggio Emilia. His research activity has essentially focused on the following areas: discourse analysis, corpus linguistics and argumentation studies. In particular, his research interests and related publications have concentrated on legal, academic and news discourse. His recent publications include: 'In Other Words, ...': A Corpus-based Study of Reformulation in Judicial Discourse (*Hermès*), 2011; *The 'Other's' Gaze. The Discursive Construction of Journalists' Professional Identity across Italy and the US*, BrownWalker Press, 2012; and 'Such a reaction would spread all over the cell like a forest fire': A Corpus Study of Argument by Analogy in Scientific Discourse (in C. Berkenkotter et al. (eds), *Insights into Academic Genres*, Peter Lang, 2012).

MARÍA ÁNGELES ORTS LLOPIS started her professional activity very early as a translator in the fields of Law and Economics. She holds a PhD in Modern Languages, her research interests having always been focused upon business and legal discourse. As a specialist in these fields, she has been a Visiting Scholar at several American Universities, has published a number of books and articles, and teaches various Postgraduate courses in a number of Spanish Business Schools. At the moment, she is the Associate Chair of the Translation and Interpreting Department of her University. Her most recent research and publications mainly involve contrastive legal discourse in the area of mercantile law and the economic discourse of the Global Systemic crisis.

MICHELE SALA, PhD (University of Bergamo), MA (Youngstown State University, Ohio), is a researcher in English Language and

Translation at the University of Bergamo. His research activity and major publications deal with the analysis of the linguistic, textual and pragmatic aspects of legal translation, and the application of genre and discourse analytical methods to a corpus-based study of legal-academic discourse. He has also published in the field of academic discourse (*Persuasion and Politeness in Academic Discourse* 2008), pragmatics and cognitive linguistics (*Differently Amusing* 2012).

TARJA SALMI-TOLONEN is currently a Research Fellow at the Faculty of Law, University of Turku, Finland. She has held a chair of Legal Linguistics, lectured on law and language at several universities in Finland, the US and Europe, and worked as a visiting scholar at Cambridge University, UK. She is an expert member of the Finnish Prime Minister's Language Department. She is a referee for publications on language and law. Selected publications: Persuasion in Judicial Argumentation (in Halmari *et al.* 2003), *Language and the Functions of Law* (2008), Proactive Law and Alternative Dispute Resolution Mechanisms (in Sorsa 2011), A Contract is a Speech Act (in Finnish, in Haapio *et al.* 2013).

CARMEN SANCHO GUINDA is a Senior Lecturer in the Department of Applied Linguistics at the Polytechnic University of Madrid, where she teaches English for Academic Purposes, Professional Communication, and in-service seminars for engineering teachers undertaking English-medium instruction within EU programmes. Her research focus is the interdisciplinary analysis of academic and professional discourses and genres and innovation in the teaching and learning of academic competencies. She is currently engaged in projects fostering critical and creative thought among engineering students and studying the discourse of science as a commodity. Recently she has co-edited *Stance and Voice in Written Academic Genres* with Ken Hyland (Palgrave, 2012) and *Narratives in Academic and Professional Genres* with Maurizio Gotti (Peter Lang, 2013).

IGNACIO VÁZQUEZ ORTA is Full Professor of English Linguistics at the Department of English and German Philology of the University of Zaragoza. His research interests include Pragmatics and Discourse

Analysis, Systemic Linguistics, Translation and Contrastive Studies (English-Spanish). He has recently been involved in research on generic integrity in academic and professional discourse and its uses in the construction, expression and popularisation of scientific knowledge in English. He is currently responsible for a research group called INTERLAE, which explores interpersonality in academic and professional discourse from a socio-pragmatic perspective. He has focused on writer stance in academic and arbitration discourse. He is interested in the study of professional legal discourse and in the translation of English legal documents into Spanish.

CHRISTOPHER WILLIAMS is Full Professor of English at the Department of Law of the University of Foggia, Italy. His main research interest in recent years has been in legal English with publications that have appeared in *The Verb Phrase in English: Investigating Recent Language Change with Corpora* (Cambridge University Press 2013) and *Canadian Journal of Linguistics* (2013). Besides co-editing with Maurizio Gotti *Legal Discourse across Languages and Cultures* (Peter Lang 2010), he has also co-edited with Ilse Depraetere the special issue of *English Language & Linguistics* (2010) on 'Future Time Reference in English'. He is Chief Editor of the journal *ESP Across Cultures*.

Index

Linguistic Insights

Studies in Language and Communication

This series aims to promote specialist language studies in the fields of linguistic theory and applied linguistics, by publishing volumes that focus on specific aspects of language use in one or several languages and provide valuable insights into language and communication research. A cross-disciplinary approach is favoured and most European languages are accepted.

The series includes two types of books:

- **Monographs** – featuring in-depth studies on special aspects of language theory, language analysis or language teaching.
- **Collected papers** – assembling papers from workshops, conferences or symposia.

Each volume of the series is subjected to a double peer-reviewing process.

Vol. 1 Maurizio Gotti & Marina Dossena (eds)
Modality in Specialized Texts. Selected Papers of the 1st CERLIS Conference.
421 pages. 2001. ISBN 3-906767-10-8 · US-ISBN 0-8204-5340-4

Vol. 2 Giuseppina Cortese & Philip Riley (eds)
Domain-specific English. Textual Practices across Communities and Classrooms.
420 pages. 2002. ISBN 3-906768-98-8 · US-ISBN 0-8204-5884-8

Vol. 3 Maurizio Gotti, Dorothee Heller & Marina Dossena (eds)
Conflict and Negotiation in Specialized Texts. Selected Papers of the 2nd CERLIS Conference.
470 pages. 2002. ISBN 3-906769-12-7 · US-ISBN 0-8204-5887-2

Vol. 4 Maurizio Gotti, Marina Dossena, Richard Dury, Roberta Facchinetti & Maria Lima
Variation in Central Modals. A Repertoire of Forms and Types of Usage in Middle English and Early Modern English.
364 pages. 2002. ISBN 3-906769-84-4 · US-ISBN 0-8204-5898-8

Editorial address:

Prof. Maurizio Gotti Università di Bergamo, Facoltà di Lingue e Letterature Straniere,
Via Salvecchio 19, 24129 Bergamo, Italy
Fax: 0039 035 2052789, E-Mail: m.gotti@unibg.it

Vol. 5 Stefania Nuccorini (ed.)
Phrases and Phraseology. Data and Descriptions.
187 pages. 2002. ISBN 3-906770-08-7 · US-ISBN 0-8204-5933-X

Vol. 6 Vijay Bhatia, Christopher N. Candlin & Maurizio Gotti (eds)
Legal Discourse in Multilingual and Multicultural Contexts.
Arbitration Texts in Europe.
385 pages. 2003. ISBN 3-906770-85-0 · US-ISBN 0-8204-6254-3

Vol. 7 Marina Dossena & Charles Jones (eds)
Insights into Late Modern English. 2nd edition.
378 pages. 2003, 2007.
ISBN 978-3-03911-257-9 · US-ISBN 978-0-8204-8927-8

Vol. 8 Maurizio Gotti
Specialized Discourse. Linguistic Features and Changing Conventions.
351 pages. 2003, 2005.
ISBN 3-03910-606-6 · US-ISBN 0-8204-7000-7

Vol. 9 Alan Partington, John Morley & Louann Haarman (eds)
Corpora and Discourse.
420 pages. 2004. ISBN 3-03910-026-2 · US-ISBN 0-8204-6262-4

Vol. 10 Martina Möllering
The Acquisition of German Modal Particles. A Corpus-Based Approach.
290 pages. 2004. ISBN 3-03910-043-2 · US-ISBN 0-8204-6273-X

Vol. 11 David Hart (ed.)
English Modality in Context. Diachronic Perspectives.
261 pages. 2003. ISBN 3-03910-046-7 · US-ISBN 0-8204-6852-5

Vol. 12 Wendy Swanson
Modes of Co-reference as an Indicator of Genre.
430 pages. 2003. ISBN 3-03910-052-1 · US-ISBN 0-8204-6855-X

Vol. 13 Gina Poncini
Discursive Strategies in Multicultural Business Meetings.
2nd edition. 338 pages. 2004, 2007.
ISBN 978-3-03911-296-8 · US-ISBN 978-0-8204-8937-7

Vol. 14 Christopher N. Candlin & Maurizio Gotti (eds)
Intercultural Aspects of Specialized Communication.
2nd edition. 369 pages. 2004, 2007.
ISBN 978-3-03911-258-6 · US-ISBN 978-0-8204-8926-1

Vol. 15 Gabriella Del Lungo Camiciotti & Elena Tognini Bonelli (eds)
Academic Discourse. New Insights into Evaluation.
234 pages. 2004. ISBN 3-03910-353-9 · US-ISBN 0-8204-7016-3

Vol. 16 Marina Dossena & Roger Lass (eds)
Methods and Data in English Historical Dialectology.
405 pages. 2004. ISBN 3-03910-362-8 · US-ISBN 0-8204-7018-X

Vol. 17 Judy Noguchi
The Science Review Article. An Opportune Genre in
the Construction of Science.
274 pages. 2006. ISBN 3-03910-426-8 · US-ISBN 0-8204-7034-1

Vol. 18 Giuseppina Cortese & Anna Duszak (eds)
Identity, Community, Discourse. English in Intercultural Settings.
495 pages. 2005. ISBN 3-03910-632-5 · US-ISBN 0-8204-7163-1

Vol. 19 Anna Trosborg & Poul Erik Flyvholm Jørgensen (eds)
Business Discourse. Texts and Contexts.
250 pages. 2005. ISBN 3-03910-606-6 · US-ISBN 0-8204-7000-7

Vol. 20 Christopher Williams
Tradition and Change in Legal English. Verbal Constructions in Prescriptive Texts.
2nd revised edition. 216 pages. 2005, 2007. ISBN 978-3-03911-444-3.

Vol. 21 Katarzyna Dziubalska-Kolaczyk & Joanna Przedlacka (eds)
English Pronunciation Models: A Changing Scene.
2nd edition. 476 pages. 2005, 2008. ISBN 978-3-03911-682-9.

Vol. 22 Christián Abello-Contesse, Rubén Chacón-Beltrán, M. Dolores López-Jiménez & M. Mar Torreblanca-López (eds)
Age in L2 Acquisition and Teaching.
214 pages. 2006. ISBN 3-03910-668-6 · US-ISBN 0-8204-7174-7

Vol. 23 Vijay K. Bhatia, Maurizio Gotti, Jan Engberg & Dorothee Heller (eds)
Vagueness in Normative Texts.
474 pages. 2005. ISBN 3-03910-653-8 · US-ISBN 0-8204-7169-0

Vol. 24 Paul Gillaerts & Maurizio Gotti (eds)
Genre Variation in Business Letters. 2nd printing.
407 pages. 2008. ISBN 978-3-03911-681-2.

Vol. 25 Ana María Hornero, María José Luzón & Silvia Murillo (eds)
Corpus Linguistics. Applications for the Study of English.
2nd printing. 526 pages. 2006, 2008. ISBN 978-3-03911-726-0

Vol. 26 J. Lachlan Mackenzie & María de los Ángeles Gómez-González (eds)
Studies in Functional Discourse Grammar.
259 pages. 2005. ISBN 3-03910-696-1 · US-ISBN 0-8204-7558-0

Vol. 27 Debbie G. E. Ho
Classroom Talk. Exploring the Sociocultural Structure of Formal ESL Learning.
2nd edition. 254 pages. 2006, 2007. ISBN 978-3-03911-434-4

Vol. 28 Javier Pérez-Guerra, Dolores González-Álvarez, Jorge L. Bueno-Alonso & Esperanza Rama-Martínez (eds)
'Of Varying Language and Opposing Creed'. New Insights into Late Modern English.
455 pages. 2007. ISBN 978-3-03910-788-9

Vol. 29 Francesca Bargiela-Chiappini & Maurizio Gotti (eds)
Asian Business Discourse(s).
350 pages. 2005. ISBN 3-03910-804-2 · US-ISBN 0-8204-7574-2

Vol. 30 Nicholas Brownlees (ed.)
News Discourse in Early Modern Britain. Selected Papers of CHINED 2004.
300 pages. 2006. ISBN 3-03910-805-0 · US-ISBN 0-8204-8025-8

Vol. 31 Roberta Facchinetti & Matti Rissanen (eds)
Corpus-based Studies of Diachronic English.
300 pages. 2006. ISBN 3-03910-851-4 · US-ISBN 0-8204-8040-1

Vol. 32 Marina Dossena & Susan M. Fitzmaurice (eds)
Business and Official Correspondence. Historical Investigations.
209 pages. 2006. ISBN 3-03910-880-8 · US-ISBN 0-8204-8352-4

Vol. 33 Giuliana Garzone & Srikant Sarangi (eds)
Discourse, Ideology and Specialized Communication.
494 pages. 2007. ISBN 978-3-03910-888-6

Vol. 34 Giuliana Garzone & Cornelia Ilie (eds)
The Use of English in Institutional and Business Settings.
An Intercultural Perspective.
372 pages. 2007. ISBN 978-3-03910-889-3

Vol. 35 Vijay K. Bhatia & Maurizio Gotti (eds)
Explorations in Specialized Genres.
316 pages. 2006. ISBN 3-03910-995-2 · US-ISBN 0-8204-8372-9

Vol. 36 Heribert Picht (ed.)
Modern Approaches to Terminological Theories and Applications.
432 pages. 2006. ISBN 3-03911-156-6 · US-ISBN 0-8204-8380-X

Vol. 37 Anne Wagner & Sophie Cacciaguidi-Fahy (eds)
Legal Language and the Search for Clarity / Le langage juridique et la quête de clarté.
Practice and Tools / Pratiques et instruments.
487 pages. 2006. ISBN 3-03911-169-8 · US-ISBN 0-8204-8388-5

Vol. 38 Juan Carlos Palmer-Silveira, Miguel F. Ruiz-Garrido &
Inmaculada Fortanet-Gómez (eds)
Intercultural and International Business Communication.
Theory, Research and Teaching.
2nd edition. 343 pages. 2006, 2008. ISBN 978-3-03911-680-5

Vol. 39 Christiane Dalton-Puffer, Dieter Kastovsky, Nikolaus Ritt &
Herbert Schendl (eds)
Syntax, Style and Grammatical Norms. English from 1500–2000.
250 pages. 2006. ISBN 3-03911-181-7 · US-ISBN 0-8204-8394-X

Vol. 40 Marina Dossena & Irma Taavitsainen (eds)
Diachronic Perspectives on Domain-Specific English.
280 pages. 2006. ISBN 3-03910-176-0 · US-ISBN 0-8204-8391-5

Vol. 41 John Flowerdew & Maurizio Gotti (eds)
Studies in Specialized Discourse.
293 pages. 2006. ISBN 3-03911-178-7

Vol. 42 Ken Hyland & Marina Bondi (eds)
Academic Discourse Across Disciplines.
320 pages. 2006. ISBN 3-03911-183-3 · US-ISBN 0-8204-8396-6

Vol. 43 Paul Gillaerts & Philip Shaw (eds)
The Map and the Landscape. Norms and Practices in Genre.
256 pages. 2006. ISBN 3-03911-182-5 · US-ISBN 0-8204-8395-4

Vol. 44 Maurizio Gotti & Davide Giannoni (eds)
New Trends in Specialized Discourse Analysis.
301 pages. 2006. ISBN 3-03911-184-1 · US-ISBN 0-8204-8381-8

Vol. 45 Maurizio Gotti & Françoise Salager-Meyer (eds)
Advances in Medical Discourse Analysis. Oral and Written Contexts.
492 pages. 2006. ISBN 3-03911-185-X · US-ISBN 0-8204-8382-6

Vol. 46 Maurizio Gotti & Susan Šarcević (eds)
Insights into Specialized Translation.
396 pages. 2006. ISBN 3-03911-186-8 · US-ISBN 0-8204-8383-4

Vol. 47 Khurshid Ahmad & Margaret Rogers (eds)
Evidence-based LSP. Translation, Text and Terminology.
584 pages. 2007. ISBN 978-3-03911-187-9

Vol. 48 Hao Sun & Dániel Z. Kádár (eds)
It's the Dragon's Turn. Chinese Institutional Discourses.
262 pages. 2008. ISBN 978-3-03911-175-6

Vol. 49 Cristina Suárez-Gómez
Relativization in Early English (950-1250). the Position of Relative Clauses.
149 pages. 2006. ISBN 3-03911-203-1 · US-ISBN 0-8204-8904-2

Vol. 50 Maria Vittoria Calvi & Luisa Chierichetti (eds)
Nuevas tendencias en el discurso de especialidad.
319 pages. 2006. ISBN 978-3-03911-261-6

Vol. 51 Mari Carmen Campoy & María José Luzón (eds)
Spoken Corpora in Applied Linguistics.
274 pages. 2008. ISBN 978-3-03911-275-3

Vol. 52 Konrad Ehlich & Dorothee Heller (Hrsg.)
Die Wissenschaft und ihre Sprachen.
323 pages. 2006. ISBN 978-3-03911-272-2

Vol. 53 Jingyu Zhang
The Semantic Salience Hierarchy Model. The L2 Acquisition of Psych Predicates
273 pages. 2007. ISBN 978-3-03911-300-2

Vol. 54 Norman Fairclough, Giuseppina Cortese & Patrizia Ardizzone (eds)
Discourse and Contemporary Social Change.
555 pages. 2007. ISBN 978-3-03911-276-0

Vol. 55 Jan Engberg, Marianne Grove Ditlevsen, Peter Kastberg & Martin Stegu (eds)
New Directions in LSP Teaching.
331 pages. 2007. ISBN 978-3-03911-433-7

Vol. 56 Dorothee Heller & Konrad Ehlich (Hrsg.)
Studien zur Rechtskommunikation.
322 pages. 2007. ISBN 978-3-03911-436-8

Vol. 57 Teruhiro Ishiguro & Kang-kwong Luke (eds)
Grammar in Cross-Linguistic Perspective.
The Syntax, Semantics, and Pragmatics of Japanese and Chinese.
304 pages. 2012. ISBN 978-3-03911-445-0

Vol. 58 Carmen Frehner
Email – SMS – MMS
294 pages. 2008. ISBN 978-3-03911-451-1

Vol. 59 Isabel Balteiro
The Directionality of Conversion in English. A Dia-Synchronic Study.
276 pages. 2007. ISBN 978-3-03911-241-8

Vol. 60 Maria Milagros Del Saz Rubio
English Discourse Markers of Reformulation.
237 pages. 2007. ISBN 978-3-03911-196-1

Vol. 61 Sally Burgess & Pedro Martín-Martín (eds)
English as an Additional Language in Research Publication and Communication.
259 pages. 2008. ISBN 978-3-03911-462-7

Vol. 62 Sandrine Onillon
Pratiques et représentations de l'écrit.
458 pages. 2008. ISBN 978-3-03911-464-1

Vol. 63 Hugo Bowles & Paul Seedhouse (eds)
Conversation Analysis and Language for Specific Purposes.
2nd edition. 337 pages. 2007, 2009. ISBN 978-3-0343-0045-2

Vol. 64 Vijay K. Bhatia, Christopher N. Candlin & Paola Evangelisti Allori (eds)
Language, Culture and the Law.
The Formulation of Legal Concepts across Systems and Cultures.
342 pages. 2008. ISBN 978-3-03911-470-2

Vol. 65 Jonathan Culpeper & Dániel Z. Kádár (eds)
Historical (Im)politeness.
300 pages. 2010. ISBN 978-3-03911-496-2

Vol. 66 Linda Lombardo (ed.)
Using Corpora to Learn about Language and Discourse.
237 pages. 2009. ISBN 978-3-03911-522-8

Vol. 67 Natsumi Wakamoto
Extroversion/Introversion in Foreign Language Learning.
Interactions with Learner Strategy Use.
159 pages. 2009. ISBN 978-3-03911-596-9

Vol. 68 Eva Alcón-Soler (ed.)
Learning How to Request in an Instructed Language Learning Context.
260 pages. 2008. ISBN 978-3-03911-601-0

Vol. 69 Domenico Pezzini
The Translation of Religious Texts in the Middle Ages.
428 pages. 2008. ISBN 978-3-03911-600-3

Vol. 70 Tomoko Tode
Effects of Frequency in Classroom Second Language Learning.
Quasi-experiment and stimulated-recall analysis.
195 pages. 2008. ISBN 978-3-03911-602-7

Vol. 71 Egor Tsedryk
Fusion symétrique et alternances ditransitives.
211 pages. 2009. ISBN 978-3-03911-609-6

Vol. 72 Cynthia J. Kellett Bidoli & Elana Ochse (eds)
English in International Deaf Communication.
444 pages. 2008. ISBN 978-3-03911-610-2

Vol. 73 Joan C. Beal, Carmela Nocera & Massimo Sturiale (eds)
Perspectives on Prescriptivism.
269 pages. 2008. ISBN 978-3-03911-632-4

Vol. 74 Carol Taylor Torsello, Katherine Ackerley & Erik Castello (eds)
Corpora for University Language Teachers.
308 pages. 2008. ISBN 978-3-03911-639-3

Vol. 75 María Luisa Pérez Cañado (ed.)
English Language Teaching in the European Credit Transfer System. Facing the Challenge.
251 pages. 2009. ISBN 978-3-03911-654-6

Vol. 76 Marina Dossena & Ingrid Tieken-Boon van Ostade (eds)
Studies in Late Modern English Correspondence. Methodology and Data.
291 pages. 2008. ISBN 978-3-03911-658-4

Vol. 77 Ingrid Tieken-Boon van Ostade & Wim van der Wurff (eds)
Current Issues in Late Modern English.
436 pages. 2009. ISBN 978-3-03911-660-7

Vol. 78 Marta Navarro Coy (ed.)
Practical Approaches to Foreign Language Teaching and Learning.
297 pages. 2009. ISBN 978-3-03911-661-4

Vol. 79 Qing Ma
Second Language Vocabulary Acquisition.
333 pages. 2009. ISBN 978-3-03911-666-9

Vol. 80 Martin Solly, Michelangelo Conoscenti & Sandra Campagna (eds)
Verbal/Visual Narrative Texts in Higher Education.
384 pages. 2008. ISBN 978-3-03911-672-0

Vol. 81 Meiko Matsumoto
From Simple Verbs to Periphrastic Expressions: The Historical Development of Composite Predicates, Phrasal Verbs, and Related Constructions in English.
235 pages. 2008. ISBN 978-3-03911-675-1

Vol. 82 Melinda Dooly
Doing Diversity. Teachers' Construction of Their Classroom Reality.
180 pages. 2009. ISBN 978-3-03911-687-4

Vol. 83 Victoria Guillén-Nieto, Carmen Marimón-Llorca & Chelo Vargas-Sierra (eds)
Intercultural Business Communication and Simulation and Gaming Methodology.
392 pages. 2009. ISBN 978-3-03911-688-1

Vol. 84 Maria Grazia Guido
English as a Lingua Franca in Cross-cultural Immigration Domains.
285 pages. 2008. ISBN 978-3-03911-689-8

Vol. 85 Erik Castello
Text Complexity and Reading Comprehension Tests.
352 pages. 2008. ISBN 978-3-03911-717-8

Vol. 86 Maria-Lluisa Gea-Valor, Isabel García-Izquierdo & Maria-José Esteve (eds)
Linguistic and Translation Studies in Scientific Communication.
317 pages. 2010. ISBN 978-3-0343-0069-8

Vol. 87 Carmen Navarro, Rosa Mª Rodríguez Abella, Francesca Dalle Pezze & Renzo Miotti (eds)
La comunicación especializada.
355 pages. 2008. ISBN 978-3-03911-733-8

Vol. 88 Kiriko Sato
The Development from Case-Forms to Prepositional Constructions in Old English Prose.
231 pages. 2009. ISBN 978-3-03911-763-5

Vol. 89 Dorothee Heller (Hrsg.)
Formulierungsmuster in deutscher und italienischer Fachkommunikation. Intra- und interlinguale Perspektiven.
315 pages. 2008. ISBN 978-3-03911-778-9

Vol. 90 Henning Bergenholtz, Sandro Nielsen & Sven Tarp (eds)
Lexicography at a Crossroads. Dictionaries and Encyclopedias Today, Lexicographical Tools Tomorrow.
372 pages. 2009. ISBN 978-3-03911-799-4

Vol. 91 Manouchehr Moshtagh Khorasani
The Development of Controversies. From the Early Modern Period to Online Discussion Forums.
317 pages. 2009. ISBN 978-3-3911-711-6

Vol. 92 María Luisa Carrió-Pastor (ed.)
Content and Language Integrated Learning. Cultural Diversity.
178 pages. 2009. ISBN 978-3-3911-818-2

Vol. 93 Roger Berry
Terminology in English Language Teaching. Nature and Use.
262 pages. 2010. ISBN 978-3-0343-0013-1

Vol. 94 Roberto Cagliero & Jennifer Jenkins (eds)
Discourses, Communities, and Global Englishes
240 pages. 2010. ISBN 978-3-0343-0012-4

Vol. 95 Facchinetti Roberta, Crystal David, Seidlhofer Barbara (eds)
From International to Local English – And Back Again.
268 pages. 2010. ISBN 978-3-0343-0011-7

Vol. 96 Cesare Gagliardi & Alan Maley (eds)
EIL, ELF, Global English. Teaching and Learning Issues
376 pages. 2010. ISBN 978-3-0343-0010-0

Vol. 97 Sylvie Hancil (ed.)
The Role of Prosody in Affective Speech.
403 pages. 2009. ISBN 978-3-03911-696-6

Vol. 98 Marina Dossena & Roger Lass (eds)
Studies in English and European Historical Dialectology.
257 pages. 2009. ISBN 978-3-0343-0024-7

Vol. 99 Christine Béal
Les interactions quotidiennes en français et en anglais. De l'approche comparative à l'analyse des situations interculturelles.
424 pages. 2010. ISBN 978-3-0343-0027-8

Vol. 100 Maurizio Gotti (ed.)
Commonality and Individuality in Academic Discourse.
398 pages. 2009. ISBN 978-3-0343-0023-0

Vol. 101 Javier E. Díaz Vera & Rosario Caballero (eds)
Textual Healing. Studies in Medieval English Medical, Scientific and Technical Texts.
213 pages. 2009. ISBN 978-3-03911-822-9

Vol. 102 Nuria Edo Marzá
The Specialised Lexicographical Approach. A Step further in Dictionary-making.
316 pages. 2009. ISBN 978-3-0343-0043-8

Vol. 103 Carlos Prado-Alonso, Lidia Gómez-García, Iria Pastor-Gómez & David Tizón-Couto (eds)
New Trends and Methodologies in Applied English Language Research. Diachronic, Diatopic and Contrastive Studies.
348 pages. 2009. ISBN 978-3-0343-0046-9

Vol. 104 Françoise Salager-Meyer & Beverly A. Lewin
Crossed Words. Criticism in Scholarly Writing?
371 pages. 2011. ISBN 978-3-0343-0049-0.

Vol. 105 Javier Ruano-García
Early Modern Northern English Lexis. A Literary Corpus-Based Study.
611 pages. 2010. ISBN 978-3-0343-0058-2

Vol. 106 Rafael Monroy-Casas
Systems for the Phonetic Transcription of English. Theory and Texts.
280 pages. 2011. ISBN 978-3-0343-0059-9

Vol. 107 Nicola T. Owtram
The Pragmatics of Academic Writing.
A Relevance Approach to the Analysis of Research Article Introductions.
311 pages. 2009. ISBN 978-3-0343-0060-5

Vol. 108 Yolanda Ruiz de Zarobe, Juan Manuel Sierra & Francisco Gallardo del Puerto (eds)
Content and Foreign Language Integrated Learning.
Contributions to Multilingualism in European Contexts
343 pages. 2011. ISBN 978-3-0343-0074-2

Vol. 109 Ángeles Linde López & Rosalía Crespo Jiménez (eds)
Professional English in the European context. The EHEA challenge.
374 pages. 2010. ISBN 978-3-0343-0088-9

Vol. 110 Rosalía Rodríguez-Vázquez
The Rhythm of Speech, Verse and Vocal Music. A New Theory.
394 pages. 2010. ISBN 978-3-0343-0309-5

Vol. 111 Anastasios Tsangalidis & Roberta Facchinetti (eds)
Studies on English Modality. In Honour of Frank Palmer.
392 pages. 2009. ISBN 978-3-0343-0310-1

Vol. 112 Jing Huang
Autonomy, Agency and Identity in Foreign Language Learning and Teaching.
400 pages. 2013. ISBN 978-3-0343-0370-5

Vol. 113 Mihhail Lotman & Maria-Kristiina Lotman (eds)
Frontiers in Comparative Prosody. In memoriam: Mikhail Gasparov.
426 pages. 2011. ISBN 978-3-0343-0373-6

Vol. 114 Merja Kytö, John Scahill & Harumi Tanabe (eds)
Language Change and Variation from Old English to Late Modern English.
A Festschrift for Minoji Akimoto
422 pages. 2010. ISBN 978-3-0343-0372-9

Vol. 115 Giuliana Garzone & Paola Catenaccio (eds)
Identities across Media and Modes. Discursive Perspectives.
379 pages. 2009. ISBN 978-3-0343-0386-6

Vol. 116 Elena Landone
Los marcadores del discurso y cortesía verbal en español.
390 pages. 2010. ISBN 978-3-0343-0413-9

Vol. 117 Maurizio Gotti & Christopher Williams (eds)
Legal Discourse across Languages and Cultures.
339 pages. 2010. ISBN 978-3-0343-0425-2

Vol. 118 David Hirsh
Academic Vocabulary in Context.
217 pages. 2010. ISBN 978-3-0343-0426-9

Vol. 119 Yvonne Dröschel
Lingua Franca English. The Role of Simplification and Transfer.
358 pages. 2011. ISBN 978-3-0343-0432-0

Vol. 120 Tengku Sepora Tengku Mahadi, Helia Vaezian & Mahmoud Akbari
Corpora in Translation. A Practical Guide.
135 pages. 2010. ISBN 978-3-0343-0434-4

Vol. 121 Davide Simone Giannoni & Celina Frade (eds)
Researching Language and the Law. Textual Features and Translation Issues.
278 pages. 2010. ISBN 978-3-0343-0443-6

Vol. 122 Daniel Madrid & Stephen Hughes (eds)
Studies in Bilingual Education.
472 pages. 2011. ISBN 978-3-0343-0474-0

Vol. 123 Vijay K. Bhatia, Christopher N. Candlin & Maurizio Gotti (eds)
The Discourses of Dispute Resolution.
290 pages. 2010. ISBN 978-3-0343-0476-4

Vol. 124 Davide Simone Giannoni
Mapping Academic Values in the Disciplines. A Corpus-Based Approach.
288 pages. 2010. ISBN 978-3-0343-0488-7

Vol. 125 Giuliana Garzone & James Archibald (eds)
Discourse, Identities and Roles in Specialized Communication.
419 pages. 2010. ISBN 978-3-0343-0494-8

Vol. 126 Iria Pastor-Gómez
The Status and Development of N+N Sequences in
Contemporary English Noun Phrases.
216 pages. 2011. ISBN 978-3-0343-0534-1

Vol. 127 Carlos Prado-Alonso
Full-verb Inversion in Written and Spoken English.
261 pages. 2011. ISBN 978-3-0343-0535-8

Vol. 128 Tony Harris & María Moreno Jaén (eds)
Corpus Linguistics in Language Teaching.
214 pages. 2010. ISBN 978-3-0343-0524-2

Vol. 129 Tetsuji Oda & Hiroyuki Eto (eds)
Multiple Perspectives on English Philology and History of Linguistics.
A Festschrift for Shoichi Watanabe on his 80th Birthday.
378 pages. 2010. ISBN 978-3-0343-0480-1

Vol. 130 Luisa Chierichetti & Giovanni Garofalo (eds)
Lengua y Derecho. líneas de investigación interdisciplinaria.
283 pages. 2010. 978-3-0343-0463-4

Vol. 131 Paola Evangelisti Allori & Giuliana Garzone (eds)
Discourse, Identities and Genres in Corporate Communication.
Sponsorship, Advertising and Organizational Communication.
324 pages. 2011. 978-3-0343-0591-4

Vol. 132 Leyre Ruiz de Zarobe & Yolanda Ruiz de Zarobe (eds)
Speech Acts and Politeness across Languages and Cultures.
402 pages. 2012. 978-3-0343-0611-9

Vol. 133 Thomas Christiansen
Cohesion. A Discourse Perspective.
387 pages. 2011. 978-3-0343-0619-5

Vol. 134 Giuliana Garzone & Maurizio Gotti
Discourse, Communication and the Enterprise. Genres and Trends.
451 pages. 2011. ISBN 978-3-0343-0620-1

Vol. 135 Zsuzsa Hoffmann
Ways of the World's Words.
Language Contact in the Age of Globalization.
334 pages 2011. ISBN 978-3-0343-0673-7

Vol. 136 Cecilia Varcasia (ed.)
Becoming Multilingual.
Language Learning and Language Policy between Attitudes and Identities.
213 pages. 2011. ISBN 978-3-0343-0687-5

Vol. 137 Susy Macqueen
The Emergence of Patterns in Second Language Writing.
A Sociocognitive Exploration of Lexical Trails.
325 pages. 2012. ISBN 978-3-0343-1010-9

Vol. 138 Maria Vittoria Calvi & Giovanna Mapelli (eds)
La lengua del turismo. Géneros discursivos y terminología.
365 pages. 2011. ISBN 978-3-0343-1011-6

Vol. 139 Ken Lau
Learning to Become a Professional in a Textually-Mediated World.
A Text-Oriented Study of Placement Practices.
261 pages. 2012. ISBN 978-3-0343-1016-1

Vol. 140 Sandra Campagna, Giuliana Garzone, Cornelia Ilie & Elizabeth Rowley-Jolivet (eds)
Evolving Genres in Web-mediated Communication.
337 pages. 2012. ISBN 978-3-0343-1013-0

Vol. 141 Edith Esch & Martin Solly (eds)
The Sociolinguistics of Language Education in International Contexts.
263 pages. 2012. ISBN 978-3-0343-1009-3

Vol. 142 Forthcoming.

Vol. 143 David Tizón-Couto
Left Dislocation in English. A Functional-Discoursal Approach.
416 pages. 2012. ISBN 978-3-0343-1037-6

Vol. 144 Margrethe Petersen & Jan Engberg (eds)
Current Trends in LSP Research. Aims and Methods.
323 pages. 2011. ISBN 978-3-0343-1054-3

Vol. 145 David Tizón-Couto, Beatriz Tizón-Couto, Iria Pastor-Gómez & Paula Rodríguez-Puente (eds)
New Trends and Methodologies in Applied English Language Research II.
Studies in Language Variation, Meaning and Learning.
283 pages. 2012. ISBN 978-3-0343-1061-1

Vol. 146 Rita Salvi & Hiromasa Tanaka (eds)
Intercultural Interactions in Business and Management.
306 pages. 2011. ISBN 978-3-0343-1039-0

Vol. 147 Francesco Straniero Sergio & Caterina Falbo (eds)
Breaking Ground in Corpus-based Interpreting Studies.
254 pages. 2012. ISBN 978-3-0343-1071-0

Vol. 148 Forthcoming.

Vol. 149 Vijay K. Bhatia & Paola Evangelisti Allori (eds)
Discourse and Identity in the Professions. Legal, Corporate and Institutional Citizenship.
352 pages. 2011. ISBN 978-3-0343-1079-6

Vol. 150 Maurizio Gotti (ed.)
Academic Identity Traits. A Corpus-Based Investigation.
363 pages. 2012. ISBN 978-3-0343-1141-0

Vol. 151 Priscilla Heynderickx, Sylvain Dieltjens, Geert Jacobs, Paul Gillaerts &
Elizabeth de Groot (eds)
The Language Factor in International Business.
New Perspectives on Research, Teaching and Practice.
320 pages. 2012. ISBN 978-3-0343-1090-1

Vol. 152 Paul Gillaerts, Elizabeth de Groot, Sylvain Dieltjens, Priscilla Heynderickx &
Geert Jacobs (eds)
Researching Discourse in Business Genres. Cases and Corpora.
215 pages. 2012. ISBN 978-3-0343-1092-5

Vol. 153 Yongyan Zheng
Dynamic Vocabulary Development in a Foreign Language.
262 pages. 2012. ISBN 978-3-0343-1106-9

Vol. 154 Carmen Argondizzo (ed.)
Creativity and Innovation in Language Education.
357 pages. 2012. ISBN 978-3-0343-1080-2

Vol. 155 David Hirsh (ed.)
Current Perspectives in Second Language Vocabulary Research.
180 pages. 2012. ISBN 978-3-0343-1108-3

Vol. 156 Seiji Shinkawa
Unhistorical Gender Assignment in Laȝamon's *Brut*. A Case Study of a Late Stage
in the Development of Grammatical Gender toward its Ultimate Loss.
186 pages. 2012. ISBN 978-3-0343-1124-3

Vol. 157 Yeonkwon Jung
Basics of Organizational Writing: A Critical Reading Approach.
151 pages. 2014. ISBN 978-3-0343-1137-3.

Vol. 158 Bárbara Eizaga Rebollar (ed.)
Studies in Linguistics and Cognition.
301 pages. 2012. ISBN 978-3-0343-1138-0

Vol. 159 Giuliana Garzone, Paola Catenaccio, Chiara Degano (eds)
Genre Change in the Contemporary World. Short-term Diachronic Perspectives.
329 pages. 2012. ISBN 978-3-0343-1214-1

Vol. 160 Carol Berkenkotter, Vijay K. Bhatia & Maurizio Gotti (eds)
Insights into Academic Genres.
468 pages. 2012. ISBN 978-3-0343-1211-0

Vol. 161 Beatriz Tizón-Couto
Clausal Complements in Native and Learner Spoken English. A corpus-based study with Lindsei and Vicolse. 357 pages. 2013. ISBN 978-3-0343-1184-7

Vol. 162 Patrizia Anesa
Jury Trials and the Popularization of Legal Language. A Discourse Analytical Approach.
247 pages. 2012. ISBN 978-3-0343-1231-8

Vol. 163 David Hirsh
Endangered Languages, Knowledge Systems and Belief Systems.
153 pages. 2013. ISBN 978-3-0343-1232-5

Vol. 164 Forthcoming.

Vol. 165 Julia Bamford, Franca Poppi & Davide Mazzi (eds)
Space, Place and the Discursive Construction of Identity.
367 pages. 2014. ISBN 978-3-0343-1249-3

Vol. 166 Rita Salvi & Janet Bowker (eds)
Space, Time and the Construction of Identity.
Discursive Indexicality in Cultural, Institutional and Professional Fields.
324 pages. 2013. ISBN 978-3-0343-1254-7

Vol. 167 Shunji Yamazaki & Robert Sigley (eds)
Approaching Language Variation through Corpora. A Festschrift in Honour of Toshio Saito.
421 pages. 2013. ISBN 978-3-0343-1264-6

Vol. 168 Franca Poppi
Global Interactions in English as a Lingua Franca. How written communication is changing under the influence of electronic media and new contexts of use.
249 pages. 2012. ISBN 978-3-0343-1276-9

Vol. 169 Miguel A. Aijón Oliva & María José Serrano
Style in syntax. Investigating variation in Spanish pronoun subjects.
239 pages. 2013. ISBN 978-3-0343-1244-8

Vol. 170 Forthcoming.

Vol. 171 Aleksandra Matulewska
Legilinguistic Translatology. A Parametric Approach to Legal Translation.
279 pages. 2013. ISBN 978-3-0343-1287-5

Vol. 172 Maurizio Gotti & Carmen Sancho Guinda (eds)
Narratives in Academic and Professional Genres.
513 pages. 2013. ISBN 978-3-0343-1371-1

Vol. 173 Forthcoming.

Vol. 174 Chihiro Inoue
Task Equivalence in Speaking Tests.
251 pages. 2013. ISBN 978-3-0343-1417-6

Vol. 175 Gabriel Quiroz & Pedro Patiño (eds.)
LSP in Colombia: advances and challenges.
339 pages. 2014. ISBN 978-3-0343-1434-3

Vol. 176 Catherine Resche
Economic Terms and Beyond: Capitalising on the Wealth of Notions.
How Researchers in Specialised Varieties of English Can Benefit from Focusing on Terms.
332 pages. 2013. ISBN 978-3-0343-1435-0

Vol. 177 Forthcoming.

Vol. 178 Cécile Desoutter & Caroline Mellet (dir.)
Le discours rapporté: approches linguistiques et perspectives didactiques.
270 pages. 2013. ISBN 978-3-0343-1292-9

Vol. 179 Forthcoming.

Vol. 180 Pilar Alonso
A Multi-dimensional Approach to Discourse Coherence. From Standardness to Creativity.
247 pages. 2014. ISBN 978-3-0343-1325-4

Vol. 181 Alejandro Alcaraz-Sintes & Salvador Valera-Hernández (eds)
Diachrony and Synchrony in English Corpus Linguistics.
393 pages. 2014. ISBN 978-3-0343-1326-1

Vol. 182 Forthcoming.

Vol. 183 Hajar Abdul Rahim & Shakila Abdul Manan (eds.)
English in Malaysia. Postcolonial and Beyond.
267 pages. 2014. ISBN 978-3-0343-1341-4

Vol. 184 Virginie Fasel Lauzon
Comprendre et apprendre dans l'interaction. Les séquences d'explication en classe de français langue seconde.
292 pages. 2014. ISBN 978-3-0343-1451-0

Vol. 185-186 Forthcoming.

Vol. 187 Marina Bondi & Rosa Lorés Sanz (eds)
Abstracts in Academic Discourse. Variation and Change.
361 pages. 2014. ISBN 978-3-0343-1483-1

Vol. 188 Forthcoming.

Vol. 189 Paola Evangelisti Allori (ed.)
Identities in and across Cultures.
315 pages. 2014. ISBN 978-3-0343-1458-9

Vol. 190 Forthcoming.

Vol. 191 Ruth Breeze, Maurizio Gotti & Carmen Sancho Guinda (eds)
Interpersonality in Legal Genres.
389 pages. 2014. ISBN 978-3-0343-1524-1

Vol. 192-199 Forthcoming.

Vol. 200 Maurizio Gotti & Davide S. Giannoni (eds)
Corpus Analysis for Descriptive and Pedagogical Purposes. ESP Perspectives.
432 pages. 2014. ISBN 978-3-0343-1516-6

www.ingramcontent.com/pod-product-compliance
Ingram Content Group UK Ltd.
Pitfield, Milton Keynes, MK11 3LW, UK
UKHW020201290926
15471UKWH00005B/1008

9 783034 315241